The Welfare State in Europe

The Welfare State in Europe

Challenges and Reforms

Edited by
Marco Buti

Directorate-General for Economic and Financial Affairs
European Commission, Belgium

Daniele Franco

Research Department
Bank of Italy

Lucio R. Pench

Forward Studies Unit
European Commission, Belgium

Edward Elgar
Cheltenham, UK • Northampton, MA, USA

Published by
Edward Elgar Publishing Limited
Glensanda House
Montpellier Parade
Cheltenham
Glos GL50 1UA
UK

Edward Elgar Publishing, Inc.
136 West Street
Suite 202
Northampton
Massachusetts 01060
USA

A catalogue record for this book
is available from the British Library

Library of Congress Cataloguing in Publication Data
The welfare state in Europe : challenges and reforms / edited by
    Marco Buti, Daniele Franco, Lucio R. Pench.
        Includes index.
        1. Public welfare—Europe.   2. Welfare state.   3. Welfare
        economics.   I. Buti, Marco.   II. Franco, Daniele, 1953–
III. Pench, Lucio R., 1957–   .
HV238.W45   1999
361.6'5'094—dc21   99–21911
                                                                                        CIP

ISBN 1 84064 066 9

Typeset by Manton Typesetters, Louth, Lincolnshire, UK.
Printed and bound in Great Britain by
Creative Print and Design (Wales), Ebbw Vale

Contents

Figures

Tables

Boxes

Contributors

Anthony B. Atkinson, Nuffield College, Oxford, UK

Marco Buti, Directorate-General for Economic and Financial Affairs, European Commission, Belgium

Nathalie Darnaut, Directorate-General for Economic and Financial Affairs, European Commission, Belgium

Stefan Fölster, Industrial Institute for Economic and Social Research, Stockholm, Sweden

Daniele Franco, Research Department, Bank of Italy

Robert Holzmann, Universität des Saarlandes, Germany

Assar Lindbeck, Stockholm University, Sweden

Teresa Munzi, Directorate-General for Economic and Financial Affairs, European Commission, Belgium

J. Michael Orszag, Birkbeck College, University of London, UK

Lucio R. Pench, Forward Studies Unit, European Commission, Belgium

Dennis J. Snower, Birkbeck College, University of London, UK

Gerassimos Thomas, Directorate-General for Economic and Financial Affairs, European Commission, Belgium

Abbreviations and symbols used

MEMBER STATES

EU 9   European Community excluding Greece, Spain and Portugal
EU 10   European Community excluding Spain and Portugal
EU 12– European Community, 12 member states including West Germany
EU 12+ European Community, 12 member states including Germany
EU 15+ European Community, 15 member states including Germany

CURRENCIES

DEM   German mark (Deutschmark)
DKK   Danish krone
FRF   French franc
HUF   Hungarian franc
PLZ   Polish złoty
SEK   Swedish krona

OTHER ABBREVIATIONS

AFP   Asset-funded pension
BS   Basic scheme
CADES Caisse d'amortissement de la dette sociale
CPI   Consumer price index
CSG   Contribution sociale généralisée
EMS   European Monetary System
EMU   Economic and monetary union
ES   Earnings-related scheme
Eurostat Statistical Office of the European Communities
FMI   Financial market indicator
FMR   Financial intermediation ratio
FIR   Financial interrelation ratio
GA   Government assets

GDP	Gross domestic product
GNP	Gross national product
IMF	International Monetary Fund
LCH	Life-cycle hypothesis
LE	Life expectancy
n.a.	Not available
OECD	Organization for Economic Cooperation and Development
OLG	Overlapping generations
OLS	Ordinary least squares
PAYG	Pay-as-you-go
PE	Pension expenditure
RA	Retirement age
RB	Recognition bond
RDS	Remboursement de la dette sociale
SMIC	Salaire Minimum Interprofessionel de Croissance
SSD	Social security debt
TFP	Total factor productivity
UF–FF	Unfunded–fully funded (pension schemes)

PART I

Overview

1. Reconciling the welfare state with sound public finances and high employment

Marco Buti, Daniele Franco and Lucio R. Pench

Many intellectuals in the US and Asia believe that European social welfare policies should be a blueprint for action in their own countries. But those policies, financed by high taxes and costly mandates on business, are mainly responsible for the enormous increase in European unemployment during the past decade and a half. This 'European disease' is hardly a model for other nations.

Gary Becker, 1992 Nobel laureate, Chicago University,
Business Week, 8 April 1996

Yet, as the UK and western Europe contemplate adapting more to the 'American model' it is worth noticing a more menacing side. Economic inequality has continued to widen. All the rungs on the economic ladder are now further apart than a generation ago, and the space between them continues to spread. This widening of inequality leads to distress and misery for those at or near the bottom and anxiety for those in the middle. Left unchecked it could also undermine the stability and moral authority of the nation.

Robert Reich, former US Secretary of Labour, Brandeis University,
Financial Times, 3 March 1997

INTRODUCTION[1]

1

The reform of the welfare state is one of the main policy issues in Western countries. It is of the utmost importance in the European Union, which is experiencing rapid ageing of the population and high unemployment rates. Traditional solidarity and social protection objectives are to be reconciled with population ageing, expenditure containment, and economic efficiency and competitiveness objectives.[2] Moreover, new needs, such as those of elderly citizens in long-term care and lone-parent families, are to be faced.

3

The goal of the chapters in this volume, which include academic studies presented at European Commission seminars, as well as studies produced by European Commission staff, is to enhance the debate on the state and prospects of European social protection systems and outline some reforms that could lessen budgetary pressures and improve economic efficiency.

The authors are well aware that the problems and future prospects of the social security systems of the EU member states differ substantially. This is due to differences in historical development, institutional set-up, budgetary situations, economic conditions, social attitudes, and demographic trends. Recent policies have also varied. However, in spite of these differences, European welfare states share some fundamental objectives, as well as some important challenges. The major reform options are also similar. Moreover, the essential features of the welfare state are widely supported by public opinion all over the Union: there is consensus on the need to support poor, sick, unemployed and disabled citizens, on universal rights to basic health services, and on the role of the state in regulating intergenerational redistribution.

2

This introductory chapter, which draws on the extensive economic literature on the welfare state, aims at focusing the debate at the European level. It highlights the achievements of the European welfare states, in terms of the reduction of poverty and deprivation, the capacity to cope with recessions and structural changes without social unrest, and the provision of security against risk. The chapter also highlights the substantial pressures for change stemming from budgetary and labour market problems and argues that the European welfare state cannot be maintained as it is, since population ageing and the distortionary effects of high tax rates are increasingly putting strains on social programmes. The study examines the implications of European integration on the welfare state from three different standpoints: increased factors and consumers' mobility in the internal market, the capacity of the economies to adjust to shocks in an integrated economy, and the EMU fiscal framework. Finally, it analyses some reforms that might contribute to tackling these problems.

The chapters by Anthony Atkinson (Oxford University) (Chapter 2) and Assar Lindbeck (University of Stockholm) (Chapter 3) provide a general view of the problems and prospects of European welfare states. Atkinson stresses the need for rigorous analysis of the mechanisms by which the welfare state influences economic performance. The institutional structure should be carefully taken into consideration, as well as the interaction between different policies. Reforms should be based on accurate analysis of the functioning of welfare state institutions. According to Atkinson, the positive impacts of social security on economic performance are not adequately recognized. This may depend on the theoretical framework used to analyse the effects of social security arrangements, which is generally rooted in a model of perfectly competitive markets. For instance, unemployment insurance may actually increase, rather than reduce, regular employment by inducing people to enter an employment relationship in spite of the risk of job losses. Atkinson also emphasizes that the alternatives to present welfare state arrangements may themselves have adverse effects.

Lindbeck examines the problems and the achievements of the welfare state. He particularly focuses on the dynamic aspects and highlights the fact that the effects of the welfare state evolve over time and interact strongly with each other. For instance, the disincentive effects of taxes and social benefits are initially delayed by habits and social norms, but social norms gradually adjust to the new incentive system, inducing individuals to modify their behaviour. In the end, spending may largely overshoot the levels expected when the welfare programmes were started. Lindbeck examines several marginal and radical reforms. The former include cuts in replacement rates and automatic or discretionary adjustments to shocks in demography and productivity. The latter include the shift to funded pension schemes, the introduction of a negative income tax or of an actuarially based 'drawing rights' mechanism, and the replacement of different income protection systems with a single safety net. In order to reduce disincentive and moral hazard problems, while retaining the major achievements of the welfare state, Lindbeck supports the three-pillars system: tax-financed flat-rate benefits, mandatory social insurance, and voluntary insurance.

The contributions by Stefan Fölster (Industrial Institute for Economic and Social Research, Stockholm) (Chapter 4) and Michael Orszag and Dennis Snower (Birbeck College, London) (Chapter 5) focus on how to reconcile welfare schemes with economic incentives. The basic idea is that of introducing social protection schemes designed on market-oriented lines and of strengthening the link between social contributions and benefits at the individual level.

Fölster supports the introduction of 'individual social insurance accounts'. Mandatory payments into these personal accounts with the social security system would replace most of the taxes and contributions presently financing pension, health and other social benefits. When the need arises individual benefit would be drawn out of the account (and limited by its level). At retirement the balance of the account would be taken into consideration to assess pension entitlements. These accounts would limit the demand for benefits and make workers fully aware of the value of the benefits for which they are paying contributions. Incentives to stay on benefits would be reduced. Incentives to work would be increased, since eligibility to benefits would depend on work record. The scope for the benefit principle is large: most social security spending (80 per cent in Sweden) simply smoothes income over the individual's life cycle, that is, it is insurance, not welfare.

These measures would increase work effort by reducing the incentives to stay on benefits. Along similar lines, Orszag and Snower argue for the establishment of 'welfare accounts' for all citizens. They argue that the size of a government's welfare state spending bears little relation to the level of welfare services provided in the economy and that expanding the welfare services does not necessarily mean expanding public expenditure. On these bases, Orszag and Snower outline a set of institutional changes that would prevent large welfare systems from impairing economic activity. They argue for the introduction of four 'welfare accounts' for every citizen (retirement, unemployment, human capital and health account). The government would set minimum contribution rates to the accounts. Citizens would be allowed to withdraw fixed maximum amounts per month. The accounts could be initially run on a Pay-as-you-go (PAYG) basis and later turned into a fully funded system. They would increase consumer choice about the size and composition of welfare services, promote competition between the public and the private sectors, and make redistribution of income less inefficient and vulnerable to political pressures.

The issue of pension reform is considered in the studies by Robert Holzmann (World Bank) (Chapter 6) and Gerassimos Thomas (European Commission) (Chapter 7). Holzmann examines one of the key topics of the debate on pension systems: the transition from PAYG to funded systems. He highlights the potential benefits of a shift from an unfunded to a funded pension system, such as the reduction of labour market distortions and the positive effects on saving rates and capital market development. The study outlines the complex fiscal issues raised by the transition, the liabilities towards the current generation of retirees and workers become explicit, and considers the main options for financing them. It also examines the likely effects of the transition on saving, capital accumulation and productivity. Finally, it draws several indications from the reform implemented in Chile in the 1980s, which represents the most relevant case study on the transition issue. Holzmann concludes by pointing to the feasibility and the potential efficiency of a shift towards a funded pension system or a mixed system.

Thomas examines the current institutional set-up of European pension systems and their prospects, taking present demographic scenarios and expenditure trends into consideration. Despite the reforms introduced over recent years, most European countries face substantial expenditure increases. Further reforms are therefore required. Thomas explores the implications of different reform options. While a radical shift from PAYG to funding is considered unrealistic, the paper stresses the need for further reforms of PAYG systems and for the gradual development of a funded pillar. These changes would modify the distribution of responsibilities and risks between governments, employers and employees and create a more diversified portfolio of retirement income sources. They would also produce marginally positive effects on savings and contribute to the development of financial markets. As to the impact on the labour market, Thomas points to some risks related to potential reduction of mobility and early withdrawal from the labour market.

The study by Nathalie Darnaut (European Commission) (Chapter 8) examines the problems and prospects of the French social protection system, which, in several respects, represents a 'prototype' of the European welfare states. It also provides information on the organization, expenditure levels and financing structure of the social protection systems of the EU member states. The analysis of the strengths and weaknesses of the French system highlights the complexity of modern welfare systems, the problems raised by their need for increasing financial resources, and the practical difficulties of adapting them to new demographic and economic conditions. The study focuses on the efforts to reform the French health-care system and places them in the context of the health reforms undertaken in industrialized countries. The reforms aim at controlling expenditure growth and at improving the quality of the services. The study also examines the prospects of the French pension system and points to the need for further reforms.

Finally, the study by Daniele Franco and Teresa Munzi (European Commission) (Chapter 9) examines the budgetary implications of demographic changes in EU member states over the coming decades. By outlining the effects that these changes might produce on the major social expenditure programmes, the study sets the debate on the reform of the welfare state within the more general budgetary prospects of EU member states and the fiscal framework introduced for economic and monetary union (EMU). Public expenditure projections point to the fact that up to the year 2010 the budgetary effects of demographic changes are relevant, but are far from dramatic. There are, however, reasons for anticipating policy changes. The fiscal framework introduced for EMU provides a benchmark for the adjustment of budgetary policy to the new demographic scenarios. The achievement of a 'close-to-balance' budget over the next few years, which in most countries would require substantial changes in present policies, would allow governments to meet the worsening of the demographic situation after the year 2010, when the baby-boom generation will retire, with smaller public debts. Part of the likely increases in pension and health expenditure would be offset by reductions in interest payments.

3

Some general themes underlie all the chapters in this volume: the reform efforts already under way all over Europe; the important role of labour market considerations in designing welfare state reforms; and the need for and the search for reforms allowing distributive objectives to be reconciled with expenditure containment.

Although the chapters in this volume point to the difficult problems to be tackled by European welfare states, they also show that the adjustment of welfare states to the new demographic, economic and fiscal scenarios is well under way throughout Europe. In most countries, present social policies are quite different from those implemented in previous decades. Two broad objectives can be detected behind the ongoing adjustment process of welfare states: on the one hand, the necessity to keep public finances on a sustainable course, given that social protection is the single largest area of public expenditure in all countries and also the one with the tendency to increase the fastest; on the other, the need to reduce the distortions in individual choices introduced by social programmes, which may result in under-utilization of labour, lower saving and higher government consumption than the central aims of the welfare state justify, and sometimes in the negation of these very aims. The first objective can thus be generally defined as macroeconomic, the second as microeconomic in nature. While in principle there is no contradiction between the two and both objectives can be served by the same measures, in practice the macroeconomic necessity of bringing under control the growth of social expenditure has often been the driving force of the reform process. This tendency has been reinforced by the fiscal policy framework for the entry and the operation of EMU put in place by the Maastricht Treaty.

The area of social expenditure where the change has been most evident is pensions, where projections of the existing systems had long pointed to a destabilizing potential for government financial balances. Since the mid-1980s most pension schemes have been reformed in order to restrain expenditure growth. Reducing the generosity of pension systems has typically involved rises in the standard retirement age, restrictions in indexation, and increases in qualifying periods or in contributions. Along with the general trend toward reducing expenditure one can detect measures aiming at strengthening the link between earnings and pensions, and thereby increasing incentives to work and to save. These include using a longer contribution period for the calculation of pensions, decreasing pension-credit for years without earnings and reducing special pension benefits for civil servants. The actuarial principle has received further support by at least two cases of comprehensive reform of the pension system aiming at placing it on a fully contributory basis (Sweden, Italy) and by widespread measures to encourage the development of supplementary pensions, which are typically based on the defined contribution system.

Health-care systems are also undergoing substantial changes, although the general pattern of reform is not uniform because of the substantial differences in the structure of national health-care systems. The principles of universality and equality in the access to services are in general not questioned, as evidenced also by the trend toward more tax financing in several countries. At the same time expenditure control has been pursued with tighter hospital budgets, restrictions on the supply of services and the reimbursement of drugs extension of co-responsibility payments by patients. While some of these measures can also be justified on efficiency grounds, several reforms have explicitly aimed at increasing efficiency in the use of resources and the quality of services by improving incentives on the supply side: giving patients more choice, introducing competition within the public sector and between the public and the private sector, and separating the provision and the financing of services.

Unemployment benefits are also being reformed, again with an emphasis on curbing expenditure growth and reducing perverse incentive effects, particularly on the low earners. In several countries the features of the unemployment compensation system have been modified to tighten eligibility and sometimes reduce the relative generosity of the benefits available. The integration of tax/benefits and labour policies has been pursued through targeted contribution reductions or reductions in marginal tax rates for low earners. In some cases, integrated safety-net/in work benefits have been put in place.

Reforms are gradually affecting expenditure dynamics, especially in the pension area. The updated projections reviewed and integrated by Franco and Munzi point to a ratio of pension expenditure to GDP that in most countries is increasing by less than the ratio of the old to those of working-age. In other words, the reforms already in place have already made Europe's pension systems much less generous than they used to be, even if this may not yet be evident as the new rules will typically display their effect on currently young and prime-age workers and not on those close to retirement or already retired. The changes that have already been implemented, while still not sufficient to arrest expenditure increase, offer ground for confidence in the viability of the systems, not least because in many countries public opinion has been prepared to accept substantial changes in entitlements.

4

Again, all chapters in the volume point to the need to examine jointly the welfare state and the labour market. While changes in the labour market affect the demand for benefits and the sources to fund them, benefit structures and tax rates influence labour supply and employers' decisions. On both sides, present trends are rather worrying. The rise in unemployment, particularly in long-term unemployment, and the increase of insecure forms of employment are increasing the demand for social support. Welfare subsidies and unemployment benefits, if not properly designed, produce labour supply disincentives and may result in poverty and unemployment traps. Furthermore, irrespective of the specific nature of the transfer programmes, the size of the welfare state has been considered relevant because of the tax burden implicit in its financing. The idea is that the rise in labour taxes (the tax wedge) may have been detrimental to employment via labour demand, contributing to capital–labour substitution. Essential for this line of reasoning is the condition that the tax burden is not entirely carried by workers. This may well be the case, especially in Europe, where uncompetitive labour markets and strong unions have produced 'wage resistance' and managed to shift at least part of the tax burden on to capital.

The interplay between the welfare system and labour market institutions goes deeper than this specific example. In general, institutions within the same socio-economic system tend to be interconnected, giving rise to complex interactions sometimes referred to under the notion of 'embeddedness'. In the present discussion, to the extent that job security provisions and benefit programmes respond to similar types of market failure, they are functional equivalents and can be seen as institutional substitutes. There is indeed evidence of a trade-off in Europe between the generosity of unemployment compensation and the strictness of employment protection legislation. Broadly speaking, northern countries have generous welfare systems and low firing costs, while the opposite holds in the case of Mediterranean countries; continental countries occupy an intermediate position.

While functionally equivalent in the 'workers protection' space, different combinations of job security provisions and unemployment benefits are not neutral with respect to economic and employment performance. In particular, rigid employment protection legislation and low benefits may be highly inefficient in the event of sectoral, technological and organizational shocks entailing changes in comparative advantages and requiring swift labour reallocation between firms and sectors. The underperformance of these systems in the future may be heightened as the process of globalization, market opening and economic interdependence – fostered *inter alia* by EMU and the Single Market – may well increase the frequency of such shocks in the coming years.

Several reforms are considered in this volume, with many authors pointing to the importance of strengthening the link between social contributions and benefits at the individual level. This would limit the negative effects of contributions and benefits on the labour market and employment (that is, incentives to retire early, to stay on sickness/unemployment/welfare benefits, to work in the black economy) and make the burden of contributions more tolerable and less distortive.

Member countries have also started to reconsider job security provisions with the objective of improving the functioning of labour markets. While in a number of member states important measures have been introduced, resistance by 'incumbents' and concern about the equity consequences of the liberalization have usually prevented governments from implementing radical reforms. Therefore, in many cases, the approach that has been pursued is that of reforms 'at the margin' of the labour market (such as easing the spread of temporary contracts), without touching the job security provisions of permanent workers. In some instances (for example, Spain in the 1980s), such policies have had perverse results, by leading to a further segmentation of the labour markets and strengthening insider/outsider dynamics. These negative consequences have led to a reconsideration of such policy options and more thorough reforms have been introduced in the recent period.

5

The pillars of European social policy – pension, health and education systems, unemployment benefits, labour market regulations, the entitlements for the poor and the disabled and the tax systems needed to finance them – were largely put in place or greatly extended in the years of very high growth. Present policies were designed in different economic conditions (lower social spending and lower contribution rates, lower flexibility in production, lower international competition, greater social control, and so on). By helping to distribute the benefits of growth, these policies have sustained a high level of social cohesion and favoured the research of cooperative solutions between social actors. However, as growth slowed down, a number of strains began to emerge, endangering welfare state achievements.

The European social model cannot be sustained as it is, for it is getting too expensive and it is producing negative effects on labour supply and unemployment. Through these channels the welfare state may also have a negative impact on the long-term performance of European economies. Therefore, the preservation of the fundamental features of the welfare state requires substantial reforms.

In most countries the preservation of present benefit levels and eligibility rules will require a substantial increase in the resources devoted to the welfare state. Alternatively, the stabilization of social expenditure will entail further severe cuts in benefit levels and substantial restrictions in eligibility conditions. The first option raises several problems. Although reforms strengthening the link between contributions and benefits might make the burden of contributions more tolerable and less distortive, increasing the present tax to GDP ratio would be politically difficult and economically undesirable. Increases in tax rates would also conflict with the pressures towards lower tax rates stemming from economic integration and globalization. It would also be difficult to compensate the increase in pension expenditure with cuts on other expenditure items.

The decline in the share of the young to total population offers some margins for cutting education expenditure, but health expenditure as well as expenditure for pensions and services to the elderly are likely to increase substantially. So, in the end, some containment of benefits is unavoidable. This implies a scaling down of citizens' expectations and a revision of present objectives. Further reforms might involve increases in retirement age, reductions in replacement rates, tightening of eligibility criteria. The rise in life expectancy and the improvement in the health status of elderly workers favour such steps. Provided that bold measures are introduced swiftly, the breathing-space that pension expenditure projections outline for the next few years would allow the needs of the ageing of the baby-boom generation to be met on a sounder fiscal policy footing. The ensuing reduction in interest payments would offset part of the likely increases in pension and health expenditure and allow a reduction in the changes to be implemented in present pension policies.

At the European Union level, the reform of social protection schemes by increasing incentives to work, education and job creation would allow a fuller exploitation of the potential benefits of the Single Market. By contributing to fiscal consolidation, it would help to ensure the twin objectives of sound public finance and stable money. The combined result would be higher employment and economic welfare.

A number of important issues remain largely unsettled. If we are to curb social expenditure, which benefits could actually be reduced? Should we put more emphasis on targeting benefits on the most needy? Should we withdraw the welfare state from the middle classes? Should we shift the boundary between the responsibility of the state and of the private sector? What is the scope for privatization in (a) the financing and (b) the production of social services? How to reform the functioning of labour markets, taking into account the interplay between employment regulations and welfare provisions and considering the legitimate demand for an appropriate degree of 'workers security'? Social policies have essentially been developed through incremental policy changes. For the future, and taking the political feasibility of benefit reductions into account, should we plan major reforms, or rely on a sequence of incremental reform?

The chapters in this book do not have the aim of providing definite answers to these questions. They do provide, however, a roadmap to the complex choices facing public authorities, suggest some innovative reform avenues and, first and foremost, help to put the policy debate on a sounder analytical footing.

2. ACHIEVEMENTS AND CHALLENGES

Backed by strong economic growth, social policies have contributed to making Europe, on the whole, a 'nice place to live' over the past half century. In a historical perspective, economic growth was exceptionally high in the 1950s and in the 1960s, and the subsequent period up to the 1990s still compared favourably with previous experiences in most industrial countries (Maddison, 1995). The pillars of European social policy – pension, health and education systems, unemployment benefits, labour market regulations, the entitlements for the poor and the disabled and the tax systems needed to finance them – were largely put in place or greatly extended in the years of very high growth.

By helping to distribute the benefits of growth, social policies have sustained a high level of social cohesion and favoured the research of cooperative solutions between social actors. However, as growth slowed down, a number of strains began to emerge, endangering welfare state achievements. Population ageing, changes in household structures, high unemployment, the negative effects of high tax rates on employment and rising concerns about European competitiveness in a globalized economy are adding to the pressure on social programmes throughout the EU.

This section examines the achievements and challenges facing the welfare state in Europe.[3] It begins with a brief review of the social achievements and the economic rationale of welfare systems, with particular emphasis on the comparison between the EU and North America. It then analyses two major problems that call into question the long-run sustainability of European social programmes, namely expenditure pressures and negative incentives in the labour market.

2.1 Why the Welfare State? Social Achievements and Economic Rationale

This section examines three related questions: the relative effectiveness of European welfare states in limiting poverty and inequality, their justification in terms of economic efficiency, and the relationship between welfare state and economic performance.

2.1.1 Combating poverty and discrimination
One of the greatest achievements of the welfare state is the extent to which it has reduced the incidence of poverty, by preventing individuals and

households from falling below a minimum income level, and promoted social integration, by making merit goods available to every citizen irrespective of socioeconomic status. In order to evaluate the achievements of the European social protection system, it is interesting to compare Europe with North America, which has followed a rather different approach.[4]

A more developed system of social protection has allowed Europe to combat poverty and discrimination in a much more effective way than the United States. As shown in Table 1.1, not only has Europe, on the whole, a lower incidence of 'primary poverty' (that is, poverty before taxes and trans-

Table 1.1   Incidence of poverty in the EU and North America: Sen poverty measure[1] (non-elderly families; percentage points)

	Before taxes and transfers			After taxes and transfers		
	All	Large	Single-parent	All	Large	Single-parent
Belgium (1985)	8.7	11.7	27.2	2.1	2.3	8.0
Denmark (1992)	14.6	:	:	3.1	:	1.0
Germany (1984–85)	9.8	9.6	37.1	2.8	4.3	12.8
France (1984)	10.8	24.1	27.8	4.3	3.5	8.5
Ireland (1987)	19.8	23.8	38.1	5.9	6.7	13.8
Italy (1986)	:	:	:	3.9	:	:
Netherlands (1987)	11.7	9.9	44.4	2.0	4.1	6.6
Austria (1984–85)	:	:	:	2.1	:	:
Sweden (1987)[2]	13.3	11.3	28.2	6.7	1.2	2.0
UK (1986)	18.4	28.4	61.2	5.1	8.5	9.0
EU[3]	13.2	17.0	37.7	4.4	4.4	8.7
US (1986)	13.0	24.0	42.9	10.0	19.1	29.9
Canada (1987)	12.0	16.6	43.6	7.1	8.5	21.0

Notes:
[1] The Sen index combines the share of persons in households with income below 50 per cent of median income (low-income rate), the severity of poverty as measured by the difference in income of the poor relative to the poverty line (average low-income gap) and the dispersion of income between the very poor and the not-so-poor (proxied by the Gini coefficient). The value of the index lies between 0 (no poverty) and 1 (incomes of the poor clustered around zero).
[2] As pointed out by OECD (1995c), Sweden may overestimate the number of poor families as it considers persons over 18 living with their parents as independent households.
[3] Unweighted average of available data, excluding incomplete cases.

Source: Adapted from OECD (1995c).

fers), but benefit and tax systems are more effective in alleviating it than in North America.[5] The countries with the lowest levels of poverty and, more generally, income inequality, tend to be also those with the greatest degree of social protection for the population of working age (Gottschalk and Smeeding, 1997). The difference between Europe and the United States is even more striking if one focuses on groups most at risk of poverty, namely large families and lone-parent families. Child poverty is also particularly high in the United States: about one American child in five lives in poverty. This percentage is significantly higher than those recorded in European countries (Coder et al., 1989; Förster, 1993).

Other indicators, besides poverty incidence, also point to more serious social integration problems in the United States. While in EU member states nearly all citizens are entitled to health insurance, in the United States about 15 per cent of those under 65 years of age have no insurance coverage (OECD, 1992a). Most individuals included in this group live in a precarious health-care situation and receive low-quality health care. Also, the share of the American population serving prison sentences is much higher (from 8 to 15 times) than in any EU country.[6]

The better performance of Europe compared with North America, on social grounds, is confirmed by data on trends in poverty and on the individual duration of poverty. In the United States, the share of the population under the official poverty line has increased by over 3 percentage points since the early 1970s (Haveman, 1996). In Europe, by contrast, the overall incidence of poverty has remained generally stable, even if a number of countries have seen an overall increase in (post-tax and transfer) income inequality since the 1980s, while changes in the opposite direction have been rare.

Longitudinal analyses confirm that, while there is considerable movement in and out of poverty, 'a rapid escape (after one year) from financial poverty seems more likely in countries with low poverty rates (like the Netherlands and Sweden) than in countries with high poverty rates (like Canada and the United States). In other words, there appears to be a marked inverse relationship between the incidence of poverty and escape rates' (Cantillon, 1996).[7] Moreover, according to Gramlich (1989), in the United States the spatial concentration of poverty is high and increasing.[8]

Data on the incidence of poverty over time are consistent with the much higher rise in earnings inequality in the United States than in (continental) Europe since the 1970s, and with the finding that the probability of moving upwards (and downwards) in the earnings distribution over time does not increase with the degree of earning dispersion (OECD, 1996b). Increased earnings inequality (among men) has probably been the most important factor behind rising income inequality in industrial countries since the 1980s.

Studies comparing indicators of socioeconomic mobility suggest that countries with the most developed welfare states also show a lower degree of inequality in the long run. Calculating indicators of the inequality of income – such as the Gini coefficient – over a multi-year period instead of over a single year tends to reduce inequality, but leaves the United States markedly more unequal than other countries on all measures of income (Aaberge et al., 1996). Studies measuring the correlation of the long-run economic status between father and son tend to suggest that the United States (and United Kingdom) have relatively low economic and social mobility (that is, relatively high correlation between father's and son's position in earnings distribution) compared with Germany and the Nordic countries (Björklund, 1996). In other words, empirical research does not seem to support the view that there is a trade-off between 'static' and 'dynamic' equality, whereas greater equality of opportunities can be bought at the price of higher inequality of outcomes.

Cross-country comparisons of poverty and inequality typically refer to relative income differences, as countries differ substantially in terms of (average) per capita income. However, recent calculations show that 'low-income' persons[9] living in the United States are poorer, in terms of absolute purchasing power, than similarly situated persons in each of the other 13 industrial countries, in spite of the clear advantage of the United States in terms of average and median per capita income (Gottschalk and Smeeding, 1997).

2.1.2 Reducing social risks and promoting economic change
Viewing the welfare state, and more specifically the extensive European social protection systems, mainly in terms of poverty relief and, more generally, promoting equity would be a mistake not only on economic, but also on historical, grounds. Indeed, the development of public transfer systems in most industrial countries was related not so much to the fight against poverty, *per se*, as to the general objective of providing security against the risk and hazards of life (Atkinson, 1993).[10]

Failures of private insurance markets   From an efficiency point of view, there is a strong case for government intervention to provide social insurance against risks which private insurance cannot adequately cover. A large body of theoretical literature has analysed the conditions under which private insurance markets fail. Its main conclusions with respect to welfare provisions can be summarized as follows (Barr, 1992 and 1993):

(i)   Adverse selection and moral hazard problems may prevent private insurance from covering some risks. For instance, this applies to important medical risks, where the insurer cannot readily distinguish between high-risk and low-risk individuals. In this case, a private market solution would fail to materialize if the low risks were free to opt out. While compulsory membership, making possible a pooling solution, may avoid the worst effects of adverse selection, moral hazard problems may require more extensive public intervention, such as the introduction of a social insurance scheme. More specifically, the powers of compulsion of the state are necessary to monitor and penalize the behaviour of individuals influencing the risk against which they are insured. This applies to unemployment insurance that cannot be provided by the market even for the 'best' risks.

(ii)   Private insurance requires a predictable number of winners and losers over a given period of time: it cannot cope with common shocks – in which uncertainty concerns aggregate and not just individual outcomes – or with events characterized by unpredictable probabilities. Inflationary and other macroeconomic shocks are examples of such problems.

(iii)   Social insurance can supplement market demand when non-insurance by the individual imposes costs on others, such as in health care or provision for the aged.

A social insurance system covering the entire population may also enjoy significant cost advantages, in terms of economies of scale and scope, over competing private insurance schemes. As the failures of private insurance markets typically imply an inability to tailor premiums to individual risks, social insurance will tend to contain an element of redistribution from good risks to bad risks. Compulsory membership allows governments to engage in redistribution according to equity or other objectives.

How can the efficiency effects of the welfare state be assessed?

If protection against risk, in alternative and/or in the absence of private insurance, were recognized as an essential function of the welfare state, an economic evaluation of the welfare state should focus on the effects of the increased security. Bearing in mind that risk is an unwanted activity (individuals will require increasing compensation for taking more risk), the effects can be seen both from the production and the consumption side.

From the production side, risk-taking can be considered as a 'factor of production'. Up to a certain point, risk can be transformed into higher income, as, for example, when an entrepreneur invests in a new market or a worker prepares for a new job. By reducing the amount of risk associated with any given activity, social insurance induces individuals to take up income opportunities that they might otherwise have forgone and therefore can increase welfare for society as a whole (Sinn, 1994 and 1995).

From the consumption side, the effects of increased security can be seen in terms of added 'peace of mind' for a given expected income. Under certain assumptions, these effects can be quantified. On the basis of data on German and American households for the period 1983–86, and assuming an income utility function with constant risk aversion, Bird (1995) calculates that the welfare cost of risk (that is, the amount that individuals would be willing to pay in exchange for securing their income at their expected level) corresponds to 5.4 per cent of disposable income in Germany and 8.5 per cent in the United States. This reflects the higher protection against income fluctuations available in Germany compared with the United States. According to the study, tax and transfers reduce income risk by 43 per cent in Germany and 21 per cent in the United States.

In assessing the role of the state in the provision of social protection, one should also be aware that the total level of spending on welfare services in industrial countries is not greatly influenced by whether expenditure is undertaken by the government or the private sector. For example, the difference in spending on welfare services between the United States and the Scandinavian countries is much more limited when both public and private spending are taken into account. Specifically, total spending is 35 per cent of GDP in Sweden and 28 per cent in the United States. The difference between the two countries becomes even smaller if one considers the amount of private spending on social protection plus taxes as a share of total expenditure by private households: in 1990 this attained 41.2 per cent in Sweden and 39.6 per cent in the United States (Esping-Andersen, 1996).

The case of health care is particularly noteworthy. The United States health system is much more expensive than the European systems. While in 1991, in most EU member states, total expenditure for health (public plus private) was in the 6.5 to 9 per cent range, in the United States it was about 13.4 per cent of GDP (OECD, 1994a). In spite of this, the United States system does not seem to fare better in terms of the final output, that is the health status of the population. Moreover, United States public expenditure levels are close to European levels (5.9 per cent of GDP in 1991 for the United States), but, as already mentioned, the United States system does not ensure that all citizens are entitled to health insurance (OECD, 1992a).

Welfare state and economic growth   If, to some extent, social protection can be considered as a factor of production, existing social protection systems need not imply negative consequences on output and growth. Historically, not only did the development of the welfare state actually accompany unprecedented economic growth in Europe, but also the two developments were long seen as mutually reinforcing rather than in contrast. Specifically, the welfare state was seen as strengthening economic performance because of two widely shared perceptions: the stabilizing effect of social transfers on the economic cycle and the positive contribution of social insurance to workers adjusting to economic change. More recently, the perceived relationship between economic efficiency and social justice has become more problematic and the welfare state has increasingly come under attack as being detrimental to economic performance (Pfaller et al., 1991; Boyer, 1991; Snower, 1996a).

The relationship between income distribution and growth illustrates these controversies. The topic has recently been the subject of considerable academic interest,[11] but the results are not clear-cut. Some studies conclude that inequality in the distribution of (pre-tax) personal income has a significant negative effect on growth, both in developing and developed countries (Persson and Tabellini, 1994). Inequality would reduce growth by feeding redistributive conflicts. According to other studies, once country-specific effects are removed, there is no discernible effect of pre-tax inequality on growth (Fölster and Trofimov, 1996). Both groups of studies indicate that the effects of social transfers on growth are negative. Yet another set of findings suggests that countries with larger transfer programmes tend to grow faster (Sala-i-Martin, 1996).

This section has illustrated that European welfare states have been relatively effective in limiting poverty and inequality and that their existence is also consistent with economic efficiency considerations. Moreover, it has been shown that the relationship between welfare state and economic performance is more ambiguous than many seem to believe.[12] This broadly positive assessment of the welfare state does not necessarily imply that the present size and structure of European social protection systems are in any way optimal, or that the present efficiency and equity objectives could not be achieved with a leaner welfare state. Nor does this assessment imply that the present structure is the best suited to tackle future economic and social challenges. It only implies that, in outlining reforms of the European social protection systems, one should be careful in safeguarding their most important achievements (see Section 4).

2.2 Pressures for Change

Today's economy and society are dramatically different from those at the time in which modern welfare states were established. A view of the demographic and other structural changes that have affected Europe over the past three decades is provided in Table 1.2. The most evident implications of these changes on the working and the sustainability of the welfare state are related to budgetary and labour market imbalances.[13]

2.2.1 Budgetary strains
Over the period 1970–94, the ratio of social protection expenditure to GDP in the EU increased from 19 per cent to 28.5 per cent.[14] In most member states,

Table 1.2   Demography, household structure and the labour market in the EU

	1960	1998
Life expectancy at birth (number of years)		
men	67.4	74.6
women	72.9	80.9
Life expectancy at 65 (number of years)		
men	12.7	15.6
women	15.1	19.4
Total fertility rate		
(number of children for each woman)	2.6	1.5
Incidence of single-parent households (%)	7	16[2]
Incidence of one-person households (%)	14	27[2]
Number of divorces/100 marriages	6.8	36.1
Unemployment rate (%)	2.5	10.0
Workers on temporary contracts (%)[3]		
men	4	12
women	6	14
Workers on part-time contracts (%)[3]		
men	1	6
women	22	33
Social expenditure/GDP (%)	19.0[1]	28.7

Notes:
[1]   Data refer to 1970.
[2]   Data refer to 1990.
[3]   Start of period data refer to 1975.

Sources: Eurostat. Data refer to EUR 15.

social protection expenditure now represents more than a quarter of GDP and about half of public expenditure.

To some extent, the increase in welfare spending reflects the rise in European living standards: 'after all these welfare services are not inferior goods; the demand for them rises as people's incomes and wealth increase' (Orszag and Snower, 1997). However, this trend in spending, which has already contributed to substantial increases in tax and contribution rates, cannot continue indefinitely. Reforms are urgently required to check expenditure growth, which is fuelled by several factors common to most industrial countries: population ageing, changes in household structure, high unemployment and cost increases.

Population ageing   Changes in birth rates, life expectancy and migration flows are changing the size as well as the structure of the population of EU member states (European Commission, 1995c and 1996c; and Eurostat, 1996). The increase in the old-age dependency ratio, which is reaching historically unprecedented levels, is one of the most evident and important trends.

In the coming decades, demographic changes will affect public budgets, through their effects on the demand for public services and transfers and, indirectly, through their effects on macroeconomic and structural factors.[15] Public health and pension systems will bear much of this pressure, since their expenditure is highly dependent on the population age structure. According to national pension expenditure projections, over the period 1995–2030, under unchanged policy, the ratio of public pension expenditure to GDP in the EU will increase on average by 3 to 4 percentage points.[16]

Substantial pressures are also expected on expenditure for health care (Leibfritz et al., 1995) and services for the elderly,[17] especially in the light of the growing number of very old citizens with need for costly care. Although the expected decline in the share of young people in total population might reduce the demand for public services and transfers in other areas – namely basic education, maternity and child allowances – there is a widespread consensus that overall demographic changes tend to increase public expenditure and produce negative effects on public budgets (see Heller et al., 1986; OECD, 1988a; Leibfritz et al., 1995; Franco and Munzi, 1997). These effects will vary considerably across the EU according to different national demographic trends and public expenditure structure.

Changes in household structure   Family structures are changing rapidly. Households are becoming more fragmented (see Table 1.2). The increase in the number of lone parents and, more generally, the reduction in the size of households, tend to increase the proportion of households facing difficult economic conditions and the demand for welfare state services and transfers (OECD, 1990a and 1994b). The impact of changing family patterns is visible in most industrial countries through the relative increase in the social assistance or safety net component of the welfare state, particularly concerning young people and lone parents.[18] Household fragmentation tends to justify greater individualization of welfare benefits, also on grounds of horizontal equity (equal treatment for equal situation), which in turn implies higher spending.

High and persistent unemployment   Unemployment rates in Europe are considerably higher than those recorded in past decades: in 1998 the average rate in the EU (10 per cent) was four times higher than that in the 1960s (see Table 1.2). Unemployment spells are also much longer than in the past (see Section 2.2.2). High unemployment increases public expenditure on unemployment benefits and social assistance and reduces tax revenues. It also tends to increase pension expenditure, as the actual retirement age falls under the pressure of demands for early retirement or disability pensions. As a consequence, the effectiveness of reforms, aimed at cutting pension expenditure by increasing statutory retirement age, is reduced.

Cost pressures   The production of services directly provided or financed by the welfare state is subject to the 'Baumol disease of personal services'. As they consist mainly of personal services whose productivity grows slowly – because they are essentially provided through labour input – the cost of welfare state services is bound to increase relative to the cost of other commodities. This implies that in order to satisfy a rising demand society should allocate a rising share of national income to the welfare state (Snower, 1993 and 1994b). While globalization of services and intelligence-intensive technological progress may, in principle, help in keeping costs down in some services, recent experience seems to show that these developments also entail 'product innovation', which stimulates an even greater demand on the part of the public (for example, in health care).

In conclusion, given the expected changes in demographic structure and the other factors mentioned above, the preservation of present benefit levels and eligibility rules will require a substantial increase in national resources allocated to social security systems. Alternatively, the stabilization of social expenditure will entail severe cuts in benefit levels and substantial restrictions in eligibility. Both these options are difficult: the first implies persuading citizens to pay higher taxes and accepting higher disincentive effects; the second implies a revision of present objectives and a scaling-down of citizens' expectations.

2.2.2   Labour market problems

The labour market and the welfare state are closely linked. While labour market changes affect the demand for benefits and the sources to fund them, tax and benefit structures influence the behaviour of individuals in the labour market (see, for instance, OECD, 1995b). Demand and supply of labour are also affected by employment protection legislation, which can be considered an integral part of the European welfare state 'package'.[19]

The changing relationship between welfare state and labour market   Present European welfare systems – based on budgetary transfers to support workers during spells of unemployment, and job security legislation to ensure a relatively high degree of employment stability – were conceived in a situation of low and essentially cyclical unemployment; standardized production carried out by a relatively unskilled workforce; collective bargaining arrangements with various degrees of centralization and compression of wage structures; and one breadwinner per family (see, for example, Esping-Andersen, 1996). In this context, it was natural to have welfare services and transfers largely concentrated in the first and last part of a worker's life (covering basic education and retirement pensions) and in providing social insurance for temporary unemployment spells.[20]

The current and foreseeable features of the economic environment are gradually undermining all these elements.

In the EU there are about 18 million people unemployed. In most countries unemployment has been increasing from one economic cycle to the next. According to surveys, a further 9 million people are not registered as unemployed, but would be willing to sign up for a job if labour market prospects improve. The average participation rate in Europe is around 60 per cent, compared with more than 70 per cent in the United States. Furthermore, half of the unemployed have been out of work for more than a year and half of them have low educational levels.

Mass production is quickly being replaced by flexible, customer-oriented production: traditional Taylorist factories are giving way to 'holistic' firms characterized by more horizontal structures. As argued by Lindbeck and Snower (1996), the premium on workers' versatility, entailed by the new firm organization, is leading to a widening dispersion of wages within seemingly identical workers' groups, over and above the inequality-enhancing effect of skill-biased technological progress. This process, by increasing the importance of 'personalized' wage incentives, is putting strain on collective bargaining arrangements, based on the principle of equal pay for equal work. The weight of services, accounting for more than half of private employment and continuously increasing, adds to the difficulties of collective bargaining, as production units tend to be smaller in the tertiary sector. The reduction in firm size, evident since the 1970s even in manufacturing, works in the same direction.

The one-breadwinner-per-household model, which dominated in the 1950s and 1960s, is being progressively eroded. As documented by Webb (1995), in the UK, where this process has gone relatively further, in the period 1961–63 almost seven households out of ten included only one worker. This share collapsed to just above three out of ten at the beginning of the 1990s. On the contrary, the share of the two-worker household increased over the same period from 28 to 55 per cent. This process has gone hand in hand with a rising polarization of work distribution: the share of households without people working increased from 4 per cent at the beginning of the 1960s to 13 per cent in the early 1990s. At the same time, the second earner is often a part-timer, with a less stable job, being paid a relatively low wage (Gregg and Wadsworth, 1996).

Unemployment compensation   Unemployment benefits and unemployment assistance fulfil the basic objectives of, respectively, social insurance against loss of income due to (involuntary) job termination and social assistance, ensuring a minimum living standard. As explained above, the provision of public unemployment insurance can be justified on efficiency grounds, since private unemployment insurance may not be feasible due to information asymmetries in the insurance market. Unemployment compensation can also bring economic benefits in terms of more efficient job matching, as job-seekers can spend more time on searching for the job openings in which they will be more productive, and increase human capital accumulation by workers facing uncertain demand for firm-specific services.

However, unemployment compensation and, more generally, tax and transfer programmes are perceived as having potentially serious distortionary effects on the working of the labour market, resulting in an increase in the equilibrium rate of unemployment. More specifically, a high level and duration of benefits can reduce search effort on the part of the unemployed, work effort on the part of the employed and increase the bargaining power of insiders. In particular, at the low end of the wage scale, the effect of net transfers may be such as to remove any pecuniary incentive for the jobless to become employed (unemployment trap) or for the low-paid to increase work effort (poverty trap). These effects will generally result in an increase in the reservation wage. Furthermore, taxes and charges levied to finance unemployment compensation and the welfare state will tend to reduce the real wage that businesses can afford to pay to workers at any level of employment, thereby affecting negatively the demand for labour.[21]

Are these potential effects borne out by empirical evidence? Attention should be drawn to the following points:[22]

(i)   The estimated effects of the levels of benefits on the length of unemployment are relatively modest (estimated elasticity of unemployment with respect to benefits below one) according to a number of studies. In some European countries, replacement ratios are high and, as a consequence, the disincentives are potentially important, mainly for low-wage and 'fringe' workers as well as families with children.

(ii) The duration of benefit is generally estimated to have a significant effect on the length of unemployment.[23]

(iii) National institutional characteristics can considerably influence the effect of unemployment compensation: the tighter the administration of benefits, especially concerning job-search requirements, the lower the effect.

(iv) Unemployment compensation not only affects the probability of leaving unemployment for employment but also the whole range of labour market transitions. For example, a cut in benefits (or a tightening of eligibility requirements) will also tend to reduce unemployment by increasing withdrawals from the labour force (or participation in government training schemes).

In conclusion, although the recent surge in unemployment has gone hand in hand with a reduction in the generosity of benefit systems and it is difficult to attribute the bulk of European unemployment to benefit-induced disincentives, welfare systems and their financing appear to aggravate unemployment and have a significant effect on its persistence. The effects of benefits on work incentives become greater if account is taken of the corresponding increase in the tax burden (that is, by considering the marginal effective tax rates), with taxes on earned or labour income being the most damaging. This applies especially to low-skilled workers.

Labour market regulations   The general case for relaxing labour market regulations, for example pertaining to hiring and firing workers, is similar to the case for streamlining unemployment compensation, and is subject to analogous qualifications. Besides possibly increasing the equilibrium rate of unemployment by raising the power of insiders, employment protection is generally supposed to reduce the speed of adjustment of (un)employment to its long-run level following a shock (Jackman et al., 1996).

At the same time, some forms of labour market rigidity can be rationalized as substitutes for insurance that the markets cannot provide.[24] Employment stability provisions can also be seen as enhancing investment in match-specific human capital, which would not be undertaken in a *laissez-faire* world for fear of opportunistic behaviour (Alogoskoufis et al., 1995). Finally, it is also argued that the monopsony power of employers – the power to restrict labour demand in order to push down wages – is important and labour market regulations are required to restrain its use (Gregg and Manning, 1996).

To the extent that both labour market regulations and welfare provisions respond to the same types of market failures, they can also be seen as substitutes. It has been observed that 'labour market policy regimes work like communicating pipelines' (Schmid, 1995, p. 57): the relative underdevelopment of one set of policies tends to result in others being put in place to replace it. Thus, for example, the relatively high degree of labour market rigidities in some countries may be related to the limited development of the unemployment compensation system.

At the same time, it must be recognized that current labour market rigidities in Europe are too pervasive to be justified on efficiency grounds alone. Efficiency considerations would suggest compensating uninsurable losses through taxes and transfers rather than by placing constraints on the allocation and/or price of labour. Even more than welfare provisions, therefore, labour market rigidities probably call for a 'political economy' rationale, that is, one that explicitly recognizes the need for policies to be sustained by sufficiently strong coalitions.[25]

Views on the importance of regulations on labour market outcomes differ among economists. Empirically, it has proved difficult to establish the existence of a significant long-term effect of specific regulations on labour market adjustments (Blank and Freeman, 1993). Restrictions on hiring and firing, by increasing turnover costs, tend to make employment and unemployment more resistant to cyclical fluctuations. The result is a reduction in the variability of employment, but not necessarily the average level of employment (Bentolila and Bertola, 1990).

This neutral view of the impact of labour market regulations on employment and unemployment has been challenged recently on the basis of a number of relatively new features of the economic environment in the industrialized world. Specifically:

(i)   hiring and firing costs result in a 'zone of inaction' following a demand shock. But if a large shake-out of labour does occur, for example in the case of a deep and prolonged recession as experienced by many countries in the 1980s and in the 1990s, a return of demand to its pre-shock state may be insufficient to restore employment to its earlier levels (Diaz and Snower, 1996);

(ii)   restrictions such as seniority rules, by treating workers as close substitutes for each other, may hamper the organizational innovations required by new technologies (Lindbeck, 1994c);

(iii) high turnover costs may reduce technological innovation and hence productivity and competitiveness in the long term. A country with regulations making the reallocation of labour very costly will tend to produce a lower share of innovative, but riskier, goods and have a relatively lower investment in R&D (Saint-Paul, 1996).[26]

In conclusion, a critical examination of labour market regulations would probably confirm the view that 'existing legislation was better adapted to conditions in the past than to today's world with large macroeconomic disturbances, high and persistent unemployment, rapid structural change, great uncertainty, and increasing heterogeneity of jobs and workers' (Lindbeck, 1994c, p. 73).

3. IMPLICATIONS OF INCREASING ECONOMIC INTEGRATION

European welfare states will also be affected by increasing economic interdependence. The deepening of integration worldwide and in Europe will intensify some of the pressure highlighted in the previous section and add some additional constraints.

The implications on European welfare states of increasing integration can be analysed from three different standpoints:

  (i)   increased factor and consumer mobility;
 (ii)   economic adjustments in an integrated economy;
(iii)   the quest for budgetary discipline.

3.1 Factor and Consumer Mobility

Economic integration increases the mobility of productive factors and may also increase the mobility of the consumers of social services.

Factor mobility

Economic integration, which is expected to deepen in Europe after the introduction of the single currency, by stepping up factor mobility, may increase revenue losses arising from the movement of tax bases towards countries applying lower tax rates. A situation of fiscal degradation could be made worse by fiscal competition among countries and regions, which might reduce tax rates in order to attract productive factors. These trends would primarily affect capital income taxation and corporate taxation, but labour and consumption taxes would also be influenced.

The empirical research on the effects of tax degradation and competition on revenue trends in the EU member states is still in its infancy (Hoeller et al., 1996). Although, over recent years, tax to GDP ratios have remained broadly constant, the distribution of the tax burden on different factors in the EU has changed substantially along lines consistent with fiscal degradation and competition. Over the period 1980–94, while the implicit tax rate on employees' income increased on average from 34.7 to 40.5 per cent, the implicit rate on other productive factor income declined from 44.1 to 35.2 per cent (European Commission, 1996b).

Future trends are also uncertain. Some economists take the view that, if unmitigated tax competition is allowed in the internal market, 'the New York City effect will be the death of European welfare states' (Sinn, 1990). While this view is perhaps extreme, in a context of mobile tax bases and competition between jurisdictions, further increases in the tax to GDP ratios appear unlikely. Attempts to shift even further the burden of funding public expenditure on to labour would reinforce the negative effects on employment highlighted above.

The role of benefit taxation (user charges and so on) is bound to increase, while that of the ability to pay taxation is likely to be restrained. An increasing share of revenue will come from taxpayers covering the cost of the specific services provided to them. To the extent that social protection provides insurance (rather than simply redistributing income), mobile but risk-averse workers will value it as a service. Therefore, while quasi-actuarial social insurance will survive labour market integration, social assistance will come under increasing pressure (Atkinson, 1992). Several recent pension reforms are moving this way (see Section 4.1), as well as the proposals by Fölster and Orszag and Snower considered in Section 4.2.3.

The gradual transformation of taxes into pure-benefit taxes seems a likely scenario particularly for the taxation of business, with firms increasingly shopping across jurisdictions within the single market in search of the best tax and service package. Empirical evidence, based on the United States experience, points to relatively low interregional (interstate) elasticities of economic activity (employment or value added) with respect to (aggregate) tax levels (between 0.2 and 0.6); however, elasticities become higher when public services are included in the analysis, and intraregional (intrastate) elasticities are much higher (four times as much or more) than interregional ones. This suggests that, with other cost variables similar among different locations, taxation plays an important role in location decisions (Wasylenko, 1997).

Consumer mobility

Increased economic integration may also increase the mobility of consumers of welfare state services. Citizens may have an incentive to move to countries that provide higher benefits and better services or they may demand services produced in other member states.

Welfare migration, which may push towards lowering the level of services, is not likely to reach sizeable dimensions (Ermisch, 1991). In the United States it is discernible, but not important. States are therefore able to keep different levels of benefits. Labour mobility in Europe, both across and within countries, is markedly lower than in the United States. Hence it is likely that also in the future European governments will be in a position to pursue tax and transfer policies according to national preferences. This conclusion is supported by the experience of Switzerland, a small country with a linguistically diverse population, where local authorities (cantons) are responsible for a high (and increasing) share of government transfers (Begg et al., 1993; Hoeller et al., 1996).[27]

An increasing number of citizens is also likely to demand services produced in other countries, without necessarily living there. This may apply particularly to health and insurance services.[28] This trend would provide incentives to improve the quality of services and increase efficiency. In the long run, it might also lead to some harmonization of national social protection systems.

3.2 Economic Adjustment in an Integrated Economy

Economic and monetary integration will affect the way European economies adjust to shocks. First, in economic and monetary union (EMU), the nominal exchange rate will not be available as an adjustment tool in the event of country-specific shocks. Second, globalization and the internal market are likely to change the nature of shocks. Last, but not least, the behaviour of wage and price setters is also likely to be affected. The functioning of the welfare state has important implications for the way these changes translate into employment/unemployment outcomes.[29]

It is argued that in the short term, following the occurrence of a given shock, the availability of the nominal exchange rate can enhance the effectiveness of the adjustment to the new equilibrium. Adverse country-specific shocks require a depreciation of the real exchange rate to avoid negative fluctuations in unemployment. If wages to do not adjust smoothly to the new conditions, a depreciation of the nominal exchange rate can arguably work in 'front-loading' the required real exchange rate adjustment. This presupposes, however, that exchange rates tend to move predictably in response to macroeconomic imbalances. Experience and empirical evidence indicate that, in a world of free capital movements, exchange rates tend to be driven by financial considerations, which are unrelated to such macroeconomic imbalances. Empirical evidence also suggests that European countries are characterized by a relatively high degree of real wage rigidity, that is, a relatively fast response of wages to prices changes coupled with a relatively low sensitivity to unemployment. If wages react quickly to price rises, a nominal exchange rate depreciation is bound to be less effective in inducing an equivalent change in the real exchange rate and more likely to trigger an inflationary spiral.

More generally, globalization and higher trade integration are likely to have wider consequences for the dynamics of European economies. More open and transparent markets may increase 'contestability' and spur organizational and technological innovation, thereby leading to a higher frequency of industry-specific shocks. Moreover, the internal market rules, coupled with a tough competition policy, will reduce the scope for defensive industrial policies by member countries that have been intensively used in the past, in order to cushion negative shocks and preserve occupational levels. These effects, which cannot be tackled through nominal exchange rate variations, may require more frequent changes in relative wages and a smooth reallocation of labour across sectors and regions.

At the same time, the competition-enhancing effects of economic integration are likely to impose more discipline on wage and price setters. This should mean both a more effective adjustment to shocks and a lower equilibrium level of unemployment.

Welfare state provisions have mixed effects in this context: employment protection legislation may hamper the shift of labour resources from declining to rising industries; analogously, unemployment compensation, by reducing job-search activity and enhancing insiders' power, may increase real wage rigidity. However, social insurance, by easing the transition, can render reallocation more feasible. Other welfare state programmes (that is, training and active labour market policies, as well as housing policy) also play an important role in fostering labour mobility and industrial adjustment.

Better mobility-friendly welfare services, coupled with less rigid hiring and firing rules and an improvement of the conditionality of unemployment benefits (better incentives, job-search requirement, and the like) would enhance the ability of labour markets to respond to shocks. Although the mobility-oriented revision of the welfare state should primarily involve labour market policies and unemployment benefits, all schemes should be re-examined. For instance, the obstacles to labour mobility arising from pension systems should be gradually removed (by reducing the segmentation of the system into different schemes or ensuring the portability of contributions). Housing policies should also be systematically reconsidered.

3.3 The Quest for Budgetary Discipline

Solid budgetary discipline is an essential condition for the success of EMU. A sound budgetary position before joining the single currency and budgetary prudence once in EMU are at the core of the budgetary policy provisions of the Maastricht Treaty.

It should be stressed that, as pointed out above, European budgetary trends would require substantial corrections. The budgetary framework for EMU outlines policy changes that several countries would in any case have implemented. In some cases, it may accelerate policy changes by increasing the pressure to take a more long-term view in evaluating the costs and benefits of different policies.

Given that further increases in the ratio of tax revenues to GDP do not seem feasible, because of the implications of economic integration on revenues (Section 3.1), future budgetary adjustments will have to be concentrated on expenditure items. Any correction of present expenditure trends will necessarily involve social protection expenditure, which represents about two-thirds of public expenditure net of interest payments in EU member states and, for the reasons outlined in Section 2.2.1, tends to increase faster than other expenditure items.

Over the next few years, pressure on welfare spending will be exerted by the further reduction of the deficit towards a balanced budget, as provided for by the Stability and Growth Pact.[30] This implies that governments will have to run large primary surpluses in normal economic conditions. An indication of the size of the surpluses is provided by the amount of interest payments (an average expenditure of 4.6 percentage points of GDP in 1998).

Over a longer time span, further substantial policy changes will be required in order to maintain the 'close-to-balance' position, particularly after the year 2010, and to population ageing determining unsustainable deficits and debt levels (Franco and Munzi, 1997). More specifically, action should be taken to offset the budgetary effects of the demographic changes outlined in Section 2.2.1. In the long run, welfare state transfers may also have to compete with competitiveness-enhancing spending priorities, such as infrastructure investment, and may require a revision of their internal composition, with a greater concentration on education and human capital improvement.

One point should be stressed. Although the close-to-balance rule is introduced in connection with EMU, its implementation will also allow member states to meet the deterioration of the demographic situation after the year 2010 with smaller public debts and lower interest burdens. Governments will be forced to use the demographic 'breathing-space' to meet on a sounder fiscal policy position the ageing of the baby-boom generation.[31]

4.   THE REFORM PROCESS

According to opinion polls, throughout the Union there is widespread support for the essential features of the welfare state: universal rights to basic health and educational services, support for poor, sick, unemployed and disabled citizens, and an adequate level of intergenerational redistribution guaranteed by the state. It is widely felt that reforms should not impair these achievements and fundamental features.

However, the continuation of present social protection policies would require increases in tax rates that would negatively affect labour supply and unemployment, might have a negative impact on the long-term performance of European economies, and would conflict with the pressures for lower tax rates stemming from economic integration and the globalization of economic activities. Across Europe, policy-makers are, therefore, confronted with the

task of curbing expenditure growth while preserving the fundamental features of social protection systems and facing new needs, such as those of
elderly citizens in long-term care and lone-parent families.

This section focuses on three specific aspects of the reform issue. First, it
shows that the adjustment process of social policies to the new demographic
and economic conditions is already under way, although it is far from completion. Then it considers three possible reform lines: the transition from
pay-as-you-go (PAYG) to funded pension schemes, the shift from unemployment benefits towards employment subsidies and changes in the design of
social protection in order to strengthen their efficiency. Finally, it examines
some aspects of the implementation of the reform process and points to the
problems of welfare state retrenchment.

4.1 Reforms are Under Way

In most countries, present social policies are quite different from those implemented in previous decades.[32] The phase of extension of coverage and
improvement of benefits is over, although in a few countries the lagged effects
of past extensions and improvements are still affecting expenditure growth.

This change is quite evident for pension systems. Since the mid-1980s,
most pension schemes have been reformed in order to reduce pension expenditure. Major reforms were introduced in Austria (1985, 1988 and 1993),
Germany (1989), Italy (1992 and 1995), France (1993), Greece (1990 and
1992), Portugal (1993), Sweden (1994) and the United Kingdom (1986 and
1994). Reforms involve less generous benefit indexation rules, increases in
standard retirement age, reductions in replacement rates, tightening of eligibility criteria for disability benefits and pension credits for years with limited
or null contributions, curtailing or abolishing of public sector employees'
special pension benefits, and lengthening of contribution periods required for
pension eligibility. In several countries, reforms, by cutting eligibility and
transfer ratios,[33] have brought the expected increases in the ratio of pension
expenditure to GDP firmly below the expected increases in the old-age dependency ratio. Cost containment was just one of the objectives of the reforms,
which also aimed at making the system more able to tolerate demographic
change, more transparent in its distributive effects, and less distortive in its
effects on individuals' choices.[34]

Health-care systems are undergoing substantial changes, although the general pattern of reform is less uniform (European Commission, 1995a; OECD,
1990b, 1994c and 1995a). This is due to substantial differences in the structure of national health-care systems and the role of the public sector in the
provision and financing of health care. While the principles of universality
and equality in the access to services were not questioned, expenditure con-

trol has been pursued with a wide variety of instruments: tighter hospital budgets, restrictions on the supply of services (hospital beds, new entrants in medical education, new technologies), restrictions on the reimbursement of drugs (with negative and positive lists and reference price systems), increase in cost-sharing. Several reforms aimed at increasing efficiency in the use of resources and quality of services by modifying incentives at the micro-level: giving patients more choice (Sweden), introducing competition within the public sector and between the public and the private sector (the United Kingdom), separating the provision and the financing of services (the United Kingdom), relying more on contracts as an instrument to allocate resources among providers, shifting responsibilities towards regional and local administrative levels (Finland and Italy).

Unemployment benefits are also being reformed throughout the EU, with the emphasis on curbing expenditure growth and dependency on social protection. However, institutional changes in most member states fall short of a radical overhaul of the current systems. Efforts have also been made to curb abuses. Eligibility criteria have been tightened, with stricter definitions of availability for work and tougher sanctions on those refusing to take up a job (or a training course) applied in several countries (such as Denmark, Finland, Germany, Sweden and the United Kingdom). The duration of benefits and/or replacement ratios have been reduced in an attempt to curb alleged work disincentives (Denmark, Ireland, the Netherlands, Spain and Sweden). Countries featuring in-work benefits to top up low wages (Ireland and the United Kingdom) have introduced changes aimed at minimizing the risk of poverty traps, such as higher earning thresholds and the gradual phasing out of benefits. More generally, action to curb high marginal effective tax rates has been taken in several countries (such as Denmark, France, Ireland, the Netherlands, Sweden and the United Kingdom). Overall tax wedges on labour have also been reduced (for example in the Netherlands).

In conclusion, the adjustment of European welfare states to the new demographic scenarios is under way, with reforms gradually affecting expenditure dynamics, especially in the pensions area. The changes that have already been implemented, while still not sufficient to arrest expenditure increase, offer some scope for optimism, since in many countries public opinion has been prepared to accept substantial changes in entitlements. The adjustment to a more competitive economic environment raises more difficult problems: while some reforms have improved the incentive structure in the pensions and health area, much still remains to be done. Several pension schemes still provide incentives to retire early. The effects of the reforms in the health-care sector are far from clear; moreover, the direction of further reforms is still not well defined. The incentive problems related to unemployment and other transfers would also require substantial improvements in tax-benefit systems.

4.2   Which New Reforms?

Introducing further reforms to allow European welfare states to cope with new needs and constraints raises a number of difficult issues. How far can social expenditure be constrained without impairing the main objectives of present policies? Can reforms fully offset the effects of ageing on spending or should increases in revenues and cuts in other budgetary items also be planned? Which benefits could actually be reduced? Should more emphasis be put on systemic reforms or on punctual changes of the parameters of the present system (for example by tightening eligibility rules and reducing transfer ratios)? Should the targeting of benefits on the most needy be revised or the welfare state be withdrawn from the middle classes? Should the boundary between the responsibility of the state and that of the private sector be shifted? What is the scope for privatization in the financing and the production of social services?

Providing answers to these questions goes well beyond the scope of the paper.[35] This section takes a narrower approach by considering three reform lines that aim at reducing the role of the public sector in providing pensions, overcoming the inefficiencies of unemployment benefit systems, and improving the incentives produced by social protection systems.

4.2.1   From PAYG to funding

The reform of pension systems, which absorb a large share of social protection expenditure and are particularly affected by population ageing, is at the core of the adaptation of the welfare state to new economic and demographic conditions. It is fundamental for ensuring durable fiscal consolidation and for improving the conditions of European labour markets.

As reported in Section 2.2.1, in spite of these reform efforts, which will partly offset the effects of demographic trends, in most countries the preservation of present pension benefit levels and eligibility rules will require a substantial increase in the national resources devoted to pension systems. Alternatively, the stabilization of pension expenditure will require further severe cuts in pension benefit levels and substantial restrictions in pension eligibility.

The first option raises several problems. Although reforms strengthening the link between contributions and benefits might make the burden of contributions more tolerable and less distortive, adding 3 to 4 points to the present tax to GDP ratio would be extremely difficult for the reasons pointed out at the beginning of Section 4.

It would also be difficult to compensate for the increase in pension expenditure with cuts on other expenditure items. The decline in the share of the young to the total population offers some margins for cutting education expenditure, but health expenditure and expenditure for services to the elderly are likely to increase substantially (Franco and Munzi, 1997). So, in the end, containment of benefits is likely to be the primary instrument for guaranteeing the solvency of PAYG pension systems. This implies a scaling down of citizens' expectations and a revision of present objectives. Further reforms might involve changes in indexation rules, increases in retirement age, reductions in replacement rates, and tightening of eligibility criteria (Thomas, 1997). As mentioned in Section 4.1, examples of such piecemeal reforms have, in the past, demonstrated in several countries the effectiveness of such measures in slowing down pension expenditure dynamics.

The increasing role of funding In several countries, the relative weight of PAYG and funded schemes is changing, with the latter schemes gradually becoming more important. While there is a widespread consensus that the role of funded schemes should be increased, there are no clear indications about its optimum size (OECD, 1992b; World Bank, 1994; Davis, 1995).

Economic considerations point to the desirability of pension systems that include both PAYG and funded schemes, since both types of scheme are subject to different risks and returns (Fornero, 1995). PAYG schemes are superior in the alleviation of poverty and the provision of insurance against inflation and investment risks. On the other hand, they are vulnerable to population ageing and decline in employment. Governments may also default on promises based on optimistic assumptions. Funded schemes produce lower distortionary effects in the labour market. They may also contribute to the development of financial markets (Davis, 1996) and provide workers with higher returns to contributions in a situation in which the real interest rate is higher than the rate of growth of employment and real wages. On the other hand, they are vulnerable to inflation and investment risks and have relatively high administration costs.

The development of funded schemes does not of itself provide a solution to the sustainability problems of the PAYG schemes, which can only be ensured through further cuts in their benefits. Supplementary funded schemes can, however, facilitate the reforms of PAYG schemes by offering to the workers the possibility to compensate for the reduction in the replacement rate resulting from the reforms. This development will lead to a partial shift of responsibility for retirement income provision from the government towards workers and employers.

As the importance of supplementary pensions increases as a share of total retirement income, it is increasingly important for governments to provide a secure environment for the efficient operation of supplementary funded schemes (European Commission, 1997a and 1997b). A regulatory framework that enables pension funds in all countries properly to diversify their assets, both domestically and internationally, should enhance returns, reduce risks arising from domestic economic cycles and reduce the negative impact on asset prices during periods of disinvestment (that is, when elderly generations run down their wealth).[36]

As illustrated in Holzmann (1997), reforms implying a large-scale switch from PAYG to funding are difficult to implement in the case of developed and mature public pension systems such as those prevailing in most EU member states. In the event of such a shift, government pension liabilities would become 'explicit', and create a stock and flow problem in public finances. The magnitude of the problem is indicated by the value of future pension liabilities already accrued by the workforce, which in most EU member states is much higher than conventional public debt (Van den Noord and Herd, 1994).[37] In order to assess the effect of a shift, it is important to examine how the deficit would be financed, as well as the timing of the shift. The burden of the transition could either fall on the current generation – which would have to pay twice through higher taxes, or lower public expenditure in other fields, in order to finance outgoing pensions, while having to pay contributions to the new funded scheme – or be distributed between current and future generations, through an increase in public deficit and debt. Both these solutions raise difficult problems.

4.2.2   Overcoming the inefficiencies of unemployment benefits

Unemployment benefits and assistance pursue efficiency and equity goals. However, as pointed out above, problems of incentive (in)compatibility and funding strain may give rise to unemployment and poverty traps. When these problems are particularly serious, unemployment benefits and transfers, instead of lifting the unemployed or the 'working poor' out of their disadvantaged status, actually contribute to its persistence.

The main policy alternatives to current unemployment benefits are the introduction of a conditional negative income tax and the replacement of unemployment benefits with employment subsidies.

A conditional negative income tax could achieve higher equity and efficiency than unemployment benefits (Snower, 1995). Income redistribution would imply that the lowest income brackets would receive transfers, which would gradually give way to taxes at higher income levels. The conditional character of the tax would be related, as for the current unemployment benefit systems, to evidence of active job search. Such a measure could be more effective for equity purposes because it can be argued that the income level rather than the employment status is a better criterion for redistribution. It could also be more employment-friendly because job search is less discouraged, as becoming employed at a low wage would lead to a loss of only a fraction of the negative income taxes, rather than all the unemployment benefits. More generally, a negative income tax may be more appropriate in overcoming the inefficiencies generated by credit constraints, which are more closely associated with low incomes than with unemployment.[38]

Several studies have argued that replacing unemployment benefits with employment subsidies would allow the same equity objectives to be pursued, while promoting employment.[39] Two main proposals have been widely discussed in the literature:

(i) Low-wage employment subsidies or targeted reductions in payroll taxes have been proposed to tackle the unskilled unemployment problem (see, for example, Drèze and Malinvaud, 1994; Phelps, 1994b and 1996; Fitoussi, 1996).

(ii) Giving the opportunity to unemployed people, especially the long-term unemployed, to use part of their unemployment benefits as employment vouchers to the firms available to hire them. Snower (1994a, 1994b, 1996b), who first put forward such proposal, dubbed it 'benefit-transfer' programme.

If these schemes were effective in taking the long-term unemployed off the dole, the newly generated tax revenue and savings in social transfers would reduce their net cost. No inflationary pressure would arise from the fall in unemployment because the wage discipline exerted by the long-term unemployed is negligible. As in the case of unemployment benefits, these schemes would have a built-in stabilization function.[40] The low-wage subsidies and the employment voucher proposals are not mutually exclusive.[41]

However, the above schemes are not without problems (see, *inter alia*, Nickell and Bell, 1995; Snower, 1996b):

(i) the increase in employment induced by subsidies should be assessed net of dead-weight costs (job-seekers who would have been offered a job anyway, given the incumbent workers' average propensity to quit and the proportion of vacancies filled by the unemployed) and substitution and displacement between the target group and incumbent workers (firms substituting one lot of workers for another or employment expansion in one set of firms displacing employment in other firms);

(ii) if the amount of the subsidy or the 'size' of the voucher is a positive function of the duration of period out of work, job search could be discouraged;

(iii) the acceptance of subsidies or vouchers might be less than intended if they are perceived by the unemployed and the employers as carrying signalling or stigma implications;

(iv) the employment impact depends on the endogenous reaction of wages:

for employment to increase, some part of the subsidy must act to reduce the cost of employing marginal workers and not to be passed on entirely to wages;[42]

(v) by raising the take-home pay and/or the employment rate of low-skilled workers relative to that of skilled workers, subsidies reduce the expected private rate of return on education and can thereby depress human capital accumulation and productivity growth.

Part of these negative effects can be attenuated through careful programme design: by giving the right to displaced workers to introduce a formal complaint leading to withdrawal of benefits; by transforming incapacity benefits into employment vouchers – thereby incurring low dead-weight costs – as proposed by Orszag and Snower (1996); by foreseeing a not-so-steep temporal profile of subsidies/vouchers to discourage job-search postponement; by offering higher subsidies/vouchers to firms that use them for training. However, they cannot be completely eliminated. Indeed, the experience of a number of EU countries that have implemented various forms of reductions in payroll taxes point to a rather weak net effect on employment.[43]

4.2.3 Improving the incentives of welfare state schemes

As pointed out above, many of the problems related to the working of social security systems are unavoidable. However, their dimension is surely exacerbated by the structure of present social schemes (Orszag and Snower, 1997). Contributions are often loosely related to benefits, so that they are largely regarded as a tax, expenditure controls frequently rely on administrative constraints rather than on built-in incentives, and redistribution and insurance features are frequently mixed and insurance schemes are utilized for inappropriate distribution objectives. As pointed out by Musgrave (1981): 'To represent as redistribution what in fact is not is undesirable as a matter of social sensibility. Moreover the acceptability for redistribution measures is limited and should not be preempted by what in fact is not a part thereof.'

In several countries, proposals have been put forward to redesign social security schemes along lines that are less distortive of individuals' choices and more transparent in their distributive effects.[44] Reforms have already been introduced or planned along the same lines. The strengthening of the contribution–benefit link is a crucial factor. These actions are expected to increase the incentive to work and, more specifically, to stay on in regular jobs (since benefits would depend on work record), to delay retirement, and to move from benefits to work. These effects would reduce the demand for benefits and allow a reduction in contribution rates and tax wedges. By making workers more aware of the value of the benefits for which they are paying contributions, they may also affect wage negotiations, for if workers are not aware of the value of non-wage benefits, they are not likely to trade lower wage increases for the continuation of present benefits.[45]

In the case of pension schemes, this line of reforms increases the role of actuarial principles: this implies shifting PAYG schemes from 'defined benefits' systems (which base pensions on earnings in the final period of work) to 'defined contribution' systems (which base pensions on contributions paid over the whole working life) and increasing the role of funded schemes (where the contribution–benefit link is typically very strong). Some recent pension reforms have been explicitly designed on the criteria outlined above: the Swedish and Italian reforms in 1994 and 1995, respectively, are going to replace the present wage-related pension with actuarial pensions based on lifetime contributions and expected life at retirement. Piecemeal changes introduced in several countries also strengthened the contribution–benefit link.

All encompassing reform proposals of benefit systems with built-in incentives that limit the demand for benefits are put forward by Fölster (1997) and Orszag and Snower (1997). Fölster suggests the introduction of 'individual social insurance accounts'. In the same vein, Orszag and Snower propose the establishment of 'welfare accounts' for each citizen covering the four main welfare functions, namely provision for retirement, unemployment compensation, human capital formation and insurance against sickness and disability. Mandatory contributions, set in an actuarially fair manner and supplemented by a degree of redistribution across individual income situations, would be made to each account, and individual withdrawals, subject to prudential monthly limits, would replace current pension, unemployment and sickness and disability benefits.

The system would reduce the incentives to stay on benefits and increase the incentive to work, as the longer people remain unemployed the lower the net balances on their unemployment accounts available for subsequent use. It would allow a reduction in contribution rates and bring social security contributions back to their insurance origins, that is, back to the benefit principle (the tax is the price for a specific public service or transfer). The scope for the benefit principle would be large, as a very large proportion of social transfers (80 per cent in Sweden) 'merely smooths income over the individual's life cycle' (Fölster, 1997).[46]

4.3   The Implementation of Reforms

As was pointed out at the beginning of this section, European welfare systems are undergoing substantial changes. However, even in countries that have experienced the so-called 'conservative revolution' of the 1980s (essentially, the United Kingdom and the United States), in spite of the widely publicized negative consequences of welfare dependence, there has not been a major overhaul of the welfare state. As Snower puts it, 'while many governments focused less attention on alleviating poverty and unemployment, the welfare state services to the middle classes remained virtually untouched. While the welfare state withered, the transfer state bloomed' (Snower, 1994b, p. 2).

Why is it proving so difficult to reform the welfare state?

First of all, from a political science standpoint, Pierson (1996) stresses the generally conservative character of democratic political institutions: the welfare state now represents the *status quo*. Hence changing it would require explicit political decisions (as opposed to non-decisions, which are more frequent in such sensitive matters).

Second, reforms may be hampered by the fact that their costs are felt immediately, while their benefits are more uncertain and accrue in the future (possibly beyond the political horizon of policy-makers). With reference to labour market regulations, radical reforms may be opposed because there may be more losers than winners (the unemployed are still a relatively small minority), the coalition in favour of them is politically very heterogeneous (skilled workers, small entrepreneurs, besides the unemployed and the inactive) and there is uncertainty about the groups that will actually gain from reforms.[47] These 'political economy' considerations, that emphasize the pivotal role of the median voter, seem relevant for welfare state provisions at large.

Third, in the most developed welfare state systems, as economic agents are more tightly linked than in decentralized market economies, reforms imply greater costs because changes in one part alter the efficiency of other parts of the system.[48]

While the build-up of the welfare state has occurred through incremental policy changes over the years, 'decrementalism' (a gradual rolling back of the frontiers of the welfare state) may not be the most effective reform strategy. A number of arguments point to the benefits of bundling policy changes in a single overall package. First of all, a global approach would help in exploiting policy complementarities that enhance the efficiency gains produced by individual policies (Coe and Snower, 1997).[49] Second, decrementalism may induce 'rule instability' (Lindbeck, 1994b and 1995) by leading to uncertainty and expectations of further changes down the road, with negative consequences on private consumption/saving behaviour. Finally, a comprehensive social pact aiming at overcoming the corporatist opposition of narrower special interests (Esping-Andersen, 1996) and a global package reform so that most voters both lose, on the benefit side, and win, on the tax side (Lindbeck, 1994a), appear more likely to gather political consensus.[50]

5. CONCLUSIONS

Richard Musgrave, in his seminal work on the theory of public finance (Musgrave, 1959), identified three basic government functions: allocation, redistribution and stabilization. The modern welfare state, especially in its west European version, has played a central role in each one of these functions: by stepping into areas characterized by lack of private insurance, it helped to correct significant market failures; a more equitable resource distribution was pursued through a host of mechanisms, both on the revenue and on the expenditure side of the budget; finally, a number of these mechanisms – namely unemployment insurance, as well as the large tax systems – acted as built-in stabilizers in recessions.

As this paper has documented, the achievements of the European welfare state are impressive: Europe's social fabric is, on the whole, much more cohesive than that of the United States and, for a long time, a large welfare state has coexisted with rapid economic growth. However, important challenges are calling into question such achievements.

A number of developments are undermining the role of the welfare state in all three government functions:

(i)   high marginal effective tax rates distort incentives and hamper the functioning of the labour market; they may have a significant role in the scale and persistence of European unemployment;

(ii) the equity objective is questioned by the presence of a large pool of long-term unemployed, who often become permanently disfranchised from the official labour market;

(iii) even the stabilization function is jeopardized as high deficits and debts reduce the room for manoeuvre and the anticyclical effectiveness of budgetary policy.

It is likely that, without major changes, such negative aspects would be reinforced in the future, as demography and other factors are likely to heighten budgetary sustainability and labour market problems. The acceleration of European economic and monetary integration also calls for important changes in the current welfare systems in order to allow them to continue to pursue their equity and efficiency goals in a changing economic environment.

The process of welfare state reform has started throughout Europe, often motivated by the budgetary consolidation objectives of the Maastricht Treaty. In several member states, recent reforms, especially in the pension area, have managed to slow down the increase of welfare spending as a share of GDP. On a number of accounts, however, the reform process has been unsatisfactory.

Besides taking insufficient account of likely future developments and their implications in terms of implicit government liabilities, the reforms have often taken too long to be implemented. This has increased the cost of transition once the new regime has been put into place. 'Political economy' considerations may explain the protracted controversies surrounding reforms. They may also explain two other shortcomings, namely, the relative penalization of the worst-off to the advantage of the middle classes in the reform of benefits and the insufficient attention to efficiency in the production of public services, such as health care.

What policy lessons can be drawn from the academic and policy debate that has been surveyed in this paper? Due to the lack of a country-specific approach, only a number of general principles that could underline future reforms can be highlighted:

(a)   Maintaining a sustainable fiscal position by adjusting welfare expenditure trends

Medium- and long-term expenditure trends should be closely monitored. Action should be taken well in advance to avoid pressure on public budgets leading to higher tax rates or deficits. More specifically, pension reforms should be announced early, so as to allow a gradual implementation; sudden changes in rules should be avoided, since they carry large adjustment costs as citizens have made their working and saving decisions under pre-reform rules. The breathing-space that pension expenditure projections outline for the next few years should be used to introduce reforms aimed at cutting benefits after 2010.

As future employment and productivity trends are uncertain, so are the resources available for financing benefits in the future. Whatever reforms are implemented, they should be flexible and allow for adjustments in expenditure dynamics. Flexibility should be built into the system with transparent and stable rules. For instance, pension replacement ratios could be automatically adjusted to changes in life expectancy, while pension indexation arrangements could take imbalances in revenue and benefit trends into consideration.

(b)   Strengthening the actuarial elements in the welfare state system

While the fundamental redistributive aims of social protection systems should be retained, their structure should be re-examined. Assistance functions should be more clearly separated from insurance functions. The design of insurance schemes should be modified on market-oriented lines, based on a closer link between contributions and benefits. At the individual level, the link between contributions and benefits should be transparent, easy to grasp and stable over time. Therefore, pensions, and, where possible, non-pension benefits, should be linked to past contributions by shifting from defined benefit systems to defined contribution systems. The introduction of individual social insurance or welfare accounts would substantially strengthen this reform process. All this would have favourable effects on incentives, wage settlements and budgetary sustainability and would limit the negative effects of contributions and benefits on employment.

(c)   Building incentive-compatible systems also on the supply side of welfare state provisions

Putting into practice the previous point would go a long way towards improving the incentive-compatibility of the welfare state system. However, not only recipients but also suppliers of welfare state services should have the right incentives in optimizing available resources. Major improvements can be achieved, in particular, in the production of health services. Efficiency gains can also be achieved in active labour market policies, such as those aiming at improving skills and supporting job search, where bureaucratic performance indicators may result in adverse selection (for example by making public employment services choose easy-to-place individuals).

(d)   Reconsidering social transfer and taxes at the low end of the wage scale

The economic position of the less skilled has deteriorated in both the United States (lower relative wages) and Europe (higher relative unemployment). In the European setting, if both higher employment rates and minimum socially acceptable incomes are deemed equally important objectives, steps should be taken to eliminate those features of the transfer and tax systems that tend to aggravate the situation. Specifically, low-wage recipients should not be discriminated against by the benefit system relative to the long-term unemployed or to persons who are not working. In turn, taxation should not penalise workers at the low end of the productivity scale.

(e)   Enhancing human capital formation

Measures to reduce rigidities in the labour market, including reduction of wage-compression mechanisms, should be coupled with strong action on the improvement of knowledge and skills. A key objective should be ensuring that all labour market entrants are equipped with basic literacy, numeracy and vocational competence. Achieving a more

even distribution of human capital is probably the best way to dispel the
fear that, with higher labour market flexibility, Europe might run into
the American working-poor syndrome.

NOTES

1. The views expressed in this chapter represent exclusively the positions of the authors and
   do not necessarily correspond to those of the European Commission. The authors wish to
   thank Dr Heinrich Matthes for his encouragement and support. They also thank for
   valuable comments Joly Dixon, Jan Schmidt, Jerôme Vignon, Hans Wijkander, as well as
   the participants in a seminar organized by the Directorate-General for Employment,
   Industrial Relations and Social Affairs to which a preliminary draft of the chapter was
   presented. Maria Davi, Ingrid Godkin, Tracy Kebble, Cecilia Mulligan and Rui Pericao
   provided excellent editorial assistance.
2. These issues are extensively considered also in several documents produced by the Directorate-General for Employment, Industrial Relations and Social Affairs. See European
   Commission (1993a, 1995a, 1995b, 1997a). See also OECD (1988b, 1994a).
3. As already pointed out in the introduction, it should be stressed that the social protection
   systems of EU member states are not homogeneous. According to Rhodes (1996), at least
   four models can be identified: the Scandinavian model (high degree of universality and
   institutionalization), the Bismarckian model (labour-market-based solutions, social insurance arrangements), the liberal Anglo-Saxon model (flat-rate provisions, extensive means
   testing), the Southern model (protection for regular workers, lack of general safety net,
   role of family in redistribution). On the specific features of the Southern model, see also
   Ferrera (1996). On the issue of convergence of European social protection systems towards a common model, see Chassard and Venturini (1995) and Grahal and Teague
   (1996).
4. For a comparative analysis of the development of the welfare state in Europe and the
   United States, see Flora and Heidenheimer (1981). See also Emerson (1988).
5. A caveat is in order when assessing the effectiveness of the welfare states in reducing
   inequality: the standard approach, comparing the distribution of net income with the
   distribution of income before taxes and transfer, fails to take into account behavioural
   responses to taxation and social transfers that are likely to result in pre-transfer and pre-
   tax income being more unequally distributed than it would be in the absence of redistributive
   policies (for example, relatively generous pension benefits inducing people to withdraw
   from work and hence forgo market income earlier than would otherwise be the case). The
   magnitude of these feedback effects is the object of considerable controversy, even if they
   do not seem to be anywhere as large as to negate the effect of redistribution. Moreover, the
   intensity of the welfare state redistributive effort cannot be plausibly taken as independent
   from other factors affecting income distribution (for example, trade unions' strength).
   These factors will tend to reduce the inequality of market outcomes and at the same time
   increase the intensity of redistribution (Pedersen, 1994).
6. In 1990 0.52 per cent of the United States adult male population was in prison. Overall, in
   the United States 6.6 per cent of the work force was under the supervision of the criminal
   justice system (in prison, on probation or parole) in 1993. Moreover, the prison population
   has been increasing by nearly 9 per cent a year since the 1980s so that 'at current rates, in
   the year 2000 the United States will have a larger share of males of working age impris-
   oned or long-term unemployed than Europe will have long-term unemployed on the dole'
   (Freeman, 1995b, p. 70).
7. Similar conclusions are reached by Duncan et al. (1993). According to this study, upward
   mobility is similar in Europe and the United States.
8. The share of the population living in areas defined as poor, according to strict definitions,

rose from about 0.5 per cent in 1970 to about 1.5 per cent of the population in 1980 with further subsequent increases; poor areas account for more than 12 per cent of the poor population.

9. 'Low-income' persons are defined as individuals in the bottom decile of the income distribution, with incomes calculated using the household as the unit of aggregation and weighting units by the number of persons in the household.

10. As pointed out by Varian (1980), redistributive systems can also be interpreted in terms of insurance, if the interests of the unborn are taken into consideration. If agents are risk averse and 'luck' determines the likelihood of being born in a wealthy or a poor family, a system guaranteeng a certain degree of equality may be preferred on insurance grounds.

11. For recent reviews of economic research on the subject, see Atkinson (1995) and Agell et al. (1997). See also Bénabou (1996).

12. As suggested by Atkinson (1997), research is likely to yield more definite conclusions at disaggregate level.

13. These issues are extensively examined in European Commission (1995b, 1997a). See also Grahal and Teague (1996).

14. The estimate for 1994 does not include Austria, Finland and Sweden. That for 1970 also excludes Greece, Portugal and Spain. See Eurostat (1996).

15. The economic effects of ageing have been examined by an extensive economic literature; see Börsch-Supan (1991, 1993), Cutler et al. (1990), Hagemann and Nicoletti (1989) and OECD (1988a, 1988c, 1996a).

16. The estimate refers to the projections carried out in the 11 EU member states that produce projections up to the year 2030. Austria, Greece, Luxembourg and Portugal are not included. See Franco and Munzi (1996). This issue is also covered in Kopits (1997) and Thomas (1997).

17. According to Prognos (1995), the contribution rate required to finance the German long-term care insurance scheme is likely to increase from 1 per cent in 1995 to 1.7 to 1.8 per cent in 2010 and 2.3 to 2.6 per cent in 2040.

18. In the early 1990s, a significant proportion of the population was relying on social assistance in all European countries: from 2 per cent in Portugal and in Luxembourg, to about 10 per cent in Finland and in France, up to 15 per cent in Ireland and in the United Kingdom (Van Ginneken, 1995). However, as social assistance systems complement in various ways social insurance systems, cross-country institutional differences are too great to allow for accurate international comparisons.

19. Some relevant issues are examined in the studies included in Gual (1996).

20. Significant differences exist between the main type of social protection systems (see note 3). The Scandinavian model tends to allocate a relatively large fraction of social protection outlays to the working-age population, including benefits and services to encourage job search among the unemployed and support for lone-parent work seekers and secondary earners. The other models, and in particular the Mediterranean model, tend to concentrate social benefits on the elderly population.

21. Implicit in this reasoning is a model of unemployment as an equilibrium outcome in imperfectly competitive labour and product markets (Phelps, 1994b). The equilibrium employment rate, and residual unemployment, is represented by the intersection of a wage-setting curve and a labour demand curve. The wage-setting curve represents the effect of efficiency wage considerations (or, alternatively, bilateral bargaining between firms and unions). It is upward-sloping as the premium over the market-clearing wage is increasing in the employment rate. The labour demand curve depicts firms' optimal price and employment decisions given the wage they face. It is downward-sloping as firms' unit costs are typically increasing in the wage paid economy-wide (or, alternatively, because firms set prices as a mark-up to marginal costs).

22. See Atkinson and Micklewright (1991) and Blöndal and Pearson (1995) for a survey of the literature.

23. According to some studies (referring to the United States situation), for a given expenditure cut in unemployment benefits, a reduction in duration has as much as twice the effect of a reduction in level (Katz and Meyer, 1990).

24. For example, in the presence of uncertainty over future product demand, it is efficient for risk-averse workers and risk-neutral firms to opt for contracts with redundancy pay. Informational constraints about workers' productivity or demand conditions, or the simple possibility of firm bankruptcy, may then require some form of state intervention on firing costs (Booth, 1996).

25. Thus, for example, minimum wage regulations, coupled with restrictions on hiring and firing, can be interpreted as devices to increase the convergence of interests within the 'core' of employed workers at the expense of the 'periphery' of the unemployed and the workers with the highest qualifications (Saint-Paul, 1995a and 1995b): wage compression tends to make the median voter richer relative to the average and job security tends to make the minority of losers identifiable in advance.

26. This prediction is consistent with widespread, but largely anecdotal, evidence on the different types of R&D spending in Europe and in the United States (more process innovation in the former, more product innovation in the latter). For an opposite view of the effects of labour market regulations on productivity, one may point to the widespread interpretation of the German model according to which firms have been induced to invest heavily in productivity-enhancing technologies to cope with the high labour costs. In this approach, flexible labour markets, by leading to a fall in the price of low-skilled labour, may give rise to Snower's 'low-skill, bad-job trap' (Snower, 1994c).

27. Although cross-country labour mobility is likely to remain low throughout the European Union for the foreseeable future, regional mobility (for example between the Nordic countries) may be expected to reach significant dimensions. Tentative conclusions can be drawn from the experience of the integrated Nordic labour market (citizens of Denmark, Finland, Iceland, Norway and Sweden have had the right to settle anywhere in the area without either residence or work permits since 1954; Nordic immigrants are treated the same as native residents by the national authorities and information on work opportunities is shared across the area). Studies find that intra-Nordic migration is significantly responsive to real wage and unemployment differentials, with potential mobility being the strongest among the highest educated and the largest disincentive effect being the extensive safety net for the unemployed (Hutchinson and Kletzer, 1995). At European level, in the future, some form of coordination of national benefit systems might be necessary in order to prevent individuals from adjusting their geographical location over their life cycle on the basis of specific features of benefit systems (Lindbeck, 1997).

28. As to development of a single market in supplementary pensions, see European Commission (1997b).

29. For a discussion of adjustment under EMU, with particular reference to employment/unemployment outcomes, see Viñals and Jimeno (1996).

30. The 'close-to-balance' rule would allow member states to retain budgetary stabilizers without going beyond the 3 per cent threshold in the event of recession (see Buti et al., 1997).

31. More specifically, part of the increase in pension and health expenditure determined by population ageing would be offset by a reduction in interest payments on the public debt. According to some preliminary estimates carried out in Franco and Munzi (1997), about half of the increase in public expenditure determined by population ageing in heavily indebted countries might be offset by the reduction in interest payments on public debt determined by the implementation of the close-to-balance rule.

32. For a description of recent reforms, see European Commission (1993a, 1995a). The reforms recently undertaken and planned in France are extensively examined in Darnaut (1997), who also highlights the problems raised by their implementation.

33. Respectively, the ratio of the number of pensions to the number of elderly citizens and the ratio of the average pension to the average wage.

34. This applies particularly to the recent Italian and Swedish pension reforms, which share the same general objectives and main features. See, respectively, Artoni and Zanardi (1996) and Ministry of Health and Social Affairs (1994).

35. For an analysis of the problems raised by the reform of the French welfare system, see Darnaut (1997).

36. Several other problems raised by a larger reliance on supplementary schemes should be carefully examined (for example protection against fraud, effects on labour mobility, administration costs).

37. For a review, see Franco (1995), Chand and Jaeger (1996), and Roseveare et al. (1996).

38. In a simple numerical exercise, Snower (1995) finds that a switch from unemployment benefits to a negative conditional income tax in the EU would raise the average income of individuals receiving support by about 8 per cent and cut the number of unemployed by around 7 per cent. However, as recent reforms of benefit systems in EU countries (by foreseeing a gradual withdrawal of benefits) are attenuating the inefficiencies pointed out above, the estimated implications of an outright switch to conditional negative income tax are likely to be biased upwards.

39. The economic rationale for employment subsidies is the existence of a gap between social and private benefits from an increase in employment of disadvantaged workers in a situation of involuntary unemployment. From the point of view of the individual employer, it makes sense to avoid creating jobs for which the marginal product falls below (minimum) wage costs. But this calculation does not consider the additional benefits that accrue to the economy as a whole from putting to work an unemployed person willing to accept a job. The share of payroll taxes out of the minimum wage provides a first approximation of the size of the gap (Phelps, 1996; Drèze and Sneessens, 1996).

40. The above proposals have entered the political arena both at EU and national level. The 1993 White Paper (European Commission, 1993b) proposed targeted reductions in non-wage labour costs amounting to 1 per cent of GDP, financed through a CO_2 tax. The White Paper also proposed a complementary strategy, aimed at raising the demand for labour-intensive services in sectors sheltered from international competition (for example, assistance to the elderly, personal and public safety). A further study explored this strategy in more detail, including simulation of possible measures (European Commission, 1996d). More generally, the importance of the reform of tax and benefit systems in the fight against unemployment in Europe was retained as a major policy conclusion of the Ecofin report to the European Council in Madrid in December 1994 (European Commission, 1995d). A number of EU countries have included these policies in their employment strategies, though, so far, with programmes of rather limited scale (for example, the benefit-transfer programme inspired the British Workstart pilot scheme introduced in 1993).

41. On the basis of a number of simplifying assumptions, Snower and Phelps (1995) estimated that converting unemployment benefits into employment vouchers could reduce EU unemployment by as much as 20 per cent, or 2 percentage points in percentage of the labour force. They also estimated that, by targeting on low-paid workers subsidies amounting to 1 per cent of GDP, unemployment could be reduced by 2 additional percentage points. The results depend on a number of parameters, notably the 'voucher effectiveness ratio' capturing the equivalence between a temporary voucher and a wage reduction of the same amount. For an exercise of the same type concerning most OECD countries, see Snower (1996b).

42. Subsidies produce different results depending on the degree of responsiveness of wages to unemployment. This is explicitly recognized by Phelps (1996, p. 240) in comparing the American and the European situation: 'I suppose that the main benefit of wage subsidies in the USA will take the form of higher wage rates, with a less important effect on unemployment. The reason is that "wage rigidity" is relatively small there, which means that the wage curve is relatively steep. And the main benefit of the wage subsidies on the European continent will take the form of lower unemployment rates – more workers demanded at those rigid real wages – with little improvement in wage rates. The reason, again, is that wage rigidity is relatively great in Europe, so the wage curve is relatively flat.'

43. However, in less than perfectly competitive labour markets, the rise in the number of employable workers and a higher turnover of incumbents may be beneficial *per se*: a number of long-term unemployed would be brought back into the labour market and

newly displaced workers, since they have a better chance to find a new job, would exert a more effective wage discipline pressure on insiders.

44. See, for instance, Ministry of Health and Social Affairs (1994).
45. In this respect, the United States case, where contributions to company-based health and pension schemes are an important part of wage negotiations, is particularly relevant. Any increase in health-care costs can more easily influence wage negotiations.
46. Some reforms along these lines have already been introduced in some non-European countries. Individual social insurance accounts have been introduced in Chile (unemployment insurance) and Singapore (medical insurance).
47. See Saint-Paul (1995a, 1995b) and Alogoskoufis et al. (1995).
48. This seems particularly relevant in the fully fledged Nordic variant of the welfare state: with reference to Sweden, there appears to exist a 'highly interrelated welfare state and economy in which many parts fit together (be they subsidies, taxes, collective bargaining, wage compression, etc.) in ways that maintained high employment and wage compression, that offset work disincentives from welfare benefits and high taxes, and that ultimately helped eliminate poverty' (Freeman, 1995a, p. 18).
49. However, as pointed out above in the case of unemployment benefits and job protection, welfare provisions may, in some cases, be substitutes instead of complementary. See also Atkinson (1997).
50. As Lindbeck points out, 'by making sufficiently many decisions simultaneously, it would even be difficult to some unemployed workers, it conferred benefits on other firms and other workers, but the beneficiaries calculate the distributional consequences of a "package reform"' (Lindbeck, 1994a, p. 17).

REFERENCES

Aaberge, R., Björklund, A., Jäntti, M., Palme, M., Pedersen, P.J., Smith, N. and Wennemo, T. (1996), 'Income inequality and income mobility in the Scandinavian countries compared to the United States', *Statistics Norway Research Department Discussion Papers*, No 168.

Agell, J., Lindh, T. and Ohlsson, H. (1997), 'Growth and the public sector. A critical review essay', *European Journal of Political Economy*, **18**, 33–52.

Alogoskoufis, G., Bean, C., Bertola, G., Cohen, D., Dolado, J. and Saint-Paul, G. (1995), *Unemployment: Choices for Europe*, London: CEPR.

Artoni, R. and Zanardi, A. (1996), 'The evolution of the Italian pension system', in MIRE, *Comparing social welfare systems in southern Europe.*

Atkinson, A.B. (1992), 'Towards a European social safety net?', *Fiscal Studies*, No. 13.

Atkinson, A.B. (1993), 'On targeting social security. Theory and western experience with family benefits', *Discussion Papers, No. 99*, Suntory–Toyota Centre for Economics and Related Disciplines, London.

Atkinson, A.B. (1995), 'The welfare state and economic performance', *Discussion Papers, No. 109*, Suntory–Toyota Centre for Economics and Related Disciplines, London.

Atkinson, A.B. (1997), 'The economics of the welfare state: an incomplete debate', this book, Ch. 2.

Atkinson, A.B. and Micklewright, J. (1991), 'Unemployment compensation and labour market transitions. A critical review', *Journal of Economic Literature*, **29**, 1679–727.

Barr, N. (1992), 'Economic theory and the welfare state: a survey and interpretation', *Journal of Economic Literature*, **30**, 741–803.

Barr, N. (1993), *The Economics of the Welfare State*, Oxford: Oxford University Press.

Begg, D., Cremer, J., Danthine, J.-P., Edwards, J., Grilli, V., Neven, D., Seabright, P., Sinn, H.-W., Venables, A. and Wyplosz, C. (1993), *Making Sense of Subsidiarity: How Much Centralisation for Europe?* London: CEPR.

Bénabou, R. (1996), 'Inequality and growth', *CEPR Discussion Paper*, No 1450, July.

Bentolila, S. and Bertola, G. (1990), 'Firing costs and labour demand: how bad is Eurosclerosis?', *Review of Economic Studies*, **57** (3), 381–402.

Bird, E.J. (1995), 'An exploratory comparison of income risk in Germany and in the United States', *Review of Income and Wealth*, **41**.

Björklund, A. (1996), 'Intergenerational earnings and class mobility', paper prepared for the conference 'Generations and welfare. Problems, prospects and policies', Helsinki, 17 and 18 October 1996.

Blank, R.M. and Freeman, R.B. (1993), 'Evaluating the connection between social protection and economic flexibility', *NBER Working Papers*, No. 4338.

Blöndal, S. and Pearson, M. (1995), 'Unemployment and other non-employment benefits', *Oxford Review of Economic Policy*, **11** (1), 136–69.

Booth, A.L. (1996), 'An analysis of firing costs and their implications for employment policy', in Snower, D.J. and de la Dehesa, G. (eds), *Unemployment Policy. Government Options for the Labour Market*, Cambridge: Cambridge University Press.

Börsch-Supan, A. (1991), 'Ageing population', *Economic Policy*, April, 103–39.

Börsch-Supan, A. (1993), 'Ageing in Germany and the United States: international comparisons', *NBER Working Papers*, No. 4530.

Boyer, M. (1991), 'Justice sociale et performances économiques. De l'alliance cachée au conflit ouvert?', paper prepared for the Commissariat Général au Plan's conference 'Justice sociale et inégalité', Paris, 20–22 June 1991.

Buti, M., Franco, D. and Ongena, H. (1997), 'Budgetary policies during recessions: retrospective application of the "Stability and Growth Pact" to the post-war period', *Economic Papers*, DG II, No. 121, European Commission, May.

Cantillon, B. (1996), 'The challenge of poverty and exclusion', discussion paper prepared for the conference 'Beyond 2000: the new social policy agenda', OECD, Paris.

Chand, S.K. and Jaeger, A. (1996), 'Ageing populations and public pension schemes', *IMF Occasional Paper*, No. 147.

Chassard, Y. and Venturini, P. (1995), 'La dimension européenne de la protection sociale', *Droit Social*, No. 9/10, September–October, 772–8.

Coder, J., Rainwater, L. and Smeeding, T. (1989), 'Inequality among children and elderly in ten modern nations: the United States in an international context', *American Economic Review, Papers and Proceedings*, **79** (2), 320–24.

Coe, D. and Snower, D.J. (1997), 'Policy complementarities: the case for fundamental labour market reform', *IMF Staff Papers*, **44** (1), 1–35.

Cutler, D.M., Poterba, J., Sheiner, L.M. and Summers, L.H. (1990), 'An ageing society: opportunity or challenge', *Brookings Papers on Economic Activity*, No. 1.

Darnaut, N. (1997), 'Reform in the social security system in France: challenges and prospects', this book, Ch. 8.

Davis, E.P. (1995), *Pension funds, Retirement-income Security and Capital Markets – An International Perspective*, Oxford: Oxford University Press.

Davis, E.P. (1996), 'The role of institutional investors in the evolution of financial structure and behaviour', paper presented at the conference 'The future of the financial system', Reserve Bank of Australia, Sydney, 8 and 9 July 1996.

Diaz, M.P. and Snower, D.J. (1996), 'Employment, macroeconomic fluctuations and job security', *CEPR Discussion Paper*, No. 1430, July.

Drèze, J.H. and Malinvaud, E. (1994), 'Growth and employment: the scope for a European initiative', *European Economy – Reports and Studies*, No. 1, 75–106.

Drèze, J.H. and Sneessens, H. (1996), 'Low-skilled unemployment', in Snower, D.J. and de la Dehesa, G. (eds), *Unemployment Policy. Government options for the Labour Market*, Cambridge: Cambridge University Press.

Duncan, G., Gustafsson, B., Hauser, R., Schmauss, G., Messinger, H., Muffels, R., Nolan, B. and Ray, J.-C. (1993), 'Poverty dynamics in eight countries', *Journal of Population Economics*, No. 6, 215–34.

Emerson, M. (1988), *What model for Europe?*, Cambridge, MA: MIT Press.

Ermisch, J. (1991), 'European integration and external constraints on social policy: is a social charter necessary?', *National Institute Economic Review*, May, 93–109.

Esping-Andersen, G. (1996), 'Welfare states at the end of the century: the impact of labour market, family and demographic change', discussion paper prepared for the conference 'Beyond 2000: the new social policy agenda', OECD, Paris.

European Commission (1993a), *Social protection in Europe*, Brussels.

European Commission (1993b), 'Growth, competitiveness, employment – The challenges and ways forward into the 21st century – White Paper', Brussels, December.

European Commission (1995a), *Social Protection in Europe*, Brussels.

European Commission (1995b), *The Future of Social Protection: A Framework for a European Debate*, Brussels.

European Commission (1995c), 'Report on the demographic situation of the European Union in 1994', Brussels.

European Commission (1995d), *Local Employment and Development Initiatives. An Investigation in the European Union*, Brussels.

European Commission (1996b), 'Fiscalité dans l'Union européenne – Rapport sur l'évolution des systèmes fiscaux', Brussels.

European Commission (1996c), 'Report on the demographic situation of the European Union in 1995', Brussels.

European Commission (1996d), 'Madrid employment report – Contribution of the Ecofin Council', *European Economy*, Supplement A, No. 3, March.

European Commission (1997a), *Modernising and Improving Social Protection in the Union*, Brussels.

European Commission (1997b), 'Supplementary pensions in the single market – A Green Paper', Brussels.

Eurostat (1995), *Demographic Statistics*, Luxembourg.

Eurostat (1996), *Social Protection Expenditure and Receipts 1980–1994*, Luxembourg.

Ferrera, M. (1996), 'The "southern model" of welfare in social Europe', *Journal of European Social Policy*, 1.

Fitoussi, J.-P. (1996), 'Substitutabilities vs complementarities between structural and macroeconomic policies', in OECD proceedings, *Macroeconomic policies and structural reform*, Paris.

Flora, P. and Heidenheimer, A.J. (1981), *The Development of Welfare States in Europe and America*, New Brunswick, NJ: Transaction Books.

Fölster, S. (1997), 'Social insurance based on personal savings accounts: a possible reform strategy for overburdened welfare states', this book, Ch. 4.

Fölster, S. and Trofimov, G. (1996), 'Does equality promote growth?', mimeo.

Fornero, E. (1995), 'Totally unfunded vs partially funded pension systems: the case of Italy', *Ricerche Economiche*, No. 49, 357–74.

Förster, M.F. (1993), 'Measurement of low incomes and poverty in a perspective of international comparisons', *OECD Labour Market and Social Policy Occasional Papers*, No. 14.

Franco, D. (1995), 'Pension liabilities – Their use and misuse in the assessment of fiscal policies', *Economic Papers*, No. 110, DG II, European Commission.

Franco, D. and Munzi, T. (1996), 'Pension expenditure prospects in the European Union: a survey of national projections', *European Economy*, No. 3.

Franco, D. and Munzi, T. (1997), 'Ageing and fiscal policies in the European Union', this book, Ch. 9.

Freeman, R.B. (1995a), 'The large welfare state as a system', *American Economic Review, Papers and Proceedings*, **85** (2), 16–21.

Freeman, R.B. (1995b), 'The limits of wage flexibility to curing unemployment', *Oxford Review of Economic Policy*, **11**, 63–72.

Gottschalk, P. and Smeeding, T.M. (1997), 'Cross-national comparisons of earnings and income inequality', *Journal of Economic Literature*, **35**, 633–87.

Grahal, J. and Teague, P. (1996), 'Is the European social model fragmenting?', *Economics Department Working Paper*, No. 351, University of London, June.

Gramlich, E.M. (1989), 'Economists' views of the welfare system', *American Economic Review, Papers and Proceedings*, **79**, 191–6.

Gregg, P. and Manning, A. (1966), 'Labour market regulation and unemployment' in Snower, D.J. and de la Dehesa, G. (eds), *Unemployment policy. Government options for the labour market*, Cambridge: Cambridge University Press.

Gregg, P. and Wadsworth, J. (1996), 'Mind the gap, please? The changing nature of entry jobs in Britain', *Centre for Economic Performance Working Paper*, No. 796, April.

Gual, J. (1996), *The Social Challenge of Job Creation – Combating Unemployment in Europe*, Cheltenham: Edward Elgar.

Hagemann, R.P. and Nicoletti, G. (1989), 'Ageing populations: economic effects and implications for public finance', *OECD Department of Economics and Statistics Working Paper*, No. 61.

Haveman, R. (1996), 'Employment growth and social protection: can we have both?', discussion paper prepared for the conference 'Beyond 2000: the new social policy agenda', OECD, Paris.

Heller, P.S., Hemming, R. and Kohnert, P. (1986), 'Ageing and social expenditure in the major industrialised countries, 1980–2025', *IMF Occasional Papers*, No. 47.

Hoeller, P., Louppe, M.-O. and Vergriete, P. (1996), 'Fiscal relations within the European Union', *Economics Department Working Paper*, No. 163, OCSE.

Holzmann, R. (1997), 'On economic benefits and fiscal requirements of moving from unfunded to funded pensions', this book, Ch. 6.

Hutchinson, M.M. and Kletzer, K.M. (1995), 'Fiscal convergence criteria, factor mobility and credibility in transition to monetary union in Europe', in Eichengreen, B., Frieden, J. and von Hagen, J., *Monetary and fiscal policy in an integrated Europe*, Berlin: Springer-Verlag.

Jackman, R., Layard, R. and Nickell, S. (1996), 'Combating unemployment: is flexibility enough?', *Discussion Paper*, No. 293, LSE Centre for Economic Performance, March.

Katz, L. and Meyer, B.D. (1990), 'The Impact of the potential duration of unemploy-

52 *Overview*

ment benefits on the duration of unemployment', *Journal of Public Economics*, **41**, 209–90.

Kopits, G. (1997), 'Are Europe's social security finances compatible with EMU?', *IMF Paper on Policy Analysis and Assessment*, No. 3, February.

Leibfritz, W., Roseveare, D., Fore, D. and Wurzel, E. (1995), 'Ageing populations, pension systems and government budgets: how do they affect saving?', *OECD Working Paper*, No. 156.

Lindbeck, A. (1994a), 'Overshooting, reform and retreat of the welfare state', *The Economist*, **142**, 1–19.

Lindbeck, A. (1994b), 'Uncertainty under the welfare state – Policy-induced risks', *Institute for International Economic Studies Seminar Paper*, No. 576, July.

Lindbeck, A. (1994c), 'The welfare state and the employment problem', *American Economic Review, Papers and Proceedings*, **84**, 71–5.

Lindbeck, A. (1995), 'Hazardous welfare state dynamics', *American Economic Review, Papers and Proceedings*, **85**, 9–15.

Lindbeck, A. (1997), 'Welfare state dynamics', this book, Ch. 3.

Lindbeck, A. and Snower, D.J. (1996), 'Reorganisation of firms and labour market inequality', *CEPR Discussion Paper*, No. 1375, March.

Maddison, A. (1995), *L'économie mondiale 1820–1992. Analyse et statistique*, Paris: OECD.

Ministry of Health and Social Affairs (1994), 'Pension reform in Sweden – A short summary', proposal of the Working Group on Pensions in 1994, Stockholm.

Musgrave, R. (1959), *The Theory of Public Finance*, New York: McGraw-Hill.

Musgrave, R. (1981), 'A reappraisal of social security financing', in Skidmore, F. (ed.), Social Security Financing, Cambridge, MA: MIT Press.

Nickell, S. and Bell, B. (1995), 'The collapse in demand for the unskilled and unemployment across the OECD', *Oxford Review of Economic Policy*, **11**, 40–62.

OECD (1988a), *Ageing Populations*, Paris.

OECD (1988b), *The Future of Social Protection*, Paris.

OECD (1988c), *Reforming Public Pensions*, Paris.

OECD (1990a), *Lone-parent Families*, Paris.

OECD (1990b), *Health Care Systems in Transition*, Paris.

OECD (1992a), *US Health Care at the Cross-roads*, Paris.

OECD (1992b), *Private Pensions and Public Policy*, Paris.

OECD (1994a), *New Orientations for Social Policy*, Paris.

OECD (1994b), *Caring for Frail Elderly People*, Paris.

OECD (1994c), *The Reform of the Health Care System – A Review of Seventeen OECD Countries*, Paris.

OECD (1995a), *New Directions in Health Care Policy*, Paris.

OECD (1995b), *The Transition from Work to Retirement*, Paris.

OECD (1995c), *Social Transfers: Spending Patterns, Institutional Arrangements and Policy Reforms*, Paris.

OECD (1996a), *Ageing in OECD Countries – A Critical Policy Challenge*, Paris.

OECD (1996b), *The Distribution of Earnings in Selected OECD Countries*, Paris.

Orszag, J.M. and Snower, D.J. (1996), 'Incapacity benefits versus benefit transfers', *CEPR Discussion Paper*, No. 1471, September.

Orszag, J.M. and Snower, D.J. (1997), 'Expanding the welfare system: a proposal for reform', this book, Ch. 5.

Pedersen, A. W. (1994), 'The welfare state and inequality: still no answer to the big questions', mimeo, European University Institute, Florence.

Persson, T. and Tabellini, G. (1994), 'Is inequality harmful for growth?', *American Economic Review*, **84**, 600–621.

Pfaller, A., Gough, I. and Therborn, G. (1991), *Can the Welfare State Compete? A Comparative Study of Five Capitalist Countries*, London: Macmillan.

Phelps, E.S. (1994a), *Structural Slumps. The Modern Theory of Unemployment, Interest and Assets*, Cambridge, MA: Harvard University Press.

Phelps, E.S. (1994b), 'Low-wage employment subsidies versus the welfare state', *American Economic Review, Papers and Proceedings*, **84**, 54–8.

Phelps, E.S. (1996), 'Wage subsidy programmes. Alternative designs', in Snower, D.J. and de la Dehesa, G. (eds), *Unemployment Policy. Government Options for the Labour Market*, Cambridge: Cambridge University Press.

Pierson, P. (1996), 'The new politics of the welfare state', *World Politics*, **48**, 143–79.

Prognos (1995), *Prognos-Gutachten 1995 – Perspektiven der gesetzlichen Rentenversicherung für Gesamtdeutschland vor dem Hintergrund veränderter politischer und ökonomischer Rahmbedingungen*, Verband Deutscher Rentenversicherungsträger, DRV-Schriften, Vol. 4, April.

Rhodes, M. (1996), 'A new social contract? Globalisation and west European welfare states', *European University Institute Working Paper*, No. 43.

Roseveare, D., Leibfritz, W., Fore, D. and Wurzel, E. (1996), 'Ageing populations, pension systems and government budgets: simulations for 20 OECD countries', *OECD Economics Department Working Papers*, No. 168.

Saint-Paul, G. (1995a), 'Labour market institutions and the cohesion of the middle class', *CEPR Discussion Paper*, No. 1298, November.

Saint-Paul, G. (1995b), 'Reforming Europe's labour market: political issues', *CEPR Discussion Paper*, No. 1223, August.

Saint-Paul, G. (1996), 'Employment protection, international specialisation, and innovation', *CEPR Discussion Paper*, No. 1338, January.

Sala-i-Martin, X. (1996), 'Transfers, social safety nets, and economic growth', *IMF Working Paper*, No. 40, April.

Schmid, G. (1995), 'Institutional incentives to prevent unemployment. Unemployment insurance and active labour market policy in a comparative perspective', *Journal of Socio-Economics*, **24**, 51–103.

Sinn, H.-W. (1990), 'Tax harmonisation and competition in Europe', *European Economic Review*, **34**, 489–504.

Sinn, H.-W. (1994), 'A theory of the welfare state', *NBER Working Papers*, No. 4856.

Sinn, H.-W. (1995), 'Social insurance, incentives and risk-taking', paper prepared for the 51st Congress of the International Institute of Public Finance, entitled 'The changing role of the public sector: transitions in the 1990s', Lisbon, 21–24 August 1995.

Snower, D.J. (1993), 'The future of the welfare state', *Economic Journal*, **103**, 700–717.

Snower, D.J. (1994a), 'Converting unemployment benefits into employment subsidies', *American Economic Review, Papers and Proceedings*, **84** (2), 65–70.

Snower, D.J. (1994b), 'What is the domain of the welfare state?', *CEPR Discussion Paper*, No. 1018.

Snower, D.J. (1994c), 'Low-skill, bad-job trap', *CEPR Discussion Paper*, No. 999, September.

Snower, D.J. (1995), 'Unemployment benefits versus conditional negative income tax', *IMF Working Paper*, No. 96, July.

Snower, D.J. (1996a), 'Challenges to social cohesion and approaches to policy reform', paper prepared for the OECD conference 'Economic flexibility and societal cohesion in the 21st century', Paris, 16 December 1996.

Snower, D.J. (1996b), 'The simple theory of benefits transfers', in Snower, D.J. and de la Dehesa, G. (eds), *Unemployment Policy. Government Options for the Labour Market*, Cambridge: Cambridge University Press.

Snower, D.J. and Phelps, E.S. (1995), 'Halving European unemployment through hiring vouchers and employment tax credits', mimeo, July.

Thomas, G. (1997), 'Retirement income financing reform – A general issues paper', this book, Ch. 7.

Van den Noord, P. and Herd, R. (1994), 'Estimating pension liabilities: a methodological framework', *Economic Studies*, No. 23, OECD, Winter, 131–66.

Van Ginneken, W. (1995), 'Social protection in Europe. Trends and policy issues', paper prepared for the 51st Congress of the International Institute of Public Finance, entitled 'The changing role of the public sector: transitions in the 1990s', Lisbon, 21–24 August 1995.

Varian, H.R. (1980), 'Redistributive taxation as social Insurance', *Journal of Public Economics*, **14**, 49–68.

Viñals, J. and Jimeno, J.F. (1996), 'Monetary union and unemployment', *CEPR Discussion Paper*, No. 96.

Wasylenko, M. (1997), 'Taxation and economic development: the state of the economic literature', *New England Economic Review*, March/April.

Webb, S. (1995), 'Social security policy in a changing labour market', *Oxford Review of Economic Policy*, **11**, 11–26.

World Bank (1994), *Averting the Old-age Crisis*, Washington, DC: World Bank.

Part II

The Economic Effects of the Welfare State:
Two Views

2. The economics of the welfare state: an incomplete debate

Anthony B. Atkinson

1. INTRODUCTION

The present debate about the welfare state is highly important, not least for the millions of people for whom it is an essential part of their lives, both today and in the future. It is very much to be welcomed that economists have turned their attention to this once neglected area of policy. Government spending on the welfare state, particularly the social transfers on which I focus here, forms a major part of the budget of European countries. When seeking the causes of lagging economic performance – high unemployment and slow growth – it is understandable that one should ask whether Europe's welfare state is a burden on the economy. At the same time, the debate remains, in my view, seriously incomplete. In this chapter, I argue that there are at least six aspects which need further consideration:

(i)   the mechanisms by which the welfare state affects economic performance need to be spelled out explicitly;

(ii) a range of distinct yardsticks are being implicitly applied, often with different implications;

(iii) according to these yardsticks, social transfers may have positive as well as negative effects on economic performance;

(iv) the welfare state is embedded in a wider social system, and we need to consider the interrelation with different policies, including the alternatives to the present welfare state, which may themselves have adverse economic consequences;

(v)   individual behaviour evolves over time in response to transfers, as does government policy itself, so that reform of the welfare state should be seen as a dynamic process, where the measures currently discussed may, in turn, be replaced;

(vi) criticism of the welfare state has also come from those concerned that it is failing to meet its basic objectives of alleviating poverty, redistributing income, and guaranteeing individual security.

This chapter develops these points in turn; they are not original, but they are, in my view, underrepresented in the public debate.

In commenting on the future of the welfare state, it is hard to avoid being biased by the experience of one's own country, and I am no exception. The analysis of social transfers presented here is undoubtedly influenced by the United Kingdom viewpoint from which I write. Historically, the welfare state has developed in different ways in different European countries. The Nordic tradition is not the same as that in, say, Germany, and the German system, in turn, does not look like that in the United Kingdom. It is for this reason misleading to talk about 'the European welfare state'; and the policy reform appropriate to one country may be irrelevant, or damaging, in another.

The diversity of European Union countries is well illustrated by the projections of public pension expenditure recently published in *European Economy* (Franco and Munzi, 1996), showing projected state spending on pensions as a proportion of GDP. We know that this figure is predicted to be high in Germany – around 17.5 per cent in the year 2030 – and in the Netherlands and France, but this is not true in all countries, notably in the United Kingdom, where the figure is little more than 5 per cent. (In all cases I have taken the best-case scenarios.) This makes a great deal of difference when considering the future. People who call for a reduction in spending on the welfare state of 1 or 2 per cent of GDP, with pensions being a principal target, must recognize that such a reduction would have very different implications in different member states.

2.   THE UNDERLYING MECHANISMS

Much of the case for cutting welfare state spending appears to be based on cross-country comparisons of economic performance. Europe, it is alleged, has higher unemployment than the United States on account of its generous social transfers. Countries with large welfare states, it is asserted, grow more slowly. Elsewhere (Atkinson, 1995) I have reviewed the aggregate empirical evidence about the relation between growth of GDP and spending on social security. The results are divided and can be interpreted in different ways. In my view, aggregate growth studies, interesting though they may be, cannot on their own provide a reliable guide to the likely consequences of rolling back the welfare state. Most importantly, I do not find it satisfactory to work with what is purely a 'black box', in the sense that we have no indication as to the mechanisms that are envisaged. Sandmo, after a cautious summary of the aggregate empirical evidence about a possible trade-off between growth and social security ('the adoption of the Nordic model of social security does not have catastrophic consequences for economic growth, nor is it a guarantee of economic success'), goes on to say that 'theoretical hypotheses and data analysis at this level do not reveal the more basic structural features of the economy. To understand the connections that there *may* be, we need first of all to look into the theoretical underpinnings of the trade-off hypothesis, and, secondly, to consider whether there may be some arguments that point in the opposite direction' (Sandmo, 1994, p. 4).

We need an explicit theoretical structure with sufficient microeconomic detail. Otherwise, it is not possible to interpret observed aggregate regularities, even if they can be firmly established.

In providing such a theoretical framework, it is important that it should be sufficiently rich to allow for the institutional structure of the welfare state. While all modelling must abstract from the details of social security provision, which can be arcane in the extreme, we must be sure that the abstraction does not neglect important economic features. In the analysis of social security, this often appears to be the case, key elements of the law and its administration being missing from the typical economic model. Unemployment benefit provides an illustration of the neglect of an important institutional structure. Economic models regularly assume that the only relevant condition for the receipt of benefit is that of being unemployed. In fact, in the typical unemployment insurance programme, benefit is subject to contribution conditions, is paid for a limited duration, and is monitored to check that the person is making genuine efforts to seek employment (see Atkinson and Micklewright, 1991). Benefit may be refused where the person entered unemployment voluntarily or as a result of industrial misconduct, and a person may be disqualified for refusing job offers. Of course, the conditions are only administered imperfectly, but they are – at least in some countries – an important part of the reality of being unemployed.

The conditions for the receipt of unemployment insurance not only reduce its coverage, but also affect the relationship between transfers and the working of the economy. The standard job-search model, for example, assumes that workers can reject job offers which offer less than a specified wage. Such a reservation wage strategy can, however, lead to the person being disqualified from benefit. A second example is provided by the general equilibrium formulation of the jobsearch model by Albrecht and Axell (1984). This makes a most valuable contribution by endogenizing the wage offer distribution, but the assumptions made about the operation of unemployment benefit ignore its institutional structure. In the model, the unemployed consist entirely of those who have not held a job, which means that they cannot satisfy the usual contribution conditions attached to unemployment insurance. In addition, they have rejected a low-wage job offer, for which they would risk being disqualified. A third example is provided by a different labour market model: the shirking version of the efficiency wage hypothesis advanced by Shapiro and Stiglitz (1984), among others. Worker effort depends on the risk of being fired, and the cost of being fired is assumed to be that the worker has to live on unemployment benefit. But dismissal for shirking is likely to lead to disqualification from benefit. Employers have a strong incentive to report job loss resulting from misconduct in so far as there are statutory redundancy payments, because this would reduce employer liability. Workers who shirk cannot take it for granted that they would receive unemployment benefit.

As these examples illustrate, the economic modelling needs to be appropriate to the purpose at hand, and cannot ignore the very institutional features which have been introduced to help overcome the disincentive effects with which economists are concerned.

3.   YARDSTICKS APPLIED TO PERFORMANCE

One great virtue of economic theory is that it brings to the fore questions which may otherwise remain in the background. This applies especially to the implicit standards by which performance is being judged. What exactly are the yardsticks that we are using when assessing economic performance?

Suppose that we take the aggregate labour market model that appears to underlie much discussion. The demand for labour is determined by competitive, profit-maximizing firms; the supply of labour by workers depends on their alternative opportunities, taken here to be home production: as the wage rises, a larger fraction prefer market work. Transfers are paid to pensioners, financed by a social security payroll tax. A cut in the level of transfers, allowing a reduction in the tax rate, lowers the cost of employing labour, and hence leads to a higher level of market employment and market output.

This model is not a very realistic account of modern labour markets, but serves to identify a number of issues.

3.1   GDP versus Welfare

First, is market output (GDP) really the appropriate performance indicator? Along with the reduced labour supply comes increased home production. The professors who paint their own houses rather than write books are still producing. This is not just an accounting point. Much of public debate confuses the potential damage that taxes may do by distorting the working of the market, and by reducing output (or employment, or investment, or some other target economic variable). The distortion arises, in the simple model set out above, from the 'wedge' between the cost of labour to the employer and the opportunity cost to the employee. The distortion would be eliminated if the tax were zero. On the other hand, this would not maximize market output.

If it is being argued that the welfare state is driving people out of the market economy, then we should be told whether this is undesirable because it leads to an inefficient allocation of resources or because it reduces GDP. The numerical measure of the cost may be seriously affected. The distortionary loss from a small tax, for example, is only second order in magnitude, whereas the output effect is first order. This distinction has been drawn clearly by Lindbeck, who argues that we should focus not on 'the "positive economics issue" of whether work effort falls or rises in response to some government action, but rather ... on the "welfare economics issue" of whether deviations are created, or raised, between the social and private return on (marginal) work effort' (Lindbeck, 1981, p. 31).

As he recognizes, however, social judgements may not be based on purely welfarist concerns. The considerations which enter social decision criteria may not be confined to individual welfare levels. Governments appear to be interested, for instance, in the level of economic development which a country has attained, as witnessed by objectives such as modernizing the economy. For this purpose, the level of GDP may be a reasonable first approximation; alternatively, there may be other 'target variables', such as employment or the rate of growth.

3.2 Tax Cost versus Specific Impact

The cost in lost output, or reduced welfare, in the model described above arises on account of the existence of taxation: it is a tax cost argument. The reason for the tax (that is, financing transfers) is not, as such, material. The welfare state may represent a particularly large item in the budget, but the tax cost is the same as if the spending were on overseas aid or military defence. By the same token, tax expenditures have an identical impact to that of direct spending. Allowances against income taxation may play the same role as cash transfers, in that both increase the tax rate necessary. A higher tax exemption for the elderly reduces the overall tax receipts, as do child tax allowances. Replacing child income tax allowances by a cash child benefit may appear to increase the size of the welfare state, but have no effect on the tax rate which has to be levied on income.

Social transfers have been criticized in both ways: that they add to the financing problems of the government, and that, even if free, they adversely affect the working of the labour or other markets. The paper entitled 'Growth and employment: the scope for a European initiative', prepared by Drèze and Malinvaud, lists three major objections:

(i) measures of income protection or social insurance introduce undesired rigidities in the functioning of labour markets;

(ii)   welfare programmes increase the size of government at a risk of inefficiency; their funding enhances the amount of revenue to be raised, and so the magnitude of tax distortions;

(iii) welfare programmes may lead to cumulative deficits and mounting public debts. (Drèze and Malinvaud, 1994, p. 95)

The second and third criticisms refer to the budgetary impact; the first refers to the specific features of social transfers. They clearly have different implications. The budgetary criticism can be countered by proposing alternative expenditure cuts, but the specific criticism requires us to look at how the transfers actually work.

3.3   Contributions and Benefits

The social transfer programme outlined above in the simple labour market model is purely redistributive: the taxpayers and the beneficiaries are distinct people. To the extent that taxpayers perceive a link between the taxes paid and future benefits, the economic effect may be moderated. Where there is a contributory social insurance scheme covering those in paid employment, the labour supply decision is based on comparing the value of home output with the wage rate, net of tax and expected benefit from future receipt of the transfer. It is the full remuneration package, including the social wage, that is relevant. This can, of course, be oversold. When Lloyd George introduced national insurance in the United Kingdom in 1911, he used the phrase 'ninepence for fourpence' to persuade people of the merits of the scheme, the grounds being that the employee contributed fourpence but the employer threepence and the state twopence (Grigg, 1978, p. 325). Eliding the fact that these contributions too should enter the equation was clearly not legitimate, however successful it was as political rhetoric. Moreover, when considering the value placed on future receipt of social transfers, an element is the political risk associated with the continuance of the scheme (see, for example, Diamond, 1993; Lindbeck, 1995a). People may therefore heavily discount the prospect of future benefits. It is important to know how far the economic impact of the welfare state arises on account of the neglect or discounting of its benefits.

To summarize, if the welfare state is being criticized for its negative effect on economic performance, then we must clarify:

(i)   whether it is a distortionary cost, or a reduction in a target variable like GDP or the rate of growth;

(ii)   whether it is the budgetary cost which causes the damage, or the specific features of the social programmes; and

(iii)   whether the damage arises because people discount or ignore the benefits, or whether it happens even if (or because) people expect confidently to receive the programme benefits.

4.   POSITIVE AS WELL AS NEGATIVE EFFECTS

The idea that the welfare state may have positive as well as negative consequences for economic performance will not come as a totally alien idea to most non-economists. Historically, social insurance grew up as a complement to the modern employment relationship, guaranteeing workers against catastrophic loss of income through accident, sickness or unemployment, and hence providing an incentive for people to enter industrial employment (Atkinson, 1996, ch. 11). In current times, as mature economies transform, it is recognized that people may be more willing to take risks, to retrain, and to change jobs, in a society in which there is adequate social protection. As argued by Abramovitz, 'the enlargement of the government's economic role, including its support of income minima, health care, social insurance, and other elements of the welfare state, was … not just a question of compassionate regard … It was, and is – up to a point – a part of the productivity growth process itself' (Abramovitz, 1981, pp. 2–3).

This refers to the impact on a target variable – the rate of growth of output; the same argument has been made in terms of welfare efficiency by Schmähl:

> It would be one-sided and dangerous to view social policy merely … as something that disturbs the market process … It is far rather a question of organising social security in such a way as to minimise losses in efficiency while at the same time making a positive contribution towards that efficiency, so that we avoid being confronted by a "big trade-off". (Schmähl, 1995, p. 27)

The welfare state can work with, rather than against, the grain of economic policy.

The emphasis by economists on the purely negative economic effects of the welfare state can be attributed to the theoretical framework adopted in much policy analysis, which remains rooted in a model of perfectly competitive and perfectly clearing markets, like that in the previous section. In this first-best situation, any real-world tax or transfer necessarily causes a loss of efficiency. Put another way, the theoretical framework incorporates none of the contingencies for which the welfare state exists. There is no uninsured uncertainty in the model, and no involuntary unemployment; nor is the future introduced in any meaningful way. The whole purpose of welfare state provision is missing from the theoretical model.

Recognition that the real-world economy departs from the competitive equilibrium model does not necessarily imply that the welfare state takes on a benign role. It is conceivable that state intervention reinforces, rather than corrects, departures from full employment. Unemployment insurance may make it more attractive for workers to queue for union jobs, increasing the 'natural' rate of unemployment. (This interaction is discussed further in the next section.) But this is not true of all departures from the competitive equilibrium model, and there are many forms that such departures could take. Once we leave the comfortable world of the Arrow–Debreu model, the conclusions often depend sensitively on the precise assumptions made. Other starting points, reflecting recent advances in economic theory such as those on imperfect information stressed by Barr (1992), provide a different perspective. For reasons that are now well understood, private insurance may be incomplete; if social insurance is scaled back, then workers may not be able to obtain comparable private cover.

The assessment of social security's economic impact depends on the criterion applied, as argued in Section 3. A positive role may more commonly be found when the government has specific economic target variables. To take one example, a government may legitimately be concerned with the integration of its citizens into the regular labour force. Suppose that we consider a situation where people choose between, on the one hand, regular formal employment, covered by social security, and, on the other hand, informal self-employment (or irregular employment). A regular employee is either engaged or laid off with no wage (and no possibility of returning to self-employment). The demand for labour is determined by profit-maximizing competitive firms which face uncertainty about demand for their product: there is either a boom or a slump. They contract with a certain number of workers, all of whom are engaged in a boom, but some of whom may be laid off in a slump. There is state unemployment insurance, financed by a tax on wages. Firms observe that there is a 'going rate' of expected wage payments, which they have to match in order to attract workers, where this going rate depends on the level of benefit and on the tax rate.

What is the impact of unemployment insurance? In a context like that just outlined, the tax reduces total employment. On the other hand, when we allow for the unemployment benefit, we can see that this acts as a subsidy to employment, increasing the total number of workers contracted. It is true that the extent of lay-off unemployment is increased, an aspect that has been emphasised by Feldstein (1976) and others, but that has to be set against the increased number of workers contracted, and it is possible that the overall impact of the benefit is a rise in average regular employment. The model, oversimplified though it may be, shows how, if it is regular employment that is our concern, unemployment insurance may be functional rather than dysfunctional. People have to be induced to enter the employment relationship, with the attendant risk of total loss of income, and this has to be compensated for either by wages or by the 'social wage'. If the government cuts back on the social wage, then the wage paid by employers has to rise, and the number of workers contracted is reduced.

Economists have, in my view, been preoccupied by the negative effects of the welfare state, and have failed to recognize sufficiently the positive impacts of social security on economic performance. The aim of reform should not be blanket dismissal of social transfers but should include the identification and strengthening of the positive elements.

5.   WIDER SOCIAL SYSTEM AND THE INTERRELATION BETWEEN DIFFERENT POLICIES

The welfare state is embedded in a wider social and economic system, as has been emphasized by Freeman (1995), and can only be interpreted in that light. Where state spending is small, other forms of provision are significant. In the United Kingdom, for example, a larger role is played than in most countries by employer pensions and by personal pensions, both of which permit contracting out of the state second-tier pension. This means that one cannot read across to the levels of spending in other countries. It does not make sense to suppose that social transfer spending in Sweden, say, could be reduced to the level in the United States, without considering all the other differences in the two countries. This point is illustrated by the calculations of the cost of social protection (income transfers plus health care) given in the Netherlands by the Ministry of Social Affairs and Employment (1996). They show that net public spending was indeed much higher in Sweden (34 per cent of GDP in 1993) than in the United States (15 per cent of GDP), but that private spending in the United States was higher by 9 per cent of GDP, reducing the gap very substantially. The total expenditure in the United States was 27 per cent of GDP, a figure which was very similar to that in Denmark (29 per cent) and Germany (31 per cent).

Taking a wider view of the position of the welfare state leads to the recognition that there may be interactions with other areas of government policy. This is well illustrated by the work of Alesina and Perotti (1994), where they show the interdependence between the welfare state, in the form of a tax on wages, and unionized labour markets. In their model, if the labour market were competitive, the tax would be borne by workers (it would be a purely lump-sum tax). It is the existence of trade unions which leads to a wage which is a mark-up on the reservation wage, and hence unemployment, in which case the tax does reduce employment. It is the interaction between union bargaining power and the welfare state which leads to the adverse effect on employment. This has the important implication that labour market reforms may be an alternative to cuts in benefit. If a government opts for labour market flexibility, and substantially reduces union power, then this may allay concerns about the economic impact of the welfare state. This conclusion is the opposite of that reached by Coe and Snower (1997), who argue that a wide range of labour market policies are complementary, rather than substitutes. They reach this result in a different labour market model, illustrating the point made earlier about the sensitivity of the findings to the choice of assumptions.

Put the other way round, where governments do cut back a public transfer programme, then this may have implications for other parts of the system. To take one example, those advocating abolition of the pay-as-you-go state pension do not usually propose that nothing takes its place. Critics typically wish to see an enhanced role for funded private pensions, combined with a residual state safety net. The thrust of the World Bank (1994) document, *Averting the Old-age Crisis*, with its three-pillar approach, is in this direction. The public pillar would remain, but with the limited object of alleviating old-age poverty, and there would be a mandatory funded second pillar, privately managed. (The third pillar is additional voluntary savings.)

Such changes in policy would, however, have economic repercussions. The growth of private pension funds has consequences for the working of the capital market. If greater targeting means replacing universal pensions by means-tested benefits, then this affects the incentives faced by households. Developing the latter point, suppose that the level of state pension provided to those with no other resources is left unchanged but that the state benefit is progressively withdrawn from those with other sources of income. The pension ceases to be universal and becomes an 'assistance pension'. In a limiting case, the state benefit represents a minimum income guarantee, and is reduced one for one with other resources. Such a reform promises to reduce total public expenditure while still meeting the anti-poverty objective (providing the guarantee is set at a sufficient level). But the test of resources changes the intertemporal budget constraint faced by the individual. People who prior to retirement foresee that increased savings lead to reduced state transfers may adjust their saving behaviour. In the case of the minimum income guarantee, they in effect face a choice. Either they save sufficient to be completely independent in old age or they reduce their savings to zero and rely solely on the state benefit. Such a policy move towards assistance pensions, while reducing total welfare state spending, creates a 'savings trap' (Atkinson, 1996, ch. 16). The savings of at least a section of society will be reduced, and there will inevitably be concerns about the polarization of the elderly into rich and poor.

We have, therefore, to look at proposed reforms 'in the round'.

6. DYNAMICS OF REFORM

In a series of recent articles, Lindbeck (1995a, 1995b) has stressed the dynamics of individual behavioural response to social transfers, arguing that disincentive effects are likely to be larger in the long run than in the short run, not least because behaviour is restricted by social norms regarding the work ethic which evolve slowly over time. Such norms may also affect attitudes towards claiming benefits, and thus the issue of the non-take-up of means-tested benefits (Cowell, 1986). We have to allow for the fact that the feasibility set faced by the government is evolving over time. What was feasible in the 1960s may not be in the 1990s; equally, what appears realistic, or unrealistic, today may not be so in the year 2020. Dynamics are also important on the side of the government. Adopting a public choice perspective, we have to recognize that there are lagged adjustments in the political process. Reforms made in response to current pressures may be later reversed by politicians responding to the problems created by today's reforms.

Seen first from the standpoint of policy design, the existence of lagged reactions means that governments have to anticipate such adjustments of household behaviour, to avoid 'overshooting' (Lindbeck, 1994). The design of such a policy does, however, depend on the determinants of social norms, and the extent to which they embody expectations about future welfare state policy. This is very much uncharted territory for economists, particularly when we consider other dimensions of social norms such as attitudes towards redistribution.

A public choice perspective lends further interest to the dynamics. Suppose that the scale of the welfare state, and the associated tax rate, is adjusted towards that preferred by the median voter, and the preferred level depends on the degree of confidence that promised benefits will be paid. Suppose that the degree of confidence feeds on itself but falls if the tax rate is felt to be unsustainably high. There may then be three possible equilibria:

(i)   with 100 per cent confidence and the median voter's preferred tax rate;
(ii)   an interior solution, which is a saddlepoint and not therefore generally attained; and
(iii)   no taxation and zero confidence.

The outcome depends on the initial conditions, and by the same token is subject to the influence of extraneous shocks. Lindbeck (1995a) rightly draws attention to the sensitivity to macroeconomic shocks, but there may be others. Suppose that the economy is approaching the equilibrium (i), with a high level of confidence and the tax rate rising to its long-run value. Alarms are then raised, by economists perhaps, about the hazards of the welfare state.

This causes an instantaneous drop in public confidence, and, as a result, the economy then diverges towards the zero tax, zero welfare state equilibrium. There are many different stories that one could tell, but the above version allows economists, normally shy of surfacing in their own theories, to make an appearance in the model of the political process.

7.   THE OTHER CRITIQUE

Recent critiques do not usually recognize that the post-war welfare state has been the subject of attack for several decades – on the grounds that it is failing to meet the objectives of alleviating poverty, redistributing income, and guaranteeing individual security. Social security has been criticized for inadequate coverage, excluding significant groups of the population, for being founded on an outdated model of the male breadwinner, and for failing to adapt to new forms of poverty.

This attack may reinforce that based on economic performance, opening up the opportunity of improvement on both counts. Scope undoubtedly exists to make social security both more effective and less economically costly. Measures to raise the net incomes of the families of low-paid workers may alleviate poverty, reduce the disincentive to take such jobs, and increase investment in the human capital of their children. But there is also likely to be conflict. The attempt to square adequate benefits with reduced budgetary cost has led governments towards means-tested benefits. In the United Kingdom, for instance, they have sought to help families by means-tested family credit, limited to those with low total family incomes, while the universal child benefit has been eroded. But means-tested benefits create poverty traps, with high marginal tax rates. There is an endemic problem of non-take-up, so that a significant minority do not claim the benefit to which they are entitled. On the other hand, the alternatives are expensive. Child benefit is, after all, directed at objectives in addition to alleviating poverty, in particular redistributing income towards families with children. Child benefit can be seen as a basic income for children, and the idea of a basic income for all, adults as well as children, has received a lot of support. It has the attraction of being neutral with respect to employment and other decisions: the same payment is made irrespective of employment status. The cost is, however, a sizeable increase in the tax rate on all income.

There are difficult choices to be made. The recent economic literature has contributed to debating these choices by highlighting the implications for economic performance. We should not, however, overlook the effect of proposed reforms on the incomes of individuals and their families. Here, too, economists have contributed through the development of quantitative models, measuring the impact on today's population and on future generations. Such models are now widely used by national governments, and a Europe-wide tax benefit model, Euromod, is currently being studied by a team of researchers from all 15 member states (Sutherland et al., 1995). It is only by using such models that one can, for example, determine the extent to which the consequences for the poor of welfare state reforms can be mitigated by accompanying measures.

8. CONCLUDING COMMENT

The *status quo* has no particular claim on our attention, and governments cannot, and should not, wait for certainty before carrying out reforms. But the importance of reforms of the welfare state and their implications for the lives of all citizens are so great that there should be a full debate.

REFERENCES

Abramovitz, M. (1981), 'Welfare quandaries and productivity concerns', *American Economic Review*, **71**, 1–17.

Albrecht, J.W. and Axell, B. (1984), 'An equilibrium model of search unemployment', *Journal of Political Economy*, **92**, 824–40.

Alesina, A. and Perotti, R. (1994), 'The welfare state and competitiveness', *NBER Working Paper*, No. 4810.

Atkinson, A.B. (1995), 'The welfare state and economic performance', *National Tax Journal*, **48**, 171–98.

Atkinson, A.B. (1996), *Incomes and the Welfare State*, Cambridge: Cambridge University Press.

Atkinson, A.B. (forthcoming), *The Economic Consequences of Rolling Back the Welfare State*, Cambridge, MA: MIT Press.

Atkinson, A.B. and Micklewright, J. (1991), 'Unemployment compensation and labour market transitions: a critical review', *Journal of Economic Literature*, **29**, 1679–727.

Barr, N. (1992), 'Economic theory and the welfare state: a survey and interpretation', *Journal of Economic Literature*, **30**, 741–803.

Coe, D.T. and Snower, D.J. (1997), 'Policy complementarities: the case for fundamental labour market reform', *CEPR Discussion Paper*, No. 1585.

Cowell, F.A. (1986), 'Welfare benefits and the economics of take-up', *TIDI Discussion Paper* 89, LSE.

Diamond, P.A. (1993), 'Insulation of pensions from political risk', conference on mandatory pensions, Santiago, Chile.

Drèze, J.H. and Malinvaud, E. (1994), 'Growth and employment: the scope for a European initiative', *European Economy*, No. 1, 77–106.

Feldstein, M.S. (1976), 'Temporary lay-offs in the theory of unemployment', *Journal of Political Economy*, **84**, 937–57.

Franco, D. and Munzi, T. (1996), 'Public pension expenditure prospects in the European Union: a survey of national projections', *European Economy*, No. 3, 1–126.

Freeman, R.B. (1995), 'The large welfare state as a system', *American Economic Review, Papers and Proceedings*, **85**, 16–21.

Grigg, J. (1978), *Lloyd George: The People's Champion 1902–1911*, London: Eyre Methuen.

Lindbeck, A. (1981), 'Work disincentives in the welfare state', reprinted in Lindbeck, A., *The Welfare State*, Aldershot: Edward Elgar, pp. 27–76.

Lindbeck, A. (1994), 'Overshooting, reform and retreat of the welfare state', *The Economist*, **142**, 1–19.

Lindbeck, A. (1995a), 'Hazardous welfare state dynamics', *American Economic Review, Papers and Proceedings*, **85**, 9–15.

Lindbeck, A. (1995b), 'Welfare state disincentives with endogenous habits and norms', *Scandinavian Journal of Economics*, **97**, 477–94.

Lindbeck, A. (1997), 'Welfare state dynamics', this book, ch. 3.

Ministry of Social Affairs and Employment (1996), *The Dutch Welfare State from an International and Economic Perspective*, The Hague.

Sandmo, A. (1994), 'Social security and economic growth', international colloquy entitled 'The Nordic model of social security in a European perspective', Lillehammer, Norway.

Schmähl, W. (1995), 'Social security and competitiveness', *Social Security Tomorrow: Permanence and Change*, International Social Security Association, *Studies and Research*, No. 36, Geneva, pp. 19–28.

Shapiro, C. and Stiglitz, J.E. (1984), 'Equilibrium unemployment as a worker discipline device', *American Economic Review*, **74**, 433–44.

Sutherland, H. et al. (1995), Euromod: *A proposal*, Cambridge: Microsimulation Unit.

World Bank (1994), *Averting the Old-age Crisis*, Washington, DC: World Bank.

3. Welfare state dynamics

Assar Lindbeck

1. INTRODUCTION[1]

This chapter deals, in a general way, with the achievements and problems of welfare state arrangements in western Europe. These arrangements naturally differ among countries. In particular, the extent to which countries rely on four basic institutions – the state, the firm, the family and the market – varies greatly. This is the case both for systems of income security, that is, transfers over the life cycle, and for provision of various types of services, such as health care, childcare and old-age care.

With respect to income security, the most important difference between countries is probably between the reliance on a common safety net, that is, flat-rate benefits tied to specific contingencies; means-tested benefits, that is, benefits that are lost by higher income; and income protection, that is, benefits that rise by higher income in the past. With respect to services to households, the most important difference is probably between countries in which the government provides such services, such as the Nordic countries, and countries in which these services are mainly provided by the family or the private market.

Another important distinction is between corporatist welfare states, where benefits are connected to labour contracts, and universal welfare states in which benefits are tied to citizenship. This distinction is blurred, however, by recent tendencies in corporatist welfare states to extend coverage to citizens who have a rather weak attachment to the labour market, and in universal welfare states to tie benefits to previous or contemporary work under the slogan 'workfare' rather than 'welfare'. The degree of generosity of benefits is another important distinction. Naturally, the lower the benefit levels in the compulsory state-operated systems, the stronger the incentives for citizens to complement these systems with voluntary market solutions, in the form of private saving and private (though possibly collective) insurance arrangements.

While acknowledging these differences in welfare state arrangements between nations, this chapter mainly deals with issues that are common to most countries in western Europe. The emphasis will be on 'dynamic' issues, that is, the achievements and problems of the welfare state that evolve over time, often with important interaction between several different variables. Let me begin, however, with a number of more familiar 'static' aspects.

2. STATIC ASPECTS

The most obvious achievements of the modern welfare state are probably: (i) to redistribute income over the life cycle of the individual, and, in this context, equalize the distribution of yearly income between individuals and households; (ii) to reduce income risk; (iii) to stimulate the consumption of various social services, often with strong elements of investment in human capital; and (iv) to mitigate poverty. In some countries, welfare state arrangements have also (v) equalized the overall distribution of disposable lifetime income, that is, wealth, among individuals, and also the distribution of specific social services. This enumeration of achievements illustrates the common view that welfare state arrangements may be motivated on both efficiency grounds (the first three achievements just mentioned) and distributional grounds (the last two).

How, then, can we be sure that similar redistributions of income over the life cycle, reductions of income risks, and investment in human capital would not have taken place even without welfare state arrangements, that is, on a voluntary basis? The 'paternalistic' answer, obviously, is that many individuals are myopic, and that they would therefore not have chosen equally elaborate economic security on their own. Economists, however, tend to emphasize various deficiencies of voluntary market solutions to problems of economic security. The most obvious examples are perhaps difficulties in borrowing with human capital as collateral, and high administrative costs of voluntary insurance policies. Compulsory social security may also overcome tendencies towards free-riding by individuals who expect the government to help them out if they encounter economic difficulties in the future. It is also a method to prevent 'cream-skimming' by insurance companies when they are able to identify low-risk individuals, and a technique to avoid adverse selection when insurance companies are not able to make this kind of identification. There is also general agreement among economists that various positive externalities of investment in human capital tend to make such investment suboptimal without government interventions, for instance in the form of loan guarantees and subsidies to prenatal care, education and perhaps also child care.

But how do we know that welfare state arrangements have in fact equalized the distribution of disposable income among individuals? One piece of evidence is that the dispersion of disposable income in most OECD countries is much smaller than the dispersion of factor income – and this holds not only for the overall income distribution but also for its lower tail. Moreover, there is very little evidence that benefits and taxes, designed to equalize the distribution of disposable income, have been shifted to factor prices, making the distribution of factor income more dispersed. Indeed, in most countries, the factor income distribution among citizens of active working age tended to become more even during the period when the welfare state arrangements were being built up in the first decades after World War II.

The most widely discussed problem regarding welfare state arrangements probably concerns the static efficiency costs associated with the financing of the welfare state, that is, distortions generated by various tax wedges, which are often measured by the marginal costs of public funds. My only point on this well-known issue would be to emphasize the pervasiveness of such disincentive effects. In addition to frequently studied (substitution) effects on hours of work, and somewhat less frequently studied effects on private saving and investment in physical capital, it is also important to consider the effects on, for instance, do-it-yourself work, the barter of goods and services, the intensity and quality of work, the investment in human capital, the choice of job, the allocation of investment in real and human capital, tax avoidance, tax evasion, and so on. Unfortunately, our empirical knowledge of these matters is fragmented, and sometimes even anecdotal. In the United States, the marginal costs of public funds are often estimated at about US$1.2 to 1.3 per dollar of additional spending. This means that higher government spending can be motivated if it is believed to be worth more than US$1.2 to 1.3 to society per extra dollar spent. In Sweden during the 1980s, the marginal costs of public funds have usually been estimated at between US$1.5 and 2.5. Such studies are, however, rather unreliable. Moreover, they cover only a very limited number of distortions, often only the effects on hours of work, which means that the actual costs may be considerably higher.

Distortions directly connected with welfare state benefits are no less pervasive. Means-tested benefits are bound to create 'benefit wedges', that is, implicit tax wedges, resulting in poverty traps for some low-income groups. The most severe problem inherent in various benefit systems is probably that, like private insurance, they are plagued with moral hazard, as the individual is able to adjust his or her own behaviour to qualify for benefits. Outright benefit-cheating is also bound to occur. Among major welfare state arrangements, problems of moral hazard and cheating seem to be particularly pervasive in the case of sick benefits, work-injury benefits, financial support to single parents (particularly mothers), subsidized early retirement (disability pensions), and unemployment benefits.[2]

There are, of course, strong social and humanitarian reasons for being generous to individuals with low incomes, regardless of whether this is a permanent or temporary situation. Indeed, that is one reason why welfare state arrangements have been built up in the first place. However, basic dilemmas are that the more generous the welfare state is to people who are sick, the more individuals will stay away from work even when they are healthy (but perhaps tired or bored); the more favourable the conditions for subsidized early-retirement pensions, the more individuals will choose to live on such pensions; the more generous we are to the unemployed, the higher long-term unemployment is likely to be; and the more generous we are to single mothers and their children, the more single mothers we are likely to have in the long run. The difficult problem, therefore, is how to strike a balance between the social value of income protection and redistribution, on the one hand, and the risk of moral hazard, cheating and tax distortions, on the other hand.

However, rather than dwelling on these static aspects, I would like to concentrate on effects of a more dynamic nature. By that I mean effects that evolve over time and interact strongly with each other, possibly in the form of virtuous or vicious circles.

3.   DYNAMIC ACHIEVEMENTS

Starting with dynamic achievements, it is likely that government subsidization of investment in human capital will result not only in a rise in the future level of GDP, but also in faster long-term GDP growth, as asserted by contemporary theories of endogenous growth. This should be the result not only for education and general health care, but also for policies that mitigate child poverty and provide specific social services such as prenatal care and better nutrition for mothers and children. Indeed, improvements in these fields seem to be transmitted over generations within the family (Haveman and Wolfe, 1993).

Another potentially important dynamic contribution of welfare state arrangements is to bring various minority groups into ordinary work, and hence to mitigate what is often called 'social exclusion', manifested in long-term open unemployment, withdrawal from the labour force, or highly unstable and uncertain job prospects. This contribution presupposes, of course, that long-term benefit dependency can be avoided. This is more likely to be the case if the policy were to rely on work-oriented welfare state arrangements, so-called 'workfare', rather than on pure transfer payments.

Policies that counteract social exclusion may also, in a long-term perspective, mitigate the development of cultures of criminal behaviour such as street crime, burglary, physical violence and drug addiction (see Hagen, 1994). Poor labour force attachment is, in fact, often regarded as a key factor that embeds crimes in poor neighbourhoods (see Wilson, 1987). Indeed, it is often argued that, compared with the United States, the more ambitious welfare state arrangements in western Europe help explain the smaller incidence of such phenomena in the latter area (see Coder et al., 1989; Jäntti and Danziger, 1994).

The emergence of long-term dynamic effects such as these was already a basic notion in Gunnar Myrdal's *An American Dilemma* (1944, Appendix 3), where he emphasized the possibilities of what he called processes of 'cumulative causation' between variables such as 'employment, wages, housing, nutrition, clothing, health, education, stability in family relations, manners, cleanliness, orderliness, trustworthiness, law observance, loyalty to society at large, absence of criminality, and so on'. Long-term productivity-enhancing welfare state policies, and policies that stimulate labour force participation in the private sector, also expand the tax base in the long run. This would help finance the welfare state in the first place – which is an obvious example of a virtuous circle.[3] Once again, such effects presuppose that welfare state policies do not result in long-term benefit dependency. Labour supply in some countries is also enhanced by tying the individual's right to social benefits to work – to previous work in the case of pensions, sickness benefits and paid maternity leave, and to current work in the case of subsidized child care.

It has also been argued that an even distribution of income mitigates social conflicts (Alesina and Rodrik, 1994) and reduces the political pressure to redistribute disposable income further by way of distortionary political interventions (Meltzer and Scott, 1981; Persson and Tabellini, 1994). Another common view is that welfare state arrangements make citizens more willing to accept a reallocation of resources in response to changes in technology, product demand and international competition, and even perhaps contribute to making citizens more sympathetic to the market system. This argument is based on the idea that individuals cling less to previous jobs if society provides a solid safety net.

Welfare state policies may also have profound long-term consequences for the role of the family in society. Some family-oriented welfare states on the European continent tend to support the traditional family, in the sense that married women are encouraged to work in their homes rather than in the open market. Examples of such countries are Austria, the Netherlands, Switzerland, and to a considerable extent also Germany. This result is accentuated by high marginal tax wedges, which favour household work rather than work in the market.

The consequences for the family are more complex in 'individual-centred' welfare states, for example the Nordic countries. High marginal tax rates in these countries inevitably also create substitution effects in favour of household work. But incentives in the opposite direction are created in several of these countries by the subsidization of child care, medical care and the care of the elderly outside the household. In some countries, labour force partici- pation of married women is also stimulated by the separate assessment of income taxes for husband and wife, which lowers the marginal income tax rate for the 'second' income earner in the household. Another example is positive income (or rather liquidity) effects on labour supply by a combina- tion of high average tax rates and the provision of benefits 'in kind' that cannot be transformed into money income, which often makes it difficult to finance the family on the basis of one income earner only.

Thus, in countries with a combination of high marginal tax rates, strict work requirements and subsidized child care outside the home, labour force participation may very well be high for married women. But the average number of working hours per year per individual would be expected to be rather low, in particular if the benefit systems are far from actuarially fair. Strongly subsidized child care and old-age care may also keep up the birth rate in such societies.

It is, of course, a question of values whether we are in favour of family- oriented or individual-oriented welfare states – or if we prefer, in conformity with non-paternalistic principles, to opt for welfare state arrangements that are intended to be neutral with respect to the division of labour between household work and market activities, as well as to the division of work between family members.

4.   DYNAMIC PROBLEMS

The dynamic achievements of the welfare state should be compared with various dynamic problems. For instance, the positive effects of the subsidization of investment in human capital are counteracted by the reduced return on such an investment because of marginal taxes on labour income, in particular if the tax system is progressive. Similarly, broad marginal tax wedges on the return on physical assets tend to reduce the accumulation of such assets. It is, by contrast, often argued that policies with negative effects on domestic saving do not harm domestic investment in physical assets in a world of free international capital movements. This, I believe, is a mistaken view. One reason is that there seems to be a home bias regarding the supply of funds to physical investment, in the sense that foreign saving is not a perfect substitute for domestic saving when it comes to the financing of domestic investment. In particular, it is likely that small and medium-sized firms are favoured by domestically supplied financial capital – equity capital as well as loans – because of various information problems in capital and credit markets. For instance, providers of financial capital require detailed knowledge of the entrepreneurs to whom they supply funds, and this knowledge is difficult to acquire 'long distance'. A more important point is, perhaps, that private entrepreneurs, particularly small ones, are likely to have preferences for capital that is controlled either by themselves or by people whom they know. Thus both capital taxes that reduce the return on private saving and welfare state arrangements that reduce the need for the household to save would be expected to thwart the entry and growth of small private firms.

More wide-ranging dynamic problems may also arise in connection with welfare state policies. I have hypothesized elsewhere (Lindbeck, 1995; Lindbeck et al., 1995) that the full realization of various disincentive effects of taxes and benefits is likely to be delayed because habits and social norms constrain individual behaviour. Before the build-up of generous welfare state arrangements, work and saving were crucial for the living standard of the individual, and indeed often even for his survival. It may be hypothesized that today's habits and social norms are, at least partly, a result of incentive and control systems in the past. However, as increased marginal tax wedges and more generous benefits in recent decades have reduced the return on work, and also made individual saving less imperative, it is likely that habits and social norms gradually adjust to the new incentive system. Moreover, as more individuals abandon previously obeyed social norms, it will be easier for others to do the same. In other words, it is likely that interaction between economic incentives and social norms contributes to a dynamic process by which individuals gradually adjust their behaviour to a new incentive structure. Such delayed effects were probably not anticipated by politicians when today's welfare state arrangements were decided. Therefore, it is tempting to argue that the welfare state will easily 'overshoot', in the sense that welfare state spending will expand more than politicians had originally planned.

In the previous section on dynamic achievements of the welfare state, I mentioned that welfare state arrangements may raise the acceptance among citizens of continuing reallocation of labour. However, reallocation is often resisted even in advanced welfare states (including in my own country, Sweden), and citizens ask for regional subsidies to allow them to stay where they are. Moreover, we cannot really be sure that reductions in income inequality, when brought about by policy actions, will necessarily mitigate social conflicts and reduce the political pressure for further redistributions through taxes, transfers and regulations. The appetite for redistributions may even increase by the amount of redistributions implemented earlier. One reason is that such policy actions politicize distributional issues by making people believe that income differences, rather than constituting an indispensable element of a well-functioning market system, are arbitrarily determined in the political process. This is, in fact, my own interpretation of the Swedish experience of redistribution policy after World War II. Indeed, it seems that the political discussion in Sweden has increasingly focused on remaining inequalities, and the demands to reduce them, regardless of how small they have become.

So far I have dealt with problematic behaviour adjustments in connection with welfare state arrangements. Another potentially serious dynamic problem is that the welfare state is not very robust to macroeconomic and demographic shocks. More specifically, it is obvious that the welfare state has been financially undermined by the slowdown of long-term GDP growth of the last two decades. After all, the welfare state arrangements decided on during the first decades after World War II were based on the assumption of fast economic growth, probably around 4 per cent per year. The architects of the modern welfare state also based their decisions on overoptimistic expectations concerning demography. Serious problems have therefore been created by the rising life expectancy of old people. The welfare state crisis became acute in some countries in the 1980s and early 1990s in connection with strongly negative macroeconomic shocks which threw large groups of citizens into various safety nets, and induced others to withdraw from the labour force. These developments may also have speeded up the earlier-mentioned long-term weakening of social norms against living on various types of benefits.

If these hypotheses make sense, it is important to take early warning signals about disincentive effects and lack of robustness seriously, rather than to wait until academic research has shown, without doubt, that the welfare state is in trouble. The problem is rather similar to the emergence of environmental disturbances, which often also build up only gradually, but may be suddenly speeded up by abrupt shocks. In both cases, it is dangerous to wait until problems have conclusively been proven to exist, as it takes time to reverse the process.

Traditionally, automatic budget responses to fluctuations in GDP have been assumed to stabilize aggregate employment by keeping up the disposable income of households during recessions. There is some concern today, however, that the automatic stabilizer may turn into an automatic destabilizer in deep recessions in countries with exceptionally generous welfare state arrangements. The reason is that galloping government debt may create great uncertainty both among lenders and households regarding the ability of the government to live up to its previous commitments. As a result, lenders are likely to require higher interest rates on their loans to the government, and households may increase their saving in the middle of a deep recession. However, it is likely that the automatic fiscal stabilizer functions as traditionally assumed during normal business fluctuations.

Recent employment experiences in western Europe also suggest that the equilibrium unemployment rate, that is, the rate at which the aggregate wage (or price) increase is constant, has been raised by generous welfare state arrangements. These arrangements are also likely to have made high unemployment more persistent after unemployment-creating shocks. The reasons for these effects are not only that the jobless workers are encouraged to search longer when they are entitled to generous unemployment benefits for longer periods of time. Workers also tend to become more aggressive in their wage demands when the incomes received when out of work are higher.

Some welfare state arrangements also tend to reduce the hiring of labour. An example is strict job security legislation that tends to stabilize the employment level at whatever levels happen to exist. Strict job security legislation, that is, high costs of hiring and firing workers, also raises the market powers of those who already have a job, so-called 'insiders' relative to 'outsiders', that is, workers without a job. This also tends to boost the real wage rate, as insiders are then able to push up their wages above the reservation wage of outsiders without losing their jobs. High minimum wages, rigid relative wages and wide tax wedges also tend both to raise equilibrium unemployment and to increase unemployment persistence.

5. MARGINAL REFORMS

On the basis of accumulated, though highly fragmented, evidence from various countries, it should be clear that the welfare state is experiencing serious problems, and that there is a strong case for welfare state reforms. The only relevant question is how to bring them about. Indeed, reforms and retreats are already under way in several OECD countries. I will start with what may be called marginal reforms, and then shift the focus to more radical ones. Marginal reforms often aim to reduce tax and benefit wedges, to mitigate moral hazard, to fight cheating with taxes and benefits, and to make the existing system more robust to shocks. Radical reforms, on the other hand, aim to overhaul the basic structure of the welfare state arrangements.

Perhaps the most obvious marginal reform would be to cut benefit levels. Stronger actuarial elements in various social security systems would also help reduce economic disincentives, as the marginal tax wedges would then shrink. It is important to note that the systems can be made more actuarially fair without shifting to funded systems, though the return on the contributions will then deviate from the mark-off interest rate. Future benefits 'simply' have to be tied to the value of previously paid contributions. Such contributions – defined as pay-as-you-go systems – are perhaps easiest to achieve for old-age and early-retirement pensions.[4]

It is also useful to have the same replacement rates in all benefit systems between which the individual can move at his own discretion. Otherwise, some individuals will simply choose to apply for the most favourable type of benefit. Well-known examples are shifts between sick leave, work-injury benefits and disability pensions. Strict eligibility requirements for receiving benefits, and stiff controls that these requirements are satisfied, are also important. The need for controls is, of course, smaller the lower the benefit levels, and vice versa. There are, however, practical limits to controls, which are probably more effective against cheating than against moral hazard.

To avoid overinsurance, it is also useful to put caps on total insurance benefits in each system, that is, on the levels of compulsory plus private insurance benefits. Otherwise, the compulsory system may be exposed to negative external effects via moral hazard and cheating in the voluntary system. Such caps are not necessary in the old-age pension system, however, as moral hazard hardly arises in this case.

When considering methods that would allow welfare state arrangements to adjust better to shocks in demography and productivity, a basic issue is the extent to which such adjustments should be automatic or discretionary.[5] In a pension system, for instance, an obvious way to achieve automatic adjustments to demographic shocks is to tie the normal pension age to the life expectancy of the population. To provide automatic protection against a slowdown in productivity growth, the pension benefits could be formally tied to the per capita disposable income, or per capita consumption, of the active population (see Merton, 1983). Similar automatic adjustment mechanisms may also be constructed for other parts of a social security system. For instance, either the contribution or the benefits of an unemployment insurance system may be automatically tied to the unemployment rate. In a sick-pay system, contributions and benefits may be formally tied to the number of sick days either for specific groups of people or for the population as a whole. Automatic adjustments have the advantage of being somewhat more predictable than discretionary adjustments. Automatic adjustment mechanisms may, therefore, reduce the risk of discretionary political interventions, that is, they may reduce the 'political risks' in the social insurance systems.

An obvious weakness of automatic adjustment mechanisms of this aggregate type is that they may make it difficult to establish a tight relation between contributions and benefits for the individual. Relative benefits for different individuals could, however, still be tied to previously paid contributions, even if average benefits are tied to the average disposable income of the contemporary working population.

It is important to realize that reforms in the social insurance systems have wide effects in society. For instance, policies that raise the pension age, which is an important way of preventing the pension system from collapsing in some countries, are likely to increase the supply of labour in the 55 to 70 age group. If these people are to get jobs, however, the functioning of the labour market, including the formation of relative wages, has to be much more flexible. The institutional obstacle to part-time work must also be reduced to prevent many individuals in this group from being unemployed.

Incentive problems also extend to the provision of social services, in the sense that it has proven difficult to achieve efficiency and freedom of choice when the government monopolies provide such services. Services also suffer from Baumol's law, according to which the costs of many types of labour-intensive services tend to increase relative to the costs of goods or services for which productivity growth is faster. This will create even more severe financial problems for the welfare state, and force politicians to define their priorities more carefully. Obvious ways of mitigating these problems are either administrative reforms of public sector agencies or the opening up of competition with private and cooperative institutions – or both. The first option includes methods such as administrative decentralization, cash limits and comparison of the performance of different units in the public sector (that is, benchmark competition). The second option requires free entry and an end to the discrimination of actual and potential competitors to public sector agencies. To mitigate distributional problems in connection with freer competition, a voucher system is perhaps the most obvious device.

Some of these welfare state reforms are also likely to reduce long-term unemployment. The most obvious example is perhaps less generous unemployment benefits, including lower replacement ratios, shorter benefit periods and stronger actuarial elements in the financing of the system. Less rigid job security legislation would be expected to have similar effects in countries with heavy unemployment.

Many of the marginal reforms discussed here may well have distributional consequences that are not happily received by the general public. There are, however, well-known methods to mitigate some of these consequences. These methods include lower income taxes, or so-called 'in-work benefits' for people who otherwise may become 'working poor', reduced payroll taxes for low-productivity workers, tax favours, or subsidies, for the purchases of labour-intensive household services, the option of transforming unemployment benefits to vouchers by which unemployed workers can 'buy' jobs from firms, subsidies for the training of unemployed workers and perhaps also for low-productivity workers in general, apprenticeship systems for the young, and so on. Each of these measures is connected with various drawbacks, but these have to be compared with either not being able to reform the welfare state at all or with a much wider dispersion of disposable income.

6. RADICAL REFORMS

The considerations above focused on marginal reforms within an approximately given structure of welfare state arrangements. More recently, however, there has also been some discussion of changes of the basic structure of the welfare state.

Examples of radical alternatives are:

  (i)   to replace a system of income protection with a safety net that is common to all (flat-rate benefits);
 (ii)   to shift from a pay-as-you-go to a funded social insurance system, possibly combined with partial or total privatization, while keeping insurance compulsory;
(iii)   to replace a complex social security system, in which benefits are tied to specific contingencies, with a negative income tax (a so-called 'gradient system'); or
 (iv)   to replace a traditional social security system with actuarially based lifetime drawing rights, that is, forced-saving accounts, whereby an individual is free to draw, at his own discretion, on an individual account which comprises compulsory fees accumulated over his working life.

Each of these radical reforms has specific advantages and drawbacks. A shift to a common safety net, that is, the 'back-to-Beveridge strategy', has the advantage of being financially inexpensive for the government. Such a system is also attractive if we want individuals to take considerable personal responsibility in the form of voluntary saving and insurance policies, which is often believed to reduce the risk of individuals becoming passive. A clear disadvantage of this strategy is that the administrative costs are higher in private insurance systems than in compulsory social insurance systems.

Funded systems not only have the advantage of being (more or less) actuarially fair (which means that wide tax wedges are avoided), but are also likely to have a favourable effect on aggregate national saving, at least during a period of transition. It is also reasonable to assume that subjectively felt property rights are stronger in a funded system than in a pay-as-you-go system, in the sense that the risk of political intervention is smaller. Thus a funded system is probably politically more stable than a pay-as-you-go system. However, the individuals would instead be exposed to more capital market risks. It is also important when a shift to funding is implemented. An abrupt rise in aggregate national saving in the midst of a deep recession would only serve to worsen the recession. It is also important that a rise in aggregate saving is combined with policies that encourage physical investment or a rise in the current account surplus, or both.

In addition to well-known transition problems (such as some generations having to finance two parallel systems), a government-implemented funded system also raises the difficult issue of who should administrate and control the funds. It is theoretically possible for the funds to be managed in such a way that their managers, and hence also politicians and public sector bureaucrats, do not interfere in either the allocation of the assets or the control of the firms in which the funds are invested. Theoretically, for instance, it may be possible to legislate that the funds should hold 'market portfolios', or invest only in mutual funds.

However, it is naive to believe that future politicians will necessarily adhere to such rules. They can simply amend legislation in the future so as to control the funds and/or exert power over firms in which the funds have shares. In other words, there is a great risk that a funded, government-operated social security system will, in reality, sooner or later develop into a system with strong government control of both capital markets and individual firms. It is much easier for politicians to use an instrument that already exists, that is, government-created funds, to exercise power over the capital market and firms, than to engage in open socialization with the explicit purpose of taking control of the private sector.

The Swedish experience is instructive from this point of view. When the supplementary pension system was introduced in Sweden in 1959, it was explicitly stated that the buffer funds created by the new system should not be used to buy shares in private firms. Nevertheless, new decisions have been taken over the years to do just that. Moreover, Swedish politicians have not chosen index funds or mutual funds, and the government-appointed boards of the funds have, in fact, used the voting rights of the shares held by the buffer funds to intervene in firms. From time to time, politicians and labour union leaders have also suggested that the pension funds should buy more shares and be used more systematically as instruments for centralized industrial policies. Those who want to limit the risk of future socialization of firms, therefore, have good reason to object to a shift to a government-operated funded social security system.

What about a shift to a negative income tax, which is a popular idea among some economists? One main advantage would be that extremely high implicit marginal tax rates, that is, poverty traps, may be avoided for low-income earners. But such a system is very expensive because of the thickness of the tail left in the factor income distribution in most countries, which requires the imposition of quite high tax rates on the rest of the population. As a result, the marginal tax distortions would simply move up along the income distribution, which may create more incentive problems than it solves.

There is, however, an even more serious problem associated with a negative income tax. It may create new generations of 'drifters', living on government handouts. Thus a negative income tax may, over time, result in a demise of habits and social norms in favour of work and saving (for instance among the younger generation). Such risks are probably smaller in the case of social security systems in which the benefits are tied to well-defined contingencies (Lindbeck, 1994). A negative income tax may, therefore, also develop into a 'hippie subsidy'.

A system of drawing rights, finally, would allow the individual to draw on an account in the public sector for well-defined contingencies, for instance in connection with education, training, sickness or unemployment, though less would then be available later on, ultimately for pensions (Fölster, 1997). However, such a system requires complementary risk insurance, as different individuals are exposed to quite different risks, such as sickness, permanent invalidism, unemployment. It would also be necessary to put a strict ceiling on how much the individual is allowed to draw before retirement age in order to avoid myopic behaviour and free-riding. Experiences in Singapore and Chile suggest that a system of this type is at least administratively feasible.

Some of these radical reforms may also have distributional consequences that are not regarded as acceptable. Complementary redistributional reforms will then be necessary, such as those discussed at the end of the previous section.

7. CONSEQUENCES OF THE EUROPEAN UNION AND EMU

So far, I have discussed the welfare state in a national perspective only. How, then, does increased international economic integration influence the functioning of the welfare state? More specifically, what are the consequences of the European Union (EU) and a future economic and monetary union (EMU) for the west European welfare states?

One important implication for national welfare states of free mobility of financial capital between member states is that an individual country cannot finance its own welfare state spending by considerably higher taxes on capital than those existing in other countries. As labour is much less mobile than capital, it is possible to let taxes on labour income deviate more. However, it is likely that labour mobility will increase in the future, which will make it more difficult for a national government to depress after-tax wages much below what corresponding workers receive in other countries, in particular for well-trained labour with an international labour market and a good knowledge of foreign languages.

The establishment of a monetary union will have additional consequences. Such a union cannot function well without increased mobility of labour over the national borders and more flexible real and relative wages. Otherwise, economic shocks will result in even more serious unemployment problems than those already existing in western Europe today. Thus individual countries within a monetary union have to take strong measures that facilitate both international labour mobility and flexible real and relative wages. But if countries succeed in raising labour mobility, this will further constrain the national autonomy in distributional policies. In this sense, a monetary union will indirectly further constrain the redistributional ambitions of national welfare state arrangements. If countries instead fail to raise international labour mobility and flexibility of real and relative wages, the shift to a monetary union is more likely to accentuate the serious unemployment problem of western Europe.

Increased international mobility of labour also necessitates some coordination of the national benefit systems. For instance, it will be necessary to prevent individuals from adjusting their geographical location over their life cycle on the basis of differences in the national benefit systems by choosing to live in low-tax nations when young and healthy, and in countries with high benefits and highly subsidized old-age care and health care after retirement. A basic policy issue, therefore, is whether individuals should be allowed to carry their 'earned' benefits with them wherever they move within Europe, or if they should receive the same benefits as other individuals in the country in which they are living at that time. The first alternative is obviously more compatible with the idea of actuarially fair systems than the second alternative. It is easier to implement the first alternative for social insurance benefits than for public services, such as health care and old-age care. Another example of a necessary coordination of national rules concerns measures to ensure the protection of workers' pension rights in relation to supplementary and occupational schemes when they move to another member state.

It is likely, however, that the European Union will, in fact, try to harmonize national welfare state rules much more than is really necessary for these various reasons. The official argument for such harmonization is that this is necessary to prevent social dumping. The idea seems to be that international competition is distorted if working conditions differ among countries. This is a rather dubious proposition since the total production costs are what are important. How these are distributed on wage and non-wage costs is actually immaterial from the point of view of international competitiveness. If the determination of wages can be left to national agents and institutions, so can non-wage costs.

Nevertheless, a process of harmonization of welfare state arrangements has already started within the European Union – as an element of the social dimension. Examples are contemplated restrictions on temporary and part-time work, more generous rules for parental leave, regulations that limit the rights of firms to contract out work, rules for the placing of a worker with another company or in another plant in another member country, and so on. Whatever arguments there may be for each of these interventions, the overall effect will be further to reduce flexibility in the European labour markets, making it even more difficult to reduce mass unemployment.

8.   CONCLUSION

Reforms of the welfare state have to be designed both to make it more robust to exogenous shocks, and to reduce problems of disincentives, moral hazard and cheating. The difficult problem is how this can be done without seriously damaging the achievements of the welfare state. Thus it is important to find a proper combination of redistribution, insurance and incentives.

   In view of these complex considerations, it is natural that welfare state reform proposals include combinations of different elements. The most celebrated combination in contemporary reform proposals is perhaps a three-pillared system consisting of:

   (i)   tax-financed flat-rate benefits, that is, a safety net, at the 'bottom' for well-defined contingencies such as sickness, unemployment and old age. Such a system, of course, has then to be combined with discretionary social assistance for people who, for various reasons, cannot support themselves;

   (ii) a supplementary system of mandatory social insurance designed for income protection, with strong actuarial elements in order to minimize tax wedges. This system may include some funding, provided it is possible to guarantee both individual ownership of the assets and private management of the funds, outside the reach of politicians;

   (iii) voluntary saving and insurance policies 'at the top', which may include both collective and individual insurance.

The first pillar, which may be strongly redistributive, need not be institutionally separate from the second, more actuarial, pillar; the two may be administratively combined. However, it is important that the first two pillars are constructed in ways that make them robust to shocks of economic growth, changes in demography and political interventions. Methods to achieve this have been discussed in the paper.

   A three-pillared system of this type would also pool political risks and market risks. This is perhaps as much economic security as can be achieved in an uncertain world. When such reforms are designed, it is also important to design the system in such a way that the serious unemployment problem in western Europe is mitigated rather than accentuated. I have indicated how this may be brought about.

The increased heterogeneity of the population in many countries also requires that social services in the future become better adjusted to the needs of the individual. This can only be achieved if the consumers of such services are given a greater say, that is, if they can exert influence both by voice and exit. The latter, of course, requires alternatives, for example competition. Moreover, in the future the elderly will be much more selective than former generations of elderly people, partly because they are better educated and healthier. They will also have considerable financial resources at their disposal, which will enable them to pay for services and accentuate their insistence on choosing for themselves.

To summarize: the European welfare states are confronted with serious problems. Reform proposals are likely to abound. There is, however, a tendency among some adherents of generous welfare state arrangements to shut their eyes to the serious problems with which the welfare state is likely to be confronted in the future. It must, however, be wiser to reform the welfare state now than to wait until the problems have become more serious. Indeed, if current and expected future problems regarding the welfare state are not mitigated soon, its economic foundations may crumble. Even more drastic reforms and retreats of various welfare state arrangements would then be necessary.

NOTES

1. Several points in this paper are developed in more detail in Lindbeck 1995, 1996a, 1996b and 1996c.
2. Some figures for Sweden may illustrate the issue. For instance, in the 1980s, when the replacement ratio in the sick benefit system was above 90 per cent of previous income (up to a ceiling), people stayed away from work for alleged sickness for about 25 days per year on average. In connection with lower compensation levels and stricter social control (after employers took over the payments of benefits for the first two weeks), the number of sick days fell dramatically, probably to 11 days. The deep recession in the early 1990s also appears to have contributed to this development. When the administrative controls were relaxed in the work-injury system (with 100 per cent replacement rates) around 1980, government spending for work-injury insurance increased by a factor of four in real terms after a few years.
   The number of individuals receiving subsidised early retirement (originally designed for disabled persons) amounted to about 8 per cent of the labour force in Sweden in the 1980s – long before full employment broke down. (The figure is higher in some other countries, such as Italy and the Netherlands.) Generous compensation levels for the unemployed in Sweden did not constitute a serious problem as long as unemployment was very low. But it became a problem when total unemployment (open unemployment

plus individuals in Labour Market Board activities) reached about 13 per cent in the early 1990s.
3. For recent emphasis on positive interrelations between social achievements and economic efficiency, see, for instance, Glyn and Miliband (1994).
4. In a system of work-injury benefits, actuarial elements may be introduced by varying the contributions from firms in accordance with work-injury risks ('experience rating'). In the unemployment benefit system, actuarial elements may be instituted by differentiating the fees by sectors and professions in accordance with unemployment risks.
5. This issue is discussed in Diamond (1996).

REFERENCES

Alesina, A. and Rodrik, D. (1994), 'Distributive politics and economic growth', *Quarterly Journal of Economics*, **109**, May, 465–90.

Coder, J., Rainwater, L. and Sweeding, T. (1989), 'Inequality among children and elderly in ten modern nations; The United States in an international context', *American Economic Review*, **79** (2), 320–24.

Diamond, P. (1996), 'The structure of social security', *Journal of Economic Perspectives*, **10** (3), 67–88.

Fölster, S. (1997), 'Social insurance based on personal saving accounts: a possible reform strategy for overburdened welfare states?', this book, ch. 4.

Glyn, A. and Miliband, D. (eds) (1994), *Paying for Inequality*, London: IPPR/Rivers Oram Press.

Hagen, J. (1994), 'Crime, inequality and efficiency', in Glyn, A. and Miliband, D. (eds), *Paying for Inequality*, London: IPPR/Rivers Oram Press.

Haveman, R. and Wolfe, B. (1993), 'Children's prospects and children's policy', *Journal of Economic Perspectives*, **7** (4), 153–74.

Jäntti, M. and Danziger, S. (1994), 'Child poverty in Sweden and the United States: the effects of social transfers and parental labour force participation', mimeo, Academy of Finland, October.

Lindbeck, A. (1994), 'Overshooting reform and retreat of the welfare state', *The Economist*, **104** (1), 1–19.

Lindbeck, A. (1995), 'Incentives in the welfare state – Lessons for would-be welfare states', lecture given at the International Economic Association Congress in Tunis, December 1995, Macmillan.

Lindbeck, A. (1996a), 'The future of the European welfare state – within the economic and monetary union', the 19th Congress of the Instituto Español de Analistas Financieros in Barcelona, September 1996.

Lindbeck, A. (1996b), 'Full employment and the welfare state', Frank E. Seidman Award Lecture, Memphis, September 1996.

Lindbeck, A. (1996c), 'The west European employment problem', *Weltwirtschaftliches Archiv*, December 1996.

Lindbeck, A., Nyberg, S. and Weibull, J.W. (1995), 'Endogenous social norms and the welfare state', *IIES Seminar Paper*, No. 608, Stockholm.

Meltzer, A. and Scott, R. (1981), 'A rational theory of the size of government', *Journal of Political Economy*, **89**, 914–27.

Merton, R. (1983), 'On the role of social security as a means for efficient risk-bearing in an economy where human capital is not tradable', in Bodie, Z. and Shoven, J.B. (eds), *Financial Aspects of the US Pension System*, Chicago: Chicago University Press.

Myrdal, G. (1944), *An American Dilemma*, New York: Carnegie Foundation.

Persson, T. and Tabellini, G. (1994), 'Is inequality harmful for growth?', *American Economic Review*, **84**, June, 600–621.

Wilson, W.J. (1987), *The Truly Disadvantaged: The Inner City, the Underclass and Public Policy*, Chicago: Chicago University Press.

PART III

Improving Incentives in the Welfare State

4. Social insurance based on personal savings accounts: a possible reform strategy for overburdened welfare states?

Stefan Fölster

1. INTRODUCTION[1]

A central dilemma for overburdened welfare states is that many proposed reform strategies either lead to higher marginal effects of taxes and subsidies (called the marginal tax rate from here onwards) or deepen poverty. Cutbacks, for example, that maintain the standard of living of the poorest reduce benefits more for those with medium or higher incomes. This tends to make social insurance less actuarial and thus raises the marginal tax rate. Cutbacks that actually reduce the marginal tax rate generally imply that people have to rely more on own saving and private insurance and this typically hurts low-income groups who face the highest risks of, for example, unemployment and sickness.

This dilemma can to some extent be resolved by building social insurance around a personal savings account. Detailed simulations indicate that it is quite possible to design a combination of mandatory personal savings and insurance that slashes the marginal tax considerably and yet maintains or even improves upon the economic security offered by welfare states.

Such a claim may at first seem surprising. Social insurance based on personal savings has often been viewed as incompatible with the aims of western welfare states, partly because countries like Singapore that have savings-account-based systems provide very little redistribution.[2] Yet there are good theoretical reasons why a savings account can also increase efficiency in a system with extensive redistribution.

The basic idea is that mandatory payments into a personal savings account replace most of the taxes currently used to finance unemployment benefits, sickness benefits, parental leave, pensions and all other social insurances. When the need arises, people are allowed to withdraw from their account instead of receiving benefits. At retirement the balance on the account is converted into an annuity that determines the pension level. Various insurance elements which are described below provide protection for those who deplete their account, typically due to a combination of low wage and frequent spells of income loss.

One reason why savings accounts may be an increasingly interesting feature in a welfare system is that life styles have changed considerably over the past century. When welfare systems were conceived in most western countries, only a small portion of adult life was spent not working, and most of that could be ascribed to insurable events. Today, more than half of a typical person's life is spent in spells of non-work that are often highly predictable, even planned, and hardly qualify as insurable events. In fact, studies from several welfare states indicate that a mere 20 to 25 per cent of social transfers actually redistribute between individuals, thus covering the two central aims of the welfare state of providing insurance and equality. The remaining 75 to 80 per cent merely smooth income over the individual's life cycle (ESO, 1994).

Importantly, the arguments for a savings-account-based insurance outlined below do not require a funded system, but arise even in a pay-as-you-go system with simulated accounts on which drawing rights are accumulated. If one chooses to convert an extant pay-as-you-go system into a system of funded personal savings accounts, there are additional opportunities and risks that are not treated here.[3]

1.1 Lower Marginal Taxes

Introducing a savings account into social insurance lowers marginal taxes for two reasons. First, programmes that provide income-smoothing over the life cycle are most commonly entitlement systems in which benefits are poorly related to contributions, thus creating a tax wedge. A savings account explicitly records individuals' deposits and withdrawals, thus avoiding most of the tax wedges created by quirks in entitlement rules.

Second, to the extent that social insurance deals with insurable events, both tax-financed transfers and actuarial insurance face a dilemma. Payment of the tax or insurance premium – as well as payment of the benefit – must be conditional on declared income. This implies a clear presence of moral hazard. At least some individuals are able to abuse the transfer system or insurance by voluntarily earning less or by earning undeclared income. The presence of moral hazard implies that even an actuarial insurance gives rise to disincentives that are equivalent to marginal effects of taxes and subsidies. Unemployment compensation, for example, reduces incentives to work regardless of whether the compensation is provided by an actuarial insurance or a tax-financed system.

Moral hazard can be addressed by introducing a deductible. The size of the deductible is limited, however, by the desire of welfare states to maintain a minimum standard of living. Thus, for people with a wage close to the acceptable minimum standard, the deductible is effectively constrained to zero.[4]

Social insurance based on a personal savings account addresses this problem by using the account to shift premium payments and deductibles from periods where the individual has a low income to other time periods during which the individual may have greater incentives or ability to earn a higher income. As a result, the savings account allows a greater deductible than standard actuarial insurance, without compromising the minimum standard of living in any period.[5]

To study the importance of these two effects on the marginal tax rate, a simulation of introducing a savings-account-based social policy in Sweden is presented below.

1.2 Increased Economic Security

Increasingly, cutbacks in welfare states imply that people with low incomes face increasing economic risks. At the same time, these groups often have less access to borrowing and other means of spreading extraordinary costs over time. As a result, low-income groups increasingly live in economic insecurity, even when they manage on average. The introduction of an account will provide these groups with a better instrument for smoothing income over time.[6]

More importantly, a savings account is an excellent device for keeping track of which individuals fare poorly throughout life. Instead of insuring each type of mishap separately, as most current systems do, a savings account allows an insurance that best protects those who are affected by a combination of low income and frequent income losses over most of their lives. A redistribution and insurance mechanism that accomplishes this can be designed in many different ways. One approach is illustrated by describing the two mechanisms that were used in the simulation reported below.

(a) Life income insurance
The balance that has accumulated on the account at the time of retirement is converted into an annuity, thus determining the individual's pension rights. At that time, claims against the life income insurance are also calculated. Paralleling most social insurance systems, the life income insurance grants a person who has saved little on his account because he chose not to work at all throughout life only the lowest guaranteed pension. In contrast, a person who has worked part of his life, but has then been unemployed or disabled,

receives a higher guaranteed pension, but not as much as he would have had if he had worked and built up a balance on the account.

(b) Liquidity insurance

The savings account guarantees liquidity in the sense that withdrawals from the account can be made even when the balance is zero or negative. Withdrawals are regulated and administered much like benefit payments in other social insurance systems. In addition, a limit to the debt that can be accumulated on the account is assumed, for the same reason that bankruptcy laws allow write-offs of debt. Too large a debt burden makes it improbable that the individual can ever repay the debt. When the debt limit is reached, withdrawals from the account are covered by public (non-actuarial) insurance.

This chapter focuses on the effects that arise in a pay-as-you-go system with simulated accounts. In particular, the question is how much marginal taxes may be reduced in a realistic setting without jeopardizing the aims of the welfare state. A simple model of social insurance is set out in Section 2 and is used as a basis for the simulations reported in Section 3.

2.   A MODEL OF SOCIAL INSURANCE

Assume initially that there is symmetric information between the individual and the insurer: at the beginning of each period both know the individual's wage w_t during period t as well as expected future values of w_t. The individual pays m_t which can be either a tax or an insurance premium. After that he learns his actual income y_t which may be lower than w_t due to income losses. At the same time, new information about the likelihood of future income losses is revealed. He then receives compensation x_t for income losses and consumes c_t. Between periods the person earns interest $1 + r$, and for simplicity it is assumed that the discount factor β equals $1/(1 + r)$. The argument is not affected by different values or varying interest rates.

Expectations, conditional on time t information before y_t is revealed, are denoted E_t. Thus $E_0 y_0$ refers to the expected value of y_0 in the first half of period 0, before y_0 is revealed.

Consumers maximize a standard intertemporal utility function:

$$\max E_0 \sum_{t=0}^{\infty} \beta^t u(c_t) \tag{4.1}$$

Assume initially that there is no moral hazard. The individual cannot avoid declaring income, reduce work effort or otherwise influence own income losses.

A universal welfare state system will typically finance social insurance with an income-related tax or non-actuarial insurance premium, $m_t = \tau y_t$. The tax rate τ is assumed to be proportional and constant over time. In return, the individual receives a compensation $x_t = (w_t - y_t)(1 - \tau)$. Suppose that in this system the initial expected value of tax payments must balance the expected payments of compensations:

$$E_0 \sum_{t=0}^{\infty} \beta^t \tau y_t = E_0 \sum_{t=0}^{\infty} \beta^t (w_t - y_t)(1-\tau) \qquad (4.2)$$

If w_t were constant and the information about expected values of y_t remained constant, this would constitute an efficient arrangement. Given a concave utility function, the individual's utility is maximized with a constant consumption stream, in this case $w_t (1 - \tau)$.

In fact, however, w_t can vary and information on expected values changes between periods. As a result, the tax an individual pays in any period will differ from the actuarial premium. In addition, the consumption stream is no longer constant, and therefore no longer pares to optimal even though the state would care nothing about rearranging payments to provide a constant consumption stream.

A similar problem arises for a voluntary insurance.[7] Assume that the insurer is risk-neutral and competitive, and can borrow or lend at the interest rate r. Risk-neutrality implies that individual income loss is a perfectly diversifiable risk. Competition among insurers is assumed to imply zero economic profits. Then the Pareto-optimal insurance contract can easily be found under the assumption that complete contingent claims' markets exist. At time 0 the individual sells claims to his income stream and buys contingent claims to cover income losses. Then the individual's time 0 budget constraint is

$$E_0 \sum_{t=0}^{\infty} \beta^t c_t = E_0 \sum_{t=0}^{\infty} \beta^t y_t \qquad (4.3)$$

Maximizing utility (4.1) subject to this constraint yields first-order conditions that specify a constant consumption level c at every date and in every welfare state. Solving the budget constraint with constant consumption gives

$$c = r\beta E_0 \sum_{t=0}^{\infty} \beta^t y_t \qquad (4.4)$$

The time 0 contingent claim contract is, however, not time-consistent. As soon as new information on expected values of future y_t is revealed, insurers will try to get rid of individuals with deteriorating prospects. This effect could possibly be avoided with the help of regulation. What is worse is what happens if the individual's prospects improve. The individual will then cancel the insurance, making it impossible for the insurer to cross-subsidize those with income losses. Thus a voluntary social insurance requires lifetime ties in order to work. Such lifetime ties to private insurers are probably in conflict with legal principles in most current welfare states.

Cochrane (1995) suggests a mechanism for the related case of health insurance that could solve the problem of time-inconsistency. The essence of the approach is to adjust the insurance premium in every period to reflect changed information on expected income losses, and at the same time require side payments each period that reflect the present value of changes in expectations of income losses. Thus an individual whose prospects deteriorate would receive a payment from the insurance company equalling the net present value of increases in future income losses. Vice versa, the individual would have to make a payment to the insurance company if prospects improved.

In order to enforce the contract in a situation where individuals can go bankrupt, Cochrane's mechanism requires a savings account in which savings at any time equal the possible payment that a client may have to make to the insurance company. Thus the time-inconsistency problem can potentially be solved with the help of a savings account.

An obvious way around the time-inconsistency problem in both Cochrane's mechanism and the universal welfare state arrangement is to introduce a mandatory, public, actuarial insurance. The insurance premiums would then be set as implied by (4.3) and (4.4), while the time-consistency problem would be suppressed since it would be impossible to switch insurance company.

So far, however, the analysis misses the essence of the welfare state dilemma. Social insurance, whether privately or publicly arranged, remains susceptible to moral hazard. In fact, the presence of moral hazard is the main motivation for attempting to keep marginal tax effects low in social insurance.

Assume that an individual can influence his income stream in a way that the state or insurer cannot detect, for example by pretending to be sick or unable to find employment. Let the new income stream y_t' be the result of the individual's utility maximization. Let utility be a function $u(c_t', l(y_t - y_t'))$ of consumption c_t' and the additional leisure $l(.)$ that the individual gains by manipulating his income from y_t to y_t'. The utility function satisfies that for a constant consumption level a voluntary income loss is preferred, since it allows more leisure. This implies that $y_t' < y_t$. Further, if x_t' compensates for the entire income loss s.t. $x_t' = (w_t - y_t')(1 - \tau)$, then the individual's utility maximization implies $y_t'(x_t') = y_t'((w_t - y_t')(1 - \tau)) = 0$.

In order to avoid this, a deductible must be introduced. We assume that the deductible is determined by a rule D that assigns a particular D_t in every time period, conditional on variables such as w_t, y_t' and other variables, but not on y_t which is assumed to be unknown to the state or insurer. The compensation paid is then $x_t' = (w_t - y_t')(1 - \tau) - D_t$.

Assume a public, mandatory, actuarial insurance that, apart from the deductible, allows a constant consumption stream. Going through the same steps that led up to (4.4), the individual's consumption in any period with moral hazard and a deductible becomes

$$c_t' = -D_t + r\beta E_0 \sum_{t=0}^{\infty} \beta^t (y_t' + D_t) \qquad (4.5)$$

Since y_t' is decreasing in D_t, a lower deductible lowers the individual's consumption stream. Since the insurer or the state still makes zero profit and is therefore indifferent to the size of the deductible, the socially optimal design of the system can be found by maximizing the individual's utility w.r.t. the rule D that determines the size of the deductible in each period.

In doing so, there is an important constraint. In each period the individual must have a minimum to live on – call it MIN. This limits the size of the deductible. The maximization problem is then as in (4.6), where y' as defined above is the individual's optimal choice of declared income.

$$\max E_0 \sum_{t=0}^{\infty} \beta^t u(c_t' y_t, l(y_t - y_t'))$$

$$\text{s.t. } D_t \leq (y_t'(1 - \tau) - \text{MIN})/(w - y_t')(1 - \tau) \qquad (4.6)$$

Since the condition must be met for any y_t', it is clear that it is quite restrictive.

The constraint can be made less restrictive, however, by introducing a savings account. We assume a very simple version of the savings-account-based social insurance. Assume that a deposit is made on the savings account in any period in which income y_t' exceeds MIN and the balance on the account is below some maximum amount. The balance on the account is, in a sense, the individual's money, and the individual earns interest. In every period an annuity based on the balance in the account is returned to the individual.[8] Yet the individual's expected value of making the mandatory deposits on the account is, of course, smaller than the actual deposits since expected future withdrawals must be taken into account.

The size of the deposit on the account in any period is A_t and the maximum amount is governed by a rule A which we do not need to specify to make the point.

Similarly, withdrawals from the account are governed by a rule V that determines a withdrawal V_t in any period. The withdrawal is zero if either the balance on the account is zero or if the constraint in (4.5) is met. In this case the insurance takes over. Otherwise the withdrawal V_t is positive. Since this means that the deductible can be completely or partly paid with a withdrawal, the new restriction for the maximization problem (4.6) becomes

$$D_t \leq (y_t'(1-\tau) - \text{MIN} + V_t)/(w_t - y_t')(1-\tau) \qquad (4.7)$$

Clearly this constraint is less restrictive, which means that the deductible can be made larger due to the account than would otherwise be possible.

The model does not say much about the size of the effect. Intuitively it is obvious, however, that this depends on the probability distributions of w_t and y_t'. If the world divides into individuals that never have an income loss $(y_t' = w_t)$ and individuals that have a complete income loss in every period, then the account will make little difference. Those with persistent income losses persistently have $V_t = 0$ so that (4.7) is identical to the restriction in (4.6).

The potential for reducing marginal tax effects with the help of savings-account-based social insurance is investigated for the case of Sweden in the following simulation.

3. A SIMULATION

The simulation analyses a comprehensive reform of the entire Swedish social insurance system. This is important since social insurance programmes often interact in ways that make it misleading to look only at the effect of reforms on one programme at a time.

A limitation is that the simulations only show the direct effects of the choice of social insurance system on marginal tax effects and income distribution. In reality these direct effects then yield indirect effects on, for example, labour supply and take-up rates in the social insurance programmes, which, in turn, influence the average person's marginal tax rates and income distribution. These indirect effects are not calculated here. Since empirical estimates of individuals' adjustment to changing marginal tax rates vary widely, any assumptions about the size of these effects would be quite *ad hoc*. Instead, our simulation of direct effects lends itself to the interpretation that a change of social insurance system that, for a given income distribution, induces the largest direct reduction of marginal tax rates also induces the most favourable indirect effects.

The simulation is described in four steps. First, the construction of the life cycles is explained. Then the implementation of the personal savings account and an alternative actuarial insurance are described. Finally, simulation results are shown.

3.1 The Simulated Life Cycles

The calculation is based on a simulated population of 1000 persons. It is also assumed that all incomes and prices remain as in 1990 in real terms. Life cycles begin at age 20 and end at death.

There are four steps in the construction of the simulated population:

1. The distribution of pre-tax simulated wages is first determined. The simulated population is divided into six groups (male or female with no secondary education, secondary education and tertiary education respectively) using the frequency distributions in the actual population.[9] For each group the mean wage in year t is determined as

$$m_t = m_g + \theta_t - \delta t^2 \qquad (4.8)$$

This yields the typical parabolic income pattern over time. m_g is a constant that differs for each of the six groups. In addition, the individual's wage w_{it} differs from the mean by a random-walk process. Let u_{it} be a random variable which is distributed independently of income and previous proportional changes; then if $z_{it} = \log(w_{it}/m_t)$ the generating process can be written as

$$z_{it} - z_{i,t-1} = u_{it} \qquad (4.9)$$

If u_{it} has a constant variance of σ_u^2 and if σ_t^2 denotes the variance of z_{it} then (4.9) implies that

$$\sigma_t^2 = \sigma_0^2 + t\sigma_u^2 \qquad (4.10)$$

and the variance of the logarithms of income in each year grows linearly over time. Therefore, information on the variance of earnings in different age groups provides estimates of (4.10).

   Estimates of the parameters in (4.8) and (4.10) were jointly estimated using a maximum likelihood method (as done, for example, in Cameron and Creedy, 1995).[10] The simulated wage distributions are consistent with estimates obtained in various studies that analyse wage panel data.[11] Note that in our simulations we assume that there is no productivity growth.

2. To generate lifetime earnings, first the pre-tax wage is calculated for each individual, rewriting (4.9) as

$$w_{it} = w_{i,t-1} \exp[(m_t - m_{t-1}) + u_{it}] \qquad (4.11)$$

This can be used to generate the w_{it}s given a set of random variations from an $N(0, \sigma_u^2)$ distribution.[12] Capital income and capital taxation are ignored in the simulation of individual income streams, but enter the state's balanced budget requirement described later.

Subsequently, after-tax earnings I_{it} are calculated as

$$I_{it} = \begin{cases} w_{it} - T(\mathbf{X}_{it}) + B(\mathbf{X}_{it}) & \text{if } i \text{ is working} \\[2mm] -T(\mathbf{X}_{it}) + B(\mathbf{X}_{it}) & \text{if } i \text{ is sick, retired, on parental leave, in tertiary education, involuntarily unemployed, or voluntarily not working.} \end{cases}$$

Here $T(.)$ is a schedule of taxes and/or deposits on the personal account, and $B(.)$ is a schedule of benefits and/or withdrawals from the personal account. Both depend on a vector $\mathbf{X}_{it}$ that describes the individuals' history in terms of earnings, employment record, number and age of children and other aspects that determine tax and benefit rates. These are described further below and in the appendix. Family history, which is typically the most complicated part in a life-cycle simulation, has been considerably simplified here. Since Swedish tax and benefit rules are geared, with few exceptions, towards the individual, with no regard to marital status, we have for the most part ignored marital status.[13] Thus individuals in the life-cycle model are not 'matched' to each other to create families. Each individual has children with a certain probability and bears half the costs associated with children, for example child-care fees.

3. It is assumed that all people retire at 65 years of age, unless they fall ill and enter early retirement. The age of death is determined randomly according to the actual distribution of mortality. This differs for men and women, but is assumed to be independent of other variables.

4. Sickness, voluntary and involuntary unemployment, parental leave, and tertiary education are determined as follows. We assume that spells of sickness are equally likely for all categories at all stages in life, but that the duration of spells varies according to a probability table which depends on sex, age, current income, and the share of the previous five years during which the individual has been either sick or unemployed.[14] Spells of sickness beyond three years are assumed to imply early retirement. Individuals who retire early are assumed not to work at all until they reach the age of 65 when all individuals enter normal retirement. Spells of involuntary unemployment and voluntary non-work are ran-

domly assigned based on probability tables where the length of the spell depends on age, income, sex and the share of the previous five years during which the individual has been either sick or unemployed.[15] The occurrence of childbirth is determined randomly according to the actual distribution. It is assumed that when a child is born a mother is on parental leave for 90 per cent of 1.25 years (the time compensated by parental leave insurance) and a father for 10 per cent of 1.25 years. This corresponds to aggregate statistics. Participation in tertiary education is determined randomly according to aggregate frequencies as described above. A person engaged in tertiary education is assumed to participate for five years, during age 20 to 24.

A weakness of such simulation models is that they do not capture all cross-effects well. For example, no account is taken of how education may affect sickness or the probability of having children. As one measure of robustness, however, a study using an alternative technique – creating life cycles by splicing together panel data – yielded similar distribution of lifetime income, unemployment and sickness (ESO, 1994).

Using the simulated income pattern and the simulated work history, payments into the social insurance in the form of payroll taxes and income taxes are calculated. Then income before and after transfers is derived.[16] Based on these data, it is then easy to ascertain amounts transferred between individuals on a lifetime basis. Since we assume constant real prices and wages, the real interest rate (r) earned on savings in the personal savings account is assumed to be low, only 2 per cent. The simulation is not affected by whether the personal savings account is organized as a pay-as-you-go system or a reserve system since changes in the savings rate are not endogenized.

3.2 Design of the Personal Savings Account

There are many ways to implement the concept of a savings-account-based social insurance. The intention here is to design a savings-account-based social insurance that provides the same income distribution and economic security as the current Swedish social insurance system, but significantly lowers marginal tax effects. In fact, the rules governing the personal savings account are rigged to give exactly the same disposable income y_{it} as the current system up to the age of 65. At age 65 the balance on the personal savings account is converted into an annuity, and thus determines the pension level, subject to the insurance elements described further below.

Up to the age of 65, payments into the personal savings account are mandatory and would be collected much as taxes are today. For comparability it is also assumed that the sum of mandatory payments into the account

(A_{it}), insurance premiums $(S_{it}, S_{it}, < 0$ for premiums, $S_{it} > 0$ for compensation), and taxes in the savings account system (T_{it}^{CA}) equal taxes paid in the current system for each individual (T_{it}):

$$T_{it} = A_{it} - S_{it} + T_{it}^{CA} \qquad (4.13)$$

The insurance premium is not entirely equivalent to a tax since it has an actuarial element. Higher income, leading to higher deposits on the account, and higher insurance premiums also imply higher guaranteed pensions.[17] Withdrawals from the personal savings account (V_{it}) and insurance compensation (S_{it}) are regulated and vary with the cause of income loss, previous income and other factors, just as benefit levels (B_{it}) do in the current system:

$$B_{it} = V_{it} + S_{it} \qquad (4.14)$$

The personal savings account as constructed here incorporates the two insurance elements, briefly described above. The exact tax and social insurance rules applied in the simulation are shown in the appendix.

(a) Life income insurance

The balance on the personal savings account accumulates as $\sum_{t=1}(A_{it} - V_{it})$ $(1 + r)$ up to the age of 65 when it is converted into an annuity, thus determining the individual's pension. At that time claims against the life income insurance are also calculated. The life income insurance accumulates guaranteed pension rights throughout life. This bears some resemblance to private pension plans that guarantee some pension even if the return on invested savings develops poorly.

The guaranteed pension is calculated as a linear function of a minimum pension level that everyone is guaranteed, and a fraction of the average payments into the account over the 47 years between age 18 and 65.

$$\text{Guaranteed pension} = \text{Minimum pension} + g\sum_{18} A_{it}/47$$

When the guaranteed pension exceeds the annuity calculated on the balance of the personal savings account at age 65, then the insurance pays a compensation amounting to the difference between the guaranteed pension and the annuity.

Two important redistributionary flows in the current system are retained in the personal savings account system. One is that there is a redistribution from men to women who would otherwise receive lower pensions since they tend to live longer.[18] The other is that there is a transfer from people who do not have children to people who have children.[19]

(b) Liquidity insurance

The personal savings account guarantees liquidity in the sense that withdrawals from the account can be made even when the balance is zero or negative. In addition, a limit to the debt (LIM) that can be accumulated on the personal savings account is assumed, for the same reason that bankruptcy laws allow write-offs of debt. Too large a debt burden makes it improbable that the individual can ever repay the debt, and thus reduces incentives to achieve gainful employment. When the debt limit is reached, withdrawals from the account that the individual is eligible for are compensated by the insurance.

A constraint applied in the simulation is that the government budget balance in the savings account system is the same as in the current system. This implies that g, LIM, the minimum pension, and the size of insurance premiums are set so that the sum of insurance premiums and insurance compensations matches over all individuals and all time periods:

$$\sum_i \sum_t S_{it} = 0$$

The values that fulfil the constraint are found by numerical calibration. The minimum pension is set to the same level as in the current system, LIM = SEK – 220 000 and $g = 0.26$. These values work both for the wide and for the narrow version of the savings account. At these parameter values, it turns out that 14 per cent of all people end up using the guaranteed pension. Further, the insurance premiums are set at 21 per cent of payments into the account in the narrow version, and 19 per cent in the wide version, as explained below.

We analyse two implementations of the personal savings account, one narrow and one wide. Table 4.1 shows the range of benefit programmes encompassed by the two versions. The exact rules for the financing of each programme, and the levels of compensation paid, are supplied in the appendix. Public expenditure on various transfers is shown in gross terms (ignoring for the moment that it is often taxed and therefore partially recouped by the government). In the narrow version, public expenditure amounting to 9.25 per cent of GDP would be channelled via the personal savings account system, although a fraction of that would pay for insurance premiums rather than being deposited in individual accounts. In the wide version, public expenditure amounting to 41.8 per cent of GDP would be channelled via the personal savings account system. These figures should be compared with a total tax revenue of 48 per cent of GDP and total public expenditure of 68 per cent of GDP in 1994.

In the narrow version, neither the pension system nor provisions for the elderly are subsumed under the personal savings account system. Rather it is

Table 4.1 Benefits and public services encompassed by narrow and wide definitions of the personal savings account

Benefit	Programme's cost in terms of % of 1994 GDP	Share assumed financed via savings account[1] %
Narrow		
Unemployment benefit[2]	3.7	100
Parental leave	1.5	100
Sick benefit	1.3	100
Child benefit	1.2	100
Welfare	0.93	100
Housing benefits	0.62	100
Narrow total	9.25	100
Wide		
Pensions[3,4]	13.6	100
Housing subsidies	2.1	100
Student loans[5]	0.7	100
Education for the unemployed	1.0	100
Miscellaneous transfers[6]	2.7	100
Health care	9.6	50
Child care	2.6	100
Schooling	4.3	50
Miscellaneous subsidies and services[7]	4.7	75
Wide total (adjusted by share financed via the account)	41.8	—

Notes:
[1] Not counting public costs of insuring the account.
[2] Includes benefits for training during unemployment (AMU).
[3] Includes housing benefits to the elderly.
[4] Includes early retirement and work injury.
[5] Net of repayments.
[6] Includes, for example, transfers to divorced parents.
[7] Includes subsidies to sport and entertainment, energy, food, renovation of houses, employment, medicine and services related to these subsidies.

assumed that savings on the account are converted into an annuity at the age of 65 and added on to pensions allowed by the current pension system.[20]

In the wide version, it is assumed that the pension system is subsumed under the personal savings account system (thus working much as it will anyway after the move towards a contribution-based pension system is implemented). Again, savings on the account are converted into an annuity which constitutes the pension.

In the wide version, it is assumed that most social insurance and transfers to households are replaced completely by the account. In public services, however, payments are only partially made via the account. In health care, for example, it is assumed that fees are charged for common health services, amounting in sum to about 50 per cent of total health-care costs. These fees are financed via the account. The remaining 50 per cent are assumed to remain publicly financed, covering high-cost operations as well as a number of minor functions such as health research or disease control. In essence, this provides an additional insurance against the risk of very costly health-care needs.[21] A number of studies suggest that this type of cost-sharing could raise efficiency in health care (for example Jönsson, 1995).

Schooling in the wide version is assumed to be financed via the account covering half of total costs. The remainder is publicly financed, which can be justified by the fact that schooling presumably has positive external effects.

We assume initially that early retirement remains as in the current system. In the event of early retirement, public insurance pays 70 per cent of current wages. From this, deposits are made on the citizen account as though income were a regular wage. The balance on the account then determines old-age pension as for all other people.

Since this is a rather generous system, and the life income insurance provision in the personal savings account offers a natural alternative organization of retirement insurance, we also investigate another, less generous, possibility. In this version, in the event of early retirement, withdrawals are allowed from the account at a rate determined by the accumulated contributions in the life income insurance. This would imply that young early retirees receive lower benefits than older early retirees.

Further, it is assumed that all withdrawals from the citizen account related to care of children must be made in equal proportions from both parents' accounts. This effectively prevents families from trying to abuse the life income insurance by placing the entire burden on one parent's account.

3.3 Actuarial Insurance Without a Savings Account

As a benchmark we also perform simulations for a simple actuarial insurance without a savings account. The term actuarial insurance may be somewhat misleading. As shown in the theoretical model, a savings-account-based insurance may in the end be more actuarial than a conventional actuarial insurance in the presence of liquidity constraints.

An actuarial insurance scheme could be implemented in many different ways, depending on assumptions about the information that the insurer can use about each individual's actuarial risk. Here we use a very simple specification. It is assumed that the premium paid by each individual in any year exactly equals the expected value of compensation payments during the same year for people of the same age, sex, current income, and length of education.[22] A constraint exists, however. If the actuarial premium charged is so large that the individual's disposable income falls below the level of welfare payments, that is, the minimum acceptable living standard, then a lower premium is charged, leaving the individual with the minimum living standard.[23] In effect, the insurance is subsidized for low-income earners, and the subsidy is withdrawn as income rises.

Compensation payments paid by the actuarial insurance are assumed to equal those in the current system. The actuarial insurance is applied to the same social programmes as the narrow version of the personal savings account, thus avoiding the issue of how to deal with the pension system, health care and schooling under an actuarial insurance.

A real actuarial insurance would presumably also insure against year-to-year changes in risk in ways that we have not taken account of here. It remains unclear how that affects the result.

3.4 Simulation Results

Marginal tax rates are calculated in the simulation by letting each simulated person earn SEK 100 more during one year at a time. Then the relation between the SEK 100 increase in gross earnings and the discounted (by 2 per cent annually) sum of increased current and future net earnings y_{it} can be calculated:

$$0.01\sum_{t=j}^{\infty} y_{it}\,\frac{1}{(1+r)^{t-f}}$$

This quotient is defined as the marginal tax rate and is shown as an average over all individuals and over all time periods; $j = 18.65$ in the tables below.

Table 4.2 shows what happens when the current system is replaced by a personal savings account system. Results are shown for three versions of the personal savings account: the narrow version, the wide version, and the wide version with a less generous early-retirement provision as described above.

The marginal tax rate is calculated as explained above. It includes marginal effects in the current system of progressively increasing fees for public services and decreasing subsidies. The marginal tax rate is first shown as an average for all people and then for different income groups.[24]

Table 4.2   Marginal tax rates in a simulation of social insurance reform

	Current system	Narrow savings account	Wide savings account	Wide account with less generous early retirement	Narrow actuarial insurance
Marginal tax rate[1] in per cent					
Average for all	74	54	37	33	65
Average for deciles in terms of lifetime income					
Tenth decile	80	51	35	32	59
Fifth decile	67	53	36	32	64
Second decile	75	57	44	39	68
First decile	94	85	79	73	89
Average for deciles in terms of monthly income					
Tenth decile	79	50	35	32	50
Fifth decile	68	53	36	32	59
Second decile	73	56	44	39	75
First decile	91	61	51	49	95

Note: [1] Includes marginal effects of benefits.

Income is here defined in two ways. First, deciles for distribution of lifetime income (after taxes and subsidies) are shown. In the current system, marginal tax rates are highest for high-income earners, due to progressive taxation, and low-income earners, due to progressively reduced subsidies.

With the various versions of the personal savings account, marginal tax rates are much lower and more equal for all deciles except the first decile. The reason is that people in the first decile at retirement tend to have less on their account than the minimum guaranteed amount. As a result, they still have some incentive to earn income as this raises the guaranteed pension, but the incentive is naturally much lower than for someone who ends up with more than the guaranteed amount on the account.

Table 4.2 indicates that our implementation of the actuarial insurance does not have equally large effects on the marginal tax rate as the narrow version of the citizen account. The main reason seems to be that the constraint stating that individuals' minimum living standard should be preserved has a large effect. The groups with the lowest income in any particular year tend also to have high risks of income loss during that year even though they may have low risks and high incomes in other life periods. This implies that their insurance must be subsidized. Since increasing incomes for these groups imply a reduced subsidy, the marginal effects are very high.

Table 4.3   Life income distribution

	Current system	Narrow savings account	Wide savings account	Wide account with less generous early retirement	Narrow actuarial insurance
Gini life income (per year)	0.119	0.118	0.121	0.122	0.24
Gini annual income	0.281	0.281	0.283	0.284	0.37

Since the aim of the personal savings account system is to decrease marginal taxes without affecting income distribution too much, we show income distributions for the current system and the versions of the personal savings account system in Table 4.3. Income distribution is shown as Gini coefficients for lifetime income and for annual income, where the annual income includes benefits or withdrawals from the account in order to ensure comparability with the current system.

Clearly, overall income distribution is not much affected by a switch to the personal savings account. This is no surprise for annual income since withdrawals allowed from the account were designed to match current benefits. It is more remarkable, however, that the distribution of lifetime income remains virtually unaffected by a switch to the personal savings account. This corroborates evidence discussed above that only a small fraction of current welfare spending is actually redistributed from high-income to low-income individuals.

These results on overall income distribution do not preclude the existence of redistributionary effects between groups of people that do not perturb the overall distribution. We have performed a number of tests on such effects, but reporting these falls beyond the scope of this chapter. A rough characterization is that people who work many years at a low wage gain with personal savings accounts, which in the current system means that they pay in a lot over the course of their lifetime, but receive fairly low compensation when they are, for example, sick or unemployed. On the other hand, people who work for only a few years at a high wage, lose with personal savings accounts, which means that they receive high compensation in the current system even though they pay in rather little over the course of a lifetime.

The actuarial insurance induces a significant shift in the income distribution. It should be remembered, however, that this is based on a particular implementation of actuarial insurance that probably does not cover changes in risk levels well. In particular, it appears that risks and expected compensations are quite high during the ages 20 to 35, when many people's incomes are low. The high actuarial premiums essentially push a large fraction of this age group to the minimum standard of living.

4. CONCLUSION

Most countries already have some element of social insurance based on a mandatory savings account. Pension systems and student loans often work this way. A number of countries, among them Sweden, have recently reformed their pension systems, moving from an entitlement system to a savings-account-based system.[25] In a number of countries savings-account-based systems are also under consideration for training of both the employed and unemployed. 'Individual learning accounts' were, for example, proposed by the British Labour Party.[26]

For other types of social insurance, savings accounts are less common. One example, however, is the Chilean unemployment insurance. Newly employed there are required to save in the form of monthly instalments until savings reach a value of two months' wages. If a person becomes unemployed, the savings are paid back over a four-month period. Only after that does public assistance step in. Saved funds follow employees if they change employer. At retirement saved funds are paid out. In essence, the scheme creates a larger deductible, but helps to spread the impact over a longer time period.

More comprehensive systems of mandatory savings accounts exist in Malaysia and even more so in Singapore (see Asher, 1994).

An important question is what technical difficulties a conversion would face. A savings-account-based social insurance could be introduced for younger people only, thus leading to a gradual transition. It would be quite possible, however, to organize a simultaneous transition for all. This would require that for each type of person an account balance is imputed, depending on age, sex, accumulated tax payments and perhaps a few other variables. A mixture of these approaches is actually being used in Sweden's current pension reform.

NOTES

1. I would like to thank Dennis Snower, Assar Lindbeck, Per Lundborg and Tony Atkinson for valuable comments.
2. See Asher (1994) for a description of the Singaporean Central Provident Fund. Originally designed to increase savings and to provide retirement security, it has since been extended with a number of schemes, for example saving for medical needs, financing of higher education, insurance of dependants and a variety of other social needs.

3. Many studies find that pay-as-you-go systems imply lower national savings and aggregate capital stocks than funded systems. However, switching from a pay-as-you-go system to a funded system means that an increase in savings may be matched by an increase in public debt required to finance unfunded promises to retirees. According to some economists (for example Mitchell and Zeldes, 1996), this implies that national savings would not increase at all. Others (for example Feldstein, 1996), however, show that in a growing economy savings in the funded system will quickly outgrow the fixed sum of promises to retirees at transition. In support of this case Chile is often cited, since it managed to switch from a generous pay-as-you-go system to a funded system during the 1980s with a surprisingly mild increase in national debt and a large increase in private savings and investment.

4. Even user fees charged for subsidized public services such as child care and public health care can be seen as a deductible in the presence of moral hazard.

5. This mechanism will not work if all individuals are either always poor or always have high incomes. Studies indicate, however, that income variability is considerable in European welfare states. An OECD study (1996) shows, for example, that half of the people in the lowest income quintile in the United Kingdom in 1986 had moved to a higher income group by 1991.

6. If the personal savings accounts are funded, there is an additional way to improve the economic security channel. In conventional systems, individuals accumulate future entitlements which cannot be used to cushion credit risks or temporary liquidity squeezes that many households face, for example, when purchasing a home. In a savings-account-based social insurance, individuals can be allowed to borrow from their own savings account for home purchase, thus reducing the risks of credit and liquidity problems considerably. In the Singaporean system, this seems to have worked well for some time, and has allowed many low-income earners to purchase homes.

7. For the case of health insurance, these problems are analysed in Cochrane (1995).

8. In a model with a finite working life, the balance on the account would be returned as well at retirement.

9. The distributions of these variables are provided by the Swedish Central Office of Statistics for 1990.

10. Estimates obtained are $\sigma_0^2 = 0.173$; $\sigma_u^2 = 0.0049$; $\theta = 0.0311$; $\delta = 0.00071$; $m_{male, no\ sec\ ed} = 8.91$; $m_{male, sec\ ed} = 9.54$; $m_{male, tert\ ed} = 10.3$; $m_{female, no\ sec\ ed} = 8.70$; $m_{female, sec\ ed} = 9.14$; $m_{female, tert\ ed} = 9.8$.

11. In particular, Björklund (1993).

12. To generate wage in the first period w_{i1} for example, suppose that v_i is randomly selected from the standard normal distribution $N(0,1)$, and use $w_{i1} = \exp(m_1 + v_i \sigma_u)$.

13. An exception is social assistance payments that are conditional on the spouse's income. This is implicitly handled in the simulation by using a probability of being eligible for welfare given that the individual is out of work and does not have unemployment insurance.

14. The probability tables are provided by the Swedish Health Insurance Authority for the year 1990.

15. Data underlying the probability table are provided by the Swedish Labour Market Board.

16. Transfers are calculated in a simplified manner. Additional negotiated compensations are ignored.

17. On the other hand, there is a hidden tax due to the redistribution between men and women, and childless people and parents, explained below.

18. Female life expectancy is used to calculate the pension annuity. This means that men are undercompensated. The surplus that arises helps to finance the insurance premiums required by the system.

19. For individuals with one or no children, a sum is deducted from the citizen account at retirement before calculating the annuity. The sum equals 3.5 per cent of life earnings net of taxes for those with no children and half that for those with one child.

20. However, a fixed sum equal to the average annuity is subtracted from pensions in order to keep the sum of annuities and pensions in aggregate equal to the sum of pensions paid under the current system.

21. It is assumed that health-care costs, including costs of medicines, are financed individually up to a sum of SEK 15 000 per year via the citizen account. Costs beyond that are paid publicly. For retired people, the deductible is financed out of pensions provided this does not push them below the minimum pension level. This would imply that about 50 per cent of health-care and drug costs are financed via the account.
22. The expected value is known from the probability tables used in constructing the population, as described above.
23. The excess costs that arise to the insurance due to this constraint are financed out of tax revenue. It turns out that about 60 per cent of payments made by the insurance must be tax financed.
24. Importantly, the marginal tax calculations are based on an *ex post* reasoning. *Ex ante*, people will, of course, not know how incomes and withdrawals develop over their lifetime, so that the actually perceived marginal tax rate will be based on expectations of future developments.
25. A smaller part of contributions in the new system will be channelled into real savings accounts, while the larger part continues to work on the pay-as-you-go principle. In essence, bookkeeping accounts are built up that reflect a drawing right on future generations' payments. Individuals will have some choice as to how the real savings are to be invested.
26. In 'New deal for a lost generation', presented 15 May 1996.

REFERENCES

Asher, M.G. (1994), *Social Security in Malaysia and Singapore – Practices, Issues and Directions*, Institute of Strategic and International Studies, Malaysia.
Björklund, A. (1993), 'A comparison between actual distribution of annual and lifetime income: Sweden 1951–1989', *The Review of Income and Wealth*, **39** (4), 377–86.
Cameron, L. and Creedy, J. (1995), 'Indirect tax exemptions and the distribution of lifetime income: a simulation analysis', *The Economic Record*, **71**, 77–87.
Cochrane, J.H. (1995) 'Time-consistent health insurance', *Journal of Political Economy*, **103**, 445–75.
ESO (1994), *Skatter och Socialförsäkringar över Livscykeln – ensimuleringsmodell*, Ministry of Finance, Stockholm.
Feldstein, M. (1996), 'The missing piece in policy analysis: social security reform', *American Economic Review*, **86** (2), 1–14.
Harding, A. (1990), 'Lifetime income and redistribution in Australia: applications of a dynamic cohort microsimulation model', London School of Economics.
Jönsson, B. (1995), *Cost-sharing for Pharmaceuticals – the Swedish Reimbursement System, Sharing the Costs of Health: a multicountry perspective*, Pharmaceutical Partners for Better Healthcare, Basle, Switzerland, July 1995.
Mitchell, O.S. and Zeldes, S.P. (1996), 'Social security privatisation: a structure for analysis', *NBER Working Paper*, No. 5512.
OECD (1996), 'Employment Outlook', July, Paris.

APPENDIX

This appendix describes the tax and social insurance rules applied in the current system, the personal savings account system and the actuarial insurance.

Current System

Tax schedule: From gross income (before employer's tax) the following taxes are drawn:

Employer's tax:	35 per cent.
Income tax:	31 per cent of net income (after employer's tax) and additional 25 per cent for income over SEK 191 000 per annum.
Value added tax:	14 per cent on remaining income after employer's and income taxes. VAT rate is 19.2 per cent for most goods and services, but lower for some.

Bargained or voluntary insurance provided by the employer is ignored.

Social Insurance Benefits

Unemployment benefit:	80 per cent of previous net income up to SEK 68 000 per annum. In practice, not limited in time.
Parental leave:	80 per cent of previous net income up to SEK 231 000 per annum, paid for one year.
Sick benefit:	80 per cent of previous net income up to SEK 231 000 per annum. No compensation first day, 65 per cent second day.
Child benefit:	SEK 750 per month and child.
Welfare:	SEK 6 500 per month for an adult, SEK 2 500 per child.
Housing benefits:	Vary locally; here we assume the average figure of SEK 1100 per month for individuals with an income of SEK 6500, after that

	reduced by SEK 50 for each increase of income of SEK 100.
Pensions:	65 per cent of previous net income during 15 years with highest income. Minimum pension for those without previous income is SEK 7500 per month, which includes supplementary housing benefit.
Student loans:	During higher education, SEK 5000 per month.
Education for the unemployed:	Spread evenly over the unemployed, SEK 1500 per month.
Miscellaneous transfers:	Spread evenly over all, SEK 450 per month.
Health care:	Own average cost for fees is SEK 60 per sick day. Average system cost for health care is SEK 694 per sick day.
Child care:	System cost is SEK 61 000 per year and child. Parents pay SEK 23 000 per year and child.
Schooling:	System cost is SEK 24 000 per year and child, own costs are zero.

Personal Savings Account

The rules for allowed withdrawals from the citizen account are equivalent to the rules for size of benefits in the current social insurance as stated above. Deposits on the citizen account are calculated as equivalent to taxes paid as described below, minus premiums for the life income and liquidity insurances. Since many of the benefits in the current system are paid out of general tax revenue, it is necessary to allocate taxes to the programmes that are included in the narrow and wide versions of the citizen account. This has been done as follows. The programmes in the narrow version are assumed to be financed by the entire employers' tax except for pension contributions plus 24 per cent of direct tax revenue. The programmes in the wide version are assumed to be financed by the entire employers' tax plus 74 per cent of direct and indirect taxes.

5. Expanding the welfare system: a proposal for reform

J. Michael Orszag and Dennis J. Snower

1. INTRODUCTION

Since the early 1980s, most European welfare states have come under increasing strain. All the main traditional functions of the welfare state – social insurance, redistribution from rich to poor, life-cycle transfers, and the provision of social services such as health and education – are gradually being called into question, implicitly or explicitly. Many of the welfare state reforms implemented in Europe over the past one and a half decades have involved rolling back welfare provision. This has largely been the outcome of a top-down, dirigiste policy strategy, initiated by governments in response to their political, financial, and institutional pressures, rather than the outcome of a public movement in favour of diminished welfare state services. On the whole, the reforms have tended to occur in the wake of fiscal crises and have been justified primarily by governments' inability to continue to finance existing welfare provision.

The welfare state is therefore at a crossroads. Budgetary pressures are continuing to induce European governments to retreat from welfare state provision and finance, while economic and social pressures (skill-biased technological change, globalization, crime, drug abuse, educational under-achievement) are continuing to swell the demand for welfare services. This dilemma is a major source of disagreement between right- and left-wing parties throughout Europe.

What has made this dilemma a matter of ideological conflict is the widespread perception that policy-makers must choose between two disagreeable options on the welfare state:

(i) a 'flexible' economy with low rates of taxes and transfers, large disparities in incomes, and limited welfare state provision; and

(ii) an 'inflexible' economy with significant tax and transfer distortions, a relatively compressed distribution of incomes, and a relatively generous welfare state.

According to this view, a flexible economy is characterized by comparatively low unemployment and high efficiency, but also by economic inequality and little protection against economic and social risks; whereas the inflexible economy provides reasonable minimal standards of security against the risks of unemployment, infirmity, illness, and poverty, but it is also bedevilled by economic inefficiencies and high unemployment. Thus policy-makers often see themselves as having to choose between inequality and unemployment, between efficiency and fairness, and between economic growth and social cohesion.

We argue that this view rests on a myth, for it takes the current institutional setting of the welfare state as given, and thus blinds us to the institutional changes that could promote efficiency without harming our equity objectives. It is important to expose the myth and thereby enable policy-makers to focus on the urgent business of fundamental welfare policy reform.

The trick is to recognize that much of the welfare policy is responsible for the disagreeable choice between efficiency and equity. The current system of unemployment benefits and taxes is a good example. When unemployed people find jobs, their unemployment benefits are removed and taxes are imposed. Not surprisingly, this policy discourages the unemployed from seeking work. Within this system, a policy of restricting the benefits will reduce unemployment and create more inequality. But what usually gets overlooked is that this unemployment inequality trade-off is largely the outcome of the tax benefit system. If we changed the system, we could alleviate the disagreeable trade-off.

This chapter presents a proposal for reforming the provision and finance of welfare services – interpreted broadly to include social insurance, social services, redistribution, and life-cycle transfers. Our aim is to outline a set of complementary institutional changes that would permit an expansion of the welfare system, while at the same time promoting economic activity.

Our proposal is based on the view that it is misleading to address the public policy concern over welfare issues exclusively through an analysis of the appropriate domain of the welfare state. The reason is that the state is only one possible source of welfare services. Many of them can be carried out by firms, households, and other organizations as well. European countries differ dramatically in their division of labour in this respect. For example, many of the welfare activities shouldered by the government in Sweden are conducted by households and firms in France and Switzerland. The size of a government's welfare state spending may thus bear little relation to the level of welfare services provided in the economy. For this reason, it appears desirable to shift attention away from the welfare state to the welfare system. Expanding the welfare system does not necessarily mean expanding the welfare state.

However, reforming the welfare system involves much more than deciding on the appropriate division of labour between the government and the private sector agents in providing and financing welfare services. This division of labour depends on the complementarities between the government and the private sector agents and these complementarities, in turn, depend on the institutional structure within which welfare is provided. The government can influence the 'rules of the economic game' determining the degree to which market activity pursues public purposes. This applies as much to the provision of welfare services as it does to preserving the environment, protecting worker health and safety, and encouraging competition. The degree to which the private sector can participate in the provision and finance of the welfare system depends on the degree to which the gains from such activity are economically appropriable. Fundamental welfare state reform must involve the development of institutions that yield a socially desirable degree of appropriability.

The remainder of this chapter is organized as follows. Section 2 gives an overview of the sources of the welfare state crisis. On this basis, Section 3 summarizes the objectives of our reform proposal. Section 4 presents the proposal itself. Section 5 considers some important implications of the proposal. Section 6 concludes.

2.   SOURCES OF THE WELFARE STATE CRISIS

The main institutions of the welfare state – the redistributive systems of taxes and transfers, the pension provisions, the state-run health and education institutions, the job security regulations, the unemployment benefit systems, and various other welfare entitlements – were developed primarily in the 1950s and 1960s, when most European countries enjoyed high rates of economic growth, substantial growth of their labour forces, relatively low unemployment rates, and high rates of male labour force participation. Under these circumstances, it was relatively easy to provide social insurance, since only a small minority of citizens required unemployment benefits, incapacity payments, and other welfare support. The robust rates of economic growth made it comparatively easy for governments to redistribute income through the tax system and to provide a wide range of social services. Finally, the relatively rapid growth of the labour force facilitated the payment of generous pensions on a pay-as-you-go basis.

2.1 Productivity, Unemployment, Labour Force Participation and Ageing

After the mid-1970s, however, productivity growth fell significantly in Europe as elsewhere. As a result, the redistribution of incomes became more painful, bringing the interests of the affluent and the poor into more visible conflict. In the two decades that followed, Europe's labour markets became increasingly segmented, as the employment opportunities of unskilled workers fell significantly behind those of their skilled counterparts. In the aftermath of two oil-price shocks and various interest rate and exchange rate shocks, EC unemployment climbed remorselessly, from an average rate of 3.7 per cent in the 1970s, to 9.1 per cent in the 1980s, to around 11 per cent currently.

Over the same period, EC labour force participation fell steadily. As the number of people requiring welfare state support rose relative to the number of those supporting them, there was a steady rise in the level of taxes and transfers necessary to maintain a particular distribution of incomes. Thereby the cost of social cohesion in Europe rose. This development was reinforced by the progressive breakdown of the traditional family (creating a class of single parents facing unemployment or low-paying, insecure jobs) and the ageing of the European population (which augmented the fall in the labour force participation rate and increased the demand for health services).

These various changes have served to make the costs of the European welfare states rise substantially faster than GNP. Since the lion's share of European welfare services has traditionally been financed and provided by the state, government budgets came under progressively increasing pressure, leading governments towards an intensifying search for ways to reduce their welfare commitments.

This drive came at a time when expansions in international trade and growing capital mobility made it increasingly difficult for governments to tax multinational corporations and capital gains. Advances in information technologies made it difficult to tax the burgeoning communication and information-based services, and the increased mobility of professionals made it easier for skilled labour to escape the tax net. In a world in which unskilled labour is left as perhaps the most immobile factor of production, there is a temptation for governments to make this population group —which is in growing need of welfare support – bear an increasing share of the overall tax burden.

2.2 Inefficiency in Welfare Provision

The debate over the need to roll back the welfare state came at a time of increased awareness concerning the limitations of the state in providing public services. With the collapse of communism in eastern Europe and the former Soviet Union, the inefficiencies of public enterprises received widespread attention. This recognition, together with rising European tax burdens, led to widespread calls for government accountability and an increasing interest in the appropriate degrees of decentralization of public services. The growing concern for regional and local autonomy and for the principle of subsidiarity is also related to this development.

The efficiency problem in public enterprises often arises for much the same reasons as in some large private enterprises: eliminating waste is difficult and expensive. Unless organizations face severe competitive pressures, it is often in their best interests to be wasteful. Large parts of the European welfare states are government monopolies, facing no competition whatsoever. Under these circumstances, inefficiencies are inevitable. No number of quantitative targets and administrative controls are capable of dealing with this problem, since the services are highly heterogeneous, the public's needs are difficult to assess, and the activities of the suppliers are difficult to monitor. This is the lesson from the performance of centrally planned economies the world over. As long as the welfare states are run along central planning lines, their inefficiency will remain a fact of life.

This inefficiency is usually magnified by the 'soft' budget constraints of the welfare state. Unemployment benefits, pensions, national health, and public education are commonly financed through general taxes, and thus the government bodies providing these services often face no sharp, objective standards whereby the costs of these services are brought into relation with the associated benefits. The soft budget constraints also serve as an entry barrier discouraging private sector provision of welfare services. As long as it is possible for the government to use its tax-levying power to finance welfare services, it can always drive private providers out of business; and the private providers, knowing this, do not seek to enter. Under these circumstances, it is also impossible to induce the private sector financial services industry to contribute to the financing of the welfare system.

The soft budget constraints help explain why the prices of welfare services tend to be gravely distorted. In the face of massive cross-subsidization among the different domains of the welfare system, there is little incentive – even in the absence of distributional considerations – to make people's financial contributions to the system reflect the costs of the services provided.[1] To overcome this problem, it is not sufficient to introduce 'quasi-markets' in the welfare system and prices for welfare services (as, for example, the UK Conservative Government did for health provision in the late 1980s and early 1990s). Provided that the government can use its tax receipts to finance the provision of these services, it can keep the prices of state services artificially low.

2.3 The Blurring of Boundaries

Yet another source of the welfare crisis is the absence of clear boundaries between the various welfare state domains. The welfare state provides a variety of disparate services – social insurance, social services, redistribution and life-cycle transfers – that have traditionally been seen as the government's responsibility since they were allegedly undeliverable through the market mechanism. These services addressed a diversity of social needs, and there has been no compelling economic or social reason for grouping them together, other than their apparent susceptibility to market failures. However, the existing market failures in the provision and finance of welfare services are often the outcome of institutions that prevent the private sector from contributing profitably in this area.

Furthermore, the fiscal practice of grouping welfare state activities served to blur the divisions among the different welfare services. For example, unemployment insurance clearly fulfils a quite different function from income redistribution, but unemployment benefit systems are usually designed to achieve redistributional objectives. This blurring of boundaries has made welfare services particularly susceptible to political pressures. When European governments attempt to roll back the welfare state, they are often guided by the interests of the dominant voting constituencies. Thus the services most prone to cutbacks have been those that benefit the poor and the disadvantaged (who have relatively little electoral influence), while services focusing mainly on the middle class (such as pensions and education) have remained relatively unscathed. As a result, the European welfare states have shown a tendency to turn into what Lindbeck (1988) has called 'transfer states', where much of the tax revenue comes from those who are comfortably off and many of the services go to these people as well. In some countries, unemployment benefit systems and incapacity benefit systems have been changed with a view to lessening their redistributive impact and improving labour market incentives and, as a result, the social insurance aspect of these systems has also suffered. In this way, the blurring of boundaries within the welfare state has robbed governments of policy instruments whereby the different types of welfare services may be adjusted in response to the public's different types of needs.

Finally, it is wrong to think that the carousel of taxes and transfers among middle-class groups has little economic impact, just because it gives middle-class people about as much as it takes from them. On the contrary, each tax and transfer places a wedge between people's services and rewards and thereby distorts their incentives to work, invest, and save. This development has raised the cost of running the welfare state and reduced its effectiveness in providing social insurance and in redistributing income.

2.4   The Increasing Demand for Welfare Services

Despite European governments' efforts to cut back their welfare state spending, there are good reasons to believe that, over the past two decades, the need for welfare services in Europe has grown at a rate unprecedented for the post-war period. The case for redistributing income – based on the widespread European conviction that social safety nets and compressed distributions of income are important for the preservation of social cohesion – has been strengthened by the growing danger of unemployment and the increasing disparity between the job opportunities of skilled and unskilled workers. Rising youth unemployment, the increasing duration of the unemployment spells of older workers, and the falling average retirement age witnessed in many European countries must have all served to increase the need for life-cycle transfers. The decline of the extended family has reduced access to informal family-level insurance, which was an important cushion against unforeseen economic shocks and life-cycle transfers 30 years ago.

The gradual rise in European living standards must have brought with it a steadily increasing demand for public services, such as health and education and all forms of social insurance. After all, these welfare services are not inferior goods; the demand for them rises as people's income and wealth increases.[3] For this reason, welfare programmes remain broadly popular in Europe, despite their high costs.[4]

At the same time, the rising risks of unemployment and job loss – and particularly the concentration of these risks at particular times (recessions) and on particular people (the unskilled, disadvantaged, poorly educated segments of the European population) – made it steadily more difficult for financial institutions in the private sector to meet the growing needs for social insurance and life-cycle transfers. Thus, given the current institutional framework, Europeans have become steadily more dependent on the state for welfare provision.

In sum, the crisis of the welfare state reflects a supply-side failure combined with a growing demand for welfare services. The sources of the crisis – government budgetary problems, rising unemployment, falling labour force participation, ageing of the population, the inefficiencies in providing and financing welfare services, soft budget constraints, and the blurring of boundaries between the different domains of the welfare state – suggest the objectives of our reform proposal.

3.   OBJECTIVES OF THE PROPOSAL

Our proposal has the following objectives:

It aims to increase consumer choice regarding the magnitude and composition of welfare services.

The only way to ensure that welfare services meet the diverse and changing needs of the population is to give people decision-making power over which services to consume and to enable their decisions to guide the provision of these services. The failure of central planning to bring living standards in eastern Europe and the former Soviet Union into line with those in advanced market economies indicates how important it is to give consumers such decision-making power. The current European welfare states, on the whole, are organized predominantly along the central planning paradigm: governments usually decide how much to spend on health and education, how much to tax and transfer, how to structure pension provisions and employment regulations, and so on. Although the governments are elected by the citizens, local and national elections are about much more than welfare state policy and thus they are a very blunt instrument for determining such policy. The consumers usually have no mechanism whereby they can signal to their governments how to adjust the magnitude and composition of welfare services, taking all the relevant costs and benefits into account. Our proposal is meant to give them such a mechanism.

It seeks to minimize the inefficiencies associated with redistribution by separating the redistributive mechanism from the provision and finance of other welfare state services.

Redistributing income invariably means distorting people's incentives to produce and work and thereby introducing inefficiencies into the market mechanism. For, in purely individualistic terms, redistribution means rewarding some people for something they have not earned in the economic system and depriving others of what they have earned. Within a cohesive society, however, such an individualistic frame of reference is inadequate by itself. There is a widespread belief in Europe that the provision of social safety nets and the avoidance of extreme income inequalities are important social goals. But while there are many ways of pursuing these goals, it is important to choose the policy strategy that minimizes the associated inefficiencies.

In the current European welfare systems, incomes are redistributed in a wide variety of ways: through the tax system, pension system and the unemployment benefit system, and frequently also through the housing, the health, and education systems. This institutional structure is needlessly wasteful: distributing money from the employed to the unemployed, from the healthy to the sick, from the privately educated to the publicly educated, and so on, is an inefficient way of distributing money from the rich to the poor, because the rich are not invariably employed, healthy, and privately educated and the poor are not invariably in the opposite camp. Beyond that, this institutional structure makes the redistributive mechanism vulnerable to political pressures such as budgetary difficulties or organizational changes in the pension, unemployment, housing, health, and education systems. Our proposal attempts to avoid this danger by separating the redistributive mechanism from the provision and finance of other welfare services.

It aims to induce the private sector to contribute to the provision and finance of welfare services.

If the need for welfare services is rising with the passage of time whereas the ability of governments to provide these services is shrinking, it is desirable to explore whether the private sector can be enlisted to bridge the gap. There are certain welfare activities, such as redistribution of income, that will presumably remain dependent on government, although charities may be induced to play a significant role. But there are other activities, such as various forms of social insurance, social services, and life-cycle transfers, where the private sector could become usefully involved, provided that the institutional setting is appropriate. Many branches of European welfare states are constructed in such a way as to make private benefit from welfare provision impossible. The challenge is to alter the institutional structure of the welfare system so as to enable the private sector to derive rewards from involvement in the welfare system. Our proposal seeks to achieve this objective.

It is meant to promote competition between the public and private sectors in the provision and finance of welfare services.

The proposal does not aim to replace the public sector by the private sector in particular areas of welfare activity. Nor does it seek to establish 'spheres of influence' for the public and private sectors' welfare activities. On the contrary, it aims to make the welfare system 'contestable', that is, to give both the public and private sectors the ability to enter the market for welfare services. The consumers are then in a position to choose who they wish to provide and finance their welfare needs. Whenever a single agent – whether in the public or the private sector – has a monopoly on the provision or finance of any particular service, there are few incentives to avoid waste. But when it is possible for other competitors to enter the market, the incentives are greater, for then an inefficient supplier may be driven out of business. Competition between the public and private sectors may be particularly desirable with regard to welfare services such as health, education, and pensions, since the two sectors have different strengths and weaknesses in these areas.

For example, a major advantage of the government in the provision of education services is that it can trace people through the tax system and thereby avoid monitoring costs and default risks often faced by private enterprises. The private sector enterprises, on the other hand, often find it easier to provide more highly diversified products than the public sector, for example schools for children with special needs and abilities or training programmes for firms with idiosyncratic requirements.

It is self-financing.

In the current economic and political climate, welfare reform proposals that are not self-financing usually stand little chance of adoption. Beyond that, the self-financing criterion puts an important discipline on reform proposals. If resources under the current system are wasted, then a policy that eliminates the waste should be able to do so without additional expenditure of resources. Consequently, the self-financing criterion is a way of ensuring that any particular welfare reform does indeed improve efficiency. Our proposal attempts to satisfy this criterion.

4. THE PROPOSAL

4.1 The Establishment of Welfare Accounts

The proposal involves the establishment of welfare accounts for every person in a country. There would be four accounts: a retirement account (covering pensions), an unemployment account (covering unemployment support),[4] a human capital account (covering education and training), and a health account (covering insurance against sickness and disability). Instead of the current welfare state systems – where welfare services are financed predominantly out of general taxes – people would make ongoing, mandatory contributions to each of these welfare accounts. The balances in these accounts would cover people's major welfare needs.

This reform would replace the current tax and transfer system by a system of compulsory saving. When people retire, they would make withdrawals from their retirement accounts. When they become unemployed, they would make withdrawals from their unemployment account instead of claiming unemployment benefits. When they acquire skills, they could draw on their human capital account instead of receiving government grants, subsidies, and loans for education and training. If they are ill or disabled, they could draw on their health account.

4.2   Mandatory Contribution and Withdrawal Rates

An important potential problem that the government faces with a welfare account system is moral hazard: if individuals know that their government will care for them in old age, sickness, disability, and poverty regardless of the size of their account balances, they will have an incentive to make insufficient contributions to their accounts and excessive withdrawals from them. Consequently, the government must set mandatory minimum contribution rates and mandatory maximum withdrawal rates. These rates would be set in an actuarially fair manner (using a prospective benefits method such as the actuarial attained age or entry age method), so that for each of the accounts nationwide, the discounted value of the associated aggregate benefits equals the discounted value of the aggregate contributions. The mandatory contribution rates would depend on income and age.

Withdrawals from the welfare accounts would be regulated by the following simple rules. People who reach pensionable age or those who become unemployed, ill, or disabled would be entitled to withdraw fixed maximum amounts per month. Like the contribution rates, the withdrawal rates would depend on income and age.

4.3   The Provision of Welfare Services

As noted above, the private sector gains the incentive to contribute significantly to the welfare system only if the institutional structure of this system makes it impossible for the government to use the tax and transfer system to drive the private providers out of business. In order to establish the requisite institutional structure, the proposal in effect insulates the welfare system from the rest of the government's budgetary process. Specifically, the government would have two budgetary systems: one in which non-welfare expenditures (on defence, transport, environmental protection, and so on) are financed through the existing array of taxes (income taxes, VAT, capital gains taxes, and so on), and another system in which the public sector expenditures on welfare services are financed through payments from people's welfare accounts.

The government would be able to redistribute income across people's welfare accounts, but these redistributions would be constrained to being of the balanced-budget variety: total (economy-wide) taxes on each of the welfare accounts would be equal to total transfers into each of the accounts. Thereby our proposal meets one of the central challenges of welfare reform, namely: to enable the government to redistribute income from the rich to the poor without enabling it to use the tax and transfer system to finance its welfare provision and thereby discourage private sector provision. With regard to the health accounts, for example, these would balance for the economy as a whole, and thus the government could not use its tax receipts to fund public health and consequently drive down the prices of public health services, thereby keeping private providers from entering the health industry.

Rather, welfare services would be financed solely from what people chose to spend on these services out of their welfare accounts. Consequently, the government would have no incentive to manipulate the contribution rates and withdrawal rates of the welfare accounts in order to ease fiscal pressures outside the welfare state (for example, to use tax receipts from welfare accounts to finance spending on defence).

The public and private sectors would provide welfare services on an equal footing, setting prices for these services and competing with one another for the custom of the welfare account holders. For instance, with regard to health services, people's health accounts would pay for their health insurance and they could then choose the provider of their health services, whether public or private.

In order to prevent the private sector from cream-skimming (providing services only to those who are unlikely to receive large payouts and leaving the others to the public sector), private sector pricing of insurance services would need to be regulated. As in the case of many existing private insurance systems, private providers could be required to make their prices of welfare services dependent only on a small subset of characteristics, such as age and income, and to ignore all others.

The resulting competition between the public and private sectors in the provision of welfare services would encourage efficiency in welfare provision in both sectors.

4.4 Income Redistribution and Social Safety Nets

In order to moderate the distortions associated with income redistribution and the provision of social safety nets, the proposal involves redistributing income across people's accounts along the lines of a 'conditional negative income tax'. People's mandatory contributions to each of their welfare accounts would rise with their incomes. The lowest-income groups would receive transfers from the government into each of their welfare accounts. These transfers would pay all or a portion of these people's mandatory account contributions. The greater the levels of income, the lower the transfers. Eventually, at higher income levels, the transfers would give way to taxes. The conditions attached to the transfers for low-income groups would be analogous to those attached to current unemployment benefits. For instance, if the current unemployment benefit system specifies that people must provide evidence of genuine job search in order to qualify for unemployment benefits, then they must also be required to provide such evidence in order to receive the proposed transfers.

Each welfare account would have a specified minimum balance, depending on age and income. If a person's balance in one account fell beneath the specified minimum, he or she would be required to replenish that account with excess funds from the other accounts. If the balances on all accounts fell beneath the specified minima, the government would make specified deposits into these accounts from the mandatory contributions of those who are better off.

This redistributional mechanism would give rise to substantially fewer distortions than the present welfare systems. For example, with regard to the unemployment account, the conditional negative income tax mechanism would discourage job search, but by substantially less than unemployment benefits do, for when a person finds a job, he loses all his unemployment benefits, but only a fraction of his negative income taxes. Moreover, since the transfers under the negative income tax system would be conditional on proving willingness to accept work (except in cases of disability, illness, or other accepted personal circumstances), they would provide incentives for people to engage in productive activity. Finally, the proposed redistributional mechanism would be more efficient than the current systems at redistributing income from rich to poor, since unemployment benefits, training schemes, and other welfare entitlements would not be targeted exclusively at the poor, whereas the transfers under the conditional negative income tax system would be.

4.5 Voluntary Contributions and Transfers Among Welfare Accounts

People could voluntarily contribute more than the specified minimum amounts to their accounts. Indeed, they would be encouraged to do so: while their contributions would be taxed or subsidized in accordance with the conditional negative income tax scheme, withdrawals and capital income from their accounts would be taxed at preferential rates (or possibly not taxed at all). Since funds in the welfare accounts would thus have tax benefits relative to ordinary savings, individuals may choose to save more in their welfare accounts than the mandatory minimum amounts.

Employers would be encouraged to contribute to their employees' accounts at the same preferential rates as the employees. The account balances would be fully portable across employers.

If people's balances in a particular account exceeded a specified limit, they could be transferred to other welfare accounts. For example, a person with excess funds in the health account could transfer these to the human capital account to purchase training. At the end of their working lives, the remaining

balances in their unemployment and human capital accounts could be transferred into their retirement account.

Furthermore, excess funds (above the mandatory limit) could be withdrawn entirely from the accounts, but doing so would involve tax penalties
commensurate with the tax advantages of contributing to the accounts.

4.6   Recruitment and Training Vouchers

In order to provide additional incentives for employment and production,
the government would supplement the welfare accounts of long-term unemployed people who purchase government-issued employment vouchers.
Specifically, the government would provide subsidies for the long-term
unemployed to use their unemployment account withdrawals to purchase
recruitment vouchers for firms that hire them. Firms receiving the vouchers
would be reimbursed by the government through the tax system. The government would also subsidize the long-term unemployed for making
withdrawals from their human capital account to provide training vouchers
for firms that employ them and send them on nationally accredited training
programmes.[5]

The size of each person's voucher would depend on his wages earned over
the next one or two years of subsequent employment, and the firm could
claim the voucher at the end of that period. The recruitment vouchers would
reduce firms' cost of employing the long-term unemployed; the training
vouchers would reduce the cost of training them. The size of the vouchers
would be set so that they could be financed through the tax revenues from
people's first two years of subsequent employment and through the abolition
of in-work benefits.

The creation of such vouchers would enable the private sector to contribute
to the welfare system in the areas of unemployment and training. For instance, the long-term unemployed could hand their vouchers to employment
agencies – public or private – who could split the proceeds of the vouchers
with the employers. Since the size of the vouchers would depend on future
wages, the employment agencies would have the incentive not just to place
their unemployed clients, but to find the highest-paying jobs for them. Moreover, since the agencies would receive voucher payments regardless of whether
a worker trained in one firm is 'poached' by another firm, they would not face
what economists have called the 'poaching externality' (whereby firms have
insufficient incentives to train their employees, for, once the training has been
undertaken, the employees may be poached and thus some of the gains from
training would accrue to the poaching firms). Under these circumstances, the
employment agencies would have greater incentives to seek training for
unemployed people than individual employers would have.

Furthermore, the agencies could raise private funding for fighting unemployment by issuing 'voucher-backed equities and securities'. These financial instruments would be backed by the revenues of the employment agencies, derived from the unemployment and training vouchers which, in turn, are derived from the future contributions of workers to their unemployment accounts and human capital accounts.

Along the same lines, the government could supplement the retirement accounts of pensioners who purchase recruitment vouchers. These vouchers could be financed through the pensions forgone, and the size of these vouchers would depend on the size of the pensions.

4.7   The Transition from the Welfare State to the Welfare Account System

To make the transition from the current welfare state systems to the welfare account system fiscally viable, the accounts could initially be run on a pay-as-you-go basis. In this respect, the welfare accounts would be similar to savings accounts at commercial banks under a fractional reserve banking system (in which banks are required to hold only a fraction of their deposits in the form of liquid assets). Just as savings account holders in a fractional reserve banking system can make withdrawals from these accounts whenever they need to (within a specified framework of rules), even though most of their money (at any given point in time) is used for other purposes, so welfare account holders would be permitted to make withdrawals from their accounts in accordance with the specified rules, even though, at any point in time, some of the balances in one set of accounts may be used to finance the benefits derived from another set of accounts.

With the passage of time, the welfare accounts could eventually be turned into fully funded systems. This transition could proceed at quite different rates for different accounts, depending on the government's fiscal pressures. For example, it may be easier for a government to move speedily towards a fully funded system of unemployment accounts (where the intergenerational transfers are comparatively small), but to delay this transition for the retirement accounts until demographic trends turn favourable.

Furthermore, the transition to a fully funded system of retirement accounts could be eased through a reform of the timing of taxes. Currently, most pensions provide tax relief on contributions rather than on payments; but reversing the direction of tax relief – so that taxes are paid at the time of contribution rather than at the time of withdrawal – would shift tax revenues from the future to the present, to match the shift of benefits from the future to the present in the transition from a pay-as-you-go system to a fully funded one.

Once the transition towards fully funded systems is under way, people could be given discretion over who manages the funded portions of their accounts. The government and private sector financial institutions could both do so. To guard against bankruptcy, the financial activities of the latter institutions would be regulated, along lines similar to the regulation of commercial banks.

5. IMPLICATIONS

Moving from the current welfare state systems to a welfare account system may be expected to play a substantial role in reducing unemployment, encouraging labour force participation, promoting skills, reducing governments' budgetary pressures, cushioning people against economic risks, ensuring efficient provision of health and education services, providing social safety nets and redistributing incomes more efficiently.

5.1 Effects on Economic Incentives

Adopting the welfare account system would improve incentives for productive activity as well as for the efficient use and provision of welfare services. For example, moving from unemployment benefits to unemployment accounts would give people greater incentives to avoid long periods of unemployment. For the longer people remain unemployed, the lower will be their unemployment account balances and consequently the smaller the funds available to them later on. Thus the unemployment accounts generate more employment than unemployment benefits, for a given amount of income redistribution. By implication, the unemployment account contributions necessary to finance a given level of unemployment support would be lower than the taxes necessary to finance the same level of unemployment benefits.

5.2 Effects on Economic Efficiency

In general, the welfare accounts would help people to internalize both the benefits and the costs of welfare provision, and thereby discourage them from using welfare services wastefully. For instance, people would have little incentive to use health services in this way, since the more health services they purchase, the lower will be their health account balances. The same holds for education and training. The human capital accounts would be better suited than the current education and training programmes to ensuring people's lifetime employability, since the accounts could be accessed whenever employees and their employers found it maximally worthwhile. Nor would people have an incentive to use pensions wastefully, since they would have the opportunity of finding employment by using their pension withdrawals to purchase recruitment vouchers.

Since both the public and private sectors would be able to provide social services (such as health services, education and training), life-cycle transfer services (such as pensions), and social insurance (such as unemployment and disability insurance), these markets would become contestable and thereby promote the efficient provision of these services.

5.3   Encouraging Investment

The welfare account funds invested by the financial sector would stimulate investment. Indeed these funds could become a key component of EU investment: since the funds would characteristically have liabilities with relatively long durations, these funds could be used to finance long-term investments crucial for maintaining economic growth and competitiveness.

5.4   Encouraging Private Sector Financing of the Welfare System

Once the government and the private sector are competing on an equal footing in providing welfare services, it becomes possible to enlist the support of the financial services industry to provide the requisite finance. In the previous section, we indicated how the creation of recruitment and training vouchers could induce employment agencies to use voucher-backed equities and securities. Permitting the private sector to compete with the public sector in the provision of health, education, and pension services would similarly induce the financial services industry to issue equities, securities, and other financial instruments to help finance the welfare system.

Under the above-mentioned circumstances, the financial services industry would also have an incentive to contribute to the provision of insurance against major economic risks such as unemployment and fluctuations in human capital. A major reason why the private sector has no role in this area under the present system is moral hazard: if people could guarantee their incomes irrespective of whether they are employed or of whether they are trained, they would have little incentive to seek jobs and acquire skills. Insurance companies, knowing this, refuse to provide income insurance. However, adverse events – such as earthquakes, fire, theft, and so on – that are objectively monitorable and beyond the control of individual economic agents are not associated with moral hazard and thus can be insured against. Another source of moral hazard under the present system originates from government behaviour. When the government can finance unemployment benefits and public training programmes through general taxes, it is always in a position to drive private providers of unemployment and human capital insurance out of business.

However, if the government is constrained to keep each set of welfare accounts in economy-wide balance and to compete with the private sector in promoting employment and training, it is possible to create liquid claims – securities and options – whose values depend on aggregate unemployment and aggregate productivity. Since these aggregates are beyond the control of individual agents, they are not subject to moral hazard, and the claims on the aggregates can be used as a source of unemployment and human capital insurance. (See Shiller, 1993, for details of how to insure against macroeconomic fluctuations.) In this way, the private sector can become involved in expanding the welfare system in tandem with people's expanding needs.

6. CONCLUSIONS

The proposal for welfare state reform is related in spirit to the Central Provident Fund system in Singapore and the defined-contribution pensions schemes that have been implemented in Chile and Australia. The account framework is consonant with the policy proposal of Fölster (1997). The major innovation in our proposal, however, lies in its use of welfare accounts to:

(i) encourage the private sector to contribute to the provision and finance of welfare services;

(ii) increase consumer choice regarding the magnitude and composition of these services;

(iii) make the provision of social safety nets and the redistribution of income less inefficient and less vulnerable to political pressures; and

(iv) promote competition between the public and private sectors in the welfare system.

A common objection to personalized accounts is that these are allegedly tied to a fully funded system, but any rapid transition to such a system from a pay-as-you-go system may be impossible in most European countries. We have argued, however, that welfare accounts are compatible with a pay-as-you-go system, and thus the issue of the feasibility of transition may be decoupled from the issue of whether welfare accounts are socially desirable.

While people are generally resentful of their tax burden and often demeaned by the existing unemployment benefits and training programmes, they would be more willing to contribute to personalized accounts for their own purposes. The accounts would give people more freedom to meet their diverse individual needs. They would give them greater latitude to respond to changing job opportunities, finance periods of job search, acquire skills, and provide for retirement. All this could be done without creating greater inequality or increasing government expenditure.

Since the adoption of the welfare account system would stimulate employment and productivity, both employers and employees stand to gain from the switch to accounts. Retired people would gain through their ability to use their account balances to augment their pensions. The government would gain, since the removal of the distortions from the unemployment benefit system would promote new economic activity and thereby generate increased tax revenue.

NOTES

1. This is the case even in the United Kingdom, where major efforts have been made to promote market pricing of welfare services. For example, the marginal cost of participation in the UK social security system (for those who can afford it) is less than 2 per cent of the lower earnings limit of about £60 per week. This is less than one sixth of what the UK Conservative Party proposed in 1997 to refund to individuals as contributions to a Chilean-style fully funded state pension.
2. There are many illustrations of this relation. For example, using a sample of 92 countries, the World Bank (1994) finds a strongly positive relationship between pension spending as a percentage of GDP (PS) and income per capita (YCAP) measured in dollars: $PS = 0.66708 + 0.000519\,YCAP$.
3. This appears to be the case even in the United Kingdom which, in the period of Conservative rule (1979–97), undertook particularly stringent measures to roll back welfare services. For example, individuals in the British household panel survey (BHPS) were asked a number of attitudinal questions and they did not indicate either a lack of support for the welfare state or any major recent changes in attitudes. When asked whether they agreed with the statement that: 'All health care should be available free of charge to everyone regardless of their ability to pay', 81.3 per cent of respondents in the 1995–96 wave agreed or strongly agreed as compared with 84.6 per cent in 1991. When asked whether: 'It is the government's responsibility to provide a job for everyone who wants one', in 1991, 48.7 per cent of respondents strongly agreed and in 1995–96 this percentage had risen to 51.0 per cent.
4. Orszag and Snower (1997) examine the labour market implications of unemployment accounts.
5. A detailed analysis of employment vouchers is given in Orszag and Snower (1996) and Snower (1994, 1996).

REFERENCES

Fölster, S. (1997), 'Social insurance based on personal savings accounts: a possible reform strategy for overburdened welfare states', this book, ch. 4.

Lindbeck, A. (1988), 'Consequences of the advanced welfare state', *The World Economy*, **2**, 19–38.

Orszag, M. and Snower, D.J. (1996), 'A macro theory of employment vouchers', *CEPR Discussion Paper*, No. 1367, London.

Orszag, M. and Snower, D.J. (1997), 'From unemployment benefits to unemployment support accounts', discussion paper, Department of Economics, Birkbeck College, University of London.

Shiller, R.J. (1993), *Macro Markets: Creating Institutions for Managing Society's Largest Risks*, Oxford: Oxford University Press.

Snower, D.J. (1994), 'Converting unemployment benefits into employment subsidies', *American Economic Review, Papers and Proceedings*, **84** (2), 65–70.

Snower, D.J. (1996), 'The simple economics of benefit transfers', in de la Dehesa, G. and Snower, D.J. (eds), *Unemployment Policy*, Cambridge: Cambridge University Press.

World Bank (1994), *Averting the Old-age Crisis: Policies to Protect the Old and Promote Growth*, Washington, DC: World Bank.

PART IV

Pension Reforms

6. On economic benefits and fiscal requirements of moving from unfunded to funded pensions

Robert Holzmann

1. INTRODUCTION[1]

The reform of public pension systems in the member countries of the European Union and the OECD has been on the agenda for many years. The Maastricht deficit criteria and the growing perception of the negative effects of fiscal imbalances on economic performance have emphasized the need for reform of this, the biggest public expenditure programme. The necessities for an early and lasting reform of the essentially unfunded retirement income schemes are well known: population ageing, further system maturation in many countries, the likely negative labour market implications of high contribution rates and the insufficient contribution–benefit link, and the negative consequences for private and national saving.

The conventional measures to redress fiscally an unfunded pension scheme are also well known, and limited:

(i) An increase in revenues through higher contribution rates or taxes; due to rising international tax competition, and the excess burden of such a policy, it is largely excluded.

(ii) Lowering of other public expenditure such as on education or defence is not possible in view of the scope of the task, some 1 to 10 percentage points of GDP between 2000 and 2030. Such an approach would, in the United States, be equivalent to eliminating all defence spending and, in Japan, be equivalent to eliminating all spending on public services and defence (OECD, 1995).

(iii) A five-year increase in the retirement age would roughly eliminate the fiscal imbalance over the next 35 years in Japan, Germany, the United Kingdom and the United States. It would eliminate over half the imbalance in Canada, France, and Italy (OECD, 1995). However, even modest increases in the standard retirement age or the tightening of the

eligibility criteria to raise the effective retirement age have proven to
be extremely difficult politically.

(iv)   Reduction in the benefit level per retiree through lower initial pension
        benefit, lower indexation, higher taxing or enhanced means-testing;
        some or all of these measures have been applied in the recent reforms
        in EU countries, but they are unlikely to put the pension scheme on a
        sound, long-term financial footing (see Franco and Munzi, 1996; ISSA,
        1996). Those reforms were mostly driven by short-term budgetary
        considerations but less by a long-term fiscal view. For this very reason,
        pension reform remains a standing agenda in almost all industrialized
        countries.

A further reform option, namely to move to a (partially) funded scheme, is
often proposed, but rapidly rejected by the well-known argument of the
double burden on the transition generation. Several European countries, such
as the United Kingdom, Switzerland, the Netherlands, Denmark, but also
Sweden and Finland, are operating supplementary funded pensions on a
mandatory/contractual basis. However, the specifics of these countries, and
the often long-term history of the introduction of supplementary pensions,
frequently make the opponents of reforms in this direction discard the option.
The argument of a double burden has some validity, though it requires closer
investigation.

The Chilean pension reform of 1981 implied a shift from an unfunded,
publicly managed, and defined benefit scheme to a fully funded, privately
managed, and defined contribution scheme. It has increased world-wide interest
in the feasibility of such a reform and its potential benefits since this very
reform is held co-responsible for the impressive performance of the Chilean
economy since the mid-1980s. It has encouraged reformers throughout the
world to imitate, at least partially, the Chilean approach. Various countries in
Latin America such as Argentina (1994), Peru (1993), Colombia (1994),
Uruguay (1996) and Mexico (1992, 1997) have already begun to shift towards mandatory funded provisions, while others, such as Costa Rica and
Nicaragua, are likely to follow, and a few former centrally planned economies, such as Croatia, Hungary, Latvia, Poland and Slovenia, are making
preparatory steps in this direction.[2] In addition to its government-provided
pensions, Australia recently mandated employer-organized retirement savings for workers. Most of these countries do not envisage a full shift towards
funded provision, and the move towards a two-tier mandatory scheme, consisting of an unfunded and a funded tier, has been encouraged by a World
Bank report (1994).

A move towards funded pensions promises various benefits at political and
economic levels, ranging from higher credibility of such schemes to the

positive impact on financial sector development and national saving. In order to reap the potential benefits of such a shift, substantial changes to the current unfunded scheme and important support by the fiscal policy are required. An unconditional promotion of a shift from an unfunded to a partially funded retirement scheme is therefore problematic. It resembles the advice to somebody who spends too high a share of his income on housing rent to look for a smaller and cheaper flat, but also to think about buying one. This may prove very useful because of lower current spending and potential capital gains, but it may also require important shifts in intertemporal consumption behaviour. Furthermore, the buyer may be confronted by cash-flow problems when exposed to stochastic income realization. A similar problem arises for countries when shifting from an unfunded to a funded scheme, and this demands close investigation of the change in stocks and flows involved. The objective of this paper is to provide policy-makers and economists who are involved in such a pension reform with a better understanding of its fiscal task, and to highlight the main fiscal options and constraints.

The specific objectives of the paper are the following:

(i)   To highlight the potential benefits of a shift from an unfunded to a funded pension system. The ongoing discussions about reforms and recent reforms in different parts of the world have stressed various benefits at political and economic levels of such a reform. Specific advantages in the context of the EU reforms can be added.

(ii) To investigate the scope of the interrelation between fiscal stocks and flows involved in a shift from an unfunded to a fully funded pension scheme (UF–FF shift). The stocks comprise, *inter alia*, the existing commitment towards current and future retirees staying with the unfunded scheme. The fiscal flows comprise, *inter alia*, the operational deficit of the social security fund resulting from the loss of contributors, and the disbursement of the compensatory amount for those who switch.

(iii) To explore expenditure-minimizing procedures for the UF–FF shift and the appropriate timing of the shift. For political reasons, a voluntary decision by individuals to switch to the new funded system is preferable (this requires an understanding of the intertemporal decision-making process by the individual, which, by the same token, allows for an endogenous determination of the switching age while minimizing the fiscal costs).

(iv) To investigate the main options for financing the fiscal flows of such a reform, and the potential scope of revenue-enhancing measures.

(v)   To explore effects of the transition, such as the claimed favourable effect on capital accumulation, saving, total factor productivity and the use of government assets.

(vi)   To present preliminary empirical findings of the Chilean pension re-
        form and the economic and fiscal issues involved.

The structure of this chapter is as follows. Section 2 presents the potential
benefits of a move from unfunded to funded provisions. Section 3 explores
the links between stocks and flows, including the strategies for reducing the
implicit debt to be made explicit, and the individual switching decision.
Section 4 outlines the main financing options, including the potential financial sources which may result from enhanced economic growth or the use of
government assets. Section 5 summarizes empirical evidence of the Chilean
pension reform and its impact on economic growth, capital formation and
saving, including the financing of the debt made explicit. Section 6 concludes.

2.   POTENTIAL BENEFITS OF MOVING TO FUNDED PROVISIONS

For the shift towards a partially funded scheme, various potential benefits at
the political and economic policy level may be claimed. Those arguments are
influenced by the dragging reforms in western and eastern Europe, and the
apparent success of the Chilean reform of 1981 (Holzmann, 1996). In addition, for the European Union further and specific arguments for a common
move towards mandatory and funded provisions can be advanced. This section presents the core of those arguments, but does not investigate their
validity, nor the conditions under which they may apply.[3] This is partly taken
up in later sections.

   At the political level, three effects stand out. First, the approach provides
for a break in the deadlock of traditional reform attempts since it suggests a
time-consistent and hence credible reform (Holzmann, 1994). Second, the
approach isolates retirement provisions to a large extent from political inter-
ference and risk (Godoy-Arcaya and Valdés-Prieto, 1997; Diamond, 1994).
Last, but not least, it raises workers' awareness of financial issues and enterprise performance, thus reducing the dichotomy between capital and labour
(Piñera, 1991).

(i)   The observed political resistance throughout the world against the
        reforming of an unfunded scheme along conventional lines (such as a
        change in the benefit structure and an increase in retirement age)
        undoubtedly stems from distributional conflicts but seemingly also
        reflects a credibility problem (Holzmann, 1994). Politicians cannot
        make a convincing commitment that the proposed traditional reform is

a lasting one (that is, puts the scheme on a sound and long-term financial basis), and that they have no incentive to change the benefit/contribution structure for political reasons in the near future. Given this time-inconsistency problem, individuals have an incentive to oppose a traditional reform from the very beginning.

Shifting to a funded scheme can provide for a break in the deadlock of reform for three main reasons. First, by stressing the economic advantages and the positive impact on economic growth by such a reform, it allows for arguments that all can win, thus abandoning intractable zero-sum games and shifting the discussion from simple distributional concerns to efficiency and growth issues. Second, by separating explicitly the language for saving insurance (individual accounts and individual equity) from the language of redistribution and social protection, it provides for transparency. Last, but not least, such a shift reduces the scope of future opportunistic behaviour by politicians and thus enhances the incentives for individuals to agree.

(ii) The provision of public and unfunded pensions is subject to many sources of political risk (Diamond, 1994). The first and most obvious is the granting of excessive benefits to existing retirees when the system is not mature and the contribution revenue is largely insufficient to cover expenditure, and promises for future retirees that cannot be met. A second risk is depletion of accumulated assets through other use and/or low rate of returns, making the originally promised benefits not financeable. A third risk is the excessive responsiveness of benefits to short-term conditions of the government budget as currently experienced in the EU for the preparation of the third stage of economic and monetary union (EMU). A fourth risk is the excessive responsiveness of benefits to the long-run conditions of the government budget. Against this background, it is claimed that funded pension schemes '*à la* Chile' provide good isolation from the risk of oversensitivity to the state budget and the risk of excessive distribution to earlier generations. The protection against these risks is seen in the identification of individual accounts and their returns as private property, entitled to the same property rights as other assets.

(iii) Even in highly industrialized countries, most individuals receive their income from work only, thus focusing their interest on high wages and safe employment. As a result, high wages and job security are largely perceived as ways of redistributing income from capital to labour. Negative feedback on the future own-income position is mostly ignored. Furthermore, high rates of return on investment profits are often perceived as indecent and give rise to popular demand for redistribution through high taxation of capital income. Against this background, it is claimed that shifting to funded pensions attenuates the traditional conflict between capital and labour and the aversion of large parts of the population to financial markets, since workers become aware of their interest in a high rate of return (Piñera, 1991). Such a perception would be particularly strong under a defined contribution scheme where a higher rate accrued exclusively to the individual.

At the economic level, three main reform effects are claimed. First, the reform establishes a close link between contributions and benefits. It thus reduces the labour market distortions with which traditional and unfunded programmes are considered to be fraught (World Bank, 1994). Second, a shift to funded schemes furthers and accelerates financial market developments and thus increases the efficiency of resource allocation (Davis, 1995; Holzmann, 1996). Finally, the reform positively affects national saving and capital accumulation (*inter alia*, IMF, 1995). From all three effects – less distorted labour markets, better-functioning financial markets, and higher capital accumulation – and their interaction, a higher growth path should result.

(i)   In unfunded pension schemes the link between contributions and benefits is traditionally weak for several reasons: as a result of mingling distributive function and the saving insurance function of old-age income support; as a result of imposing on the scheme labour market and other pension-unrelated functions; and as a result of its unfunded nature, offering a rate of return well below the rate of return on capital investments. In consequence, individuals perceive social security contributions largely as taxes, giving rise to labour market distortions and leading to tax evasion such as informal market activities, distorted labour supply and incentives for early retirement. In view of the high and often rising social security contributions in much of Europe, these distortions are often held co-responsible for the persistent labour market problems in this part of the world. While many of these distortions, in principle, may be eliminated in a reformed unfunded scheme, it is claimed that moving towards a two-tier scheme, with a clear separation between the unfunded distributive and the funded annuity components, is a more effective and efficient approach (World Bank, 1994, ch. 7).

(ii) Despite the globalization of financial markets over the last decade, many national capital markets in Europe are still underdeveloped when assessed by some measures such as equity market capitalization, the scope and form of capital market instruments, the speed of innovation, and market structure. The final verdict on the relative advantages of bank-based (traditional in central, southern and eastern Europe) versus

market-based (traditional in Anglo-Saxon countries) financial intermediation has still not been reached, but recent developments seemingly
indicate a trend towards market-based intermediation. All countries
want to invigorate their share market as a means to further enterprise
creation, long-term investment and employment. There is also rising
theoretical and empirical support for an old conjecture that the efficiency
of financial markets has a strong bearing on economic growth.[4] Given
the impact of pension funds on the demand for capital market instruments, they may affect instrument innovation, and the market structure
to make the capital markets deeper, more liquid and competitive. A
shift towards funded retirement provisions could importantly accelerate such a development.

(iii)   The decline in total saving in the OECD area as a whole over the past
30 years or so and the long-term rise in the real interest rate which
accelerated at the beginning of the 1980s have heightened the fear of
future global capital shortages with adverse consequences for future
output (see Group of Ten, 1995; OECD, 1996a). This concern about
the future national saving rate on which ageing is likely to have a
negative impact (directly through the age-specific consumption saving
pattern, and indirectly through its budgetary consequences) adds to the
standing claim that an unfunded scheme reduces national saving (at
least transitorily until the system matures). Thus an unfunded system
reduces the capital stock and, consequently, the output level (and also
in many endogenous growth models the growth path). Against such a
background, a shift towards funded provisions would be welcome if it
increased national saving and capital formation. Such an impact is
often claimed and seemingly fostered by the Chilean reform where
national saving as a percentage of GDP increased from 8.2 per cent in
1981 to an all-time high of 27.6 per cent in 1995 (see IMF, 1995;
Holzmann, 1997b).

For the European Union, three further and important advantages may be
claimed for a common move to a mandatory two-tier system, consisting of an
unfunded basic tier, financed from general taxation/social security contributions, and a funded supplementary tier in the form of a defined contribution
plan.

(i)   Despite the creation of an internal market as of 1993, labour mobility
between the EU member states remains low; without some (modest)
mobility, the envisaged gains from specialization and economies of
scale and scope in the EU will be limited. While cultural barriers may
certainly explain part of the labour immobility, differences in pension

and other social policy legislation quite likely also have a bearing. The current coordination rules between the EU countries reduce the obstacles somewhat, but they remain fully operative as far as supplementary pensions are concerned (with regard to transportability, taxation, and so on). With rising pressure on public pensions, the importance of supplementary (individual or occupational) provisions will increase. Having a coordinated and funded second tier on a defined contribution basis, with full transferability of funds when changing the country of residence, would considerably reduce obstacles to mobility. Clearly, this would also require important steps in the area of tax coordination if tax exemptions for premiums and returns are granted, while only the pay-outs to retirees are taxed.[5] Labour mobility gains importance once a common currency is introduced, and instruments other than exchange rate adjustment are required to cope with asymmetric and country-specific shocks. Furthermore, a common scheme for all employed in each EU country would also foster labour mobility between sectors (for example between public and private sector employment) and regions in federal states.

(ii)	All European economies are exposed to the effects of globalization, including the rising (gross) capital movements for portfolio and direct investment purposes. Such a development, while allowing for a more efficient allocation of world-wide capital and thus also for domestic efficiency gains, is often opposed by the wage-earners in the EU because they experience only the disciplinary effects of mobile capital on the wage level (not the increase in labour productivity and hence wage rate, which depends on the net inflow), and not the higher capital returns. With (partially) funded pensions, all European wage-earners would also have a stake in national and world-wide capital market gains, which would lead to supporting, not opposing, the inevitable shift from the traditional stakeholder to a shareholder society.

(iii)	Finally, partial funding of pensions would also better protect the future retirees against the symmetric demographic shocks to which all European countries are exposed. With an asymmetric ageing in Europe, one could envisage a risk-pooling through intra-European migration (while keeping individual country schemes), or a common unfunded scheme (and differences in demographic developments between the states, as in the United States). However, fertility rates in western Europe have been below reproduction level for some time, and there is little indication of a reversal. East European reform countries follow this development with a lag of one to two decades, and also life expectancy is expected to increase further. Against this likely demographic scenario of a parallel ageing of European populations, funded pensions may provide some insurance: if a shift in the financing mode leads to a higher saving rate and a higher domestic capital stock, higher pension benefits should be the result; even without an increase in the European saving rate, investing part of the fund assets internationally allows increased possibilities of risk diversification and hence a higher return at given risk, or lower risk at given return.

In summary, there are seemingly many convincing arguments why European countries should think more intensively of a preferably coordinated shift away from unfunded towards funded provisions on a mandatory basis. Yet all these arguments, even if perfectly valid and empirically fostered, may not be sufficient if the central obstacle of financing the transition is not overcome.

3. DETERMINING THE FISCAL TASK: STOCKS AND FLOWS

As is well known, an unfunded pension scheme constitutes a commitment towards current retirees and workers, and thus is equivalent to a (hidden) public debt. Shifting to a funded scheme makes this implicit debt explicit, which has eventually to be repaid. The shift between implicit and explicit public debt, and the fiscal flows involved, depends on the way the transition is structured. While most theoretical papers dealing with a shift from unfunded to funded provisions are cognizant of the stock–flow link when addressing the intergenerational welfare and intertemporal macroeconomic issues, most empirical papers on such a reform concentrate on the fiscal flows only when addressing the fiscal and distributional issues involved. This section outlines the main links between stocks and flows to be taken into consideration, supported by limited empirical data, and supplemented by some heuristic simulations.

3.1 The Scope of Pension Liabilities

Given the debt nature of pension obligations, as a first step the scope of this debt has to be assessed since it determines the potential fiscal implications of a transition. Current pension expenditures are only a good indicator of existing commitments under steady-state conditions. In the case of an ageing population, rising labour force participation and pension coverage or non-mature benefit structure, the trend in current expenditure level tends to underestimate the trend in outstanding commitments.

Three main definitions of pension liabilities exist (Franco, 1995):

(i)   accrued-to-date liabilities: these represent the present value of pensions to be paid in the future on the basis of accrued rights; neither the future contributions, nor the accrual of new rights by them are considered;

(ii) current workers and pensioners' liabilities: in this case it is assumed that pension schemes continue their existence until the last contributor dies, while no new entrants are allowed; both the future contribution of existing members and their new rights are therefore allowed under current rules;

(iii) open-system liabilities: these also include the present value of contributions and pensions of new workers under current rules; the range of options extends from including only children not yet in the labour force to an infinite perspective.

Table 6.1 highlights the interrelation between the alternative definitions of pensions' liabilities, the corresponding and alternatively used concept of social security debt or wealth, and the concept of actuarial deficit, the balancing item. The difference between the three main definitions of pension liabilities reflects alternative views of which generations, and their claims, should be considered. The difference between the gross and net concept results from taking account of assets (financial reserves and present value of future contributions); the net concept is equivalent to the balancing item, the actuarial deficit. The concept of debt or wealth represents alternative views from the side of government (debt) or individuals (wealth). For example, the gross social security debt of the current generation (as seen from government) corresponds to the gross social security wealth (as seen from the individuals); and the net social security wealth corresponds to the actuarial deficit of the current generation. The concept of net/gross social security wealth was introduced into the pension discussion by Feldstein (1974).[6]

For an unfunded–fully funded pension shift (UF–FF shift), it is the first definition which is relevant, since it is the value of accrued rights which has to be compensated and thus becomes explicit debt (unless the government defaults on its pension commitments). For a given pension system, the main assumptions which determine the level of the accrued pension liabilities (or social security debt I, henceforth SSD) are the real interest rate, real wage growth, inflation rate, and survival probabilities. For countries where the public pension system has accumulated financial reserves, the existing assets have to be subtracted.

Table 6.2 illustrates the scope of the SSD for selected OECD countries in 1990. The estimates have only illustrative character and constitute a lower limit, since they often concentrate on the main schemes only (disregarding, for example, civil servants' pensions), leave out disability and survivors'

Table 6.1   *Alternative definitions of pension liabilities/social security debts or social security wealth/actuarial deficits and their interrelation*

	Assets	Liabilities	Definition of balance	Definition of liability
	Financial reserves	Present value of pensions in disbursement		
	Actuarial deficit I	Present value of future pensions due to past contributions	Actuarial deficit I	Accrued-to-date liability
1	Gross social security debt I	Gross social security debt I		
	Present value of future contributions of current workers	Present value of future pensions due to future contributions of current workers		
2	Actuarial deficit II			
1 + 2	Gross social security debt II	Gross social security debt II	Actuarial deficit I + II = Net social security wealth/debt	Current workers and pensioners' liability
	Gross social security debt of current generation	Gross social security debt of current generation		
	Present value of contributions of future generations	Present value of pensions due to contributions of future generations		
3	Actuarial deficit III			
	Gross social security debt of future generations	Gross social security debt of future generations		
1 + 2 + 3	Gross social security debt of all generations	Gross social security debt of all generations	Actuarial deficit I + II + III = Total actuarial deficit	Open system liability

Source: Own presentation.

149

Table 6.2 Net accrued pension liabilities and financial debt for selected OECD countries, 1990 (% of GDP)

Country	Gross liabilities			Existing assets	Net liabilities	Pension expenditure[1]	Gross liabilities pension expenditure	Financial liabilities	Total gross liabilities
	Retired	Workforce	Total						
	(1)	(2)	(3) = (1) + (2)	(4)	(5) = (3) – (4)	(6)	(7) = (3)/(6)	(8)	(9) = (3) + (8)
France	77	139	216	0	216	9.0	24.0	40	256
Germany	55	102	157	0	157	6.9	22.8	44	201
Italy	94	165	259	0	259	10.6	24.4	101	360
(after 1992 reform)	94	148	242	0	242	10.6	22.8	101	343
United Kingdom	58	81	139	0	139	6.6	21.1	35	174
Canada	42	71	113	8	105	3.9	29.0	73	186
Japan	51	112	163	18	145	5.7	28.6	70	233
United States	42	70	112	23	89	5.1	22.0	55	167

Notes:
[1] Only old-age pension expenditure around 1990; figures for Japan include survivors' and disability pensions.
NB: Assumptions: Pension benefits are price indexed; real earnings grow by 2 per cent; discount rate is selected at 4 per cent from 1990 to 2010, declining to 3 per cent in 2050.

Sources: Van den Noord and Herd (1994), OECD database, and own calculations.

pensions, or ignore social pensions and means-tested and related supple-
ments.[7] Nevertheless, those estimates indicate that the hidden public debt, the
SSD, is extremely important and dwarfs the explicit financial debt existing in
those countries. Comparing the SSD with the annual pension expenditure
also confirms a rule of thumb that for reasonable parameter assumptions the
ratio is in the range of 15 to 30.[8]

3.2   Reducing the Scope of the SSD to be Made Explicit

Given the actual average pension expenditure level of EU countries and of
many emerging market economies in eastern Europe of 10 per cent of GDP
and above, this amounts to an SSD of some 150 to 300 per cent of GDP, and
sometimes above, with an often rising tendency. Moreover, in the case of the
east European reform countries, the actual expenditure level is often
downward-biased through benefit and indexation caps for budgetary reasons.
Making the debt of such an amount fully explicit, and eventually having to
repay it, does not seem feasible. This begs for strategies to reduce the amount
of SSD made explicit.

(i)   Strategy I consists in reducing the SSD via a reduction of future
      commitments through an increase in the retirement age, decrease in the
      annual accrual factor or change in the indexation procedure (say, from
      wage to price indexation). In fiscal speech, the government partially
      defaults on its pension commitments.[9]
          A reform of the unfunded scheme in parallel with a partial or full
      shift to a funded scheme appears to be required in most countries since
      the unfunded schemes are essentially financially unsustainable, and a
      mere shift in the financing mechanism is of little help. So far, all
      reform countries in Latin America have adjusted eligibility and benefit
      rules before or in parallel with a shift in the financing mechanism. In
      order to reduce the amount of SSD made explicit, the reform has to be
      implemented as early as possible (discussed below).
          Figures 6.1a and 6.1b sketch the scope and changes of the SSD
      under different benefit reform options, the impact of ageing on the
      SSD, and the divergence in development between stocks and flows.
      The results are based on a heuristic overlapping generation-type simu-
      lation model which mimics the essential features of an unfunded two-tier
      pension scheme.[10]
          Benefit indexation: Starting out with price indexation under the base-
      line scenario (implying a steady-state SSD of some 160 per cent of
      GDP), with a change to wage indexation in period −10, the SSD jumps
      immediately by over 20 per cent of GDP and continues further to

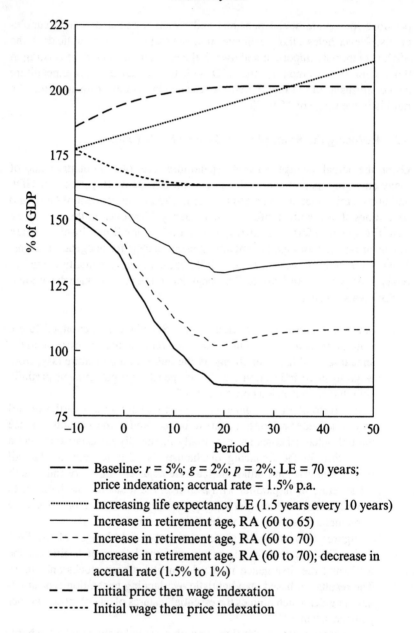

Figure 6.1a   Social security debt under alternative policy scenarios

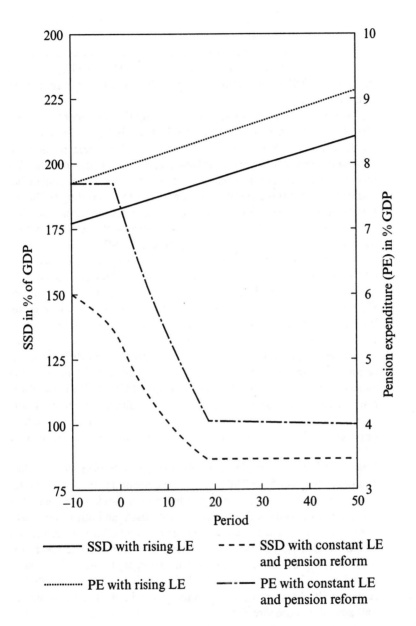

Figure 6.1b   Social security debt and current pension expenditure

increase for some 30 years until the difference from the baseline scenario reaches almost 40 per cent of GDP, or one fifth of the original
SSD level. With initial wage indexation, a change to price indexation
in period −10 leads to an immediate drop in the SSD level by some 24
per cent of GDP before gradually approaching the baseline level after
some 40 years.

Retirement age and accrual rate: Changing the retirement age from
60 to 65, or even from 60 to 70 during the periods 1 to 20 has an effect
on the SSD well before the implementation of the reform, and the
long-term impact on SSD is substantial. However, the results also
reveal that in an earnings-related scheme the effects are somewhat
compensated for if the accrual rate is not adjusted accordingly (that is,
if individuals working longer and retiring later accrue further pension
rights). Linking a strong increase in the retirement age (RA) with a
decrease in the accrual rate essentially halves the SSD.

Both changes in policy parameters and their effects on SSD are a
first indication of the importance of introducing policy changes well in
advance of a UF–FF shift if the transition costs are to be minimized.
Figure 6.1a also indicates the increase of the SSD as a result of rising
life expectancy (as of period 1). Again, SSD jumps with the future
change in life expectancy, that is, the stock effects of future changes
are immediately capitalized. Figure 6.1b exhibits this difference between stock and flow developments with regard to SSD and pension
expenditure (each measured as a percentage of GDP). While the fiscal
flow variable – the pension expenditure – is initially identical, differences in future life expectancy and policy setting have an immediate
impact on SSD. The initial difference amounts to almost 30 per cent of
GDP.

(ii) Strategy II consists in a partial shift towards a funded system, thus
making only part of the SSD explicit. The resulting (mandatory) pension scheme consists of an unfunded and a funded tier, and the
distribution between both is determined by fiscal and other considerations. Such an approach is applied in Argentina and other Latin American
countries (Queisser, 1995), and is under preparation in some east European reform countries (Latvia and Hungary), and also under
consideration in Poland, Croatia and Slovenia (see Holzmann, 1997a).
A partial UF–FF shift has both advantages and risk. The main (potential) advantages are threefold:

(a) It proportionately reduces the potential scope of the implicit debt
made explicit and can thus lead to a manageable fiscal task.
While the repayment of, say, 200 per cent of GDP in debt appears

difficult, or even impossible, the repayment of half of this amount is in the range of the Chilean pension reform.

(b) Basing retirement income on both an unfunded and a funded scheme allows for risk diversification and may be welfare-enhancing. It can be argued that the internal rate of return of an unfunded scheme – the natural growth rate – is a stochastic variable which exposes each pension cohort to an income risk. The same can be claimed for the internal rate of return of a funded scheme – the interest rate. Thus, if the covariance of both returns is lower than one, a mixed financing mechanism reduces the overall income risk and provides positive welfare effects.[11]

(c) Public and earnings-related pension schemes traditionally have a distributional and an annuity component, and it is the mingling of both and the lack of a clear contribution–benefit link which is held responsible for the various distortions inflicted by public and unfunded schemes (see, for example, Schmidt-Hebbel, 1993). Separating both components into an unfunded distribution-oriented tier and a truly earnings-related funded tier is claimed to reduce the distortions significantly (World Bank, 1994).

However, there are also (potential) risks of a partial shift only which are the following:

(a) Keeping the reduced, but traditional, unfunded tier does not contain the various sources of political risk, discussed above.

(b) Unfunded and funded tiers have different rates of return. Temporarily lower rates of return in the funded tier may exert political pressure for higher benefits under the unfunded tier in order to compensate; conversely, higher rates of return may also introduce pressure for higher unfunded benefits from those parts of the population which are little covered by the second tier.

(c) The unfunded tier is much more exposed to the ageing of the population, and the problem of long-term financing this implies.

(iii) Strategy III consists in applying an expenditure-minimizing procedure for the determination of the compensatory amount for those individuals willing to switch to the funded scheme, and hence forgoing the benefits of the unfunded one. For political considerations, the switching decision should be left to the individual. For cash-flow and economic considerations, the approximate switching cohort should be known in advance. This requires knowledge of the individual/cohort decision process, which also allows the determination of expenditure-minimizing compensation for all switchers. Put differently, setting the switching age exogenously (say, all below age 40 have to join the funded scheme) either does not conform to individual preferences and thus undermines the political support of the reform, or it reflects individual preferences but is at least as expensive as the individual voluntary decision.

The move to a funded scheme which promises a higher rate of return (and hence a higher benefit level for a given contribution rate, or an equal benefit level for a lower contribution rate) raises the question of whether compensation for a major segment of the age cohorts is required at all. If, despite the lower contribution record, the higher rate of return under the funded scheme allows the individual to achieve a benefit level at least as high as remaining with the unfunded scheme, it provides an incentive to switch to the new scheme without any compensation. Annex B outlines a simple (deterministic) approach to model the individual decision process, and the conditions under which an uncompensated switch takes place. Figure 6.2 highlights the interest rate/wage growth rate differential required in order to induce an age cohort (consisting of identical individuals with perfect foresight, hence abstracting from uncertainty and risk aversion, but including survivor probabilities, and a potential span of activity between age 21 and 60/ 65/70, and of retirement between age 61/66/71 and 100) to switch to the funded scheme. The results suggest that for reasonable rate differ-

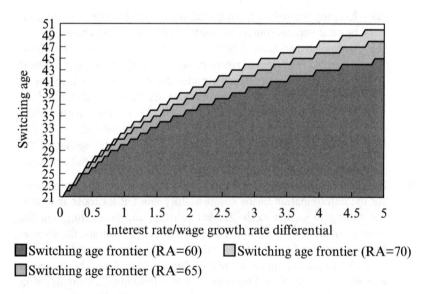

Figure 6.2   Switching age without compensation and required interest/wage rate differential

entials (say, the range of 1.5 to 3 percentage points) no compensation for individuals in the age range 33 to 44 may be required. The resulting savings, however, are likely to be limited since the present value of future benefit claims of that age segment is small.

(iv) Given the scope of the existing pension commitments, most countries will have to apply all strategies simultaneously in order to keep the resulting fiscal obligations manageable. This raises the question of an appropriate structure for the first and unfunded tier which may allow the minimization of the risks raised above.

A microeconomically ingenious approach to structure the basic and unfunded tier, going back to a suggestion by Buchanan (1968), was recently adopted in Sweden (see ISSA, 1996, p. 43) and Latvia (see Fox et al., 1996), and is also under consideration in Poland. It has the following characteristics.

The new unfunded tier is a 'notionally defined contribution' scheme. The system starts by giving everyone paying the social security contribution an account. As contributions to the pension system are paid, the account is credited, as if it were a savings account, and the accumulated capital earns a 'rate of return' equal to the growth of the average wage on which contributions are collected. At retirement, the pension paid is equal to the accumulated capital (inclusive of the notional interest rate earnings) divided by the expected post-retirement lifespan of all those of that person's age. The pension is price-indexed.

This approach has various advantages, in particular: (a) the system provides an incentive for formal labour force participation since any contribution evasion leads at the end to a lower benefit level; (b) the system is largely immune from political trickery, since any special treatment of groups has to be followed up by explicit contribution payments; (c) individuals have an incentive to stay on the labour market and to extend their working lives; (d) the system adjusts endogenously to an increase in life expectancy, since any increase will automatically lead to lower pension benefit giving rise to an incentive to retire later; (e) the benefit structure may allow an easy integration with a funded second tier of a truly defined contribution type.

The main problem of this approach is the reserve accumulation it requires against temporary adverse economic shocks, and, most importantly, against the ageing of the population. Since the system is an unfunded one, but promises a rate of return based on past average wage growth, expected changes in beneficiary/contributor ratios require corresponding financial reserves if future transfers from the state budget are to be prevented. While the calculation of a long-term expenditure-covering contribution rate is technically relatively easy, the actual accumulation of reserves and the receipt of a market-based rate of return may be constrained by political pressure for an alternative use of these funds. For this reason, an adjusted version of that 'notionally defined contribution plan', proposed by Boskin et al. (1988), may be more appropriate. In their scheme, the notional interest rate is set by actuaries, based on forecasts, so that the system is forecast to be in balance over the projection period.

3.3 Speed of Transition, Timing of Reforms and Cash-flow Considerations

(i) The speed of transition is determined by the decision at which age a switch to the funded scheme should take place. There are two extreme options. Under the radical option, all commitments – for those who have just entered the labour force to those who are already retired – are compensated. Thus the total SSD is made explicit in one stroke and has to be financed on the financial market; the cash-flow requirements equal the SSD. Under the minimal option, only the new entrants to the labour market participate in the funded scheme. This reduces the cash-flow requirements to the rising operational deficit (the difference between revenue and expenditure), since the expenditure remains for many years while the contributions decrease continuously. As a result, the transition is only completed once the last eligible person dies (after some 80 years). Most reforms will choose a switching age among the current working generation, say age 40, as a compromise between considerations to speed up transition and cash-flow limitations.

Figures 6.3a–6.5a highlight the change in the composition of the total public pension debt under different assumptions about the age of the switching cohort and over time. The decision takes place at the end of period 0 and the switch in period 1. Since the interest rate in this simulation is set equal to the growth rate, the overall debt level in per cent of GDP remains unchanged, only the composition of debt becomes different.[12] The corresponding b figures exhibit the cash-flow requirements of those changes: the operational deficit, the compensation for forgone unfunded benefits (paid at retirement, or at death to the survivors when active), and the interests on the now explicit fiscal debt.

In Figure 6.3a all workers below retirement age shift to the funded (earnings-related) scheme and are compensated for their accrued pension rights by recognition bonds (RBs). These bonds earn the market rate of return (equal to the rate of discount) and are disbursed at retirement (inclusive of the accumulated interest earnings). The affiliation to the basic scheme remains unchanged for all workers. As a

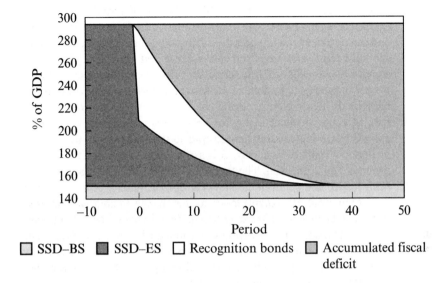

Figure 6.3a   *Total public pension debt (r = g = p = 2%; switching until RA = 60)*

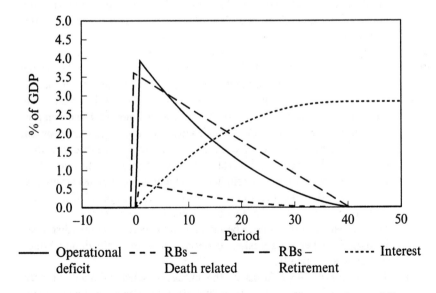

Figure 6.3b   *Cash-flow requirements during transition (r = g = p = 2%; switching until RA = 60)*

result, almost two thirds of the SSD of the earnings-related scheme is exchanged against RBs. The overall amount of RBs decreases with the retirement of each cohort and the redemption of each bond. The corresponding cash-flow requirement is presented in Figure 6.3b. The expenditure consist of four elements: the operational deficit since the earnings-related system is left with no contributors but all retirees, the RBs disbursed to the retiring cohort in each year, the value of the RBs of those workers dying before retirement (and for which it is assumed that this value is handed over to the family), and the interest on the now explicit fiscal debt. It is assumed that all cash-flow requirements are debt financed. The total cash-flow requirement is extremely front-loaded and peaks in the first year of transition.

In Figure 6.4 all workers prior to the change remain with the old system and hence no RBs are required. The change in the debt composition takes place between SSD and accumulated deficits which consists of the operational deficit and interest payments only. The cash-flow requirement is very much back-loaded and peaks after 40 years. The transition is completed only after 80 years.

In Figure 6.5 a medium scenario is presented since only workers of 41 years of age or below switch to the new system. Since their acquired rights under the unfunded scheme are relatively low, so is the level of RBs issued for compensation. Consequently the 'recognition bond carrot' is slim and long. As a result of this intermediate switching approach, the cash-flow requirements are largely centred, peaking after 20 years.

Figures 6.3–6.5 demonstrate the trade-off between the speed of transition and the timing of the cash-flow requirement. The faster the envisaged transition, the more the cash-flow requirement is front-loaded.

Under the assumption of the above simulation – that the interest rate r equals the growth rate g – no deficit in the economic sense emerges from the UF–FF shift since the liability position of the government remains unchanged. In the more relevant case of $r > g$, a true transition deficit emerges which is equivalent to interest rate/growth rate difference times the SSD made explicit. A capitalization of that true transition deficit would make the financial debt in percentage of GDP grow without bounds, violating the conventional solvency condition for the government, and thus has to be financed by general revenue (discussed below). In a perfect foresight economy, it is the only deficit which matters economically.

(ii) The timing of the reforms of the unfunded scheme linked with the switch to a funded scheme is of primary importance for the economic costs of transition, and the size and path of the cash flows involved. The

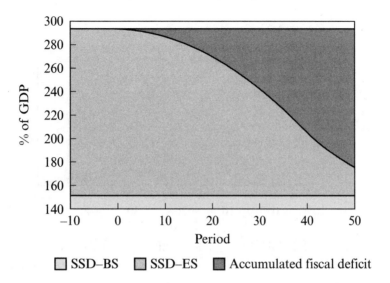

Figure 6.4a   *Total public pension debt (*r = g = p = 2%; new entrants only)*

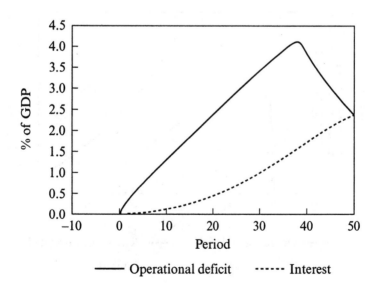

Figure 6.4b   *Cash-flow requirements during transition (*r = g = p = 2%; new entrants only)*

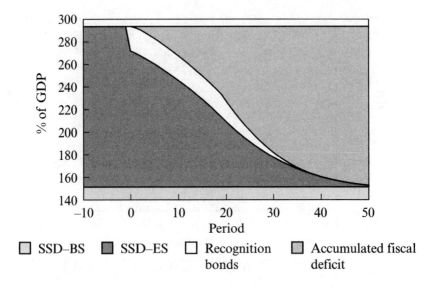

Figure 6.5a   *Total public pension debt (*r = g = p = 2%*; switching below age 42)*

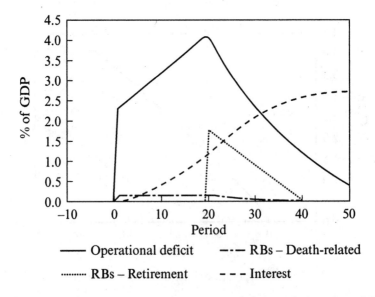

Figure 6.5b   *Cash-flow requirements during transition (*r = g = p = 2%*; switching below age 42)*

reform of the unfunded scheme serves, *inter alia*, to reduce the outstanding social security debt. Consequently, such a reform should be in place before the shift towards the funded scheme: this reduces the implicit debt to be made explicit, and hence the fiscal flow requirements involved. Figures 6.6 and 6.7 highlight the importance of an early reform under the assumption that the real interest rate is 5 per cent (that is, the discount rate and rate of return of the funded scheme), and that the prices and real wages increase by 2 per cent per annum (the latter rate is equal to the rate of return from the unfunded scheme since no population growth is assumed). In both figures an identical reform of the unfunded scheme takes place: an increase in the retirement age from 60 to 70 over a span of 20 years/periods (with an increase by one year every two years for computational reasons) and a reduction in the annual accrual rate from 1.5 to 1 per cent over the same time-span. The only difference is the timing of the reform. In Figure 6.6, the reform starts 20 years before the switch to the funded scheme, and hence is completed at the time of shifting from the earnings-related unfunded to the earnings-related funded scheme; in Figure 6.7, the reform starts concurrently with the shift. The switching decision by the individuals, and hence the age cohorts concerned, is endogenously determined, with no compensation paid. This results in a switch of all cohorts aged 44 or below under both reforms (since anybody aged 44 or below at the time of reform in any case retires at age 70).

Figures 6.6 and 6.7 indicate the importance of an early reform. In Figure 6.6a – the early reform scenario – the SSD (for both the basic and earnings-related schemes) is almost halved at a time of the financing shift, and the SSD of the earnings-related scheme made explicit is a mere 42 per cent of GDP. The operational deficit (Figure 6.6b) is front-loaded and reaches a maximum of some 2 per cent of GDP after 30 years; the true transition deficit, which has to be budgetary financed in order to avoid an increase in financial debt, rises slowly from slightly below to above 1 percentage point of GDP. The slight initial fluctuations are due to the discontinuous increase in the retirement age. This result contrasts with the late reform scenario (Figure 6.7). Due to the parallel implementation of benefit and financing reform, the SSD continues to decrease initially, albeit slightly, and remains constant once the reform is fully effective in period 20. The implicit SSD made explicit amounts to almost 82 per cent of GDP. Also, the operational deficit and true transition deficit exhibit a higher path. The fluctuations in the latter are due to the discontinuous increase in the retirement age (one year every two calendar years); while keeping the total debt constant, this reduces the budgetary financing requirement every second year.

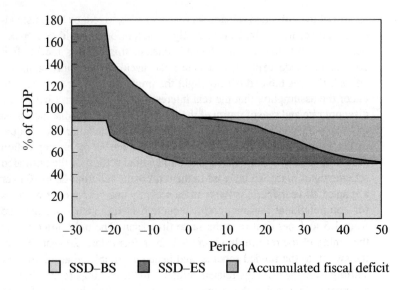

Figure 6.6a   Total public pension debt (r = 5%; g = p = 2%; unfunded benefit reform in period –20 to –1)

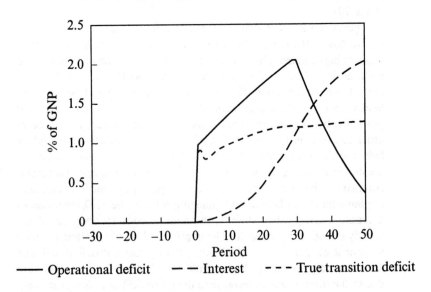

Figure 6.6b   Cash-flow requirements and true transition deficit (r = 5%; g = p = 2%; unfunded benefit reform in period –20 to –1)

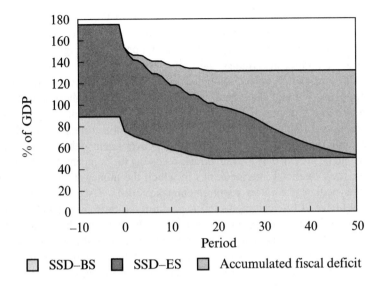

Figure 6.7a   *Total public pension debt (r = 5%; g = p = 2%; unfunded benefit reform in period 0 to 19)*

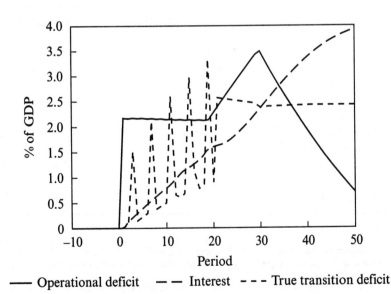

Figure 6.7b   *Cash-flow requirements and true transition deficit (r = 5%; g = p = 2%; unfunded benefit reform in period 0 to 19)*

(iii)   Cash-flow considerations are also important for the timing of the disbursement of the compensatory amount, if such a payment is required. The results in Figure 6.2 were derived in a perfect foresight economy; however, under uncertainty and risk aversion, individuals may not be willing to switch unless some compensation is provided (as has been done in all Latin American reforms so far). The highest cash-flow requirement occurs if the compensation is paid at switching age. It amounts to the disbursement and financing of the corresponding SSD for all switchers, but the financing of government debt instruments would be provided by the individuals receiving the compensation amount (or their financial intermediaries in which the money is invested). An intermediate cash-flow requirement takes place if the compensation (inclusive of interest payments) is paid only at retirement (such as the recognition bonds in the Chilean reform). In this case, the payment is distributed over the span of all switching cohorts and under a model-like setting the bonds mature with each switching cohort retiring. The minimum cash-flow requirement occurs if, further on, the recognition bonds are annuitized at retirement (similar to the compensatory pen-

Table 6.3   *Shifting from unfunded to funded pensions: the restructuring of SSD*

	Chile (1981)		Colombia (1994)	
	% of GDP	%	% of GDP	%
Social security debt				
of unreformed system[1]	n.a.		125.7	
Reform of unfunded scheme	n.a.		–37.6[2]	
Reformed unfunded scheme	n.a.		–4.5	
Social security debt				
made explicit	126.0	100	83.6	100
Operational deficit[3]	99.9	79	69.2	83
Compensation amount[3]	26.1	21	14.4	17

Notes:
[1]   Calculated from accumulated deficits under alternative scenario simulations and the assumption of interest rate equal to the economic growth rate. See Schmidt-Hebbel (1995).
[2]   Includes effects from higher contribution rates besides increased retirement age and changes in benefit structure.
[3]   Calculated from the discounted flow projections under the assumption that the interest rate equals the economic growth rate.

Sources: Arrau (1992), Schmidt-Hebbel (1995), and own calculations.

sion in the Argentinian reform). In this case, the cash-flow requirement is restricted to the sum of the annuity payments and spread to the year when the last pensioner dies. Thus, in fact, the RB or annuity solution is equivalent to a forced credit by the switching individuals.

Table 6.3 attempts to summarise the reform-induced changes in the composition of the SSD for Chile and Colombia. Both reforms entail a similar estimated level of the SSD to be made explicit, and in both countries the corresponding fiscal flows are predominantly generated by the operation deficit.

3.4 Transition and Financial Market Reactions

A temporary widening of the fiscal deficit which results from a (partial) UF–FF shift and which merely reflects a redistribution of total debt between implicit and explicit liabilities should have little effect on the pure interest rate. The capital stock and national saving are only marginally affected by such a deficit; any additional credit demand by government is supplied by the saving of the newly established funded provisions. Also, there should be no negative direct impact on the balance of payments.

With regard to reaction of the (international) financial markets, and a change in the risk premium in response to higher fiscal deficit and debt levels, however, the question goes unanswered. Since the total public debt remains unchanged, *a priori*, one would expect any risk premium to remain unchanged too. Yet financial markets may not be interested in the total debt, but only in the financial debt since any risk premium reflects the default probability of the latter. The result will thus depend on the assessment of the default probability by financial markets with regard to both kinds of debt (implicit and explicit), and their interaction.

If financial markets perceive that a government will never default on its pension obligations (that is, introduce a reform of the unfunded tier which reduces its commitments towards current retirees and workforce), with a rising SSD the risk of a default on its financial debt should increase since the set of policy options to repay that debt is reduced (there is less scope for tax increases, but scope for inflation tax since pension benefits are typically secured in real terms). Accordingly, a rise in the SSD should increase the risk premium on financial debt, while a decline should reduce it. On the other hand, if financial markets are convinced that a government will first default on the pension commitment before defaulting on its financial obligations, the level of the SSD and thus any change should be inconsequential for the imposed risk premium on financial market debt. In such a case, however, a reform of the pension system which reduces the implicit debt, but increases the stock of financial debt, would tend to increase the risk premium, with negative impacts on the budget and the economy. If the default on both kinds of debt is considered equally likely, the risk premium should be driven by the size of the total debt.

There is no empirical evidence on all three conjectures. The concentration of the drafters of the Maastricht Treaty on the financial debt (and deficit) when formulating the fiscal criteria for participation in the European economic and monetary union to be started in 1999 is consistent with the second conjecture, since no regard is given to important differences in SSD among the member countries (see Table 6.2).[13] If this conjecture were true and the European Union would strictly control for financial debt and deficit only, this could constrain future reform attempts among those EU countries with already a fragile fiscal condition; it could also have important consequences for central and east European countries against their endeavour to join the EU in the near future. Many of these countries are making preparations, or at least plans, for a partial UF–FF shift, but are afraid of adverse financial markets and/or EU reactions. Similar concerns are also raised with regard to the reaction of international financial institutions (like the International Monetary Fund) to a reform-induced widening of the fiscal stance.

4. OPTIONS FOR FINANCING THE TRANSITION

Shifting from an unfunded to a funded scheme raises the issue of the repayment of the implicit debt of the unfunded pension scheme and the burdening of the transition generation, or of all future generations. For this reason, countries have generally rejected this reform option since both a higher explicit debt level and budgetary financing through a contractionary fiscal stance were excluded. However, the welfare economic issue of a 'Pareto-improving transition', that is, making at least one generation better off and no other worse off, receives a different assessment once economic externalities of the reform are taken into account. The fiscal issues of Pareto-improving financing of the debt conversion have to be set against the background of intergenerational redistribution, changes in efficiency of taxation and macroeconomic effects. This section outlines the main financing options under both neoclassical and endogenous growth considerations, including the use of privatization proceeds.

4.1 Debt and Budgetary Financing in a Neoclassical World

Whatever the transition path chosen, radical or minimal, a UF–FF shift will burden at least one generation unless the economic benefits generated by such a reform allow for a full compensation of the transition generation(s). In the conventional neoclassical world, an unfunded pension scheme is Pareto-efficient even when the interest rate permanently exceeds the natural growth rate if the given scheme does not create economic distortions; for example, it is financed via lump-sum taxes and provides lump-sum transfers. Although only the first generation gains and all later generations are worse off, there exists no mechanism to reverse the situation without the welfare position of at least one generation deteriorating (Breyer, 1989). The result is intuitively and immediately understandable, since it amounts to an application of the second basic theorem of welfare economics: any lump-sum redistribution of income entails an allocation which is different but also Pareto-efficient (Homburg, 1990).

(i) There are two well-known fiscal alternatives to finance a transition – pure debt financing and pure budgetary financing – with known and less known effects.

Under pure debt financing, all the SSD made explicit is added to the financial debt since no debt repayment takes place. Nevertheless, the budget is affected since a higher revenue or lower expenditure level is required to finance the true transition deficit resulting from an interest rate/economic growth rate difference. Otherwise, as noted above, the explicit (and thus total) debt grows without bounds (in absolute terms and in per cent of GDP). In industrialized countries, the interest rate/ growth rate difference ranges between some 2 and 6 per cent,[14] giving rise to a long-term true transition deficit of 1 to 3 per cent of GDP if only SSD of some 50 per cent of GDP (roughly a quarter of the total SSD) were to be made explicit and not repaid. This is a permanent burden resulting from transition which is distributed over all future generations.

Under pure budgetary financing (through higher revenue or lower expenditure, keeping the sustainable fiscal position constant), the government combines a pension reform with a contractionary fiscal policy. The later policy reverses the initial intergenerational distribution, and burdens the transition generation in favour of all future generations. In the setting of a traditional overlapping generations (OLG) model, such a policy causes first-order increases in the level of national saving, capital, output and real wages. These increases rise with the share of pensioners in the population and the degree of closeness of the economy, and fall with the prevalence of voluntary intergenerational transfers (see, for example, Schmidt-Hebbel, 1993).

(ii) The costs of transition can be reduced or even eliminated under both debt and budgetary financing if the new pension scheme exhibits lower negative externalities compared with the unreformed scheme. Lower negative externalities can be motivated by the many distortions an unfunded scheme may exert on intertemporal consumption or on labour supply decisions, resulting in an excess burden. Through the UF–FF shift, the reduction or elimination of the excess burden may be used to repay the implicit debt of an unfunded scheme within finite time (Homburg, 1990). Since public pension schemes and the way they are financed quite definitely entail numerous distortions, a change in the funding mechanism may thus actually improve welfare. The conclusion rests, however, on the assumption that the funded scheme is less distortionary for individual saving decisions and labour supply than the unfunded one. Yet such a result is not necessarily linked with the funding procedure but, under the assumption of elastic labour supply, is typically related to an inadequate benefit–contribution link of unfunded schemes. Public and earnings-related pension schemes traditionally have a distributional and annuity component, and it is the mingling of both components and the lack of a clear contribution–benefit link which is claimed to be responsible for the distortions (Schmidt-Hebbel, 1993; World Bank, 1994). However, these distortions may also be reduced in an unfunded scheme, by separating both components more clearly as, for example, in a two-tier scheme with a basic tax-financed flat-rate scheme (of a universal or assistance type) taking care of distributional and poverty considerations, and a fully earnings-related one, financed by earmarked contributions only; albeit at theoretical level, it remains unclear if such a separation always creates fewer distortions than a well-conceived traditional social insurance scheme. The basic component will exist in any alternative concept and the incurred distortions are the inevitable consequence of introducing distributional activities, and forced saving always affects labour supply in a distortive manner unless assumptions about perfect credit markets are made, allowing individuals to borrow freely against their future labour and pension income. Then the remaining, potentially avoidable, distortions are reduced to the effects of an alternative funding mechanism. These effects may exist since a non-distortionary pension scheme requires actuarial neutrality which can be achieved in an unfunded scheme only if the implicit rate of return (the natural rate of growth) equals the rate of interest (that is, the golden rule of growth holds – Breyer and Straub, 1993; Perraudin and Pujol, 1995). Put differently, a pension system can still entail a sizeable net tax on labour even if the contribution–benefit link is tight, provided that the system's implicit rate of return is below that of the market.[15]

Simulation studies with OLG models *à la* Auerbach and Kotlikoff (1987) suggest that the welfare gains resulting from the elimination of labour market distortions are comparatively small. A model calibrated on the German pension system exhibits welfare gains of some 9 per cent of lifetime resources to future generations if the transition generation is not compensated. With compensation, the welfare gains to future generations are reduced to some 2 per cent (Raffelhüschen, 1993). Simulations by Kotlikoff (1995) provide higher welfare gains to future generations of 4.5 per cent (while compensating the transition generation) when assuming that the benefit–tax linkage is low, that the initial tax structure features a progressive income tax, and that consumption tax is used to finance the transition. However, when the initial tax structure is a proportionate income tax, the tax–benefit linkage is strong, when income taxes are raised to finance the transition, and when the transition generation is fully compensated, there is a 3.1 per cent welfare loss to future generations.

(iii) The considerations in traditional OLG models highlight the critical assumption for a Pareto-improving transition in a neoclassical model setting, namely that the benefit–tax link of the system to be replaced is weak, and that general taxation (income or consumption tax) is at the margin less distortionary than social security contributions (payroll taxation). This is not necessarily the case in a closed economy, and even less so in an open economy. Furthermore, the net efficiency gain declines with the incidence of worker-consumption myopia.

In a closed economy setting, the results depend on the particular structure of preferences. Simulation results indicate that for particular parameter combinations a shift between wage and income taxation produce predominantly, but not always, efficiency gains (Auerbach and Kotlikoff, 1987), and Auerbach et al. (1983) conclude from second-best theory that income taxation will not always be more efficient than wage or payroll taxation.

In an open economy, the probability of net efficiency gains is likely to be further reduced. With capital much more mobile than labour, the effective taxation of capital income is reduced or even eliminated so that the tax incidence falls essentially on the less mobile factors of production (labour and land). In consequence, shifting from payroll taxation to general taxation as part of the pension reform may not change the tax incidence and the distortionary effects but only the way taxes are levied.

The welfare economic effects become even more uncertain if social security contributions are used to finance the cash requirements of transition. Such an approach is under consideration in various countries of eastern Europe (see Holzmann, 1997a), and has recently also been proposed for Spain (Piñera and Weinstein, 1996). It consists of curtailing the expenditure for the unfunded tier (through an increase in retirement age and change in the benefit structure) while keeping the contribution rate for switchers and non-switchers until the implicit debt made explicit is repaid. Since this approach further loosens the contribution–benefit link for both switchers and non-switchers, the excess burden of the wage taxation is likely to increase.

Summing up, under a traditional neoclassical setting, the financing of a UF–FF shift is technically feasible but difficult to justify in economic terms: the long-term welfare gains are small and can be achieved only through the burdening of the transition generation unless net efficiency gains through the corresponding shift in the mode of taxation are realized. The likelihood of those gains, however, is small. Thus additional positive economic effects of such a pension reform are required in order to justify such a shift in welfare economic terms, and provide the necessary financing in fiscal terms. They may be found in the impact on economic growth.

4.2   Debt and Budgetary Financing under (Endogenous) Growth Effects

There are four main avenues by which a UF–FF shift may introduce positive externalities, leading to a higher growth rate than otherwise: (1) a higher employment level; (2) a higher national saving rate; (3) a higher rate of capital accumulation; and (4) a higher rate of technical progress. While effects (2) and (3) are identical in a closed economy, in an open economy they can diverge. All four effects (or a subset) can interact and strengthen each other once considerations of endogenous growth are taken into account.

The central economic benefit which is claimed to result from a UF–FF shift is its impact on financial market developments, which in turn influences positively capital formation, saving and economic growth.[16] In addition, an improved financial market may result in higher productivity, leading to a temporary rise in technical progress. Furthermore, embedding those considerations in endogenous growth theory, improved financial markets may permanently lead to a higher growth rate than otherwise. In consequence, the enhanced economic resources may allow for a Pareto-improving repayment of the SSD made explicit.

(i)   For the link of pension reform, financial market development and economic growth, the channels of economic effects and their empirical magnitude are important. Yet, our understanding of the pension fund–financial market link and the financial market–economic growth link is still weak and its modelling in its infancy.

   As regards the impact of pension funds on financial market developments, the central claim is that their specific demand for financial market instruments (with regard to risk, liquidity and maturity), their addition to existing financial market intermediaries (such as banks and insurance companies), and the (potential) competitive set-up of pension funds makes the financial market broader and deeper, more liquid and more competitive. A casual comparison between financial markets in countries with strong and weak traditions in funded pension arrangements (say, the Anglo-Saxon countries and most of continental Europe) supports such a view, but so far is little substantiated by modelling and empirical data (see Davis, 1995).

The claim that the effectiveness of financial markets and the level (or rate of growth) of real activity are closely related, however, is not new and empirical investigations have been undertaken for decades.[17] Against the background of neoclassical growth theory these studies could argue only for temporary efficiency effects resulting from financial market developments. More recent developments in growth theory allow for level as well as growth path effects.

However, these recent models concentrate on specific aspects of financial markets and their impact on real activity: for example, financial markets provide liquidity, allowing a shift from current liquid, but unproductive, assets towards less liquid, but more productive, assets (Bencivenga and Smith, 1991; Levine, 1991; Bencivenga et al., 1996); or, financial markets promote the acquisition and the dissemination of information allowing for better resource and risk allocation (see, for example, Diamond, 1984; Greenwood and Jovanovic, 1990); or, financial markets permit agents to increase specialization, shifting away from specialized and less productive technologies (Cooley and Smith, 1993; Saint-Paul, 1992).

All these models cover important aspects of financial markets and their impact on real activity, providing important analytical insight on issues raised by the literature for decades. However, they all fall short of providing a comprehensive framework of the different effects of financial markets and of empirically testable relationships. This still awaits future work. Various recent empirical papers demonstrate the link between financial variables, financial sector reform and economic growth and efficiency (such as Levine and Zervos, 1996; Johnston and Pazarbasioglu, 1995), but their econometric specifications are little linked to an underlying theoretical model.

(ii) To introduce potential growth effects of financial market developments in an EG model in a simple manner, borrowing from Villanueva (1993), the following structure is proposed:[18]

$$dK/dt = s(\kappa, \dots)Y - \delta K,$$
$$\text{with } \partial s/\partial \kappa > 0 \qquad (6.1)$$

$$dT/dt = \alpha(\kappa, \dots)K/L + \lambda T,$$
$$\text{with } \alpha > 0, \ \partial\alpha/\partial\kappa > 0 \tag{6.2}$$

The saving ratio s (that is, investment ratio in a closed economy) is positively related to variable measuring the depth, liquidity, and maturity of financial markets, summarized in the parameter κ. Further variables which may influence the domestic saving rate are public saving behaviour or tax regulations. Also the change in technical progress dT/dt is not only dependent on the exogenously given rate of labour-augmenting technical change λ, but also on an efficiency variable α, which interacts multiplicatively with the capital/labour ratio. $\alpha(\kappa, \dots)$ depends on the financial market variable κ and also on other variables traditionally quoted in the literature (such as level of export orientation and share of education expenditure in the budget). λ captures other growth effects not explicitly detailed in the model.[19]

In this model, the steady-state growth rate of the economy depends positively on the level of κ

$$[(dT/dt)/Y]^* = s(\kappa, \dots)f(k^*)/k^* - \delta \tag{6.3a}$$
$$= \alpha(\kappa, \dots)k^* + \lambda + n = g^*(k^*) \tag{6.3b}$$

with k^* the steady-state capital intensity measured in efficiency units of labour.[20] The model leads to the traditional result for $\alpha = 0$. With $\alpha > 0$, however, a higher saving rate leads not only to an increase in the optimal capital/labour ratio (as in the traditional growth models), but also to a higher steady-state growth rate, which in traditional models is not influenced by the saving rate.

A further important property of the model under an optimal consumption plan (that is, $\partial c^*/\partial s = 0$) is that both the steady-state growth rate and optimal net return on capital are higher than the exogenous rates of technical progress and population growth:

$$f'(k^*) - \delta = g^*(k^*) + \alpha(\kappa, \dots)k^*$$
$$= \lambda + n + 2\alpha(\kappa, \dots)k^* \tag{6.4}$$

Under such a golden-rule condition, the optimal rate of return is higher than $\lambda + n$ when $\alpha > 0$ because of two factors: the impact of higher savings (that is, capital accumulation) on the equilibrium growth rate, and the required compensation of capital for a higher equilibrium output growth induced by the efficiency term $\alpha(\kappa, \dots)k^*$.

This difference between the old and new growth path – $2\alpha(\kappa, \dots)k^*$ – may be used to finance the transition, that is, to repay the implicit debt without burdening the transition generation. Compensating the transition generation by the conventional rate of return of an unfunded scheme only (that is, by $\lambda + n$, assuming that α was zero prior to the UF–FF shift), while using part of the growth differential for financing the transition, allows, in principle, for the construction of a Pareto-superior UF–FF transition.[21] One approach could be to pay wages (and pensions) to individuals according to the old growth path until the growth differential allowed the repayment of the implicit debt. Since in a competitive setting the marginal product of each worker increases at the same rate as his or her efficiency, $g^*(k^*) - n$, in order to capture the full growth differential, this requires the use of lump-sum taxation to ensure Pareto-indifference for the transition generation until the social security debt is repaid.

(iii)   For the repayment of the public debt, however, additional fiscal considerations are required. Additional resources resulting from higher growth can be captured by the government only in a non-distortionary manner if lump-sum taxation could be applied. In such a case, all additional resources (compared to the benchmark of no pension reform) could be used to repay the SSD in a Pareto-efficient manner. This does not apply, however, in the case of distortionary taxation, the empirically relevant case: essentially constant tax rates on an enhanced tax base allow the capturing of only part of the enhanced economic resources if an increase in tax-related distortions should be prevented. Thus, in order to maximize consumption utility (through consumption smoothing) while minimizing tax distortion (through tax smoothing) would favour a temporary widening of the reform-induced fiscal stance, and gradual repayment in the years thereafter.

4.3   The Use of Privatization Assets

European Union countries with a strong tradition of a large public sector (such as Austria, France and Italy), and even more the former centrally planned economies, have important government assets (public enterprises, land, and so on). In principle, these assets can be used to co-finance a UF–FF shift. In economic terms, government assets (GAs) are exchanged against government liabilities (SSD). Since selling those assets on a large scale on the market often proves difficult, in particular in the emerging market economies of eastern Europe, this has led to various proposals to swap the GAs for SSD. Compared with a free distribution of assets to the population via vouchers, as has been done in several east European reform countries such as the Czech Republic, Bulgaria, Poland and Russia, the net asset position of the government would remain unchanged, whereas under the first approach, the net asset position would deteriorate and would have to be compensated for via future increased taxes. While such a swap in accounting terms is easy, it poses important problems with regard to intergenerational equity, liquidity and corporate governance, and the scope of the swap is likely to be limited.

Very tentative calculations for eastern Europe suggest a potential range of some 3 to 70 per cent of social security debt which could be compensated for by government assets (Holzmann, 1994). Empirical data on Hungary and Poland indicate that an actual ratio is rather to be found in the lower range, around 5 to 10 per cent. The 1994 plan in Hungary was to transfer assets worth some HUF 400 billion to the social security fund (roughly equivalent to the level of pension expenditure, or 12 per cent of GDP, or 10 per cent of privatizable assets). The Polish privatization plan originally envisaged a transfer of 20 per cent of government assets to the social security fund(s). According to the latest plan, the assets to be transferred could amount to PLZ 50 billion (as valued by the Ministry of Privatization), or only PLZ 25 billion (as estimated by the Ministry of Finance). This compares with pension expenditure of PLZ 35.7 billion in 1994 (some 15 per cent of GDP) or an estimated SSD of around PLZ 900 billion (some 380 per cent of GDP). In consequence, only some 5 per cent (or less) of the SSD could be swapped.

These estimates are of similar magnitude to those calculated for some Latin American reform countries. To co-finance the Colombian pension reform, Schmidt-Hebbel (1995) quotes an estimate of the percentage value of privatization revenue of 10 per cent of GDP; this compares with the long-term financing requirements of 83.6 per cent of GDP (the SSD made explicit).

The scope for a GA/SSD swap in the member countries of the European Union seems even more limited. Recently, in order to comply with the Maastricht debt criteria, all EU countries started to sell government assets to reduce the debt ratio towards the 60 per cent debt limit (in per cent of GDP), leading in 1994 for the average of the EU to a negative residual in the general government debt/deficit position of some 0.4 per cent of GDP (that is, the government debt level changed less than indicated by the deficit level, a proxy for the privatization effort; see Holzmann et al. 1996).

In summary, very tentative calculations and information suggest that only a relatively small portion of current public pension obligations could be exchanged even if major parts of government assets were used to finance the transition.

5. FINANCING THE TRANSITION: THE CHILEAN EXPERIENCE

The experience of the Chilean pension reform of 1981[22] has received wide international attention, as many domestic and foreign observers hold this very reform co-responsible for the excellent economic performance since the mid-1980s (see Table 6.4). If confirmed, that experience could serve as an example of a Pareto-improving transition from an unfunded to funded pension scheme. Yet, the claimed link between the UF–FF shift, financial market developments, capital formation and saving, and economic growth has been subjected to little empirical investigation. This section reports on the pertinent findings by the author which are presented comprehensively in Holzmann (1996). The results are consistent with the hypothesis of a pension reform–financial market–economic growth link, but also highlight the role of the restrictive fiscal stance applied.

5.1 Pension Reform and Financial Market Developments

A central claim about the effects of the Chilean pension reform is its contribution to the development of the financial sector (see, for example, IMF, 1995). The general hypothesis is that the rising investment needs of the pension funds, the instruments thereby created, and the competitive set-up of the privately managed pension funds made the financial market deeper, more liquid, competitive and efficient. In turn, this very development is conjectured to have contributed to higher saving, capital accumulation and economic efficiency (that is, technical progress) and thus economic growth. In order to measure that link in a first step, various indicators of financial market development are constructed (FMIs);[23] in a second step the impact of the development of pension fund (AFPs) assets on those indicators is statistically investigated; in a third step the impact of the FMI on total factor productivity and capital stock accumulation is econometrically tested (for details, see Holzmann, 1996).

Essentially all investigated FMIs exhibit a strong upward movement due to the banking crisis of 1981–83 having been resolved (Figure 6.8). The correlation between AFP assets and FMIs, and between AFP shares in total traded shares and FMIs, is very strong with coefficients in simple regressions close to 1 and R^2 of 0.9 or above. At a monthly level, there is also a strong correlation between the turnover in asset trade (in bonds, shares, and so on) and the level of assets held by the pension funds at the end of the month (as a proxy for turnover since no such data are available), with a break around the turn of 1984/85. Before 1985, the correlation is zero or negative, except for the trade in assets with fixed return ($\rho = 0.65$); this corresponds to the period

Table 6.4 Chile: macroeconomic indicators and pension fund performance, 1970–95

			Macroeconomic indicators		
	GDP growth real (%)	Inflation CPI (December–December) (%)	Unemployment rate (October–December) (%)	Real exchange rate[1]	Private saving rate (% of GDP)
1970	2.1	34.9	5.7	48.5	8.9
1971	9.0	22.1	3.9	45.2	11.8
1972	-1.2	163.3	3.3	41.9	12.2
1973	-5.6	508.4	5.0	62.7	7.7
1974	1.0	375.9	9.5	95.0	17.6
1975	-13.3	340.7	14.9	123.8	-0.6
1976	3.2	174.3	12.7	111.4	9.0
1977	8.3	63.5	11.8	100.0	6.7
1978	7.8	30.3	14.2	119.3	7.7
1979	7.1	38.9	13.6	122.9	6.1
1980	7.7	31.2	10.4	106.5	6.5
1981	6.7	9.5	11.3	92.6	2.7
1982	-13.4	20.7	19.6	103.3	4.1
1983	-3.5	23.1	14.6	124.0	7.2
1984	6.1	23.0	13.9	129.6	4.9
1985	3.5	26.4	12.0	159.2	8.7
1986	5.6	17.4	8.8	175.1	10.7
1987	6.6	21.5	7.9	182.7	15.2
1988	7.3	12.7	6.3	194.7	17.2
1989	9.9	21.4	5.3	190.2	16.5
1990	3.3	27.3	5.7	197.4	19.4
1991	7.3	18.7	5.3	186.3	19.9

			AFP assets (% of market assets)	
1992	11.0	12.7	4.4	165.4	19.4
1993	6.3	12.2	4.5	168.7	19.2
1994	4.2	8.9	5.9	160.5	20.7
1995	8.5	8.2	4.7	156.9	20.8

Pension fund (AFP) performance

	Rate of return (real) (%)	AFP assets (% of GDP)	AFP assets (% of market assets)	
			Enterprise bonds	Shares
1981	21.3	0.9	0.4	0.0
1982	28.8	3.6	0.9	0.0
1983	21.3	6.4	8.4	0.0
1984	3.5	8.6	10.2	0.0
1985	13.4	10.6	7.7	0.0
1986	12.3	12.7	11.1	2.0
1987	5.4	14.2	27.1	3.2
1988	6.4	15.1	46.0	4.2
1989	6.9	17.7	47.5	4.8
1990	11.5	24.3	58.2	5.5
1991	29.7	30.4	60.8	8.3
1992	3.1	30.6	61.0	10.1
1993	16.2	37.3	56.7	11.4
1994	18.2	41.1	57.2	10.6
1995	-2.5	38.8	–	–

Note: [1] An increase indicates a real deprecation of the domestic currency (1977 = 100).

Sources: Central Bank of Chile, monthly bulletin, and Superintendency of AFP, statistical bulletin.

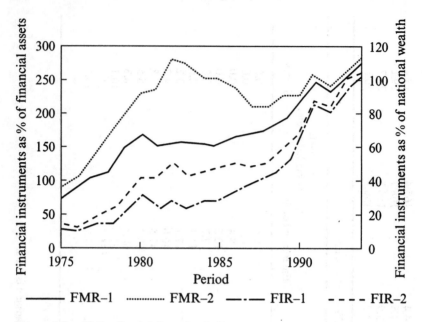

Figure 6.8   Chile: financial market indicators

when pension funds were restricted to the holding of debt instruments. For the period January 1985 to June 1995, the correlation between the monthly turnover in each asset and the stock of pension fund assets at month-end is always above 0.9. This empirical evidence is consistent with the claim that pension funds made the financial markets deeper and more liquid. Using yearly data for asset mispricing indicators (Korajczyk, 1996) and indicators of pension fund assets, the statistical analysis is consistent with the claim that the pension fund activities enhanced efficiency and risk allocation.[24] With the gradual relaxation of regulations for pension fund investments, their portfolio has also become more diversified, providing important financing instruments for the private sector. Various econometric evidence suggests that pension funds are operating efficiently and the selected portfolio, given the restrictions on asset investments which are only gradually lifted, is on the (restricted) efficiency frontier (Walker, 1991a and 1991b; Zuñiga-Maldonado, 1992). In a competitive environment, this may constitute indirect proof of the overall efficiency of the financial system. Yet all this evidence does not establish watertight proof that the establishment of pension funds has been the decisive factor for the impressive development of financial markets since the mid-1980s. The empirical evidence is only consistent with the claim.

5.2 Financial Market Developments and Economic Growth

To test econometrically the impact of FMIs on technical progress (measured via the total factor productivity (TFP), that is, the residual in the growth accounting equation) and capital accumulation (the change in capital stock, K per cent), in view of the limited number of observations (maximum 1975 to 1994) a rather simple econometric specification, with few other explanatory variables, has to be applied. The unemployment rate (UER) and its change (ΔUER) is a proxy to capture the strong cyclical effects during the initial period of investigation, respectively to measure income expectations and their change. The lagged FMI variables (with an Almon-lag-type structure) are normalized to the respective sample average of 1 in order to allow for a direct interpretation of the coefficients. The results are presented in Tables 6.5 and 6.6.

To estimate the impact of $FMIs$ on total factor productivity, this basic specification is applied, with lagged TFP and the unemployment rate to capture catch-up and cyclical effects, leading to a very satisfying statistical fit (Table 6.5). Adding the financial market indicators improves the overall fit, yielding for the lagged FMI variables coefficients which are significant at the 5 per cent level and below, while reducing the significance of the constant. The estimated parameter values prove to be robust for different specifications and time periods of estimation (not shown), and the lagged impact of financial market indicators (compared with including contemporaneous effects, which prove statistically totally insignificant) gives confidence in the causality. Taken at face value, the results would suggest strong effects of financial market developments on TFP. Using the (long-run) point estimates and assuming an equilibrium unemployment rate of 5 per cent, the exogenous technical progress would amount to some 1 per cent, to which around 1 per cent of technical progress generated by financial market developments are added, yielding a long-term annual TFP of around 2 per cent. The estimated FMI effect of around 1 per cent is likely to proxy other effects, which may be highly correlated with financial market developments, such as reductions in exchange rate restrictions and increasing openness of the economy. Given data restrictions, the separation of these effects is not currently possible.

With regard to $FMIs$ and capital formation, the econometric testing suggests that the change in capital stock follows an adjustment process, with the lagged variable entering very significantly, and this is also influenced by cyclical effects, or expectations about future income developments, measured by the unemployment rate (Table 6.6). Entering the lagged FMI variables leads to an improvement in the equation fit and to coefficients which are consistent in sign and significant at the 5 per cent level and below. Again, taking the (long-run) point estimates for the FIR/FMR variables at face value,

Table 6.5 Chile: total factor productivity and financial market developments

Endogenous variable: TFP	Constant	TFP(-1)	Unemployment rate	ΔUER(-2)	FMI(-1)	
EQ(1)	0.055	-0.125	-0.566	-0.569	—	$R^2 = 0.871$
	(4.38)	(1.66)	(4.77)	(4.42)		DW = 1.77
EQ(2)	0.025	-0.175	-0.374	-0.679	0.013	$R^2_c = 0.916$
$FMI_{-1} = \Delta FIR1$	(1.47)	(1.72)	(2.87)	(5.73)	(2.32)	DW = 1.48
EQ(3)	0.0349	-0.132	-0.462	-0.703	0.010	$R^2_c = 0.908$
$FMI_{-1} = \Delta FIR2$	(2.28)	(1.53)	(3.96)	(5.34)	(2.02)	DW = 1.75
EQ(4)	0.042	-0.260	-0.509	-0.541	0.012	$R^2_c = 0.964$
$FMI_{-1} = \Delta FMR1$	(5.54)	(3.69)	(7.67)	(7.58)	(5.01)	DW = 2.48
EQ(5)	0.055	-0.119	-0.613	-0.645	0.005	$R^2_c = 0.926$
$FMI_{-1} = \Delta FMR2$	(5.48)	(1.86)	(6.38)	(6.07)	(2.70)	DW = 2.43

Note: OLS; period of estimation: 1979–94, with lagged variables for FMI estimator starting as of 1975. Absolute *t* values in parentheses.

Table 6.6   Chile: capital formation and financial market developments

Endogenous variable: $K\%$	Constant	$K\%(-1)$	UER	$FMI(-1)$	
EQ(6)	0.030	0.79	−0.21		$R^2_c = 0.945$
	(5.10)	(9.11)	(5.14)		DW = 1.63
EQ(7)	0.026	0.526	−0.175	0.008	$R^2_c = 0.962$
$FMI_{-1} = \Delta FIR1$	(4.78)	(3.74)	(4.38)	(2.19)	DW = 1.92
EQ(8)	0.033	0.565	−0.247	0.007	$R^2_c = 0.963$
$FMI_{-1} = \Delta FIR2$	(6.33)	(4.64)	(6.38)	(2.28)	DW = 2.21
EQ(9)	0.026	0.746	−0.193	0.004	$R^2_c = 0.966$
$FMI_{-1} = \Delta FMR1$	(5.17)	(10.3)	(5.55)	(2.61)	DW = 2.00
EQ(10)	0.038	0.684	−0.295	0.005	$R^2_c = 0.969$
$FMI_{-1} = \Delta FMR2$	(6.95)	(8.88)	(6.78)	(2.85)	DW = 2.37

Note: OLS; period of estimation: 1979–94, with lagged variables for FMI estimator starting as of 1975. Absolute *t* values in parentheses.

the long-term increase in capital stock is some +5 per cent, reduced by an assumed long-term unemployment rate of 5 per cent by 1 percentage point, but increased by the enhanced financial markets by 0.5 to 1.0 percentage points, or some one eighth to one quarter of its 'natural' level. This result suggests that there may be sizeable effects of financial market developments on the formation of the capital stock which have to be added to the effects of *TFP* in their growth consequences.

Putting the low and high parameter estimates for the *FMIs* on total factor productivity and capital accumulation together with a crude estimate for labour market effects[25] into a growth-accounting equation provides a first indication about the possible overall growth effects of the pension reform (Table 6.7). Taken at face value, the result suggests that the reform may have increased the growth rate by some 1 to 3 percentage points per annum. If such an effect were to be permanent, in a very crude estimate, the result suggests that this would allow Chile to repay the social security debt made explicit of around 100 per cent of GDP in some 33 to 100 years, without burdening the transition generation, if all the additional economic resources can be captured by the government in a non-distortionary manner, and if the individuals can be compensated along the old growth path. With an actual and unchanged share of budgetary revenue in GDP of around one third, the government captures less and the repayment period increases to some 100 to 300 years. In view of the cash-flow requirements of the transition (operational deficit and redemption of recognition bonds) of some 5 per cent of

*Table 6.7   Chile: the impact of the pension reform on the economic growth
            rate (%)*

	Low estimate	High estimate
Through *TFP*[1]	0.4	1.1
Through capital formation[2]	0.5	0.6
Through labour market[3]	0.0	1.1
Total	1.0	2.9

Notes:
[1] Implied long-run parameter estimates for *FMI* variable in EQ(2) and EQ(5), Table 6.5.
[2] Implied long-run parameter estimates for capital formation variable in EQ(7) and EQ(9),
     Table 6.6, times capital elasticity of 0.35.
[3] High estimate: difference between employment and population growth of 1.7 per cent per
     annum during period 1980–94 times labour elasticity of 0.65.

Source: Own calculations based on Tables 6.5 and 6.6.

GDP, but additional budgetary revenue (at constant revenue share of one
third) of only one third of 1 per cent to 1 per cent of GDP, this would suggest
a transitory rise in the explicit fiscal debt. Yet the data suggest otherwise.

5.3   Pension Reform and Fiscal Stance

The cash-flow requirements amounting to some 5 per cent of GDP per annum
are essentially financed from budgetary resources. Figure 6.9 highlights the
contribution of fiscal performance and public saving to support the transition
from an unfunded to a funded pension scheme. The difference between
current general government revenue and expenditure in Figure 6.9 measures
public saving which became negative only during the initial four years of
transition (1982–85) before the pre-reform rate of public saving of some 5
per cent of GDP was again re-established. In view of the declining share of
current revenue as a percentage of GDP due to various tax reforms and tax
rate cuts, strengthening of the fiscal stance was achieved by programme
reforms and expenditure cuts (see Larraín, 1991; Marshall and Schmidt-
Hebbel, 1994). The new democratic government which came into office in
1989 has stabilized the expenditure level but not reversed it. In general, a
restrictive fiscal policy which pays off government debt through higher taxes
or lower expenditure and hence shifts resources from current to future generations encourages higher saving and capital formation. In addition,
international evidence suggests that private saving also reacts to the form of
fiscal retrenchment – higher taxes or lower expenditure – with the private

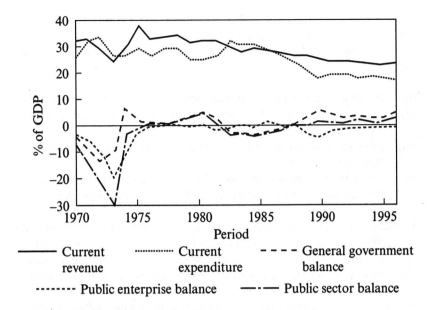

Figure 6.9   Chile: fiscal stance, 1970–95

saving rate reacting positively and significantly to a fall in general government current expenditure (Masson et al., 1995). That feature is also dominant in the Chilean budgetary policy and may thus have strengthened the rise in private saving.[26]

In summary, the Chilean experience suggests a positive and sizeable impact of pension reform on economic growth, allowing, in principle, a Pareto-improving transition, since the additional economic resources may permit the payment of the social security debt made explicit in the long run. However, the Chilean government decided to repay that debt earlier through fiscal retrenchment, thus burdening the transition generation. Yet this very tight fiscal stance may have also contributed to the outstanding economic performance, through the crowding-in of private investment, and a higher credibility of the overall economic reform programme in and outside Chile.

6.   CONCLUDING REMARKS

The transition from an unfunded to a funded pension scheme creates a formidable task for fiscal policy. The liabilities towards the current generation of retirees and workers resulting from unfunded pension provisions constitute a huge hidden public debt. Making this implicit social security debt fully explicit, thus reversing the initial redistribution towards the current generation, is for most countries quite probably beyond their political, economic and fiscal capacity. Thus, a transition requires various simultaneous steps such as:

(i)   the benefit reform of the unfunded scheme, reducing the implicit debt;
(ii)   a redesign of the basic tier remaining unfunded to minimize distortions on factor markets;
(iii)   a design of the timing and form of the debt made explicit and the fiscal flows involved; and
(iv)   a careful calculation of the compensation amount to render the switching decision by individual workers voluntary but cost-effective.

Theoretical considerations and the Chilean experience strongly suggest the feasibility and potential Pareto-efficiency of such an approach. The unfunded–fully funded shift can make an important contribution to financial market developments which, in turn, impact very positively on total productivity, capital accumulation, labour market performance, and thus economic growth. The latter can generate enhanced economic resources which allow the repayment of the debt made explicit. While a long-term increase in the economic growth rate allows, in principle, a medium-term increase in the explicit public debt to be repaid in the future out of enhanced resources, negative financial market reactions to a higher explicit fiscal debt and macroeconomic considerations may warrant a more contractionary fiscal stance from the very beginning. As suggested by the Chilean example, this requires major reforms of other public expenditure and revenue programmes.

Expectations about the potential benefits of such a reform approach, together with the inability to reform the unfunded scheme along conventional lines, have motivated many reform countries in eastern Europe to initiate reform considerations and partly already draft laws in this direction. A two-tier mandatory pension scheme, consisting of a reformed and reduced unfunded and a newly introduced funded tier, currently constitutes the reform design in those countries. Yet, as regards the fiscal requirements for such a UF–FF shift, more thoughts and efforts have to be given. However, if successful, the reform approach in the future member countries of the European Union could stimulate and invigorate the reform discussion in the Union itself.

NOTES

1. An earlier version of this paper was presented at the seminar of the Fiscal Affairs Department of the International Monetary Fund (IMF) while I was an academic scholar in the summer of 1995; revised versions under slightly different titles were presented at the

ECLAC Fiscal Seminar (Santiago de Chile, January 1996), a seminar on the future of social security by the European Commission (Brussels, June 1996), and a seminar by the Institute of Contemporary German Studies of the Johns Hopkins University (Washington, DC, October 1996). I am indebted to the participants in those seminars for constructive critiques and valuable suggestions.

2. For a survey of the recent Latin American pension reform attempts, see Queisser (1995); for a survey and assessment of the current reform discussion in eastern Europe, see Holzmann (1997a).

3. Hence this chapter falls short of an analysis of the potential risks of funded schemes (such as full or partial default, moral hazard, and so on), of the financial market requirements (including regulatory and supervisory needs), of the economic impact (such as the change in incorporate governance), or of distributional effects. However, even a cursory exposition of those issues is beyond the scope of this chapter.

   For a critical review of alternative approaches to reform of the public pension scheme against the background of recent countries' experiences, see Diamond (1996); for financial market issues of funded pension schemes, see Davis (1995).

4. For references, see the papers in *The World Bank Economic Review 1996*, vol. 10.

5. For a recent discussion and further literature on taxing funded pension schemes and budgetary policy, see Franco (1996).

6. In the steady state, with an actuarially fair pension system without financial reserves, both accrued-to-date liabilities (the gross social security debt I) and the net social wealth coincide, since the present value of further liabilities resulting from future contributions and the present value of future contributions cancel out.

7. The overall pension expenditure in most OECD countries is much higher and national estimates of the (net) social security debt arrive at values which are up to 50 per cent above the presented ones (see Franco, 1995).

8. The upper estimate of this multiple can be cross-checked under the assumption of wage growth equal to the interest rate, and a constant demographic structure. With, on average, some 10 to 20 years of retirement spell, the accrued obligation amounts to 5 to 10 times the annual expenditure. In addition, the accrued obligation with regard to the current working generations has to be taken into account. With some 30 to 40 years of average activity, the accrued obligation amounts to some 15 to 20 times the annual expenditure. Taking both upper estimates for the retired and working generation together results in accrued obligations of 30 times the annual expenditure. Of course, price indexation instead of wage indexation (or a positive interest–wage growth difference) reduces this estimate.

9. The view of partial default when downward-adjusting an unfunded pension scheme is not universally shared. Some claim that when a pension scheme is simply a public benefit programme, financed from general taxation, a downward revision in generosity through benefit cuts and reduced eligibility is standard procedure for the government which has to cope with its intertemporal budget constraint (and temporal imbalances between revenue and expenditure). This view is well supported. However, things get more complicated when individuals pay specific contributions and expect future specific benefits in exchange. Under such a setting one may claim that property rights are established (indeed, in some European countries pension rights receive such a status in the ruling of the constitutional court). Then the dividing line between property rights established through the purchase of government bonds and the payment of pension contributions becomes thin or non-existent. While in the case of bonds the partial non-repayment of principal (and interests) is generally considered a partial default, the imposition of an inflation tax or changes in the tax treatment of interest revenue may not; economically, however, they are equivalent. The same difference or similarity emerges in the case of pension benefits, say, between a direct cut in benefits and a reduction in benefit indexation. Some argue that a difference exists when the contributions are too low to buy future high benefits, and hence individuals should have rationally expected a later adjustment in benefits initially promised; thus such an adjustment constitutes no default. Yet the same argument could also be made with regard to government bonds, if the government promises a high interest rate

(because of a high risk premium) but given its budgetary stance it is not able to deliver, and hence downward adjusts its commitments (that is, it partially defaults).

10. The model has been calibrated to reflect economies with a comprehensive two-tier pension system consisting of a basic tier and an earnings-related tier. Under the baseline assumption, the life expectancy (LE) is 70 years, the basic tier amounts to 20 per cent of average wage, the accrual rate in the earnings-related tier to 1.5 per cent per annum, and the retirement age is 60. This results in an average replacement rate of some 50 per cent (net of contribution payments), a contribution rate on net wages of some 30 per cent, and an expenditure share of some 9 per cent of GDP. The baseline scenario implies an SSD of some 163 per cent of GDP, with a real interest/real growth rate differential of 3 percentage points. Reducing this gap to 2 percentage points increases the SSD by some 30 percentage points of GDP. For the motivation of the specific model approach and basic model features, see Annex A.

11. For Austrian evidence of a negative covariance between the internal rate of return of the public scheme and the market rate of interest, see Holzmann (1988b).

12. Under the steady-state conditions assumed in the model, the implicit SSD grows with the national wage bill (equal to the growth rate of GDP), while the SSD made explicit grows with the interest rate if cash-flow requirements are debt-financed. This leaves the total debt in per cent of GDP unchanged.

13. The Maastricht Treaty as the latest step in the process of European integration schedules the completion of the European internal market by introducing a common currency around the turn of the century. To be allowed to participate in the European economic and monetary union, a member state of the EU must fulfil five conditions signalling nominal economic convergence, the famous convergence criteria. Three are monetary criteria (on inflation, long-term interest rates and exchange rates) and two are fiscal criteria: a 'sustainable government financial position' deemed necessary for participation in EMU is checked by observing how public deficit and public debt, both measured in per cent of GDP, stand relative to official reference values of 3 per cent and 60 per cent. Contrary to the monetary criteria, the fiscal criteria are not only entry conditions for joining EMU, but they are also valid as fiscal restrictions once a country participates in EMU. For most EU countries, the fiscal criteria constitute the binding constraint. For a critical assessment of the Maastricht fiscal criteria, see Holzmann et al. (1996).

14. Feldstein (1996) calculates for the United States in the period since 1960 a difference of 6.7 percentage points, based on the real pre-tax return on non-financial corporate capital averaging 9.3 per cent, with the annual rate of growth of real wages and salaries (the implicit rate of return of the unfunded scheme) averaging 2.6 per cent. This estimate is upward-biased compared with a long-term government bond interest rate/economic growth rate differential. Still, his very conservative risk adjustment yields a difference of 3.8 per cent.

15. The implicit tax of an unfunded scheme which results from an interest rate/wage growth rate differential (taken as the rates of return of the unfunded and funded scheme, respectively) can be high. For a given contribution rate, comparing the benefit level of a funded and unfunded scheme under different interest rate/wage growth rate differentials provides an indication of the size of the implicit tax. For a replacement rate of 50 per cent, the required contribution rate of an unfunded scheme is some 22 per cent under standard survival probabilities, a potential working spell of 21 to 65, and a potential retirement spell of 66 to 100. With such a contribution rate, an individual could achieve a replacement rate of 108 per cent with a rate differential of 2 percentage points, and a replacement rate of 160 per cent with a rate differential of 3 percentage points. This corresponds to an implicit tax of 54 per cent and 69 per cent respectively (calculated as the replacement rate of funded minus replacement rate of unfunded scheme divided by that of the funded one).

16. At the labour market level, the type of pension scheme (UF–FF) and the perceived contribution–benefit link can determine the distribution of labour supply between the formal and informal sectors. If the latter is less productive, a pension reform which moves labour supply to the formal sector will enhance overall productivity and in an endogenous growth model can lead to a higher growth path (Corsetti, 1994).

17. See, for example, Goldsmith (1969), McKinnon (1973) and Shaw (1973).
18. The other equations of this growth model are traditional and specify the output Y via a production function with constant returns of scale to capital K and labour N (man-hours in efficiency units)

$$Y = F(K,N) = Nf(k)$$

an exogenous growth rate n of population/employed (in man-hours L)

$$dL/dt = nL$$

a definition equation between N and L via the technical change multiplier T

$$N = TL, \text{ and}$$

the capital coefficient

$$k = K/N$$

d(.)/dt is the time derivative and δ the rate of depreciation of capital.
19. Since the model features an external effect, the solution to the social planner's problem will not necessarily coincide with the competitive equilibrium in the decentralized economy. In the latter, each agent will take K/L, the economy-wide ratio of capital per head as given, thus ignoring the effect of his or her investment decision on the rate of technological progress. In consequence, in a decentralized economy individuals tend to overinvest and output to grow more rapidly, but consumption per efficiency unit is lower because a larger share of output has to be devoted to keeping K/L at its steady-state value. However, if the social planner chooses a saving rate below the one in the decentralized solution, his choice will become binding and the central and decentral outcome will coincide if an appropriate non-distortive enforcement mechanism can be found (such as auctioning of the saving/investment volume). If the social planner chooses a higher saving rate, the decentralized solution will prevail. For the following, we consider the social planner's solution, implicitly assuming that government sets the saving rate below the one derived in the decentralized economy.
20. This result is valid for both environments but the steady-state capital intensity in the competitive equilibrium k^{**} tends to exceed the planner's solution k^*.
21. In the decentralized solution the net rate of return with externalities is $f'(k^*) - \delta = \lambda + n + \alpha(\kappa, \dots)k^*$, still leaving a growth differential of $\alpha(\kappa, \dots)k^*$ for compensation of the transition generation.
22. In a nutshell, the Chilean reform consisted of a shift from a conventional unfunded and defined benefit plan to a funded defined contribution plan, in replacing public administration of the programme with private administration of competing pension funds (AFPs – asset-funded pensions), and in separating the social assistance element from the mandated saving element of retirement provisions. Government involvement remains high with regard to supervision and regulation of the new mandatory but funded scheme, the guarantee of minimum benefits, and the financing of the transition. Otherwise, the market is allowed to play its role. For a detailed survey and analysis of the Chilean pension reform in English, see Diamond and Valdés-Prieto (1993).
23. The financial market indicators constructed and presented in this chapter are the following: the FIR (financial interrelation ratio) compares the scope of financial instruments with net wealth of the economy (approximated by the capital stock); the FMR (financial intermediation ratio) compares the scope of financial instruments with the assets of the financial institutions. Two alternative measures of financial instruments are considered and thus four FMIs are calculated.
24. The mispricing indicators measure the actual performance of financial assets compared with a reference performance based on alternative model calculations. If the pension fund

activities improve the performance of the financial market, the mispricing should decrease with enhanced fund activities. The simple correlation coefficients between the mispricing and pension fund indicators prove to be the correct sign, are statistically significant at the 5 per cent error level, and range between –0.27 and –0.52.

25. The impact of pension reform on labour market performance was not econometrically investigated. Yet, since 1980, the growth rate of the labour force was 1.7 percentage points per annum above the growth rate of the working population, the value which is taken for deriving the high-growth estimate.

26. With regard to the impact of pension reform on private saving, the empirical evidence suggests a reverse causality from higher economic growth to higher saving since – contrary to the conventional view – the direct saving effect of the reform is low, initially even negative; see Holzmann (1996 and 1997b).

REFERENCES

Arrau, P. (1991), 'La reforma previsional Chilena y su financiamento durante la transition', *Coleccion Estudios Cieplan*, **32**, June, 5–44.

Arrau, P. (1992), 'El nuevo régimen previsional Chileno', *Fundación Friedrich Ebert de Colombia (Fescol, ed.): Régimenes Pensionales*, Santafé de Bogotá, Columbia.

Arrau, P. and Schmidt-Hebbel, K. (1993), 'Macroeconomic and intergenerational welfare effects of a transition from pay-as-you-go to fully funded pensions', background paper for the World Bank study on old-age security, Washington, DC (mimeo).

Auerbach, A. L. and Kotlikoff, L. (1987), *Dynamic Fiscal Policy*, Cambridge: Cambridge University Press.

Auerbach, A., Kotlikoff, L.J. and Skinner, J. (1983), 'The efficiency gains from dynamic tax reform', *International Economic Review*, **23** (3).

Bencivenga, V. and Smith, B. (1991), 'Financial intermediation and endogenous growth', *Review of Economic Studies*, **58**, 195–209.

Bencivenga, V., Smith, B. and Starr, R. (1996), 'Equity markets, transaction costs, and capital accumulation, an illustration', *The World Bank Economic Review 1996*, **10** (2), 241–65.

Boskin, M., Kotlikoff, L.J. and Shoven, J.B. (1988), 'Personal security accounts: a proposal for fundamental social security reform', in Wachter, S.M. (ed.), *Social security and private pensions*, Lexington, MA: Lexington Books, pp. 112–52.

Breyer, F. (1989), 'On the intergenerational Pareto-efficiency of pay-as-you-go financed pension systems', *Journal of Institutional and Theoretical Economics*, **145**, 643–58.

Breyer, F. and Straub, M. (1993), 'Welfare effects of unfunded pension systems when labour supply is endogenous', *Journal of Public Economics*, **50**, 77–91.

Buchanan, J. (1968), 'Social insurance in a growing economy: a proposal for a radical reform', *National Tax Journal*, **21** (4), 386–95.

Cooley, T. and Smith, B. (1993), 'Financial markets, specialisation and learning by doing', mimeo.

Corsetti, G. (1994), 'An endogenous growth model of social security and the size of the informal sector', *Revista de Analisis Economico*, **9** (1), 57–76.

Davis, E.P. (1995), *Pension Funds: Retirement-income Security, and Capital Markets – An International Perspective*, Oxford: Clarendon Press.

Diamond, D.W. (1984), 'Financial intermediation and delegated monitoring', *Review of Economic Studies*, **51** (3), 393–414.

Diamond, P. (1994), 'Isolation of pensions from political risk', *NBER Working Paper*, No. 4895, October; forthcoming in Valdés-Prieto, S. (ed.), *The Economics of Pensions: Principles, Policies, and International Experience*, Cambridge: Cambridge University Press.

Diamond, P. (1996), 'Proposals to restructure social security', *Journal of Economic Perspectives*, **10** (3), Summer, 67–88.

Diamond, P. and Valdés-Prieto, S. (1993), 'Social security reforms in Chile', Instituto de Economía de la Pontificia, Universidad Católica de Chile, documento de trabajo No. 161, October.

Feldstein, M. (1974), 'Social security, induced retirement and aggregate capital accumulation', *Journal of Political Economy*, **82** (5), 905–26.

Feldstein, M. (1996), 'The missing piece in policy analysis: social security reform', *American Economic Review, Papers and Proceedings*, **86** (2), 1–14.

Fox, L., Palmer, E. and McIsaac, D. (1996), 'Latvian pension reform', mimeo, World Bank, May.

Franco, D. (1995), 'Pension liabilities – Their use and misuse in the assessment of fiscal policies', European Commission, *Economic Papers*, No. 110, May.

Franco, D. (1996), 'The taxation of funded pension schemes and budgetary policy', European Commission, *Economic Papers*, No. 117, September.

Franco, D. and Munzi, T. (1996), 'Public pension expenditure prospects in the European Union: a survey of national projections', *European Economy – Reports and Studies*, No. 3, 'Ageing and pension expenditure prospects in the western world', European Commission, DG II, Brussels – Luxembourg, pp. 1–126.

Godoy-Arcaya, O. and Valdés-Prieto, S. (1997), 'Democracy and pensions in Chile – Experience with two systems', forthcoming in Valdés-Prieto, S. (ed.), *The Economics of Pensions: Principles, Policies and International Experience*, Cambridge: Cambridge University Press.

Goldsmith, R. (1969), *Financial Structure and Development*, New Haven, CT: Yale University Press.

Greenwood, J. and Jovanovic, B. (1990), 'Financial development, growth and the distribution of income', *Journal of Political Economy*, **98** (5), 1076–107.

Group of Ten (1995), 'Saving, investment and real interest rate', mimeo, October.

Heller, P., Hemming, R. and Kohnert, P. (1987), 'Ageing and social expenditure in the major industrial countries, 1980–2025', *IMF Occasional Papers*, No. 72.

Holzmann, R. (1988a), *Reforming public pensions*, OECD, Paris.

Holzmann, R. (ed.) (1988b), 'Ökonomische Analyse der Sozialversicherung', *Schriftenreihe des Ludwig Boltzmann Instituts für ökonomische Analysen*, Vol. 3, Vienna: Manz.

Holzmann, R. (1994), 'Funded and private pensions for eastern European countries in transition', *Revista de Analisis Economico*, **9** (1), 169–210.

Holzmann, R. (1996), 'Pension reform, financial market development and economic growth – Preliminary evidence for Chile?', *IMF Working Paper*, WP/96/90, August.

Holzmann, R. (1997a), 'Pension reform in central and eastern Europe: necessity, approaches and open questions', Ludwig Boltzmann Institute for Economic Analysis, Research Paper No. 9701, January.

Holzmann, R. (1997b), 'Pension reform and national saving: the Chilean experience', in IRELA (ed.), *Domestic Savings: The Key to Sustained Development in Latin America*, Madrid, forthcoming.

Holzmann, R., Hervé, Y. and Demmel, R. (1996), 'The Maastricht fiscal criteria: required but ineffective?', *Empirica*, **23** (1), 25–58.

Homburg, S. (1990), 'The efficiency of unfunded pension schemes', *Journal of Institutional and Theoretical Economics*, **146**, 640–47.

IMF (1995), *World Economic Outlook*, Washington, DC, May.

ISSA (1996), 'Developments and trends in social security, 1993–1995', *International Social Security Review*, **49** (2).

Johnston, R. B. and Pazarbasioglu, C. (1995), 'Linkages between financial variables, financial sector reform and economic growth and efficiency', *IMF Working Paper*, WP/95/103, October.

Kenc, T. and Perraudin, W. (1996), 'Pension systems in Europe: a general equilibrium study', Institute for Financial Research, *Working Paper*, IFR18, March.

Keyfitz, N. (1977), *Applied Mathematical Demography*, 2nd edn, New York: Springer.

Korajczyk, R. (1996), 'Measuring integration of developed and emerging stock markets', Northwestern University, *The World Bank Economic Review 1996*, **10** (2), 267–89.

Kotlikoff, L.J. (1995), 'Privatisation of social security: how it works and why it matters', NBER, mimeo.

Larraín, F. (1991), 'Public sector behaviour in a highly indebted country – The contrasting Chilean experience', in Larraín, F. and Selowsky, M. (eds), *The Public Sector and the Latin American Crisis*, San Francisco: ICS Press, pp. 89–136.

Levine, R. (1991), 'Stock markets, growth, and tax policy", *Journal of Finance*, **64** (4), 1445–65.

Levine, R. and Zervos, S. (1996), 'Policy, stock market development and long-run growth – Part I', *The World Bank Economic Review*, **10** (2), 323–39.

Marshall, J. and Schmidt-Hebbel, K. (1994), 'Chile: fiscal adjustment and successful performance', in Easterly, W., Rodriguez, C.-A. and Schmidt-Hebbel, K. (eds), *Public Sector Deficits and Macroeconomic Performance*, Oxford: Oxford University Press for the World Bank, pp. 167–224.

Masson, R.R., Bayoumi, T. and Samiei, H. (1995), 'International evidence on the determinants of private saving', *IMF Working Paper*, WP/95/51, May.

McKinnon, R.I. (1973), *Money and Capital in Economic Development*, Washington, DC: Brookings Institution.

OECD (1995), *Economic Outlook*, 57, Paris, May.

OECD (1996a), *Economic Outlook*, 59, Paris, May.

OECD (1996b), *Future Global Capital Shortages: Real Threat or Pure Fiction?*, Paris.

Perraudin, W. and Pujol, T. (1995), 'Framework for the analysis of pension and unemployment benefit reform in Poland', *IMF Staff Papers*, **41** (4), 643–74.

Piñera, J. (1991), *El Cascabel al Gato*, Santiago de Chile: Ziag-Zag.

Piñera, J. and Weinstein, A. (1996), *Una propuesta de reforma del sistema de pensiones en España*, Madrid: Circulo de Empresarios.

Queisser, M. (1995), 'Chile and beyond: the second-generation pension reforms in Latin America', *International Social Security Review*, **48** (3–4), 41–58.

Raffelhüschen, B. (1993), 'Funding social security through Pareto-optimal conversion policies', *Journal of Economics*, Supplement 7, pp. 105–31.

Saint-Paul, G. (1992), 'Technological choice, finance markets and economic development', *European Economic Review*, **36**, pp. 763–81.

Schmidt-Hebbel, K. (1993), 'Pension reform transitions from State pay-as-you-go to privately managed fully funded Systems', mimeo, World Bank.

Schmidt-Hebbel, K. (1995), 'Colombia's pension reform – Fiscal and macroeconomic implications', *World Bank Discussion Paper*, 314, Washington, DC.

Shaw, E.S. (1973), *Financial Deepening in Economic Development*, New York: Oxford University Press.

Valdés-Prieto, S. (ed.) (1997), *The Economics of Pensions: Principles, Policies and International Experience*, Cambridge: Cambridge University Press.

Van den Noord, P. and Herd, R. (1994), 'Estimating pension liabilities – A methodological framework', *OECD Economic Studies*, 23, 131–66.

Villanueva, D. (1993), 'Openness, human development, and fiscal policies: effects on economic growth and speed of adjustment', *IMF Working Paper*, WP/93/59, July.

Walker, E. (1991a), *Desempeño financiero de las carteras accionarias de los fondos de pensiones – ¿Es desventajoso ser grande?*, Instituto de Economía de la Pontificia, Universidad Católica de Chile, documento de trabajo No. 136.

Walker, E. (1991b), *Desempeño financiero de las carteras de renta fija de los fondos de pensiones - ¿Es desventajoso ser grande?*, Instituto de Economía de la Pontificia, Universidad Católica de Chile, documento de trabajo No. 137.

World Bank (1994), *Averting the Old Age Crisis: Policies to Protect the Old and Promote Growth*, New York: Oxford University Press.

Zuñiga-Maldonado, F. (1992), *Desempeño de los fondos de pensiones: impacto de las restricciones legales*, Instituto de Economía de la Pontificia, Universidad Católica de Chile, tesis de grado No. 97.

ANNEX A   THE APPLIED SIMULATION MODEL

In order to investigate the impact and effects of pension reform on the economy, OLG models *à la* Auerbach and Kotlikoff have been established as a main instrument, and are widely used (for example, Arrau, 1991; Arrau and Schmidt-Hebbel, 1993; Schmidt-Hebbel, 1993 and 1995; Perraudin and Pujol, 1995; Kenc and Perraudin, 1996). These OLG models provide important insights into economic intertemporal interactions, but also have severe limitations. Primarily, in their current structure they allow only for one control variable – consumption. This excludes the investigation of other decision processes, such as switching between funded and unfunded schemes. Second, the models are based on a deterministic lifetime (say, until age 75). Non-deterministic lifetimes and hence the use of survival probabilities are important to gauge the full effects of different indexation procedures or the actuarial effects on switching decisions. Third, the current OLG models do not allow one to investigate the effects of ageing on the SSD and the transition costs. Last, but not least, the model type is a very cumbersome and time-consuming instrument to investigate different options of pension reform.

For these reasons, a somewhat different model type is applied, which may be described as an overlapping cohort model in an open economy (that is, we assume a given interest rate, wage profile, and so on). This spreadsheet-based model views the period –50 to +120, with cohorts aged 21 to 100. It consists of a demographic module (using synthetic survival probabilities – see Keyfitz, 1977), a labour market module (allowing for formal and informal activities), a simple output market module (allowing the calculation of GDP), a pension module (covering both funded and unfunded pensions), and a fiscal module. It is highly parametrized and allows for the investigation of a wide range of assumptions, both economic and pension related. Most important, it allows for the endogenous and expenditure minimising selection of the switching age as a result of a cohort decision process.

The model allows the analysis of a wide range of reform options and their fiscal implications. The drawback of spreadsheet-based model implementation is the long calculation time for each simulation.

ANNEX B   INDIVIDUAL SWITCHING DECISION AND COMPENSATORY AMOUNT

To derive the compensatory amount which is required to initiate a switch from unfunded to funded earnings-related pensions, a simple, perfect-foresight economy is assumed. The result can also be derived under rational expectations and risk-neutrality. For the decision to switch from an unfunded to a funded system, it is assumed that at the decision date T (end of period), each (identical) individual in the age cohort of age A compares the present value of expected lifetime resources LTR at retirement age RA under the unfunded and funded schemes:

$$LTRU(A)_{RA} <> LTRF(A)_{RA} \qquad (6A.1)$$

If the present value of lifetime resources under the funded scheme exceeds that of the unfunded, a switch takes place. The steering variable for the government is the compensatory amount $CP(A)_{RA}$ paid at retirement.

The lifetime resources under the unfunded scheme consist of the gross wage compensation minus the contributions to the basic and earnings-related system while active, and the basic and earnings-related benefits while retired. Other forms of taxation are ignored.

$$
\begin{aligned}
LTRU(A)_{RA} = & \left[\sum_{a=21}^{A} w_a(1 - c_a^{ub} - c_a^{ue})(1+r)^{A-a} \right] S(A,RA)(1+r)^{RA-A} \\
& + \sum_{a=A+1}^{RA} w_a(1 - c_a^{ub} - c_a^{ue})S(A,a)(1+r)^{RA-a} \qquad (6A.2) \\
& + \sum_{a=RA+1}^{100} (b_a^{ub} + b_a^{ue})S(A,a)(1+r)^{RA-a}
\end{aligned}
$$

$$
\begin{aligned}
LTRF(A)_{RA} = & \left[\sum_{a=21}^{A} w_a(1 - c_a^{ub} - c_a^{ue})(1+r)^{A-a} \right] S(A,RA)(1+r)^{RA-A} \\
& + CP(A)_{RA} + \sum_{a=A+1}^{RA} w_a(1 - c_a^{ub} - c_a^{fe})S(A,a)(1+r)^{RA-a} \qquad (6A.3) \\
& + \sum_{a=RA+1}^{100} (b_a^{ub} + b_a^{fe})S(A,a)(1+r)^{RA-a}
\end{aligned}
$$

where w the gross wage/contribution base, c^i the contribution rates for the unfunded basic (*ub*), unfunded earnings-related (*ue*), and funded earnings-related (*fe*) schemes, respectively, r the interest rate (for simplicity held constant), $S(A, a)$ the survival probability from age A to age a; and b^i the corresponding benefits under the different schemes. The maximum age is set at 100, and wages and benefits are assumed to be paid at the end of the period. For ease of notation, the retirement age, *RA*, is the last year of activity.

Since the net wage until the decision age *A* is the same under both options – the first term in equations (6A.2) and (6A.3) – it cancels out in both equations; the same is true for basic contribution and benefit above the decision age *A*. Consequently, the switching decision problem can be reduced to

$$\sum_{a=RA+1}^{100} b_a^{ue} S(A,a)(1+r)^{RA-a} - \sum_{a=A+1}^{RA} w_a c_a^{ue} S(A,a)(1+r)^{RA-a}$$
$$< CP(A)_{RA} + \sum_{a=RA+1}^{100} b_a^{fe} S(A,a)(1+r)^{RA-a} - \sum_{a=A+1}^{RA} w_a c_a^{fe} S(A,a)(1+r)^{RA-a} \tag{6A.4}$$

For equal contribution rates under the unfunded and funded schemes, the terms for the contribution payment cancel out and equation (6A.4) can be rewritten as

$$CP(A)RA > \sum_{a=RA+1}^{100} (b_a^{ue} - b_a^{fe}) S(A,a)(1+r)^{RA-a} \tag{6A.5}$$

where b_a^{ue} is the unfunded benefit under full contribution record (depending on the internal rate of return of an unfunded scheme), and b_a^{fe} is the funded benefit under the reduced contribution record since switching age (depending on the interest rate r).

From equation (6A.5) the lowering impact of a higher interest rate on the compensatory amount can be immediately deducted. First, and obviously, it increases the discount factor. Second, and more important, while a higher interest rate leaves the unfunded benefit b_a^{ue} unchanged, it increases unambiguously the value of the funded benefit b_a^{fe} and hence the difference between both. Despite a shorter contribution record to the funded scheme, for a high enough interest rate, the difference will become negative. For a given interest rate, the change in sign will increase with the length of the contribution record, that is, the lower the switching age. Hence, if the rate of return for the funded scheme is well above that of the unfunded one, for a large section of the younger age cohort the compensatory amount can be zero while initiating a switch.

7. Retirement income financing reform – a general issues paper

Gerassimos Thomas

1. INTRODUCTION

Demographic and public finance considerations have triggered a series of reforms in social security programmes in most EU member states over the last ten years. With regard to pay-as-you-go pension schemes, reforms have mostly focused on the reduction of benefits and on an effort to make schemes more actuarially fair. This has resulted in increases in effective retirement age and reductions in replacement ratios. Contribution rates have also been increased.

In several countries, however, the adequacy of these reforms, in terms of relaxing the pressure on public finances, is proving inadequate and it is therefore argued that further reforms will be necessary in order to ensure the sustainability of the public pension schemes. As future benefits would inevitably be negatively affected, reforms are likely to be accompanied by measures that facilitate the development of supplementary funded pension schemes in order for employees to be able to maintain their expected level of retirement income. In a small group of European countries (Denmark, Ireland, the Netherlands and the United Kingdom), supplementary funded pension schemes are already well developed and account for a large share of retirement income financing, but in the majority of member states supplementary schemes play either a very marginal role or are operating on a pay-as-you-go basis.

This paper aims to discuss the major challenges and reform options faced by EU governments, as well as the key economic issues that must be taken into account in the debate over further retirement income financing reforms.

2. CURRENT INSTITUTIONAL SET-UP

Pension systems in the EU member states were set up at different points in time and their development in terms of population coverage and benefit structure have proceeded at different speeds. Overall, most public EU pension systems have now stopped their expansion but the maturity of their liabilities varies considerably from country to country.

Overall, workers rely for income provision in old age on a number of sources:[1]

First pillar	Flat-rate, social security pensions (pay-as-you-go), earnings-related, defined benefit (pay-as-you-go/funded)
Second pillar	Supplementary pension schemes, defined benefit or defined contribution (pay-as-you-go/funded)
Third pillar	Individual precautionary savings, life-insurance-based savings plans, residential property ownership, family support, and so on.

Public pay-as-you-go schemes (mainly first-pillar) are financed through contributions by current employees (and employers) and through budget transfers. Pension benefits are calculated on the basis of a formula fixed in advance and are usually dependent on years of service and average/final salary. Pension income after retirement is usually indexed to inflation or to current wages. The link between contributions made during working life and benefits received after retirement varies substantially from system to system. Where the link is weak, contribution rates are likely to be perceived as a labour tax and may distort resource allocation.

Public pay-as-you-go schemes provide for forced retirement saving, redistribution of income from high to low lifetime earners and allow for intergenerational risk-sharing. The underlying assumption is that public pay-as-you-go schemes are superior in providing insurance against earning shocks, longevity and inflation risk. On the other hand, as liabilities are backed up by the power of governments to tax, public pay-as-you-go schemes are vulnerable to political risk, as governments may fail to honour their promises in full or raise contributions due to, for example, adverse developments in demography and public finances.

Funded schemes, on the other hand (in their majority voluntary, supplementary second-pillar schemes), collect and invest employees' contributions on a pooled basis for eventual payment in the form of annuities or lump sums. Defined contribution schemes are funded through regular employee contributions and provide benefits dependent solely on the return on assets invested. Consequently, pension income is subject to inflation and investment risk (and return). Defined contribution schemes cannot provide insurance against earnings loss, although it is possible that investment returns might prove, in practice, superior to earnings growth (see Section 4.3). In defined benefit schemes, on the other hand, benefits are covered by the sponsor (company or occupational scheme) which takes over inflation and investment risk. The employee remains exposed to the bankruptcy (and fraud) risk.

Defined contribution schemes cannot provide intergenerational risk-sharing as it is impossible to write contracts with unborn future generations. Defined benefit schemes, on the other hand, allow for some income redistribution among the members of the scheme.

Funded schemes provide a closer link than pay-as-you-go schemes between contributions and future benefits and allow employees to distinguish better between contributions levied for pension provision and general taxation levied for other welfare benefits.

A major difference between defined contribution and defined benefit schemes is their portability in case of change of employment. Defined contribution schemes are usually portable as they are outside the structure of the employer's organization, while defined benefit schemes are usually non-portable as they are fully dependent on the employer. The degree of portability varies according to vesting rules.[2] Public pay-as-you-go schemes, on the other hand,

Table 7.1   The importance of second-pillar schemes

	Private sector employment coverage (early 1990s) (%)[1]	Pension fund assets as % of GDP (1993)	Supplementary pensions as % of total pensions (1993)
Belgium	31	3.4	8
Denmark	80	20.1	18
Germany	46	5.8	11
Spain	15	2.2	3
France[2]	Under 10	3.4	21
Ireland	40	40.1	18
Italy	5	1.2	2
Netherlands	85	88.5	32
Portugal	15	—	—
United Kingdom	75	79.4	28

Notes:
[1]   Voluntary defined benefit schemes except for Denmark, where the second pillar is compulsory and defined contribution, and the UK, where 50 per cent refers to company/occupational defined benefit schemes and 25 per cent to personal defined contribution schemes.
[2]   An additional 80 per cent of private sector employees are covered by quasi-mandatory, pay-as-you-go schemes.

Sources: Davis (1995), EFRP and European Commission.

are fully portable within countries. Cross-border portability of pension rights exists only in limited cases on the basis of bilateral agreements but is not ensured at EU level.

Table 7.1 shows the coverage of private sector employees by supplementary funded schemes (column 1) and their relative importance as a source of retirement income for the total population (column 3). It is evident from these data that the first-pillar, public pay-as-you-go pension schemes remain the dominant source of retirement income provision in the majority of EU member states.

3.   PUBLIC PENSION EXPENDITURE PROSPECTS IN THE EU

The demographic structure of European countries is changing considerably. The old-age dependency ratio (that is, the ratio of the elderly to working-age population) is increasing in most countries and reaching historically unprecedented levels. Although the long-term effects of the ageing process on public budgets are rather uncertain and depend on the way the economy and society will adapt to the process, a significant pressure for higher public expenditure is very likely to occur in the coming decades. Public pension schemes will bear much of the pressure since their expenditure is highly dependent on the age structure of the population.

In a recent paper, Franco and Munzi (1996) surveyed national projections of public pension expenditure for EU 15 for the period 1995–2030. Some countries' projections are expressed in terms of public pension expenditure to GDP (Figure 7.1) and others in terms of equilibrium contribution rates, that is, the rate required to finance all current pension expenditure from a uniform contribution levied on current labour income (Figure 7.2a and 7.2b). Projections are based on unchanged policy scenarios but take into account the major reforms that have been introduced in member states since the mid-1980s. For most countries, two scenarios (best/worst case) have been considered.

National projections are not homogeneous in the coverage of pension expenditure. Comparable estimates of the impact of pension expenditure on general government accounts have been produced on the basis of national expenditure trends and 1995 ratios of total public pension expenditure to GDP. Figures 7.3 and 7.4 present the unweighted and the weighted average[3] of the change in the ratio of pension expenditure to GDP in the 11 member states which produced projections up to 2030.

The main issues illustrated by the survey results are the following:

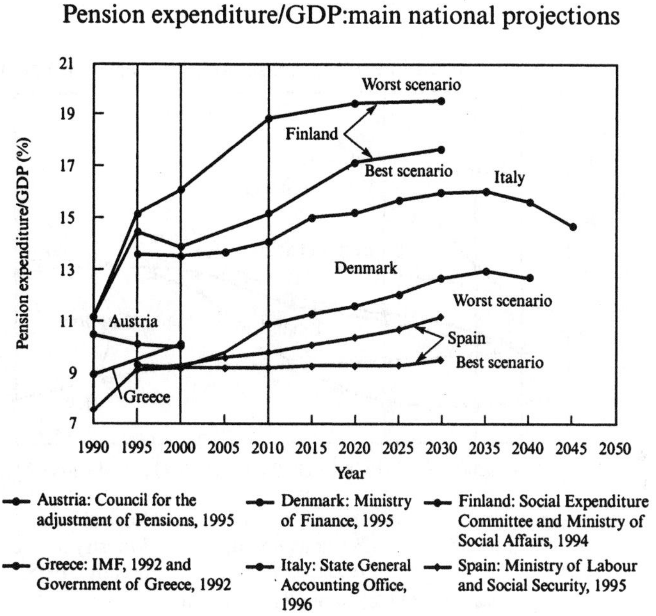

Pension expenditure/GDP:main national projections

Figure 7.1   Public pension expenditure as percentage of GDP

(i)   Over the period 1995–2000, expenditure increases stemming from public pension systems, although non-negligible, are expected to be rather limited in most countries. The ratio of pension expenditure to GDP in EU 15 is expected to increase on average by 0.1 percentage points (under favourable economic scenarios) and up to 0.4 percentage points (under unfavourable scenarios).[4]

(ii)   Over the period 2000–2010, the outlook for the pension systems becomes worse. The expenditure to GDP ratio is expected to increase in most countries in the case of favourable economic assumptions. Over the period 2000–2010, the unweighted average of pension expenditure to GDP ratios in the 13 countries for which projections up to 2010 are available will increase by 0.7 percentage points per year (under favourable assumptions) and up to 1 percentage point (under unfavourable assumptions).

(iii)   After 2010, when the baby-boom generation retires, the situation of European pension systems deteriorates more sharply. The change in the pension expenditure trend is quite radical for the countries where the ageing process is relatively slow (particularly in Ireland). Over the period 2010–30, the unweighted average of pension expenditure to GDP ratios in the 11 countries for which projections up to 2030 are available

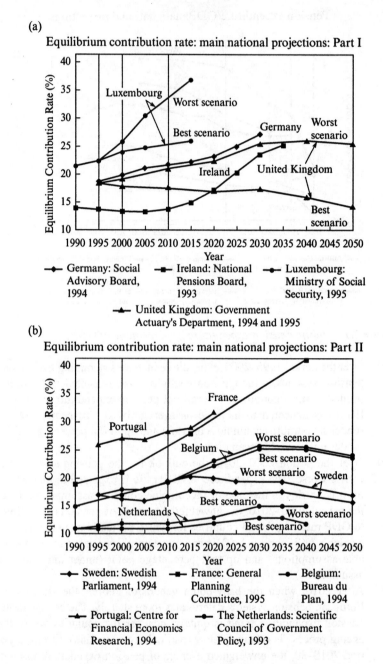

Figure 7.2   Public pension schemes' equilibrium contribution rates

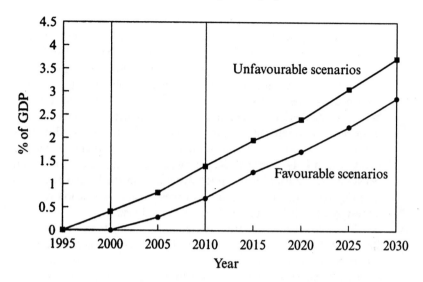

Figure 7.3   Estimates of public pension expenditure growth in the EU:
unweighted average of expenditure growth in 11 member states

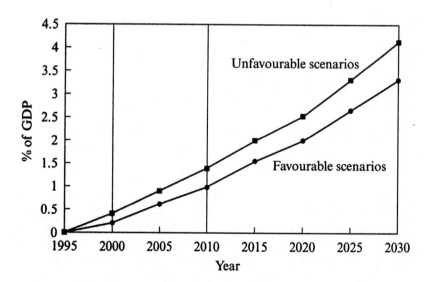

Figure 7.4   Estimates of public pension expenditure growth in the EU:
weighted average of expenditure growth in 11 member states

will increase by 2.2 percentage points (under favourable assumptions) and up to 2.6 percentage points (under unfavourable assumptions). In several countries expenditure pressures will peak in the period 2030–40.

(iv)   Over the whole period 1995–2030, expenditure pressures will be relatively strong in several countries which have not yet substantially reformed their pension systems (Belgium, Denmark, Ireland, Luxembourg, the Netherlands), and also in some countries that have already introduced large reforms (Finland, France, Germany). Expenditure increases are expected to be fairly limited (under favourable economic scenarios) in Italy, Portugal, Spain, Sweden and (in the case in which pensions are adjusted just to price dynamics) in the United Kingdom (see Figures 7.3 and 7.4). In most of these countries pension reforms largely contributed to curtailing expenditure dynamics.

(v)   By 2030, in several countries (Belgium, Finland, France, Germany, Italy and the Netherlands) the ratio of pension expenditure to GDP might be in the range of 15 to 20 per cent. Luxembourg (available projections up to 2015) is also likely to belong to this group. Expenditure would be lower in Denmark, Spain, Sweden (in the 10 to 15 per cent range), and in Ireland and the United Kingdom (below 10 per cent). Portugal (available projections up to 2020) is also likely to belong to this latter group.

4. THE CASE FOR FURTHER REFORM

The above survey results demonstrate that, despite the reforms introduced over the last decade, the current institutional set-up will lead in several countries to an increase of public pension expenditure in the future.[5] Most governments are therefore confronted with the challenge of:

(i)   ensuring the sustainability of the current public pay-as-you-go schemes;
(ii)   providing a framework that can ensure a level of retirement income that is acceptable to the labour force.

A large part of the debate on the sustainability of public schemes is currently focused on the financing mechanism of such schemes. Pensions in pay-as-you-go schemes depend on the ratio of contributing workers to pensioners (dependency ratio); in funded schemes pensions depend on the number of years of retirement relative to working age (passivity ratio). The first imply dependency of pensioners on the willingness of current employees to finance pensions through social security contributions; the second imply dependency on accumulated capital stock which is divested after retirement in order to finance individual pensions. The demographic risk increases the uncertainty for current employees (future pensioners) in the first case. Such considerations often lead to proposals to introduce radical (systemic) reforms in the public pension schemes and change their financing mechanism from pay-as-you-go to funding. Section 4.1 discusses why such a radical reform is an unrealistic option in the current public finance environment.

On the other hand, the sustainability of public pay-as-you-go schemes could be ensured through a range of piecemeal reforms like, for example, reduction in benefits, increase in contribution rates, and so on. In most countries pension policies have changed substantially over the last few years. The extension of coverage and improvement of benefits have been put on hold, although in a few countries past extensions and improvements are still affecting expenditure growth. Most countries, however, have reached a stage where future increases in the pension expenditure to GDP ratio will be at the same level or below demographic trends (the exceptions being, in the long run, France, Ireland and Luxembourg).[6] Section 4.2 discusses options for further reforms that could offset the negative impact of demographic trends.

Reforms of the public pay-as-you-go schemes will, in several countries, lead to a substantial reduction in the pension benefits provided by these schemes in the future. Ensuring adequate retirement income and maintenance of the standard of living after retirement will increasingly fall on fully funded supplementary pension schemes. Such a development will change the distribution of responsibilities and risks between government, employers and employees for retirement income provision and will create pension systems that offer a more diversified 'portfolio' of retirement income sources to the labour force (that is, public pay-as-you-go and private funded schemes). Section 4.3 discusses the advantages and risks associated with an increased reliance on supplementary funded schemes.

4.1 A Shift from Pay-as-you-go to Funding for Public Pension Systems – an Unrealistic Option

A radical (systemic) reform of the public social security scheme, with a shift from pay-as-you-go to funding, would involve significant transition costs as a government's pension liabilities would change from implicit to explicit at the time of the switch. The transition would create both stock and flow problems for the government.[7] The stock problem is related to the accrued-to-date liabilities which equal the present value of future pension liabilities that have been already accrued by the workforce, that is, it does not include future contributions or the accrual of new rights.[8]

Table 7.2 illustrates the stock problem that could be created by such a shift on the basis of estimates produced by Van den Noord and Herd (1993)[9] as a

Table 7.2   Net pension liabilities

	Accrued pension liabilities (% of 1990 GDP)	General government debt 1994 (% of GDP)
Germany	157	50.4
France	216	48.3
Italy	242	125.6
United Kingdom	139	50.3

Sources: OECD (1995); data for UK updated by Van den Noord and Herd (1994).

percentage of 1990 GDP. Irrespective of the accuracy of the absolute figures, the main message remains that the hidden public debt is extremely important and in most cases exceeds by far the explicit financial debt existing in these countries.[10]

The fiscal implications of a shift from pay-as-you-go to funding would depend on the way the transition is structured and on its timing.

In a gradual shift, only new entrants to the labour market would participate in the funded schemes. In terms of cash flow, expenditure on current and future pensioners would continue until the death of the last member of the current labour force. Similarly, contributions to pay-as-you-go schemes by current employees would also continue but would decrease over time. In terms of stock, only liabilities of current pensioners would become explicit at once, while the rest would become explicit gradually as current employees reach retirement.

In the case of a sudden shift, all members of the pension scheme and their liabilities would be shifted to the funded scheme at once. In this case all liabilities of the current scheme would become explicit, that is, the stock of government debt would increase at once. In terms of cash flow, expenditure would continue but no contributions would be coming in.

In order to estimate fully the effects of such a shift, it is important to examine how the deficit would be financed. If it is financed in full by an increase in government borrowing, the burden of the transition would be distributed over all future generations. If it is only partly financed through an increase in government borrowing and partly through an increase in taxation, the burden of the fiscal consolidation would fall on the current generation which would pay twice, while future generations would benefit.

Another issue to be considered in that respect is the reaction of financial markets. Holzmann (1996) argues that a widening of the budget deficit and an increase of debt which results purely from a redistribution of implicit and explicit liabilities should in theory have no effect on interest rates. Since total debt remains unchanged, the issue is whether financial markets price the risk premium of government securities on the basis of total or on the basis of explicit financial debt. In case financial markets perceive that governments will first default on their pension commitments before defaulting on their financial obligations, making the implicit debt explicit will increase the risk premium with negative impacts for the budget and the economy. If, on the other hand, financial markets perceive that governments will never default on their pension commitments, the implications are less clear. In principle, if financial markets have priced a no default and a no policy change scenario, the risk premium should remain unchanged. What is more likely, however, is that financial markets have taken into account the possibility of reform (at least *vis-à-vis* current employees/future pensioners). In this case making the implicit debt explicit will increase the risk premium as the set of policy options available to the government to repay its pension liabilities is reduced and the amount of financial debt is increased.

Finally, in order to estimate fully the effects of a shift to funding, it is important to examine the control and regulatory framework that the government would develop for the funded schemes.

With regard to control, pension funds should develop outside the government sector and pension fund assets should be excluded from overall fiscal targets. Given that in most cases policy-makers make non-pension tax and expenditure decisions on the basis of overall fiscal deficit, an inclusion of pension fund reserves in the fiscal deficit calculations could have distributional consequences in the long term by financing an expansion of government activities.

With regard to the regulatory framework, pension funds should not be subject to investment restrictions except for prudential reasons. In case investment restrictions are so strict that they effectively bind pension funds to invest their assets in domestic government securities,[11] pension funds would become vulnerable to demographic developments in a way that would greatly resemble that of pay-as-you-go schemes. In the future, as an increasing number of covered employees reach retirement, that is, as pension funds mature, government securities would have to be liquidated to pay for their pensions. The cost of re-financing the government debt will increase at that point, that is, a tax on future generations. Moreover, such a policy would deprive pension funds from achieving superior financial returns through investments in other asset classes and international diversification, eliminating thereby one of the major advantages of the reform. Such restrictions would, in any case, be increasingly ineffective after EMU, especially for countries participating in the euro.

Overall, the increase in financial liabilities for the public sector resulting from making the implicit pension liabilities explicit makes this shift unattractive for most governments from the fiscal point of view. A sudden shift poses problems as it would increase the (explicit) debt/GDP ratio, while a gradual transition would create constant pressure on primary balances throughout the transition period. Both would be problematic in the current fiscal environment of EU member states.

4.2 Ensuring Sustainability of the Public Pay-as-you-go Schemes

Ensuring the sustainability of current public pay-as-you-go schemes would require the implementation of further piecemeal reforms. In theory, options available include raising the contribution rates, increasing budgetary transfers, reducing benefits or a combination of these.

Increasing contribution rates to a level that would ensure equilibrium appears an unattractive solution as they are already high in most member states, particularly after the last round of reforms. Moreover, further increases in contribution would pose equity and efficiency questions. In terms of equity, contribution rates have reached such high levels that they risk undermining the overall progressivity of the tax system. Problems of intergenerational equity might also arise. In terms of efficiency, on the other hand, an increase in contribution rates would increase labour costs with negative effects on employment of, in particular, low-wage employees with relatively elastic labour supplies.

An increase in budgetary transfers does not appear a feasible option either, as most EU member states are in the process of fiscal consolidation and preparing for the third stage of EMU.

A reduction of benefits seems therefore to be the main option to be exploited. It could take the form of further reductions in average replacement rates, an extension of retirement ages or a modification of indexation arrangements. Reductions applied to accrued benefits imply in effect a partial default of the government on its obligations, a phenomenon that has already occurred during recent pension reforms in EU member states. Forward-looking reductions, however, could either be justified on other than fiscal grounds (for example, longer life expectancy for retirement age increases) or could be justified as part of an implicit 'new' contract. It is, therefore, important to examine separately the treatment of current pensioners and that of current contributors (and future pensioners). In reality, due to the political resistance of current pensioners, most of the reforms would have to be forward-looking.[12]

In a recent paper Chand and Jaeger (1996) examined the implications of different benefit reduction reforms on the pay-as-you-go schemes of the major industrialized countries. Methodologically reforms are evaluated according to their impact on contribution rates. The yardstick is a 'contribution gap' defined as the difference between an estimated sustainable contribution rate for the period 1995–2050 and the current contribution rate (including budgetary transfers) which is assumed to continue to apply in case of no policy change.

For most major industrialized countries examined, the 'contribution gap' is substantial and has to be eliminated through pension system reform (Table 7.3). Moreover, the gap (and consequently the reform task) increases the longer reforms are delayed.

Although the demographic and macroeconomic assumptions, as well as the methodology for calculation of pension liabilities (and consequently of contribution rates), differ from the ones used in the EU 15 national survey mentioned above, the results of this study illustrate quite clearly the order of magnitude of the problem and the expected effectiveness of various reform options.

Columns (2) and (3) of Table 7.4 illustrate the effects of a 5 percentage point reduction in the replacement rates for new pensioners only or for all pensioners respectively. Replacement ratios can be reduced by lowering the accrual factors or by increasing the number of years of income used for determining the average income level upon which the accrual factors would apply, or by a combination of both of the above.

Columns (4) and (5) illustrate the effects of a modification in the index provisions,[13] while columns (6) and (7) illustrate the effects of an extension in retirement age. In the first case, already announced retirement age increases are being front loaded; in the second, a unified retirement age of 67 years is applied.

Overall, the above estimates demonstrate that the sustainability of the public pay-as-you-go schemes can be ensured through a package of piecemeal reforms. The actual package of the reforms would have to differ from country to country and would depend on the structure of the pension system and the reforms already introduced in the recent past.

4.3 The Growth of Supplementary Funded Schemes – Advantages and Risks

In addition to ensuring the sustainability of the public pension schemes, governments are under increasing political pressure to ensure that current employees and future pensioners would be in a position to maintain post-retirement income at a level that will enable them to avoid a drop in their standard of living.

The development of supplementary pension schemes that operate on a fully funded basis implies, in reality, a partial shift of responsibility for retirement income provision from the government towards employees and employers (depending on the structure of the second-pillar system in each

Table 7.3 Sustainable contribution rates and contribution gaps in selected industrial countries, 1995–2050 (% of GDP)

	Projected average contribution rate, 1995–2050	Sustainable contribution rate, 1995–2050	Contribution gap	Increase in contribution gap if reforms are postponed by:		
				5 years	10 years	15 years
Industrialized countries	6.5	8.3	1.8	0.3	0.7	1.4
Canada	3.8	5.8	2.0	0.1	0.5	0.9
France	12.1	15.4	3.3	0.6	1.3	2.4
Germany	10.3	13.7	3.4	0.6	1.3	2.7
Italy	16.0	18.5	2.5	0.5	1.1	1.9
Japan	3.9	7.2	3.3	0.6	1.4	2.7
Sweden	7.1	8.0	0.9	0.1	0.2	0.4
United Kingdom	4.2	4.3	0.1	—	0.1	0.1
United States	4.7	5.5	0.8	0.1	0.2	0.5

Sources: IMF; Chand and Jaeger (1996).

Table 7.4 Effects of benefit reforms on contribution gaps in selected industrial countries (% of GDP)

	Baseline (1)	Reduction in replacement rate by 5 percentage points		Modification of indexation arrangements		Changing retirement ages	
		New pensioners only (2)	All pensioners (3)	100% CPI indexation (4)	80% CPI indexation (5)	Front-loading announced increases (6)	Unified retirement ages at 67 (7)
Industrialized countries	1.8	-0.7	-1.1	-0.5	-0.8	-0.5	-1.4
Canada	2.0	-1.0	-1.2	—	-0.4		-0.7
France	3.3	-0.9	-1.3	-0.8	-1.4	-0.4	-3.7
Germany	3.4	-1.2	-1.4	-1.9	-2.3	-0.4	-1.2
Italy	2.5	-0.7	-0.8	—	-0.2	-1.1	-5.7
Japan	3.3	-0.5	-0.7	-1.4	-1.5	-0.8	-1.6
Sweden	0.9	-1.0	-1.2	—	-0.6	—	-1.0
United Kingdom	0.1	-0.7	-0.8	—	-0.5	-0.4	-1.1
United States	0.8	-0.7	-1.2	—	-0.2	-0.3	-0.3

Sources: IMF; Chand and Jaeger (1996).

country). The basic advantage from increasing the reliance on supplementary funded schemes in a pension system is the ability to offer to employees a mixed portfolio of pay-as-you-go and funded components that maximises expected returns and diversifies risks. Under uncertain rates of economic growth and real yields, portfolio theory suggests that an optimal pension arrangement should include both pay-as-you-go and funded components.[14]

Given the absence of a private earnings insurance market, private funded schemes cannot offer contractual insurance against earnings loss at retirement. In practice, however, it is possible that investment returns might prove superior to the growth rate of labour income[15] which equals the implicit real return of a pay-as-you-go scheme.

Recent economic history indicates that real returns offered by financial markets have been superior to the implicit returns offered by pay-as-you-go schemes in most countries (Table 7.5). It could therefore be argued that funded schemes could maximize the after-tax rate of return of a given level of contributions, or minimize the necessary saving over a lifetime for a set level of benefits.

The ability of pension funds to provide positive investment returns in real terms is extremely important. Pension funds hold a substantial part of their assets in equity investments in order to hedge inflation risk. A number of studies on the long-term performance of equity investments have demonstrated that equities can provide a good hedge against inflation. It should be

Table 7.5   Real returns on pension fund portfolios, 1967–90[1]

	Estimated real portfolio return		Real average earnings growth		Real portfolio return less average earnings
Denmark	3.6	(12.7)	2.8	(3.6)	0.8
Germany	5.1	(4.4)	4.0	(3.1)	1.1
France	n.a.	n.a.	4.0		n.a.
Ireland	5.0	(11.9)	2.0		3.0
Italy	n.a.	n.a.	3.1	(4.3)	n.a.
Netherlands	4.0	(6.0)	2.4	(3.2)	1.6
Sweden	0.2	(7.6)	1.5	(3.5)	−1.3
United Kingdom	5.8	(12.5)	2.6	(2.5)	3.2

Note: [1] In parentheses are the means (standard deviations) of annual real total returns in local currency.

Source: Davis (1995), using national flow of funds data and BIS macroeconomic database (for asset returns).

stressed, however, that the performance of equities over shorter periods of time, when inflation is rising, has been less reassuring. Data for the six major OECD economies in the 1970s showed that in most countries increases in the value of equities did not keep pace with the rate of inflation. Similarly, a study[16] of the real performance of the UK stock market over 1918–84 has indicated that investors in equities have suffered real losses in periods of rising inflation and it has often taken as much as a decade before they recouped their losses.[17]

Insurance against length of life can be provided by funded schemes through the purchase of annuities at the date of retirement. The private annuity market is, however, hampered by adverse selection problems. Households have private information about mortality and those expecting to live longer are more likely to purchase annuities, while those expecting to live less long are likely to request a lump-sum payment of their pension benefit. Pay-as-you-go schemes avoid this form of adverse selection because annuitization is mandatory and all households are grouped into a single risk pool. Finally, it is worth pointing out that private annuities are usually not indexed to inflation, therefore reducing real income over time.

The structure of benefits and the risks of funded schemes vary substantially according to whether they are defined benefit or defined contribution (see also Section 2 above). In the former, inflation and investment risks are borne by the employer, and in the latter, by the employee. Moreover, the operators of the schemes vary in each case. Defined benefit schemes are administered by pension funds while defined contribution schemes are usually administered by life insurance companies which also administer proprietary third-pillar schemes. One of the disadvantages of the funded schemes is the high administration costs compared with the public pay-as-you-go schemes. The evidence from the United States and Chile shows that administration costs could be up to four times higher in a funded pension system.

As the importance of supplementary pensions increases (as a percentage of total retirement income), it is increasingly important for governments to provide a secure environment for the efficient operation of supplementary funded schemes. A regulatory framework which enables pension funds in all countries to diversify properly their assets, both domestically and internationally, should enhance returns, reduce risks arising from domestic economic cycles and reduce the negative impact on asset prices during periods of disinvestment (that is, when elderly generations realize their wealth).

The role of international diversification is particularly relevant in that respect as higher saving in the rest of the world and particularly in emerging economies could satisfy the demand for assets at that time. As shown in Table 7.6, foreign asset holdings of pension funds vary substantially across countries, due mainly to remaining restrictive government regulations for pension

Table 7.6   Pension fund foreign assets in 1994 (% of total assets)

	Total foreign	Foreign equities	Foreign bonds	Other
Belgium	35	21	12	2
Denmark	7	5	1	1
Germany	6	3	2	1
Spain	5	0	5	0
France	5	2	1	2
Ireland	37	32	4	1
Italy	5	1	3	1
Netherlands	25	16	6	3
Austria	20	8	11	1
Sweden	12	10	1	1
United Kingdom	30	24	3	3

Source: EFRP (1996).

fund investments, but are in most cases at very low levels compared with investments in domestic assets.

5.   IMPLICATIONS OF THE REFORMS

The pursuit of further reforms in the public pay-as-you-go schemes and an increased reliance on supplementary funded schemes for retirement income financing will have significant consequences for the economy as a whole. The following sections discuss some of the issues that should be addressed in the debate over the reform in each member state.

5.1   Implications for Aggregate Saving

The reform of existing public pay-as-you-go schemes and the potential growth of supplementary funded schemes could affect both the level of saving in the economy and its composition. Empirical evidence so far seems to suggest that the expansion of pension funds has only a marginal positive effect on the level of aggregate national savings, although very few studies have focused on European evidence. On the other hand, it is certain that a shift to funded schemes would alter the pattern of private and collective savings, change the distribution of demand for domestic and international financial assets and have an impact on market organization and the demand for financial services.

In the context of the current debate, it has to be kept in mind that the basic objective of a pension reform is to provide income security in old age, not to raise the saving rate. There is, none the less, a connection between pension reform and national savings since the income of the elderly ultimately depends on the amount of saving one generation makes while working and the bequest of human and physical capital it makes to its descendants.

The theoretical framework typically used for the analysis of the impact of pension system reform on savings is the life-cycle hypothesis (LCH) of consumption. According to the LCH, unless pension reform alters the total (that is, current and future) wealth of pension plan participants, it will not affect consumption. It may affect the distribution of saving between the public and private sector, but not its total amount. The LCH provides a useful tool for pension system design but its extreme assumptions[18] rarely hold in the real world.

The reform of the pay-as-you-go schemes can affect both current and future pensioners (that is, current participants) depending on the type of reforms decided in each country. In both cases public sector saving will increase, but this increase is unlikely to be fully offset by a fall in private saving. In fact, for current participants and future pensioners the decline in benefits resulting from the public scheme reform would reduce expected future income and, therefore, current employees will tend to save more in order to keep the same standard of living after retirement. Private saving might therefore also increase in this case unless such a development has been already anticipated and is already discounted in their current saving behaviour.

The way changes in the structure of the existing system would affect aggregate national saving in EU countries depends on the characteristics of financial markets and the saving behaviour of individuals. More importantly, the impact will greatly depend on the type of funded schemes existing or developed in each country, that is, defined benefit or defined contribution, on whether they are voluntary or compulsory, on their vesting and portability, on the regulatory framework and the confidence that this inspires to individuals and on the fiscal treatment and prudential regulatory framework for alternative third-pillar forms of saving instruments.

Empirical evidence from the United States and the United Kingdom suggests that growth in funded pension schemes is only partly offset by declines in discretionary personal saving. Davis (1995) reports that every unit increase in pension fund assets results in an increase in personal savings of around 0.35. The key reason for this divergence from the LCH seems to be the imperfection of credit markets which do not allow individuals to borrow in order to offset the increases in saving arising from pension contributions. The effects are generally smaller the more developed the credit markets and are also smaller for defined contribution schemes which, in a number of cases, allow individuals to borrow against their accumulated pension wealth. The degree of vesting of each scheme is also influencing the outcome.

A pension reform that aims to increase private saving through the growth of supplementary pension funds is likely to make participation in the scheme compulsory and set contribution rates at high levels. Such a policy implies substantial regulation and government intervention with varying side effects on equity and efficiency. In the case of defined contribution pension schemes, compulsory high contribution rates might discriminate against a certain type of employment. If, for example, private sector employees depend more heavily on supplementary pension schemes for their retirement income as compared with public sector employees, they will face higher compulsory saving over their working lives with adverse effects on their consumption pattern. In the case of defined benefit schemes, which are by definition actuarially fair, such a regulation would lead to an increase in offered benefits.

It is often argued that fiscal incentives could be used to promote private pension schemes with positive spillover effects on savings. Neither theoretical analysis nor empirical investigation supports the view that fiscal incentives to pension funds and other saving vehicles produce unambiguous effects on the total level of savings in the economy.

Engen et al. (1994) point out that 'saving incentive programmes that raise the after-tax return on limited amounts of assets may be a less effective way to stimulate private saving than increasing the rate of return of all savings'. In the case of ceilings in tax incentives, on the other hand, a positive impact on private saving can arise if the ceiling is higher than the desired level of saving by the employees, in which case they might be willing to save more in order to optimize the fiscal advantage.

The empirical evidence reviewed by Franco (1996) is relatively inconclusive despite the large number of studies undertaken on the subject. Most studies point to an increase of private saving due to limited substitution between various forms of saving[19] but the evidence is inconclusive with regard to total national saving (that is, once the effect of lost revenues to the state are calculated). Recent research in the United States shows, however, that the growth of tax-favoured schemes has not been at the expense of other forms of saving.[20]

5.2 Implications for Financial System Structure

The growth of pension funds will alter the demand and supply of financial assets in the economy. Overall, it will increase substantially the demand for equities, bonds and other long-term assets, which will, in turn, alter the way firms are financed in Europe. The implications for the financial system structure, capital market efficiency and corporate governance policies in each member state and the EU as a whole are likely to be far-reaching. Changes will be more profound in countries where the banking system is the dominant source of funding for firms and where capital markets are relatively underdeveloped.

There are two ways to analyse developments in these areas. One is to examine the changes induced due to the shift of assets from third-pillar savings to second-pillar supplementary funded schemes. The other is to examine changes induced by the type of supplementary pension schemes developed in each country.

In the first case, savings shifted from individual precautionary savings will be invested in different types of assets by pension funds. The change will reflect the difference in the risk frontier of individuals (who invest with an uncertain time horizon as they use savings both as additional retirement income security and for other needs), and pension funds that have a clearer liability structure and superior ways in matching these liabilities with assets.

Pension fund portfolios vary widely across countries and across institutions, but in most cases they hold a greater proportion of capital uncertain and long-term assets than households (Table 7.7). For example, equity holdings of pension funds in 1990 varied from 70 per cent of portfolio total in the United Kingdom and 48 per cent in the United States to 18 per cent in Germany. In each case, however, these holdings were higher than personal sector equity holdings, which were 12, 19 and 6 per cent respectively. On the other hand, households tend to hold a much larger proportion of liquid assets, such as cash and deposits, than institutions.

Irrespective of the type of pension fund developed in each country (that is, defined benefit or defined contribution), in the absence of restrictive regulatory provisions, the growth of pension fund assets will, in the short and medium terms, increase the demand for equities in Europe. The newly created, immature (low number of beneficiaries of retirement age) pension funds would have an interest in investing a large part of their portfolio in equities to maximize growth and protect assets against inflation. This will change with population ageing. As pension funds mature, they will have to ensure a more stable income flow from their investments, in order to pay their pension obligations. Over the long term, therefore, one can expect a relative increase in the percentage of pension fund assets invested in bonds.

The choice between defined contribution and defined benefit schemes, however, will further influence the demand for financial assets. As the liabilities of these schemes are of a qualitatively different nature, they generate different types of risks and these risks have to be hedged with different portfolios of assets.

Blake (1996) analysed the portfolios of life insurance companies, which usually administer defined contribution schemes, and pension funds, which

Table 7.7   *Pension fund and household portfolio distributions, 1990 (% shares)*

Country	Cash and deposits		Bonds		Equities		Property	Life insurance and pension funds
	Pension funds	Households	Pension funds	Households	Pension funds	Households	Pension funds	Households
Denmark	1	—	67	—	7	—	—	—
Germany	2	48	25	18	18	6	6	22
France	—	51	—	3	—	34	—	12
Italy	21	49	45	18	2	22	32	12
Netherlands	3	29	23	8	20	6	11	54
Sweden	3	—	84	—	1	—	1	—
United Kingdom	7	29	14	4	63	12	9	47
Australia	23	34	20	13	27	17	16	36
Canada	11	39	47	6	29	21	3	28
Japan	3	53	47	5	27	13	2	23
United States	9	30	36	10	46	19	—	33
Switzerland	12	—	29	—	16	—	17	—

Note: UK and Canadian households have 1 per cent foreign assets; others are zero or not recorded.

Source: Davis (1995).

Table 7.8   Asset allocation of life insurance companies and pension funds, end-1994 (%)

	Life insurance companies	Pension funds
Short-term (net)	3.2	3.4
UK government bonds	16.0	8.6
Other fixed income	7.5	2.7
UK company shares	38.8	49.0
Unit trusts	7.6	2.9
Overseas fixed income	2.7	3.3
Overseas company shares	11.6	17.0
Property	8.5	5.4
Loans, mortgages and other	4.1	7.7
Total assets (£billion)	419.5	451.0

Source: *Financial statistics*, Central Statistical Office, from Blake (1996).

usually administer defined benefit schemes, in the United Kingdom and found substantial differences in their asset allocation (Table 7.8).

Liabilities of pension funds are generally more uncertain than those of life insurance companies as they depend on wage inflation in the period up to retirement and price inflation after retirement. Table 7.8 shows that pension funds hold 69 per cent of their assets in equities (including unit trusts) and 5 per cent in property in order to ensure adequate coverage against inflation risk. Life insurance companies, on the other hand, hold a higher percentage of their assets in bonds compared with pension funds, 26 per cent against 15 per cent.[21] Although the absolute figures in Table 7.8 are influenced by the asset allocation decisions in this particular year, they demonstrate the diversity in demand for financial assets that the choice between defined benefit or defined contribution could bring.

In addition to the changes in the demand for financial assets, the growth of pension funds will have important implications for the functioning of capital markets. Pension funds, as all institutional investors, can improve capital market efficiency by stimulating competition among financial intermediaries. Pension funds require more complete, accurate and timely information on financial assets and, thereby, increase transparency in capital markets. Finally, due to their need for liquidity and sophisticated risk management, they act as a catalyst in the development of new financial instruments and enhance liquidity in capital markets.

The growth of pension funds will also have important implications for corporate governance practices. Due to the sheer size of their equity and bond investments, pension funds have a strong incentive to monitor closely the management of the companies they invest in and ensure the pursuit of shareholder value.

In most EU countries, in the absence of developed corporate bond markets, corporate debt is concentrated in the hands of banks, which exercise their control on the firm directly. Similarly, in countries with relatively undeveloped stock markets, a large proportion of firms are privately owned and shareholder control is also exercised directly. The growth of institutional investors, like pension funds, will increase the role of outsiders (as opposed to insiders) in the monitoring of the strategy and performance of the firm. Davis (1995) characterizes this development as a move from direct control via equity and debt towards market control via equity and debt.

Empirical evidence from the United States,[22] however, shows that private pension funds are not following activist corporate governance policies. In defined benefit schemes, managed inside the firm, there is a clear moral hazard issue that prevents the pension fund fiduciary from being actively involved in corporate governance of the firm in which it almost always has a large equity stake. But even for equity investments in other firms, the possibility of reciprocity makes fiduciaries in practice very prudent in actively exercising their corporate governance potential. In the case of pension funds (defined benefit or defined contribution) managed outside the firm, the moral hazard is also present as fund managers view other firms as existing or potential clients. In fact, partly due to the sheer size of their equity portfolios, the same pension fund has often been found holding stakes of both companies in a takeover process.

5.3 Implications for Labour Markets

There are several ways in which changes in the structure of a country's pension system can affect the labour market. Pension system arrangements have an impact on labour mobility and labour productivity, affect retirement age and raise equity concerns in terms of income adequacy and distribution of wealth across population groups.

Public pay-as-you-go schemes provide full portability within a country and have the same rules with regard to contribution rates. Supplementary schemes, on the other hand, differ according to whether they are defined benefit or defined contribution. Defined benefit schemes are not portable across companies or occupations as they are virtually guaranteed by the employer. Defined contribution schemes are usually portable within a country, although vesting rules might reduce their portability in the early stages of joining.

Empirical evidence, mainly from the United States, suggests that membership of a pension scheme reduces labour turnover. The probability that employees (younger and older) will remain in the same job over a five-year period is more than twice as high if employees are covered by a pension scheme. In the EU, where public pay-as-you-go schemes provide the basic source of retirement income, it is the quality (rather than the existence) of supplementary schemes, in terms of benefits offered and the contribution that the employer takes on charge, that is likely to make the difference. Occupations or companies with generous supplementary schemes usually have a lower turnover of employees, although vesting rules play an important role.

For policy-makers, the main concern should be to avoid the development of supplementary pension schemes that, one way or another, inhibit productivity growth. Back-loading in defined benefit schemes or a long vesting period in defined contribution schemes should not be used by employers (sponsors) as an instrument to reduce hiring and training costs (Pesando, 1992).

The structure of retirement benefits offered by the pension system also influences the decision to withdraw early (before the standard retirement age) from employment. Over recent years, labour market participation by older workers has been falling,[23] a paradox considering the concerns about demographic developments and the sustainability of the pension system. The forces leading to the withdrawal from employment of older workers have their origin mainly on the demand side as, for example, companies are restructuring or governments seek to open up or preserve employment opportunities for other groups (for example, the unemployed). Pension scheme arrangements, however, act on the supply side. They can contain incentives to withdraw early from employment and/or disincentives to stay in work beyond the normal retirement age. A private company defined benefit scheme can, for example, offer early-retirement benefits that are less than fully actuarially reduced and late-retirement benefits that are less than fully actuarially enhanced. Public pay-as-you-go schemes also entail such incentives for all or for certain population groups.

In terms of equity, increased reliance on supplementary pension schemes in the future implies that an individual's ability to accumulate benefits for old age would be increasingly influenced by initial endowments (such as human capital potential) and different education and wealth levels on entering the labour force. Differences in income during the working life will also have a more important effect. Employees reaching retirement age after having gone through periods of unemployment will be more vulnerable. The opportunity for employees to participate in a supplementary scheme is likely to be skewed in favour of certain groups, for example full-time employees, certain industrial sector employees, and higher income groups.

Overall, any pension system reform should be policy-coherent as the implications on labour market productivity, mobility and length of working life can be important. Moreover, attention should be given to the spillover effects on other social security measures (for example, unemployment insurance system), as reforms can sometimes lead to cross-substitution among the different benefits offered by the state.

6.   CONCLUSIONS

Demographic and public finance considerations make further piecemeal reforms of the public pay-as-you-go pension schemes necessary in order to ensure their sustainability. These reforms, however, will in several countries lead to a substantial reduction in the pension benefits provided by these schemes in the future. Ensuring adequate retirement income and maintenance of the standard of living after retirement will increasingly fall on supplementary pension schemes. Such a development will change the distribution of responsibilities and risks between government, employers and employees and will create pension systems that offer a more diversified portfolio of retirement income sources to the labour force (that is, public pay-as-you-go and private funded schemes). A reform of the pension system in that direction is likely to have marginally positive effects on aggregate saving and create positive externalities in the field of financial markets. The potential effects for the labour market are much less clear as certain risks associated with retirement income provision are likely to be transferred from the government to the employees, but so will a number of opportunities.

NOTES

1. The distinction between pillars is not always clear-cut and can differ between countries.
2. Vesting is the fixed minimum period that an employee has to be a member of a pension scheme before he/she can have a right to the benefits offered.
3. Weighted by 1995 GDP in units of purchasing power standard.
4. Figures 7.3 and 7.4 refer to the 11 countries for which estimates are available up to 2030.
5. Public pension expenditure includes old-age, disability and survival pensions. This paper mainly refers to old-age pensions, as they are the ones mostly affected by demographic developments.
6. Franco and Munzi (1996).
7. For a review of the arguments, see Holzmann (1996).
8. According to Castellino (1985) pension liabilities can be categorized as follows:

    Accrued-to-date liabilities: these represent the present value of pensions to be paid in the future on the basis of accrued rights; neither the future contributions of existing workers, nor the accrual of new rights by them are considered.
    Current workers and pensioners' liabilities: in this case it is assumed that pension schemes continue their existence until the last contributor dies, while no new entrants are allowed;

both the future contributions of existing members and their new rights are therefore included under current rules.

Open-system liabilities: these also include the present value of contributions and pensions of new employees under the assumption of current rules, the range of options extends from including only children not yet in the labour force to an infinite perspective.

9. See also Franco (1995).

10. Although more recent projections have been produced since by the OECD, IMF and others, these are the only estimates that distinguish the accrued liabilities (from those of current workers and future pensioners' liabilities), which are the only ones relevant in estimating the level of debt to become explicit when phasing out existing pay-as-you-go schemes. See Chand and Jaeger (1996) and Roseveare et al. (1996).

11. For example, a combination of restrictions to invest a maximum of 25 per cent of pension fund assets in equities (on volatility grounds) and a minimum of 80 per cent in domestic currency securities (on currency matching grounds) would effectively bind a large part of pension fund assets in domestic government bonds. Such policies become increasingly difficult to sustain in the framework of the internal market. The European Commission presented in June 1997 a Green Paper entitled 'Supplementary pensions in the single market' addressing these issues.

12. The main exception is modifications in the indexation arrangements. They have been accepted relatively easily by current pensioners and have produced a large part of expenditure reductions over the last decade.

13. In France pensions have in reality been indexed to prices since 1987; wage indexation has been constantly suspended on a yearly basis. However, this paper has assumed wage indexation in its projections.

14. For a review, see Fornero (1995).

15. Assuming a steady state and a constant contribution rate, the implicit real return of the pay-as-you-go scheme is equal to the growth rate of labour income, that is, the sum of the rates of increase of the real wage per employee (g) and of the labour force (n).

16. See Petrie and Sturm (1991).

17. It should not be forgotten that the destruction of pension fund assets by inflation in the earlier part of this century lies behind the creation of most of the current pay-as-you-go pension schemes.

18. The main assumptions are:

   (i) efficient capital market with no liquidity constraints for individuals, that is, they can borrow at any time during their working life against the security of their human wealth and therefore smooth their consumption pattern over both working and non-working life. In practice, imperfect capital markets inhibit consumers from borrowing on the back of future income, and consumer credit without collateral becomes very expensive if not impossible;

   (ii) individuals are far-sighted and have perfect information about the future in order to plan for retirement and achieve, therefore, a smooth consumption pattern over a lifetime.

19. See Dinlot (1992), Poterba et al. (1993), Venti and Wise (1994) and Feldstein (1995).

20. On empirical studies for the United States, see Engen et al. (1994), Burman et al. (1990) and Attanasio and DeLeire (1994).

21. Holdings of bonds are also dependent on the 'maturity' of the pension fund, that is, the age of employees covered; the more employees at retirement or near retirement age, the higher the holdings of fixed income assets.

22. For a survey, see Giavazzi and Battaglini (1996).

23. For an extensive discussion on this issue, see OECD (1995).

REFERENCES

Attanasio, O.P. and DeLeire, T.C. (1994), 'IRAs and household saving revisited: some new evidence', *NBER Working Paper*, No. 4900.

Blake, D. (1996), 'Portfolio choice models of pension funds and life assurance companies: similarities and differences', paper presented at conference entitled 'The role of insurance in the modern economy', Venice.

Burman, L., Cordes, J. and Ozanne, L. (1990), 'IRAs and national savings', *National Tax Journal*, No. 3.

Castellino (1985), 'C'e un secondo debito pubblico (più grande del primo)?', *Moneta e Credito*, No. 149.

Chand, S. and Jaeger, A. (1996), 'Ageing populations and public pension schemes', *IMF Occasional Paper*, No. 147.

Davis, E.P. (1995), *Pension Funds, Retirement Income Security and Capital Markets – An International Perspective*, Oxford: Oxford University Press.

Dinlot, A. (1992), 'Taxation and private pensions: costs and consequences', *OECD Private Pensions and Public Policy*, Paris.

EFRP (European Federation for Retirement Provision) (1996), *European Pension Funds – Their Impact on European Capital Markets and Competitiveness*.

Engen, E.M., Gale, W.A. and Scholz, J.K. (1994), 'Do saving incentives work?', *Brookings Paper on Economic Activity*, No. 1.

Feldstein, M. (1995), 'The effects of tax-based saving incentives on government revenue and national saving', *The Quarterly Journal of Economics*, May 1995.

Fornero, E. (1995), 'Totally unfunded versus partially funded pension systems: the case of Italy', *Richerche Economiche Università degli studi Ca' Foscari Venezia*, **49** (4).

Franco, D. (1995), 'Pension liabilities – Their use and misuse in the assessment of fiscal policies', *Economic Papers*, No. 110, European Commission, DG II.

Franco, D. (1996), 'The taxation of funded pension schemes and budgetary policy', *Economic Papers*, No. 117, European Commission, DG II.

Franco, D. and Munzi, T. (1996), 'Pension expenditure prospects in the European Union: a survey of national projections', *European Economy – Reports and Studies*, No. 3.

Giavazzi, F. and Battaglini, M. (1996), 'Privatisations and ownership structures: theory, experience and policy implications', IGIER, Università Bocconi, Milan.

Holzmann, R. (1996), 'On economic benefits and fiscal requirements of moving from unfunded to funded pensions', this book, ch. 6.

OECD (1995), 'The transition from work to retirement', *Social Policy Studies*, No. 16.

Pesando, J.E. (1992), 'The economic effects of private pensions', ch. 8 of *OECD Private Pensions and Public Policy*.

Petrie, M. and Sturm, P. (1991), 'Old age income maintenance – Basic problems and alternative responses', mimeo.

Poterba, J.M., Venti, S.F. and Wise, D.A. (1993), 'Do 401(K) contributions crowd-out other personal saving?', *NBER Working Paper*, No. 4391.

Roseveare, D., Leibfritz, W., Fore, D. and Wurzel, E. (1996), 'Ageing populations, pension systems and government budgets: simulations for 20 OECD countries', *OECD Economics Department Working Papers*, No. 168.

Van den Noord, P. and Herd, R. (1993), 'Pension liabilities in the seven major economies', *OECD Economics Department Working Papers*, No. 142.

Venti, S.F. and Wise, D.A. (1994), 'Individual response to retirement saving programmes: results from US Panel data', paper presented at the conference entitled
'Saving and retirement' in January 1995, Venice.

PART V

A Case Study

8. Reform of the social security system in France: challenges and prospects

Nathalie Darnaut

1. INTRODUCTION[1]

In all European Union member states the social protection systems experience similar developments and face, to a large extent, comparable problems. The rapid growth in social expenditure is in conflict with budgetary restraint and the need to stabilize the public finances, in order to reduce budget deficits and restore sustainability in national debt levels. In the context of EMU, the position of social finances has a direct bearing on the ability of member states to meet the fiscal convergence criteria laid down in the Maastricht Treaty, social security institutions being a major component of the general government accounts. In the medium and long term, bringing social accounts back to balance will be essential in most member states with a view to complying with the provisions of the Stability and Growth Pact. However, the ageing of the European population will put both the pay-as-you-go pension system and the health-care system under increased financial pressure. In view of this, reform of both the pension and the health-care systems has become a priority. The persistently high level of unemployment in Europe has led to reviewing government policies with the objective of making the social protection system more employment-friendly. Reforming the social protection system is essential in order, on the one hand, to strengthen incentives to produce and work and, on the other, to reduce the negative employment implications of current methods of financing benefits.

In its communications on social protection,[2] the Commission has shown that, in spite of the different characteristics of their systems, the member states could benefit from a European debate on the common challenges which they face. Reform of the social protection system is now a prominent priority in France. The French system is, to a certain extent, representative of the other European systems. It mixes the two traditions of national and socio-professional solidarity around which the social security systems of the member states have been built. The share of social protection expenditure in GDP is

229

higher in France than the European average: it was 29.2 per cent in 1993 compared with 27.5 per cent on average in the Union.[3] As in most member states, social protection resources mainly comprise social security contributions levied on wages, while the financing of pensions relies largely on pay-as-you-go pension schemes. As regards health care, the differences between the systems of the member states are more marked and reflect historical and cultural factors. However, the case of France is representative as this country ranks first within the European Union for the share of health expenditure in GDP, with a figure of 9.4 per cent in 1992.[4] Faced with budgetary restraint, France and most member states have taken steps to reform their health-care systems in recent years. The challenges and objectives of these reforms were the same but the countries gave different weights to equity, cost containment and microeconomic efficiency considerations in designing these reforms.

The reform plan presented by the French government on 15 November 1995 (Juppé plan) is a continuation of past efforts to redress the social accounts. It consists of a very ambitious plan, seeking to address short-term financial problems confronting social security in the advent of EMU, as well as long-term sustainability problems with a view to ensuring the financial viability of the system. Besides its cost-containment objective, the 1995 reform plan aims at implementing radical changes in order to adapt the health-care and pension systems to the changing economic and social environment.

The aim of this chapter is to review the current reform of the French social security system.[5] The discussion is centred on the reform of health insurance which forms the central element of the Juppé plan. After this introduction, the study is organized around five sections. Section 2 presents the main features of the French social protection system and provides an assessment of its strengths and weaknesses. Section 3 describes the measures provided for in the Juppé plan, in particular in the area of health insurance, and places it in the context of the challenges of such reforms met in the industrialized countries. Section 4 assesses the effects of the emergency measures adopted and offers some observations on the health insurance reform. Section 5 examines the prospects of the pension schemes after the recent measures taken. Finally, concluding remarks are presented in Section 6.

2.   MAIN FEATURES OF THE FRENCH SOCIAL PROTECTION SYSTEM

Founded in 1945, French social security was originally designed as a universalist system, but historical circumstances led to the continuation of special schemes from which certain employees benefited before 1945, and to the creation of independent schemes for the self-employed in the non-agricultural sector. The predominance of the schemes organized along professional lines explains the complex organization of the system and the method of its financing, based mainly on social security contributions. This method of financing creates economic distortions. Between 1970 and 1994, spending on social protection grew on average faster than economic growth but the performance of the system does not appear to be in line with the resources allocated to it. The social security system has been experiencing recurring financial crises since 1975 and steps to redress the situation have now been taken in the area of health insurance and retirement pensions.

2.1 The (Complex) Organization of the Public Insurance System

Immediately after World War II, France and the other European countries set up social security systems.[6] The aim of social security is to protect individuals against 'social risks', that is, events which prevent the acquisition of professional income (sickness, invalidity, occupational accidents, old age, unemployment) or which cause particular expenses (sickness, family responsibilities). State intervention in the area of social insurance is justified by market failure to insure against certain risks, by the presence of asymmetric information and by redistributive objectives. More generally, the objectives of protection systems are threefold: efficiency, equity and administrative feasibility (Barr, 1992).

(i) Efficiency has several aspects. On the macroeconomic level, the allocation of resources (the fraction of GDP) among social institutions must be efficient. On the microeconomic level, social policy should ensure the efficient distribution of social resources between the different benefits. Finally, this policy must minimize adverse effects on employment, labour supply and savings.

(ii) Supporting living standards is an essential objective of the social protection systems,[7] which aim at reducing poverty, preventing large and unexpected falls in living standards and enabling individuals to reallocate consumption over their life cycle. The equity objective also covers the reduction of inequality and enhancing social integration.

(iii) From an administrative point of view, the system should be simple and cheap to manage and should ensure that abuses in the allocation of benefits are limited.

Two types of social security systems have conventionally been considered: the 'Bismarckian' systems (social insurance) and the 'Beveridgian' systems (universal). In the former, protection is defined in relation to the ability to work, with administration being entrusted to representatives of the insured persons and financing being ensured by contributions levied on wages. In the latter, protection is universal, with the benefits being uniform whatever the contributory effort; the system is unique and administered by the state and financing is ensured by taxation (see Table 8.1). The French social protection system combines features of the two welfare state models, becoming a mixed system as are the majority of the European systems (see Table 8.2).

The institutional features of the French system have, to a large extent, been determined by historical circumstances. Founded by the decree of 4 October 1945, social security was originally designed according to Beveridgian principles: universal protection, unique scheme and uniform benefits. However, these broad principles rapidly had to be amended and now remain only in a watered-down form. Thus an attempt to unify the schemes failed immediately with the refusal of employees of pre-existing special schemes (miners, sailors, RATP, SNCF, Bank of France, civil servants, EDF–GDF) to join in and the desire of the self-employed (artisans, traders, liberal professions) to remain autonomous. The 1945 decrees were eventually limited to non-agricultural wage-earners and their families, covered by the general scheme (*régime général*). This explains why the social protection system appears to be a patchwork of schemes established on a socio-professional basis. This foundation on profession was subsequently reinforced by the development of supplementary pension schemes created by collective agreements. The general scheme nevertheless plays a pivotal role within this system whose unity it partially ensures through financial compensation mechanisms.

Table 8.1   The welfare state models

Main criteria	Beveridgian system	Bismarckian system	French system
Type of social protection	Universal	Socio-professional social insurance	Social insurance of a general nature
Method of administration	State	Decentralized (funds)	Decentralized under state control
Method of financing	Tax	Contributions	Taxes and contributions
Benefits granted	All-inclusive	Proportional to salary with upper limit	Proportional with social minima
Obligation for	All	Insured persons with salary below upper limit	All

Source: Viossat (1995).

Table 8.2   Typology of the social security systems

Country	Dominant system
Belgium	BM
Denmark	BV
Germany	BM
Greece	MI
Spain	MI
France	BM
Ireland	BV
Italy	MI
Luxembourg	BM
Netherlands	BM
Austria	BM
Portugal	MI
Finland	BV
Sweden	BV
United Kingdom	BV

Notes:
BV: Beveridgian system
BM: Bismarckian system
MI: mixed system

Source: European Commission (1996).

The objective of universality has been sought through the progressive generalization of the social security coverage. Since 1969, the various categories of salaried and self-employed workers have been covered against the main risks. Eventually, the objective of uniformity of benefits was abandoned except to ensure a common minimum of protection through the so-called harmonization principle.

The French system has a complex organization. The social security system, as currently understood in France,[8] consists of over 530 compulsory schemes (basic schemes and supplementary pension schemes, see Table 8.3). There are 144 basic schemes. These can be divided into four main groups: general scheme, agricultural scheme, independent schemes for the non-agricultural self-employed and special schemes. The general scheme constitutes the main fundamental scheme. It covers employees in trade and industry and numerous related categories. Providing insurance for the largest fraction of the population, it pays nearly 60 per cent of the benefits granted by the compulsory schemes and naturally constitutes the reference scheme. The

Table 8.3   The compulsory social security schemes

	Population covered	Benefits provided (billion FRF)[1]	Share of the total benefits (%)
Basic schemes:			
● General scheme	Employees in trade and industry, others	1105	57.8
● Agricultural scheme	Agricultural employees and farmers	134	7.0
● Schemes for self-employed non-agricultural workers	Self-employed non-agricultural workers	338	17.7
● Special schemes	Officials of the State and local authorities and employees from the public sector	64	3.4
Supplementary pension schemes	Employees and self-employed	269	14.1

Note: [1]   1994 data.

Sources: Commission services; French Ministry of Social Affairs.

risks covered by the general scheme are broken down into different functions (*branches*), as follows: sickness, maternity, invalidity, survivors; occupational accidents and diseases; old age; and family.

Features of the health-care system
In the organization of health care, a distinction is often made between 'national health services' and 'health insurance systems' (Eurostat, 1995). The former provide care through a single universal scheme financed by taxation; the latter are administered by independent funds organized on a territorial basis and financed mainly by contributions. The French health-care system is organized according to the health insurance system model. Almost the entire population is covered by the statutory health insurance, which is administered by funds, composed of representatives of the employers and the insured persons. The health insurance funds have relative independence under the overall control of the central government. Non-profit-making insurance companies (*mutuelles*) and private insurers play a supplementary role in covering health expenses. The financing of health insurance is ensured primarily by contributions and a proportion of the costs is paid by patients (in particular, through the *ticket modérateur* for the non-reimbursable part of the standard cost of prescriptions and consultations). Doctors are paid on a fee-for-service

Table 8.4   Typology of the health-care systems

	Institutional organization	Main source of financing	Method of service provision (dominant system)	Remuneration of the primary care doctor
Belgium	Health insurance system	Social security contributions	Non-integrated system	Fee-for-service payment
Denmark	National health service	Tax	Integrated system	Fee-for-service payment, capitation payment, others[1]
Germany	Health insurance system	Social security contributions	Non-integrated system	Fee-for-service payment
Greece	National health service	Social security contributions	Integrated system	Salary[1]
Spain	National health service	Social security contributions	Integrated system	Salary[1], others
France	Health insurance system	Social security contributions	Non-integrated system	Fee-for-service payment
Ireland	National health service	Tax	Integrated system	Fee-for-service payment, others
Italy	National health service	Social security contributions	Integrated system	Capitation payment[1]
Netherlands	Health insurance system	Social security contributions	Non-integrated system	Capitation payment,[1] fee-for-service payment
Austria	Health insurance system	Social security contributions	Non-integrated system	Fee-for-service payment,[1] capitation payment
Portugal	National health service	Social security contributions	Integrated system	Salary[1]
Finland	National health service	Tax	Integrated system	Salary,[1] partly capitation payment
Sweden	National health service	Tax	Integrated system	Salary,[1] private practice doctors paid on a fee-for-service basis
United Kingdom	National health service	Tax	Integrated system	Capitation payment,[1] fund-holding general practitioners, others

Note: [1] Access to the services of specialists after consultation with the primary care doctor.

Sources: Commission services: OCED (1992).

basis. They may practise either in sector I, where their fees are fixed under an agreement with the national health insurance fund (*caisse nationale d'assurance-maladie*), or in sector II, where they are free to set their fees. The public hospitals are financed by a global operating budget. The system is very liberal. In particular, patients are free to choose their doctor, both general practitioners and specialists, and their hospital, public or private. Four other main principles govern the exercise of independent medical practice: freedom of prescription, freedom of location, confidentiality and direct payment of fees by the patient. This last principle does not exclude the third-party payment practice in which the health insurance exempts patients from having to pay certain costs.

Table 8.4 presents a typology of the European health-care systems according to certain criteria. The two models of health-care organization, national health service and health insurance system, are found in all European countries with certain variations, in the degree of decentralization of the competent authorities, for example, or the method of financing. The links between the actors in the system – insurers, providers, and insured persons – may be organized according to two main models (OECD, 1992). In the integrated model, a single entity (the state, a local authority or an approved insurer) plays a dual role as the purchaser of services and the provider. The majority of the member states (Denmark, Greece, Spain, Ireland, Italy, Portugal, Finland, Sweden and the United Kingdom) use this model to varying degrees. In the non-integrated system, the providers are totally independent of the insurers. France and a few other European countries have a system of this type.

In Table 8.4, the health-care systems are also classified according to the main source of financing and the method of remuneration of the primary care general practitioners. This typology imperfectly reflects the diversity of the health-care systems. Other aspects are important, such as the methods of payment of the health-care providers, the level of cost-sharing by patients, and so on.

2.2   Expenditure and Performance of the System

A sustained growth in social expenditure
Social protection expenditure has long grown at a rate faster than GDP (see Table 8.5). Between 1970 and 1994, the volume of social expenditure increased on average by 4.4 per cent per year, compared with an average increase in GDP of 2.4 per cent. As a result, its share in GDP increased during this period from 17.9 to 28.6 per cent. This development did not occur at a uniform rate throughout the period (see Figure 8.1(a)). In proportion to GDP, this expenditure increased particularly in the 1970s. Its share in GDP then dropped between 1984 and 1989, with economic growth and the imple-

Table 8.5   *Growth in social security benefits and in GDP, 1970–94*
            (average annual real growth rate in %)

	Benefits	GDP
1970–75	7.1	3.5
1975–80	4.9	3.1
1980–85	4.0	1.5
1985–90	2.8	3.2
1990–94	3.1	0.8
1970–94	4.4	2.4

Sources: French Ministry of Finance; Commission services.

mentation of cost containment measures. Since 1991, the slowdown in growth has again led to a significant increase in the share of this expenditure.

The data from the Esspros system enable a comparison of social protection expenditure at European level (see Table 8.6). The weight of social expenditure in GDP is slightly higher in France than the European average and puts this country in fourth place behind Denmark, the Netherlands and Germany (including the new *Länder*). Thus, in the European Union (excluding the three new member states), social protection expenditure represented on average 27.5 per cent of GDP in 1993, compared with 29.2 per cent in France. As in the other European countries, the old-age and sickness risks constitute the two main benefit items. The share in GDP of expenditure on pensions (including survivors' pensions) in France is close to the European average, amounting to 12.7 per cent in 1993, with a Union average of 12.2 per cent. On the other hand, France is, after Germany, the country in the Union which allocates the highest share of its GDP to sickness benefits (including industrial accidents).[9] In 1993, these benefits represented on average 6.7 per cent of GDP in the Union, compared with 8.3 per cent in France and 8.8 per cent in Germany.[10]

Between 1980 and 1993, French social protection expenditure evolved on average at the same rate as in the rest of the Union (see Figure 8.1(b)). However, the growth in the volume of sickness expenditure was greater (3.6 per cent on average per year in France, compared with 2.9 per cent in EU 12). This is also true for old-age expenditure, which grew on average by 3.3 per cent per year in France in real terms, compared with 2.2 per cent in EU 12.

Determinants of expenditure growth

The factors underlying the growth differ according to whether one considers health-care expenditure or pension expenditure. The high health expenditure

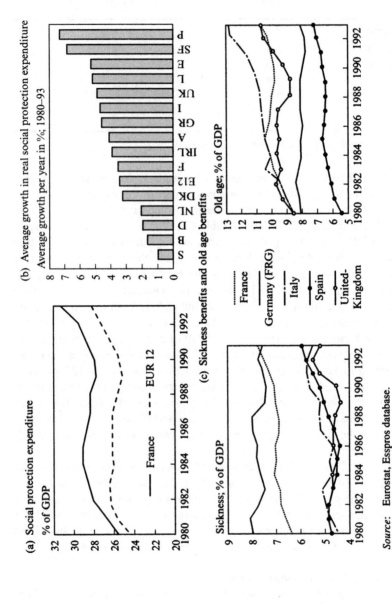

Source: Eurostat, Esspros database.

Figure 8.1 Social protection expenditure in the European Union, 1980–93

238

Table 8.6 Social protection expenditure in the European Union by function, 1980–93 (% of GDP)

	1980						1993					
	Sick.	OA	Fam.	Unem.	Others	Total	Sick.	OA	Fam.	Unem.	Others	Total
Belgium	6.6	11.0	3.0	2.4	3.5	26.5	6.5	11.9	2.1	2.6	3.2	26.3
Denmark	7.7	10.0	3.0	3.0	4.3	28.0	6.4	11.0	3.8	4.1	7.0	32.3
Germany (unified)	8.8	11.9	2.8	0.9	3.6	28.0	8.3	11.0	2.1	1.6	3.8	26.8
Greece	1.5	6.1	0.3	0.3	1.1	9.3	8.8	12.1	2.4	2.0	4.4	29.7
Spain	5.1	7.2	0.8	2.7	1.7	17.5	2.3	10.2	0.2	0.5	2.3	15.5
France	7.0	10.5	3.1	1.0	2.4	24.0	6.4	9.4	0.4	4.3	2.2	23.2
Ireland	7.3	6.2	2.3	1.6	2.3	19.7	8.3	12.7	2.8	2.0	3.4	29.2
Italy	4.9	9.9	1.4	0.4	1.4	18.0	6.2	5.7	2.6	3.0	2.9	20.4
Luxembourg	7.0	12.0	2.6	0.2	3.5	25.3	6.0	15.4	0.9	0.5	1.7	24.5
Netherlands	6.9	9.6	2.7	1.8	8.0	29.0	6.7	11.2	3.0	0.2	2.9	24.0
Portugal	3.6	4.6	0.9	0.3	2.2	11.6	7.1	11.9	1.7	2.9	8.5	32.1
United Kingdom	5.0	8.8	2.7	1.7	2.5	20.7	5.7	7.0	0.9	0.8	2.9	17.3
EU 12	6.0	10.1	2.4	1.3	3.4	23.2	5.2	11.1	3.1	1.6	5.8	26.8
EU 12 (unified)	—	—	—	—	—	—	6.5	11.9	2.0	1.9	4.3	26.6
							6.7	12.2	2.1	2.0	4.5	27.5

Notes:

Sick. = Sickness: OA = Old age; Fam. = Family; Unem. = Unemployment.

'Sickness' comprises the sickness and industrial accident functions; 'Old age' comprises old age and survivors; 'Family' comprises family and maternity; 'Others' includes the other functions (invalidity/disability, placement–vocational guidance–resettlement, housing, miscellaneous).

The social protection expenditure indicated above corresponds to benefits and does not therefore include either administration costs or other current expenditure.

EU 12: average of the 12 with FRG; EU 12 (unified): average of the 12 with Germany unified (from 1991).

The EU 12 and EU 12 (unified) averages are weighted by the GDP of the various countries.

Sources: Eurostat (1995); Esspros database.

growth is linked to a range of structural factors: increased income, population ageing, technological progress, appearance of new diseases. According to the Commissariat général du plan (1993), the direct impact of population ageing on health expenditure should not be overstressed since it would not have exceeded 0.25 points over and above the 3.3 per cent annual growth in the volume of expenditure during the 1980s, it would have reached 0.3 per cent in the 1990s and should not exceed 0.5 per cent per year during the period of acceleration of population ageing from 2000 to 2040. Advances in medical technology have also contributed to the growth in health expenditure, but their impact is difficult to evaluate.

Institutional factors have also played an essential role in the determination of expenditure. The progressive generalization of social security coverage partly explains the significant growth in expenditure. In health insurance systems such as the French one, there exists a 'moral hazard' from both the demand and supply sides (see Section 3.1). An insured patient will tend to over-consume the services covered by insurance because he or she does not pay the marginal cost of care (Cutler, 1994). As health-care providers are reimbursed for each test or procedure they perform, they are encouraged to increase the amount of care provided if the price paid is higher than the marginal cost of the service offered (Cutler, 1994). Numerous surveys and studies have revealed the existence of wastage and unnecessary expenditure in the French health-care system. In this respect, the Commissariat général du plan (1994) has underlined the need to reinforce the mechanisms of information and evaluation of the quality of care in order to encourage the actors in the health-care system to adopt more rational behaviour. The lack of coordination between the actors in the system (general practitioners, specialists, hospital system) and the medical density[11] combined with the current method of remuneration (fee-for-service payment) constitute other factors explaining the increase in health expenditure (Commissariat général du plan, 1994).

As for pension expenditure, its rapid growth is linked to the increase in life expectancy at age 60, to the continual improvement of legislation since 1945, which has led to the allocation of higher pensions to more pensioners, and to the maturing of the schemes. Generally, the organization of the system with an unclear distribution of responsibilities between the state, parliament and the social partners is undoubtedly partly responsible for the drift in expenditure.

Performance of the system
The celebration, in October 1995, of the 50th anniversary of the creation of social security in France was the occasion for a wide-ranging national debate[12] on social protection. This debate underlined the positive results achieved by the social protection system and also its weaknesses and the need for

reform. The achievements of social security are significant. Social coverage has progressively been extended to the whole population and nowadays France has one of the most extensive welfare systems in Europe. This system has also been an instrument of social justice. Thus the standard of living of the youngest pensioners is now on average at global parity with that of the working population. In particular, for all the single-pension pensioners in the general scheme who worked for the whole of their working lives, the average net pension in the private sector represented, in 1993, about 80 per cent of the average net wage paid[13] (Briet, 1995).

However, the efficiency of the system is now in question; the principal criticisms levied against it are as follows:

(i) The marked growth in health expenditure in France is not synonymous with better quality of care. Although France is in second place among the European Union countries for the share of sickness expenditure in GDP, its health-care performance is not significantly higher than that of the other European countries (see Table 8.7).[14] The male life expectancy is equal to the European average. In terms of perinatal and infant mortalities, France is a middle-ranking country. Early mortality among males (before the age of 65) is higher in France than in other countries. Similarly, the performance of the French health-care system is average compared with the other European countries in terms of the extent of health coverage.[15]

(ii) The system has proved to be powerless to correct certain inequalities, and the diversity of the schemes is itself a source of further disparities among insured persons. In the area of health insurance, coverage and contributions vary by scheme. Disparities in access to care still exist and the supply of care is unequally distributed in the country. In the area of retirement pensions, the fact that the 1993 reform applied to the general scheme and to the aligned schemes (see Section 5.1), but not to the special schemes, has contributed to the increase in disparities between private sector employees and the beneficiaries of special schemes.

(iii) Finally, the sustained growth in social expenditure, which has been faster than that of revenue, is the source of financial imbalances. The expansion of social security benefits risks crowding out other public expenditure (OECD, 1994a). The financing of social expenditure has led to an increase in social security contributions which may be the source of economic distortions (see Section 2.3.2). The restoration of the balance of social security accounts is a key element in the budgetary strategy, in particular with a view to meeting the fiscal convergence criteria laid down in the Maastricht Treaty (see Section 3.2.1).

Table 8.7 Health status and outcome indicators, 1992[1]

	Female life expectancy	Male life expectancy	Female life expectancy at age 60	Male life expectancy at age 60	Perinatal mortality[2]	Infant mortality[3]	Female potential years of life lost[4]	Male potential years of life lost[4]
France	81.3	73.1	24.4	19.2	0.82	0.68	2766.8	5904.5
Germany	79.3	72.9	22.4	18.0	0.56	0.60	2837.8	5048.9
Italy	80.4	74.0	23.1	18.6	1.04	0.83	2763.5	5081.1
Spain	80.5	73.4	23.5	19.2	0.72	0.76	2937.9	5767.7
United Kingdom	79.0	74.0	22.0	17.7	0.81	0.66	3054.2	4819.9
United States	79.0	72.3	22.9	18.7	0.87	0.85	3876.9	6960.6
Total OECD[5]	79.2	72.9	22.5	18.3	0.80	0.91	2942.3	5139.6

Notes:
1   Or latest year available.
2   Deaths in the first week of life as a percentage of live and stillbirths.
3   Deaths of children aged one year or less as a percentage of live births.
4   Deaths from all causes (excluding suicides) between ages 0 and 64; per 100 000 population; 1990 or latest year available.
5   Unweighted arithmetic average.

Source: Oxley and MacFarlan (1994).

2.3 Method of Financing and Labour Market Implications

2.3.1 Social-security-contributions-based financing

The financing of social security benefits in France is primarily based on social security contributions levied on wages. This particular feature of the system is coherent with the social insurance principle according to which the social security system was designed.

Within the European Union, the preponderance of social security contributions in the financing of social protection is not unique to France; it is rather the high level of contributions which constitutes the French specificity. In most European Union member states, the funding of social protection is ensured mainly by social security contributions (see Table 8.8); direct budgetary contributions dominate only in Denmark and, to a lesser extent, in Ireland. However, it is in France that the share of contributions is the highest, with nearly 80 per cent of social protection revenue. In addition, in France, as in the other member states, with the exception of Luxembourg and the Netherlands, the burden of social security contributions weighs proportionally more heavily on employers than on employees. Thus, in 1993, employers bore 50 per cent of the cost of financing social expenditure compared with 28.3 per cent for employees.

Between 1980 and 1993, the share of employers' contributions in total social protection revenue fell in France and generally in the European Union due to policies aiming at reducing the cost of labour and to the increase in so-called solidarity expenditure,[16] for which financing based on earnings is less justified. The counterpart to this development was a rise in employees' contributions and an increase in social-security-allocated taxes. In per cent of GDP, social security contributions are higher in France than in all other member states (see Table 8.9). In 1992, they represented 19.5 per cent of GDP in France, compared with 12 per cent on average in the European Union. However, personal income tax as a ratio to GDP is significantly lower than in most other countries (6 per cent of GDP compared with 11.1 per cent on average in the European Union). As a result, the ratio of taxes levied on earnings to GDP (basically, personal income tax and social security contributions) in France is marginally above the European average.

2.3.2 Social security financing and the cost of low-skilled labour

An increase in social security contributions, *ceteris paribus*, raises the cost of labour and has, in theory, a direct adverse effect on employment, by encouraging the substitution of capital for labour. However, in France, the marked increase in social security contributions has not led to an equivalent increase in the cost of labour. On average, increased contribution rates have led to net wage decreases. According to Cotis and Loufir (1990), social

Table 8.8 *Social protection current revenue by type (% of total)*

	Employers' contributions		Employees' contributions		Budgetary contributions		Other revenue	
	1980	1993	1980	1993	1980	1993	1980	1993
Belgium	44.5	41.5	17.8	27.4	34.0	21.0	3.7	10.0
Denmark	10.0	6.8	2.3	—	82.9	81.2	4.8	6.9
Germany	41.5	40.0	28.0	30.4	27.0	26.1	3.5	3.3
Germany (unified)	—	38.4	—	31.0	—	27.4	—	3.5
Greece	57.8	46.8	—	—	4.7	17.6	6.2	7.9
Spain	63.6	52.4	18.8	16.5	16.1	28.9	1.5	2.2
France	55.5	50.1	24.3	28.3	17.3	19.7	2.9	2.5
Ireland	24.5	23.2	11.3	15.3	63.3	60.7	1.0	0.9
Italy	60.0	49.2	13.9	17.1	23.8	30.1	2.4	3.7
Luxembourg	36.4	30.1	23.4	21.7	32.8	41.0	8.4	7.2
Netherlands	37.1	20.1	31.0	42.2	20.4	21.9	11.5	15.8
Portugal	53.2	40.3	18.7	13.7	25.4	37.2	2.7	8.8
United Kingdom	33.4	26.1	14.6	15.6	43.2	43.8	8.7	14.4
EU 12	45.4	39.8	22.0	24.5	27.9	29.6	4.7	5.9
EU 12 (unified)	—	39.3	—	24.9	—	29.9	—	6.1

Note: EU 12: average of the 12 with FRG; EU 12 (unified): average of the 12 with Germany unified.

Source: Eurostat (1995).

Table 8.9   Taxes and social security contributions in 1992 (% of GDP)

	Social security contributions	Taxes	Of which personal income taxes	Total tax revenue	Of which taxes on earnings[1]
Belgium	16.4	29.0	14.2	45.4	30.6
Denmark	1.5	47.8	26.4	49.3	27.9
Germany	15.2	24.4	11.1	39.6	26.3
Greece	12.4	28.1	4.1	40.5	16.5
Spain	13.1	22.7	8.5	35.8	21.6
France	19.5	24.2	6.0	43.6	25.5
Ireland	5.6	31.0	11.7	36.6	17.3
Italy	13.3	29.2	11.5	42.4	24.8
Luxembourg	13.7	34.7	10.8	48.4	24.5
Netherlands	18.2	28.7	11.7	46.9	29.9
Austria	14.3	29.2	9.4	43.5	23.7
Portugal	8.4	24.6	6.7	33.0	15.1
Finland	10.9	36.1	18.9	47.0	29.8
Sweden	14.4	35.6	18.0	50.0	32.4
United Kingdom	6.3	28.9	10.0	35.2	16.3
EU 15	12.0	29.4	11.1	41.4	23.1
OECD	9.9	28.9	11.5	38.8	21.4

Note:
[1]   Basically, taxes on earnings: taxes on personal income and social security contributions.

Source: OECD (1994c).

security contributions do not affect the cost of labour in the medium term but weigh on the purchasing power of net wages; this wage flexibility could be explained by the fact that employees or their representatives perceive social security contributions as deferred elements of remuneration which may be substituted for the direct wage. As a result, the cost of labour in France is close to the European average. This is evident, in particular, from the comparison of the hourly cost of labour in the manufacturing industry (see Table 8.10).

A high cost of low-skilled labour   By contrast, the cost of low-skilled labour is slightly higher in France than in the other European countries. In terms of the labour cost at the minimum wage level, France is in fourth place in the Union (excluding the three new member states), behind Denmark, Belgium

Table 8.10 *Hourly cost of labour in the manufacturing industry (France = 100)*

	1992
West Germany	123.2
Belgium	107.0
Denmark	102.5
Austria	102.1
Netherlands	101.5
Sweden	101.2
France	100.0
Italy	99.0
Finland	93.5
Luxembourg	91.4
Japan	89.2
United States	79.5
Spain	76.6
United Kingdom	68.1
Ireland	65.8
East Germany	63.6
Greece	36.1
Portugal	28.4

Source: CSERC (1996), Eurostat (1992).

and the Netherlands, and in fifth place if the minimum manual worker's wage in Germany is considered (see Table 8.11).

As noted by Foucault (1995), in the case of low-skilled workers, it has not been possible to achieve wage flexibility to compensate for increased social security contributions. From 1967 to 1983, the minimum wage (SMIC) increased significantly under the effect of adjustments specified by the law and additional increases (*coups de pouce*). As a result, the dispersion of wages increased and, as social security contributions were slightly regressive,[17] the weight of social security contributions on low wages increased. From 1979, the removal of the ceiling[18] on social security contributions helped to increase the dispersion of labour costs but did not compensate for the marked increase in the SMIC. The high level of the low-skilled labour cost is probably one of the reasons why unemployment is affecting particularly this category of workers.[19]

Labour cost and employment   Under the assumption of rigidity of real wages, the direct effects of an increase in social security contributions on employ-

Table 8.11   Labour cost at the minimum wage level (1000 FRF)

	1993
Belgium	114
Denmark	119
Germany[1]	80
Germany[2]	113
Greece	37
Spain	48
France	98
Ireland	60
Italy	96
Luxembourg	91
Netherlands	106
Portugal	25
United Kingdom	50

Notes:
[1] Corresponding to the minimum wage of the 'employee in manufacturing'.
[2] Corresponding to the minimum wage of the 'manual worker in manufacturing'.

Source: Study of the Centraal Planbureau cited in CSERC (1996).

ment depend on the elasticity of the labour demand with respect to labour cost. Empirical studies give differing estimates for this parameter. Estimates from macroeconomic data generally conclude that in France this elasticity is either zero or not significantly different from zero when the labour demand is defined over relative factor costs; or –0.5 when the labour demand is defined over the absolute level of the labour cost (CSERC, 1996). On the basis of data for the manufacturing industry, Dormont (1994) has estimated the long-term elasticity of employment with respect to labour cost at between –0.8 and –0.5.

When distinguishing between the different categories of labour, the elasticity of labour demand with respect to the cost of labour depends specifically on the possibilities of substitution between the categories. The studies conclude, in the case of France, on a fairly high substitutability between skilled labour and unskilled labour, greater than that linking each of these categories to capital (CSERC, 1996).[20] As a result, the more the reduction of social security contributions is concentrated on the low paid, the greater the potential effect on employment.

Added to the direct effect of the increase in social security contributions on labour demand are the indirect effects linked to the impact of the increase in the labour cost on the external competitiveness and the profitability of companies.

The reduction of social security contributions for the low paid Since the summer of 1993, the government has undertaken a policy of reducing social security contributions for the low paid in order to reduce the cost of low-skilled labour. Two mechanisms have been adopted: a total or partial exemption from employers' family benefit contributions (for wages less than 1.3 times the SMIC) from July 1993 and regressive exemption from employers' health insurance contributions for wages less than 1.2 times the SMIC from September 1995. The two types of reduction were merged on 1 October 1996 to form a single exemption for wages less than 1.33 times the SMIC.

Box 8.1   Social security contributions, wages and employment

In France and in most member states, social expenditure is financed in large part by contributions paid by employers. Economic theory indicates that these contributions have an adverse effect on employment through increasing the labour cost. It also shows that a transfer of contributions from employers to employees does not have any effect on the level of employment after taxation. According to this theory, which is called the invariance of incidence proposition, the replacement of an employers' tax with an employees' tax of equal magnitude has no effect on the real economy: the total after-tax cost of labour to the employer (product wage), the net wage received by the employee (consumption wage) and the level of employment are not affected by the transfer of charges (OECD, 1990).

Figure 8.B1 illustrates this theory. The curve LS indicates the amount of labour which employees are prepared to provide for the various levels of real wage. The curve LD indicates the amount of labour which is demanded by employers for the various levels of real wage. The equilibrium of the labour market is achieved at point E_0; this equilibrium position corresponds to the real wage W_0 and to the level of employment L_0. If an employees' tax is introduced, the labour supply curve shifts up to LS'; a higher real wage W_1 and a lower level of employment L_1 correspond to the new equilibrium point E_1. If a tax of a similar amount to the above is levied on employers, the labour demand curve shifts down to LD', leading to a new equilibrium real wage W_2, lower than W_0, and a level of employment L_1. For a given tax, an increase in the labour supply and a fall in the labour demand have a similar impact on employment; only the equilibrium wage level varies.

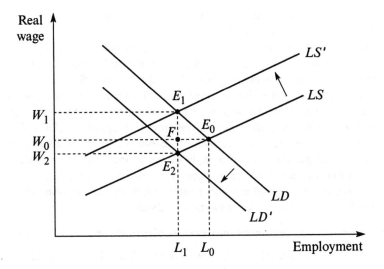

Figure 8.B1   Social security contributions, wages and employment

Whether the tax is paid by employees or employers, the level of the real product wage and that of the real consumption wage are, respectively, W_1 and W_2. The tax revenue is given by the surface $W_1E_1E_2W_2$. This is made of two elements. The surface $W_0FE_2W_2$ represents a transfer of income from employees to the state resulting from the reduction in the net real wage received by the employees; the surface $W_1E_1FW_0$ represents the loss in income of employers associated with the increase in the labour cost after taxation and the corresponding transfer of income to the state. The introduction of the tax also leads to welfare losses for the community. Employees who would want to work at the wage level corresponding to segment E_2E_0 of the labour supply curve, and the employers who want to use the amount of labour corresponding to segment E_1E_0 of the labour demand curve, cannot do this due to the taxation. The surface E_1FE_0 corresponds to the loss of welfare linked to the reduction of the producer's surplus, with the surface E_2FE_0 corresponding to the welfare loss of the employees. The magnitude of the reduction in employment, of the income and welfare losses for the employees, and employers and the level of the equilibrium wage depend on the elasticity of the labour demand and supply curves.

The invariance of incidence proposition implies that a switch from employers' to employees' taxes causes an adjustment of the nominal wage or of prices, such that the real product wage, the real consumption wage and employment return to their initial levels. However, this theory does not hold in the short term. Empirical studies (OECD, 1990) suggest, in fact, that a reduction in employers' taxes compensated for by an equivalent increase in employees' taxes is likely to reduce short-term unemployment. The short-term effects may last from five to ten years, due to wage and price adjustment lags. Even if the invariance of incidence proposition holds, the changes in the tax base can affect the allocation of resources (Moghadam, 1995). For example, employers' contributions are based on wages whereas personal or corporate taxes also apply to capital income. A switch from direct taxes to employer contributions implies an increase in the rate of taxation on employment and a reduction in capital taxation, which may lead to a substitution of capital for labour.

CSERC (1996) estimated that this measure would enable between 40 000 to 200 000 jobs to be created on a full-year basis, taking macroeconomic effects into account. Other measures for exemption from employers' contributions were adopted in 1995 in order to foster employment among the long-term unemployed (*contrat initiative-emploi*) and the development of part-time work.

Furthermore, the government is trying to diversify the resources allocated to the social security schemes so that their financing weighs less on the cost of labour. The generalized social security contribution (*contribution sociale généralisée* – CSG), levied on a wide range of incomes, was set up with this aim in 1991. The reform of the financing of health insurance undertaken in 1997 also falls within this context (see Section 3.2.3). Finally, such an adaptation of the method of financing social security, in the sense of increasing taxation of incomes rather than falling predominantly on wages, appears to be justified by the increased share of benefits related to national solidarity objectives.

2.4 The Recurring Problem of Social Deficits

Social security has been experiencing recurring financial crises since the first oil-price shock. These have resulted from the diverging development between the revenue levied on the wage bill, which is sensitive to economic fluctuations, and social expenditure, which has continued to evolve faster than economic growth (see Figure 8.2). The social security accounts were in deficit in 1981–82 and then again in 1986 (see Figure 8.3). Since 1991, the social security accounts have been continually in deficit. The social security net borrowing increased considerably in 1993 to reach FRF 100.9 billion (1.4 per cent of GDP). It remained at a high level in 1995 (1 per cent of GDP).

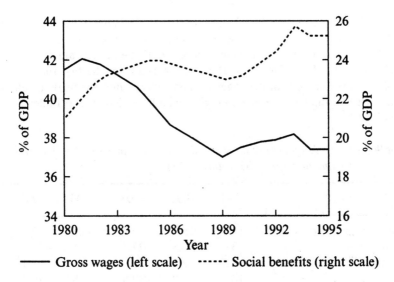

Source: Comptes de la nation (1996).

Figure 8.2 Development of social benefits and gross wages

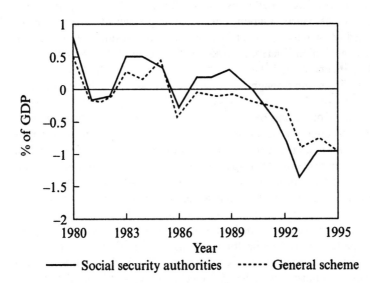

Source: Comptes de la nation (1996).

Figure 8.3 Social security net borrowing

Within the social security accounts the general scheme has a preponderant weight. This scheme has been in deficit since 1986 but its financial situation has worsened dramatically since 1990. The deficits are due to the sickness and old-age functions. However, in 1994, for the first time since 1945, all the functions of the general scheme were simultaneously in deficit and, in 1995, the family function registered a large deficit (see Tables 8.12 and 8.13).

Table 8.12   Development of the general scheme balance and breakdown by function, 1991–95 (billion FRF)

	1991	1992	1993	1994	1995
General scheme of which:	−16.6	−15.3	−56.4	−54.8	−67.3
sickness	−3.0	−6.3	−27.3	−31.5	−39.7
industrial accidents	0.5	2.1	−0.3	−0.1	1.1
old age	−18.7	−17.9	−39.5	−12.8	10.1
family	4.6	6.8	10.7	−10.4	−38.8

Source: Commission des comptes de la sécurité sociale (1996).

Efforts to consolidate health insurance   Since 1975, several plans to redress the health insurance situation have been implemented. They have mainly consisted of increases in contribution rates. As a result, the average rate of health contributions increased from 13.36 per cent of the gross wage in 1975 to 19.6 per cent in 1995. The government has also attempted to restrain health expenditure growth through increased cost-sharing, price control mechanisms, restrictions on the supply of care and global budgeting for hospitals and physicians. Controlling health expenditure was attempted first by acting on demand, through measures increasing out-of-pocket payments (increase of the *ticket modérateur*, change in the rate of reimbursement of certain pharmaceuticals, increase of the hospital fixed fee (*forfait hospitalier*), creation of sector II for free pricing of services by doctors). All these measures led to a fall in the average rate of reimbursement of health care and in the share of health costs paid by social security (see Table 8.14). Increased cost-sharing, by raising the prices of medical goods and services, should in principle induce patients to reduce health-care consumption. However, this policy had little success in terms of cost containment. This is due to the fact that the *mutuelles* and other private insurance companies pay a significant part of the health-care costs payable by patients. However, low-income patients who are poorly covered by supplementary insurance are penalized by the increase in the co-payment (Commissariat général du plan, 1994).

Table 8.13 Development of the balance of social security accounts, 1980–95 (billion FRF)

	1980	1985	1990	1995
1. Basic schemes				
General scheme	13.4	22.4	−10.4	−74.6
Unemployment benefit scheme	2.9	−3.4	4.2	20.3
Special funds	0.0	−0.2	0.3	0.3
2. Special schemes				
Special schemes for non-agricultural salaried workers	1.8	−3.8	3.2	−2.4
Supplementary schemes	5.8	6.3	13.7	−3.1
Schemes for self-employed non-agricultural workers	2.0	3.6	4.4	−2.5
Agricultural scheme	0.7	−0.7	−1.9	0.5
3. Bodies dependent on social insurance	−3.3	−7.4	−8.5	−12.1
Social security net borrowing (−)/lending (+):				
billion FRF	21.3	16.8	5.0	−73.6
% of GDP[1]	0.8	0.4	0.1	−1.0
% of GDP[2]				−0.8
General government net borrowing/lending (% of GDP)[1]	0.0	−2.9	−1.6	−5.3
General government net borrowing/lending (% of GDP)[2]				−4.8

Notes:
[1] General government/social security net borrowing according to national accounts.
[2] For 1995, general government/social security net borrowing reported by the French government in the context of the excessive deficit procedure.

Sources: Comptes de la nation (1996); French Ministry of Finance.

Prices of medical goods and services have long been subject to governmental controls. As a result, inflation has been successfully contained in the health sector; since 1945, health-care prices have risen less than overall inflation, and price levels for health services are now lower in France than in most industrial countries. Although price controls have contributed to slowing expenditure growth, they have also had perverse effects: they distort the allocation of resources and encourage the increase in the volume of health-care services.

Table 8.14   Development of the health insurance contribution rate, the reimbursement rate and the balance of the sickness function of the general scheme

	1975	1980	1985	1990	1995
Contribution rate (%)[1]	13.36	17.16	18.1	18.5	19.6
Average reimbursement rate (%)[2]	90.2	91.0	90.2	88.9	82.2
Balance of the sickness function (billion FRF)	–6.5	7.8	13.8	–9.4	–39.7

Notes:
[1] Weighted average health insurance contribution rate on wage without upper limit.
[2] Average rate of reimbursement of health care paid by health insurance; this rate differs from the average rate of health costs paid by health insurance which was 73.5 per cent in 1994.

Sources: Commission des comptes de la sécurité sociale (1996); French Ministry of Social Affairs.

The government has attempted to control health-care supply through a planning policy in the hospital sector (*carte sanitaire* – health map) and by applying a *numerus clausus* on student admission in medical schools. These actions, based on the statement that in the health sector, supply creates its own demand, have also proven to be relatively ineffective.

By contrast, global budgeting, introduced for public hospitals in 1984 and extended in 1992 to private hospitals, has proved an effective cost-containment mechanism. Until 1984, public hospitals were paid on a *per diem* and fee-for-service basis, which constituted an incentive to increase the volume of services. The introduction of global budgets for public hospitals[21] has led to a significant deceleration in expenditure growth. The share of hospital care in total medical consumption decreased from 50.5 per cent in 1985 to 47.3 per cent in 1991. However, since 1992, hospital expenditure has started to grow again more rapidly than total health expenditure: its share in total medical consumption amounted to 48.4 per cent in 1995 (SESI, 1996). While being a successful tool for containing expenditure growth, global budgeting has not promoted structural change and cost-effectiveness. Budget allocations are based on historical costs and calculated by applying the same rate of increase almost evenly to all hospitals. As a result, this procedure penalizes expanding hospitals facing growing costs, while those with shrinking services continue to receive increasing funds. Furthermore, budgets are allocated on the basis of financial and not medical criteria; therefore, the most dynamic establishments cannot demonstrate that the services they perform are more costly.

Table 8.15   Spending targets[1] and outcomes by profession (%)

	1994				1995			
	Objective		Outcome		Objective		Outcome	
	General scheme	All schemes	General scheme	All schemes	General scheme	All schemes	General scheme	All schemes
Private practice doctors	3.7	3.4	1.9	1.6	3.3	3.0	5.0	4.5
Biologists[2]	4.2	4.0	–8.2	–8.6	4.7	4.5	2.6	2.4
Nurses	4.5	4.5	3.7	3.6	3.3	3.3	3.2	2.9
Physiotherapists	5.2	5.0	2.9	2.8	3.7	3.3	4.7	4.5
Dentists	3.2	2.7			5.3	4.8	1.6	1.4
Speech therapists	No objectives				6.6	5.9	6.9	6.6
Orthoptists	No objectives				8.0	7.0	7.6	7.3

Notes:
[1] The objectifs quantifiés nationaux are set for all functions (sickness, maternity and industrial accidents) and all schemes. 'All schemes' comprises the general scheme (CNAM), the self-employed non-agricultural workers' scheme (CANAM) and the agricultural scheme (MSA).
[2] The objective for biology expenditure is set in terms of reimbursed expenses; the objectives for the other professions are set in terms of expenses presented for reimbursement.

Source: French Ministry of Social Affairs.

255

Expenditure caps have been introduced for doctors outside hospitals and other health professions. From 1991, annual spending targets (*objectifs quantifiés nationaux*) have been negotiated between the health insurance funds and certain professions: biologists, private practice nurses, physiotherapists, laboratories, doctors, and so on. This policy has produced some satisfactory results, although budget ceilings have not always been supplemented by mechanisms guaranteeing their respect (see Table 8.15). In ambulatory care, until 1996 compliance with spending targets was to be ensured by sanction mechanisms and the elimination of medically useless or dangerous health care or prescriptions (*maîtrise médicalisée des dépenses*). The marked slowdown in health expenditure observed in 1994 can be partly attributed to the existence of budget ceilings, although the health insurance recovery plan of July 1993, including a sharp increase in the *ticket modérateur*, has also had a significant effect. However, the renewed rapid rise in health expenditure recorded in 1995 has showed the limits of the mechanisms introduced and the need to reinforce them. Ambulatory care expenditure (general scheme only) rose by 5 per cent in 1995, while the expenditure target set by the medical agreement was 3.3 per cent (see Table 8.15).

3.   THE CURRENT REFORM OF THE HEALTH INSURANCE SYSTEM: THE JUPPÉ PLAN

Social security deficits are an important component of budgetary imbalances in France. Therefore, restoring social security accounts to balance has become a central element of the budgetary strategy adopted by the government from 1993 with a view to complying with the fiscal convergence criteria laid down in the Maastricht Treaty and to securing a lasting reduction in the government deficit. In this context, on 15 November 1995, the government announced a plan for a far-reaching reform of the social security system (the Juppé plan). The first part of the plan, implemented within a very short time at the beginning of 1996, consists of emergency measures intended to bring social accounts back to balance by 1997. The second part of the plan sets out the structural reforms aiming at long-term containment of social, and more specifically health, expenditure. The government therefore recognizes the need to reduce the growth in health expenditure in order to ensure the sustainability of the social protection system. Moreover, the French reform aims to introduce more equity and to improve the efficiency of the health-care system and presents similarities with the experiments carried out recently in other countries.

In the present section the economic challenges of the reform of the health-care systems in the industrialized countries are reviewed and the measures contained in the French reform plan, in particular in the area of health insurance, are analysed.

3.1 Reform of the Health-care Systems in Industrialized Countries

In most industrialized countries, the health-care systems are subject to major pressures, due mainly to the rapid growth in spending. Reforms have been undertaken in order to ensure cost control and to improve efficiency. As indicated by Jönsson (1996), despite the diversity of the institutional structures, the methods of financing the systems and the regulations in force, there are many similarities in the approaches adopted by the various countries. This section analyses the main economic issues raised by the health-care systems and the objectives pursued by the reforms.

Health care differs from other consumer goods in several respects (Weisbrod, 1991). In particular, it is characterized by a high degree of information asymmetry to the detriment of consumers, which can justify state intervention in order to protect the latter. Moreover, it affects the duration and quality of life, and is therefore considered as a social good which must be accessible to all, regardless of individuals' contributory capacity.

There are four principal questions which impinge on the economics of health:

(i) Is it necessary to control the growth of health expenditure and reduce its share of GDP?
(ii) Does the method of health-care financing have an unfavourable effect on employment?
(iii) What are the effects of the methods of financing and benefits of health care in terms of income redistribution?
(iv) What is the effect of the health-care system on the savings rate of the economy?

The high level and rapid growth of health expenditure is causing concern in most industrialized countries. It is, however, worth noting that it is the rapid growth rate of expenditure rather than its high level which is worrying (Newhouse, 1992). In recent decades, the growth rate of health expenditure has, on average, been higher than that of GDP in the majority of countries, which has led to an increase in the share of GDP devoted to this expenditure. Whereas rapid growth in other sectors of the economy is not considered to be worrying, the opposite is true for the health-care sector.

A major argument in favour of a health expenditure control policy is the desire to consolidate public finances. The reduction in public health expenditure can contribute to reducing government deficits (Cutler, 1994). The high growth in public health expenditure makes unpopular measures necessary: tax increases, reduction of other public expenditure, increase in social security contributions, reduction in benefits, increased payments by patients (Newhouse, 1994). However, concerns over the growth of health expenditure do not concern public health expenditure alone but all health expenditure, including the part financed by the private sector (Nolan, 1996).

The cost control policies implemented by most industrialized countries reflect the idea that the opportunity cost of the additional resources allocated to the health sector has become too high, and is higher than the marginal gain derived from the additional expenditure (Newhouse, 1992). According to Enthoven (1980), we have engaged in 'flatten-the-curve' medicine, where spending on medical care increases even though the additional gains from such spending are very low or non-existent. This notion is supported by studies showing that a large part of health expenditure is medically inappropriate (Chassin et al., 1987). This can be explained by the existence of moral hazard (see Section 2.1).

Newhouse (1992) emphasizes the importance of the concept of 'willingness to pay' in terms of health care. If market forces do not act to slow spending growth, at some point government intervention, such as global budget ceilings, may be desirable. The key issue in assessing these expenditure ceilings in terms of social welfare is whether consumers are willing to pay for the increase in health expenditure. In this respect, Newhouse points out that consumers have without doubt accepted to pay a large part of the additional spending entailed by technological change, implying that the welfare loss associated with the increase in expenditure may not be as large as an analysis in terms of opportunity cost might lead one to suppose. As a result, if consumers want to pay for part of the increase in health expenditure, a cost-containment policy may lead to a welfare loss by preventing care providers and consumers from making mutually advantageous exchanges.

The health-care systems and, in more general terms, the social protection systems have major implications for employment. It is less the level of social protection which matters than the design of benefit programmes and the method of financing (OECD, 1994a). The effects on the labour market are specific to each system. In the United States, the current system which links health insurance and employment contributes to limiting labour mobility (Cutler, 1994). In the case of France, increased social security contributions have helped to increase the cost of low-skilled labour and can partly explain the high level of unemployment for this category of worker (see Section 2.3.2).

All the measures affecting the financing or the provision of care necessarily have redistributing effects (Newhouse, 1994; Evans, 1996). Equity is an important objective for health-care systems; most European governments favour the egalitarian design which is based on the principles of horizontal equity ('with equal need, equal treatment') and vertical equity ('each person contributes to the financing of the system according to his contributory capacities') (Lachaud and Rochaix, 1995). The redistributing effects of the method of financing the health-care system depend on the degree of progressivity/regressivity of the system and on its various contributory components (tax, social security contributions, insurance premiums and direct payments).[22] Thus Lachaud and Rochaix (1995) show that the system of financing health care in France has a slightly regressive structure due to the weight of health insurance contributions in total resources; insurance premiums and direct payments, which are strongly regressive, have only a limited role in the financing of health care. The analyses of the equity of the European benefit systems show that inequalities in health care exist in favour of the higher-paid, that is, the frequency of unhealthy individuals is higher among the lower-paid (Lachaud and Rochaix, 1995). Newhouse (1994) shows, in the case of the Clinton health-care reform plan, that a reform of health-care financing can lead to major redistributions across industries, within industries, and also between geographical areas. Health-care reforms also have redistributing effects between care providers (Evans, 1996).

The social protection system also affects the savings rate of the economy. In particular, the method of financing social protection has major implications on the savings rate (Feldstein, 1974). The social protection system has an impact on precautionary saving, that is, saving made in response to uncertain health expenditure (Kotlikoff, 1989). Kotlikoff shows that, in the case where private insurance is not available, a public system of health insurance can have harmful effects on the savings rate, which must be compensated for by other policies.

The health-care systems of virtually all industrialized countries are confronted with similar problems, with the result that many are pursuing the same reform objectives (OECD, 1994b; Jönsson, 1996), as follows:

(i) greater equity or satisfactory and fair access for all citizens to a minimum level of health care;
(ii) containment of health expenditure growth (macroeconomic efficiency);
(iii) a more efficient use of the resources allocated to health care (microeconomic efficiency).

Jönsson (1996) underlines the need to define precisely the concepts of equity and efficiency and also stresses the possible antagonism between these two objectives.

3.2   The Juppé Plan: An Overview

3.2.1   Budgetary objectives

Social security deficits are an important component of budgetary imbalances in France. Since 1992, the social security deficit has contributed to
the increase of the general government net borrowing by approximately one
fifth of 1 percentage point in terms of GDP. In 1995, the social security net
borrowing amounted to 0.8 per cent of GDP, and the general government
net borrowing to 4.8 per cent (see Section 2.4, Table 8.12). Bringing the
social security accounts back to balance has become a central element of
the budgetary strategy of the government, aimed at ensuring compliance in
1997 with the fiscal convergence criteria laid down in the Maastricht Treaty
and achieving a sustainable position in the public finances over the medium
term.[23] This strategy, defined in the convergence programme of November
1993 and reaffirmed by the government on several occasions since then, is
based on the idea that budgetary consolidation must result from the reduction of financial imbalances in all the subsectors of the general government,
and in particular in the social security system. It is in this context that the
government presented, on 15 November 1995, a plan for a far-reaching
reform of the social protection system, involving emergency measures intended to ensure the restoration of the financial balance of the social security
accounts by 1997.[24]

3.2.2   The emergency measures

The first part of the Juppé plan consists of adjustment measures aimed at
handling the problem arising from the debt accumulated by the social security funds and at eliminating the general scheme deficit by 1997. At the time
the plan was presented, the general scheme deficit was estimated to decline
from FRF 64.5 billion (0.8 per cent of GDP) in 1995 to FRF 16.6 billion (0.2
per cent of GDP) in 1996 and to turn into a surplus of FRF 11.8 billion (0.1
per cent of GDP) in 1997. These projections were based on the macroeconomic hypotheses and revenue forecasts determined by the Commission des
comptes de la sécurité sociale in October 1995.[25]

In accordance with this plan, the accumulated social debt[26] (FRF 250
billion or 3.3 per cent of GDP) was taken over by a newly created institution,
the Caisse d'amortissement de la dette sociale (CADES), which is funded by
the proceeds of a new broad-based income tax, the *remboursement de la dette
sociale* (RDS), introduced on 1 February 1996. This tax is levied at the rate
of 0.5 per cent on all income with the exception of statutory minimum
income and income from tax-exempt savings accounts (*Livret A* and similar).[27] It was created for a period of 13 years, which corresponds to the period
of amortization of the debt.

In addition, a package of adjustment measures, consisting of revenue increases and expenditure cuts, was adopted. In total, the expenditure cuts represent over half the adjustment effort required over the two years 1996 and 1997 (see Table 8.16).

Table 8.16   Emergency measures provided for in the Juppé plan (billion FRF)

	1996	1997
Revenue measures (excluding RDS) (*ex ante*)		
Taxation of family allowances[1]	—	6.0
Increase in health insurance contributions on pensions and unemployment benefits	7.1	14.9
Penalty to the pharmaceutical industry	2.5	—
Tax on companies' insurance premiums	2.5	2.5
New resources allocated to the family branch	—	0.9
Total tax and contribution increases	12.1	24.3
Expenditure cuts (*ex ante*)		
Freezing of family allowances in 1996	2.6	2.8
Overhaul of family benefits and measures in favour of housing[2]	3.1	5.4
Control of health expenditure[3]	6.6	11.1
Savings on health insurance expenditure[4]	3.9	3.5
Savings on pension expenditure[5]	0.7	0.8
Savings on social security funds' running costs	1.5	2.0
Total expenditure cuts	18.4	25.6

Notes:
[1]   Measure abandoned.
[2]   This involves the refocusing of child benefits in favour of less well-off families, the inclusion of transfer incomes in the calculation of resource conditions for the allocation of housing benefits and family benefits, and the alignment of the methods of administration of family benefits of the state and public enterprises with those of private enterprises.
[3]   Both hospital and ambulatory care spending growth are limited to the projected inflation rate, that is, 2.1 per cent, in 1996 and 1997.
[4]   Billing of claim costs, creation of a mutual fund for the computerization of surgeries, compulsory affiliation of doctors in sector II to the national health insurance fund, and so on.
[5]   These savings would result from the limitation of the adjustment of pensions in the general scheme to 2.1 per cent in 1996 and the harmonization of the method of calculation of pensions of employees affiliated to several pension schemes with those of employees affiliated to a single scheme.

Source: French Government (1995b).

3.2.3   Reform of health insurance

The objectives of the structural measures contained in the 1995 reform plan are threefold: first, to ensure a more equitable access of citizens to health care; second, to keep health spending under control; and, third, to improve the efficiency of the health-care system so that better quality health care is delivered at a lower cost. While structural changes are undertaken in several fields (organization of the social security system, health-care system, family policy, pensions), the reform of the health insurance system constitutes the core of the whole reform.

Reorganization of social security   The reorganization of the social security system is aimed at clarifying the respective role of the state, social partners and parliament in the management of the social security system and, in particular, in controlling health expenditure growth. Its main element is the reinforcement of the legislator's powers in the social field, following the constitutional amendment of 19 February 1996. In the context of the social security financing law, parliament will each year set a national target for the growth of health expenditure, and it will also take decisions on the broad guidelines of the public health policy. On the basis of the national target, health spending objectives will then be defined for each sector (hospital, ambulatory care) and for each region. Moreover, social security funds will be reorganized to enable them better to fulfil their role of managers of the system. The composition of their boards is changed with a view to strengthening social democracy, regional associations of health insurance funds are created, and multi-year agreements setting objectives and means are concluded between the state and the national funds and are implemented at the local level by multi-year contracts between the national funds and the local funds.

Reform of health insurance and of the health-care system   The main structural changes concern the health-care system and, more precisely, the hospital and ambulatory sectors.

The hospital reform provides for the creation of regional hospital agencies charged with the management of both public and private hospitals. They are responsible for allocating regional global budgets (*dotations régionales hospitalières*) to individual hospitals; these budgets are determined on the basis of the national health insurance expenditure growth objective set by parliament. To take their decisions, regional agencies refer to accreditation reports prepared by a new national agency (Agence nationale d'accréditation et d'évaluation en santé), in charge of monitoring the quality of health care in public and private hospitals. This agency is made up of independent experts. Furthermore, multi-year contracts setting objectives and resources are concluded between each hospital and the competent regional agency. Regional agencies also have competence for hospital restructuring in order to reduce excess capacity.

In the ambulatory care sector, the reform[28] aims at long-term control of physician spending. Each year, an objective for prescription and fee spending is set by negotiation between the national health insurance funds and the doctors' unions, on the basis of the national health spending target. This objective may be broken down by health profession or by geographical area. Sanctions are foreseen if the spending targets are not met. Beginning in 1997, physicians' fees will not be raised if the spending targets have been overrun in the previous year. Moreover, in case of overshooting of the spending targets, physicians will collectively have to make reimbursements to health insurance. The medical agreement (*convention médicale*) signed between the national insurance funds and the doctors' unions defines the criteria according to which the reimbursement burden is individualized between doctors, in order not to penalize those who are more conscientious.

Another element of the reform in this sector is the reinforcement of the mechanism of *maîtrise médicalisée des dépenses*, introduced in 1993 (see Section 2.4). The medical guidelines, which define medically useless or dangerous health care or prescriptions (*références médicales opposables* – RMO), are supplemented by more efficient control mechanisms and penalties by the health-care funds. The coding of treatments and diseases is accelerated. Additional measures have been adopted. By the end of 1998, all surgeries will have to be computerized. As a result, data exchanges between doctors and health insurance funds will be made by electronic means, which will entail a reduction in the funds' operating costs. Incentives for the early retirement of physicians will be introduced, which should make it possible to stabilize the number of physicians by the year 2000. Training obligations for doctors are reinforced. The use of generic drugs is encouraged in order to keep drug prices low. These unbranded drugs, whose patents have fallen into the public domain, are sold at reduced prices as compared with the original drugs. Doctors will be encouraged to prescribe the cheapest medicines in order to comply with their spending objective.

Furthermore, tools to foster care coordination are introduced. By 1997, all insured patients will have an individual medical file which will ensure that duplication of treatment is avoided. Forms of managed care, placing general practitioners at the heart of the health of the system, are put in place on an experimental basis: *filières de soins* care channels organized around general practitioners, *réseaux de soins* care networks which pay for all care costs incurred by patients suffering from major or chronic diseases.

One of the government's priorities set out in the Juppé plan is the reform of the financing of health insurance. This reform aims at replacing part of social security contributions with a tax on a broader range of incomes. The objectives of the reform are twofold: first, to reduce the cost of labour and, second, to limit the effects of the business cycle on the financial balance of social accounts. The first measures implementing this reform have been adopted in the social security financing law of 1997 (see Section 4.1). This law provides for the reduction by 1.3 points of the rate of employee health insurance contributions. At the same time, the base of the CSG is extended to interest and capital income and some social security benefits, and the rate of the broadened CSG is raised from 2.4 per cent to 3.4 per cent. These three measures are expected to entail a revenue gain of FRF 5.2 billion for public finances on a full-year basis and an increase in net wages of 0.45 per cent. The government has not made any commitment as to the continuation of this reform.

The French plan also provides for the creation of a universal health insurance regime, with a view to improving the equity of the health-care system. This reform will guarantee the access to health insurance of all residents in France and will aim at harmonizing the benefit rights and contributions of the insured people. Currently, the sickness coverage and the rates and tax bases of health insurance contributions vary by scheme; the methods of financing the different schemes should be harmonized in the context of the reform of health insurance financing.

Finally, the plan provides for the creation of private pension funds (see Section 5.1) and a reform of family policy. The latter, designed to simplify the system of family benefits and to make it more equitable, was intended to be adopted in 1997. By early 1997, the details of the reform had yet to be specified. However, the government had renounced subjecting family allowances to personal income tax.

A rapid implementation of the reform The reinforcement of parliament's powers in the social security field, the cornerstone of the reform, required a constitutional amendment. The other provisions of the November 1995 reform plan have, for the most part, been implemented by decree; the urgency of the reform justified the use of this exceptional procedure. The emergency measures and certain structural reforms (reorganization of the social security funds, hospital reform and measures in the ambulatory sector) have been adopted according to this procedure. The other structural measures (creation of a universal health insurance scheme, reform of the health insurance financing and creation of private pension funds) have been or will be the subject of laws (see Table 8.17).

Table 8.17   Implementation of the social security reform

Measure/reform	Date	Type of measure adopted
Emergency measures		
Treatment of social security debt	1.1996	Decree
Financial rebalancing measures	1.1996	Decree
Structural reforms		
Reinforcement of parliament's power in the	2.1996	Constitutional
social security system	6.1996	amendment/organic law
Reorganization of the social security funds	4.1996	Decree
Hospital reform	4.1996	Decree
Control of ambulatory care spending	4.1996	Decree
Creation of a universal health insurance scheme	1997	Law
Reform of the health insurance financing	1997	Law[1]
Reform of family policy	1997	Law
Creation of private pension funds	2.1997	Law
Reform of special pension schemes		Reform postponed

Note: [1] The first measures implementing this reform have been adopted in the social security financing law of 1997.

Source: Commission services.

4.   SOME CONSEQUENCES OF THE JUPPÉ PLAN

This section reviews some effects of the emergency measures on public finances, growth and income distribution. It presents some observations on the health insurance reform and its potential impact with regard to the objectives pursued: health expenditure containment, equity, economic neutrality of the method of financing and improvement of the quality of care.

4.1   Macroeconomic and Redistribution Effects of the Emergency Measures

As with previous plans, the adjustment measures adopted to bring social security accounts back to balance mainly consist of increases in contributions, while expenditure cuts account for only one third of the adjustment effort (including the RDS). However, the short-term part of the plan also involves several innovations: it excludes an increase in cost-sharing by patients; it avoids increasing the cost of labour by not raising employers' contributions; it creates a new broad-based tax, like the CSG, with a wider tax base; and it increases the tax and contribution burden on specific social categories (pensioners, the unemployed, doctors) and companies (state-owned enterprises, pharmaceuticals industry, insurance companies).

As a result, the burden of the reform is not equally shared between economic agents (see Table 8.18). It weighs proportionally heavier on families.[29]

Table 8.18   Distribution of the burden of the reform (billion FRF)

	1996	1997
RDS[1]	21.5	25.0
Families	5.6	14.0
Taxation of family allowances	—	6.0
Freezing of family allowances	2.6	2.8
New resources allocated to the family function	—	0.9
Overhaul of family benefits and measures in favour of housing	2.4	3.7
Reform of maternity benefits	0.6	0.6
Pensioners/unemployed	7.8	15.7
Savings on pension expenditure	0.7	0.8
Increase in health insurance contributions	7.1	14.9
Enterprises	6.7	5.2
Penalty to the pharmaceuticals industry	2.5	—
Tax on companies' insurance premiums	2.5	2.5
Billing of claim costs	1.0	1.0
Harmonization of administration procedures for family benefits	0.7	1.7
Health professions	8.9	13.0
Savings on ambulatory care expenditure	3.3	7.2
Savings on hospital expenditure	3.3	3.9
Levies on doctors	2.3	1.9
Total (billion FRF)	50.5	72.9
Total (% of GDP)	0.7	0.9

Note: [1] *Remboursement de la dette sociale*: this tax, which is levied on all income with the exception of the social minima and income from exempt savings accounts, weighs on families and, to a lesser extent, on pensioners and the unemployed.

Source: Commission services.

Contribution increases and benefit cuts represent a burden of FRF 66 billion (that is, 0.8 per cent of GDP, including the RDS) on families, that is, over 50 per cent of the total effort required over the two years. Families are taxed via the RDS, the taxation of family allowances and the tightening of the conditions for the granting of family and housing benefits. Pensioners and the unemployed contribute about 20 per cent to the total effort required. Their taxation is justified by the low level of their health insurance contribution rates. This will result in a reduction in the relative living standard of these two social categories which are already affected by other measures (1993 reform of the pension system and 1992 reform[30] of the unemployment benefit scheme). Doctors are affected by 'sanction' measures (increases in their family and health insurance contributions) and by expenditure ceilings. The contribution demanded of enterprises represents 10 per cent of the total effort. Overall, it does not seem that the emergency measures contribute to reinforcing significantly the equity of the social transfers and contributions.[31]

A positive impact on public finances

The macroeconomic impact of the emergency measures (excluding structural reforms) in France has been estimated using the QUEST model.[32]

Table 8.19 indicates the impact on transfers to households, direct taxes and social security contributions, in percentage deviation from the control solution (situation in the absence of emergency measures). As regards monetary policy, the simulation was carried out under the hypothesis that the nominal interest rate is fixed or that the money supply is endogenous; consequently, the real rate of interest is also endogenous.

Table 8.20 presents the simulation's results. Contribution increases and cuts in benefits entail a reduction in households' real disposable income. This leads to a reduction in private consumption. The inflation rate falls slightly. Real short-term interest rates increase in the first two years and then decline.

Table 8.19 *Simulation hypotheses (deviation in relation to control in %)*

	1996	1997
Current transfers to households	−0.3	−0.4
Direct taxes	+4.0	+5.1
Social security contributions	+0.4	+0.9

Note: [1] Beyond 1997, the measures were extended by assuming that the reductions in benefits and increases in contributions programmed for 1997 would be maintained until 2005.

Source: Commission services.

Table 8.20   Impact of the emergency measures (deviation in relation to
              control in %)

	1996	1997	2005
GDP	−0.3	−0.2	−0.1
Private consumption	−0.4	−0.7	−0.4
Private investment	−1.3	−0.5	0.6
Inflation	−0.15	−0.1	0.0
Employment	−0.1	−0.2	−0.2
Government deficit (% of GDP)	−0.6	−0.9	−0.7

Source: Commission services.

The increase in real rates impinges negatively on private investment in the short term.

Overall, the emergency measures lead to a small reduction in GDP. In relation to control, the fall in GDP is 0.3 points in 1996, 0.2 points in 1997 and 0.1 points in 2005. The slowdown in activity affects employment, which falls over the whole reference period. The measures make possible a significant reduction in the general government deficit: the latter is reduced by 0.6 per cent of GDP in 1996, 0.9 per cent in 1997 and 0.7 per cent in 2005.

By comparison, the expenditure cuts and contribution increases represent an adjustment effort equivalent to 0.7 per cent and 0.9 per cent of GDP respectively in 1996 and 1997. Therefore, the reduction in the government deficit is slightly less than the yield of the emergency measures in 1996 and equal to it in 1997. In 1996, the slowdown in growth halts the fiscal consolidation. The results suggest that these measures were appropriate since they entail a significant reduction in the government deficit, although with a negative effect on growth and employment. However, it should be emphasized that the results are specific to the model and are obtained *ceteris paribus*.

Deficit objectives overshooting

In spite of the relative efficiency of the measures adopted, the government's initial objectives for the social security deficit will not be achieved. In the Juppé plan, the deficit[33] of the general scheme was projected to decrease from FRF 64.5 billion (0.8 per cent of GDP) in 1995 to FRF 16.6 billion (0.2 per cent of GDP) in 1996 and to turn into a surplus of FRF 11.8 billion (0.1 per cent of GDP) in 1997. However, in September 1996, the Commission des comptes de la sécurité sociale revised the deficit forecast for 1996 upwards, due to revenue shortfalls caused by the economic slowdown.[34] The Commission estimated that the deficit would amount to FRF 51.5 billion (0.65 per cent of GDP). The overshooting of the objectives is mainly due to disappointing economic developments. On the contrary, the yield of the emergency measures was very close to the government's initial estimates. However, implementation circumstances and the abandonment of a small number of measures (notably the contribution of doctors to the computerisation costs) caused a revenue loss of FRF 5 billion as compared with the initial estimate (see Table 8.21).

Table 8.21 *Effects of the emergency measures in 1996; comparison of the initial estimate with the revised estimate (billion FRF)*

	1996 initial estimate	1996 revised estimate
Increase in health insurance contributions on pensions and unemployment benefits	7.1	4.9
Penalty to the pharmaceuticals industry	2.5	2.5
Tax on companies' insurance premiums	2.5	2.5
Total tax and contribution increases (excluding RDS)	12.1	9.9
Freezing of family allowances in 1996	2.6	2.6
Overhaul of family benefits and measures in favour of housing	3.1	2.2
Control of health expenditure[1]	6.6	5.5
Savings on health insurance expenditure	3.9	2.8
Savings on pension expenditure	0.7	0.8
Claim costs against third parties	0.2	0.0
Savings on social security funds' running costs	1.5	1.5
Total expenditure cuts	18.4	15.6
Total measure yield in 1996	30.5	25.5

Note: [1] The estimate of the Commission des comptes is based on the hypothesis of compliance with the growth objective for the global hospital allocation and community care expenditure (+2.1 per cent) in 1996.

Sources: Commission des comptes de la sécurité sociale (1996); Commission services.

The government has therefore been prompted to take additional adjustment measures and to revise downwards its objective for the general scheme balance in 1997. The expenditure and revenue measures adopted in the social security financing law for 1997 should make it possible to reduce the deficit of the general scheme to FRF 30 billion (0.4 per cent of GDP). This law initiates the reform of the health insurance financing (see Section 3.2.2). The law provides for other revenue measures and caps health insurance expenditure at FRF 600.2 billion in 1997, that is, an increase of 0.2 per cent in real terms as compared with 1996.

The overrun of the deficit objectives contained in the Juppé plan has two consequences. First, it will be necessary to refinance the debt accumulated by social security in 1996 and 1997 (which will represent about 1 per cent of GDP at the end of 1997), and, second, the social security accounts will return to balance only in 1999, while the November 1995 plan foresaw a slight surplus as early as 1997.[35]

4.2 Implications of the Reform of the Health Insurance System

The 1995 reform preserves the main features of the French social security system. It reaffirms that social security is founded on the principle of national solidarity and it maintains the independence of the social security funds under the responsibility of social partners. As regards the health-care system, it safeguards the principles governing the exercise of independent medical practice (freedom of location, freedom of choice of doctor, freedom of prescription, fee-for-service payment, confidentiality) and the principles of the hospital system (access for all to hospitals, possibility for patients to choose between public and private hospitals).

The reform of the health insurance system raises questions as to its efficiency in terms of cost containment, equity, its consequences on employment and the quality of care.

Cost Containment
The reform should allow substantial savings to be made in the short term, but may prove insufficient as a lasting spending control.

The reform relies on supply-side measures to contain spending. Such a policy is based on the idea that, in the health sector, supply induces demand. However, as noted by Reinhardt (1989), this question is controversial. Supporting this thesis, certain economists highlight the fact that care providers exploit the lack of information on their patients in order to increase their income. By contrast, for neoclassical economists, control over resource allocation to health care is better achieved through the demand side, by letting patients discipline providers who compete against one another on the basis of price and quality (Reinhardt, 1989).

Budget ceilings are likely to halt, significantly and immediately, health spending growth. The introduction of global budgets for the main components of health expenditure may be an efficient cost-containment tool (Jönsson, 1996). The French plan recalls in certain respects the reform of the German health-care system introduced in January 1993 (Seehofer reform).[36] This reform was characterized by a tightening of budget constraints on the main items of health expenditure (ambulatory care, hospitalization, dental care and medicines). Its impact was spectacular in terms of cost containment and the system recorded a surplus in 1993 and 1994. However, by 1995, deficits had reappeared. This experiment tends to confirm the idea that it is difficult to find mechanisms allowing the growth in expenditure to be durably slowed and that, therefore, repeated state intervention through successive reforms is necessary (Commissariat général du plan, 1994).

The majority of the reforms occurring in the industrialized countries since the early 1980s have tended to reinforce the market mechanisms in the health-care sector in order to achieve a more efficient allocation of resources[37] (OECD, 1992). The Juppé plan seeks to develop competition between care providers. It provides for experimentation[38] with networks of insurers/suppliers (*réseaux de soins coordonnés*) and is inspired, in this respect, by foreign experiments. In the United Kingdom, the recent reforms of the National Health Service have also been intended to stimulate competition between care providers. The district health commissions and the fund-holding general practitioners 'purchase' care from the health professions and hospitals on behalf of their clients. In the United States, the health maintenance organizations, which constitute the most advanced method of integration between insurers and care providers, have better control of their costs due to the tight control which they exercise over the producers.

The French reform reinforces a new regulatory instrument, the *contrôle médicalisé des dépenses*. In principle, this regulatory mechanism is very attractive to doctors as the control of spending is based on medical criteria. However, its justification is not certain from either a medical or an economic point of view (Commissariat général du plan, 1994). For this mechanism to be efficient, three conditions should be met:

(i)   medical science can affirm the unnecessary nature of a medical practice and the medical guidelines can cover a significant part of the field of medical activity;

(ii)   it is possible, without excessive cost, to gather the information needed in order to evaluate the practices of doctors;

(iii)   unnecessary care is sufficiently frequent for its elimination to have a noticeable effect on spending.

In addition, the efficiency of this regulatory instrument depends on the reliability of the systems for evaluating medical practices.

Finally, it is worth noting that certain measures will lead to additional costs. In particular, the computerization of data exchanges between surgeries and funds has a cost which is not evaluated in the government's plan. For the health insurance funds alone, the distribution of smart cards to all the insurance contributors represents an investment of FRF 4 billion. The creation of a universal health insurance scheme will lead to additional costs, linked to the coverage of the people not contributing to insurance and the increase of the administration costs of the funds which will result from this. The official estimates record a cost in this field of FRF 1 billion on a full-year basis.[39] Finally, the reform provides for the creation of new structures, specifically in the hospital sector with regional hospital agencies and the Agence nationale d'accréditation et d'évaluation. It modifies the organization of health insurance funds, with the creation of regional associations. The government has not assessed the operating and investment costs of these new bodies.

As a whole, it is currently difficult to evaluate what the impact of the reform of health insurance will be in terms of control of health spending. The results obtained in 1996 appear to be encouraging. The growth in health insurance expenditure in the general scheme has declined in relation to the previous year (+3.3 per cent in 1996 compared with +4.7 per cent in 1995). The targets for hospital and ambulatory care spending have been virtually met.[40] This result has been achieved even though certain elements of the reform of the health-care system were not in place. More generally, the structural measures adopted will only produce their effects gradually. In particular, savings expected from the hospital reform, through the reduction of excess capacity, will be slow to materialize. Spending caps and the mechanisms introduced to ensure compliance with these should gradually lead to a change in physicians' behaviour, which is the only way to durably reduce spending pressures. Ultimately, the success of the reform will depend on the determination with which it is implemented. In this regard, in the event of overshooting of spending targets, it is important for the credibility of the reform that penalties and sanctions envisaged against physicians be strictly applied.

Effects contrary to equity
Certain provisions of the reform appear to be contrary to equity. The reform does not ensure the equality of treatment between physicians and the other health professions. It appears particularly strict towards private practice doctors, although they account for less than a third of health expenditure. In 1990, the ambulatory care expenditure (medical and paramedical care) represented 28.4 per cent of total health expenditure compared with 44.2 per cent for hospital expenditure. In addition, the share of ambulatory expenditure in total health expenditure is no higher in France than in the other European countries. Private practice doctors are subject to strict controls and are liable to sanctions. Certainly, the agreements signed between the funds and other health professions also provide for sanctions in the event of overshooting of

the *objectifs quantifiés nationaux*, but the mechanism appears in general to be less rigorous than for private practice doctors.

Moreover, the reform of the financing of health insurance entails transfers of charges between social groups. The reduction in the employees' health insurance contributions leads to a net income gain for employees. By contrast, other social groups have their contribution to the financing of social security increased through the broadening and increase of the CSG rate, in particular pensioners, the unemployed and property owners. The harmonization of the contributory efforts of the insured persons in the context of universal health insurance will also lead to transfers of charges to the detriment of pensioners, civil servants, employees of certain public enterprises and the self-employed.

Effects of the health insurance financing reform on the labour market
The health insurance financing reform is intended to reduce the economic distortions caused by the current method of financing. The effects on employment of such a reform are uncertain. According to IMF unpublished estimates, a reduction of 1 point in employees' social security contributions, financed by an increase in a broad-based income tax of the CSG type, would have a positive effect on employment in the short term but a negative one in the long term.

In the IMF simulation, the reduction in the employees' contributions[41] is neutral in budgetary terms in the short term; it is totally offset by the increase in a tax on all incomes. In the short term, employment increases by 0.1 per cent. The employees transfer part of the tax reductions to employers by a reduction in their gross wages. The employees' net income increases but the net rate of return on capital falls and investment declines. In the long term, employment falls by 0.2 per cent and the reform has a negative effect on the budget. These effects result from the fall in investment due to the reduction in the net rate of return on capital.

Strong resistance of the medical professions
The strike days organized by doctors and the protest movements in public hospitals, which took place at the end of 1996 and in 1997, are evidence of the strong opposition of the medical professions to the reform. These have stated their disagreement with the fee reimbursement mechanism, and have denounced the risk of the rationing of care and the attacks on the principles of independent medical practice. The reform of health insurance has been favourably welcomed only by a single doctors' association, MG France, representing general practitioners. Despite this resistance, the government has remained quite firm in the application of the reform. In particular, the doctors' unions obtained few concessions on the part of the health insurance

funds on the question of the control of medical expenditure during the negotiation of the medical agreements in early 1997.

The French reform illustrates the difficulty of restructuring the welfare
state. As shown by Wilsford (1994), health-care systems do not lend themselves to radical changes; however, far-reaching reforms are possible in
centralized systems, such as the German or French systems, provided that
favourable circumstances are present. Therefore, in the case of Germany, the
acute financial crisis created by unification and the presence of a strong
coalition in power allowed the Minister for Health, Seehofer, to implement an
ambitious reform in 1993 and to overcome the structural obstacles which had
made the previous Blüm reform fail in 1989. Similarly, Pierson (1996) concludes that the unpopularity of restrictive policies in terms of social protection
makes reforms highly improbable except under certain conditions, in particular at times of budgetary crisis and under governments in a strong electoral
position. To a certain extent, these considerations can explain the success of
the French government in implementing the reform of the social security
system. However, even in a favourable context, certain measures are difficult
to adopt, as the abandonment of both the project to tax family allowances and
the reform of the special pension schemes shows.

5.   MEDIUM- AND LONG-TERM PROSPECTS OF THE PENSION SCHEMES

As in most member states, retirement income in France is mainly financed by
pay-as-you-go schemes. The ageing of the population and the retirement of
the 'baby-boom' generation from 2005 onwards pose new challenges for
pension schemes. In France, the reform of the pension system started with the
law of 22 July 1993. However, beyond 2005, the financial prospects of the
system remain worrying. The Juppé plan has introduced a major change with
the introduction of legislation on private pension funds.

5.1   Measures Implemented in the Area of Pensions

Features of the French pension system
The pension system in France comprises a large number of pay-as-you-go
schemes (about 120 basic schemes and 400 supplementary ones).[42] They can
be broadly divided among those for private sector employees and the self-
employed, and those for public sector employees and some categories of workers
(railwaymen, miners, EDF employees, and so on). Private sector employees
have a two-level system: the general level (general scheme) and the supplementary level (*régimes complémentaires*) grouped around AGIRC (Association

générale des institutions de retraites des cadres) and ARRCO (Association des régimes de retraites complémentaires). In some cases, there is a third level. Some companies provide optional supplementary schemes (*régimes surcomplémentaires*) which are usually funded. Public sector employees are covered by different 'special schemes' which usually have only one level, although a voluntary funded scheme is also available for civil servants. A special public fund, *Fonds de solidarité vieillesse*, provides old-age benefits including a *minimum vieillesse* for citizens aged 65 or over without adequate income. In total, as in the majority of member states, private pension funds play a limited role in France as a source of retirement income.[43]

Retirement age, contribution rates and calculation of benefits may vary considerably between the different schemes. Benefits from the general scheme are determined by the number of years the beneficiary has contributed, as well as the average wage earned over a certain number of years, indexed by either changes in price levels or average wage increases. Benefits from the *régimes complémentaires* are proportional to the number of 'points' the individual accumulated before retiring. The ratio between the annual pension each point secures and its cost is known as the 'rate of return' (*rendement*) of contributions. Cumulation of pensions from different schemes is allowed. On average, retirees receive pensions from 1.5 basic schemes and 1.3 supplementary schemes (White Paper, 1991).

The rapid increase in pension expenditure in France started causing concerns during the last decade and led to increases in contributions and efforts to reduce benefits. However, no major reform was adopted until 1993.

The reform of July 1993

An important step in reforming the pension schemes was undertaken in 1993. On the basis of recommendations in the White Paper (1991), the law of 22 July 1993 reformed the method of calculation of pensions in the general scheme and in the schemes aligned to it. The reform[44] consisted of the following points:

(i)   the contribution period for a full-rate pension will be gradually increased from 150 to 160 quarters;

(ii)   the number of best years used for the calculation of the reference wage will be gradually increased from 10 to 25 years, which will have the effect of reducing the average pension paid;

(iii)   pension adjustments will be based on the consumer price index (CPI) instead of gross wage growth;

(iv)   the *Fonds de solidarité vieillesse* (FSV) is created with the main task[45] of financing the non-contributory old-age benefits resulting from national solidarity.

The next section presents an analysis of the effects of the July 1993 reform. This reform contributes to improving of financial prospects of the pension system by 2005 but leaves many questions unresolved, particularly the sustainability of the special pension schemes. The reform of these schemes is proving difficult. Provided for in the November 1995 plan, this reform was finally abandoned following strikes in the public sector at the end of 1995. Bringing these schemes back to balance was to involve, in particular, the extension from 37.5 to 40 years of the duration of contribution required to benefit from a full-rate pension.

Encouraging private pension funds

The other major provision specified by the Juppé plan concerning pensions, the introduction of legislation on private pension funds, has been implemented in spite of political difficulties. In general, such pensions funds are likely to play an increasing role in the pension systems of the member states, in order to compensate for the reduction in benefits paid by the pay-as-you-go pension schemes (Thomas, 1997).

The adoption of the law of 20 February 1997 establishing retirement savings plans[46] has led to lively debate. The question of pension funds remains controversial in France. Opposition to funded pension schemes is based on unfortunate pre-war experiences which led to the adoption of the pay-as-you-go principle for social security in 1945. Not affected directly by socio-demographic developments and the situation on the labour market, these schemes are, however, sensitive to the risk of inflation and the instability of the financial markets. The transition from contribution to funding could affect intergenerational equity (White Paper, 1991). The stimulation of savings by households may be inappropriate given the current sluggishness of consumption (Cornilleau and Sterdyniak, 1995). Be that as it may, thinking has developed in favour of private pension funds in France since 1991. The growth of the life insurance sector and of company-sponsored savings plans creates an environment favourable to the expansion of prefunded pension schemes in France (Levy, 1995). However, because of historical and cultural factors, private pension funds are likely to play only a modest role in providing retirement income compared with the basic and supplementary schemes, in contrast to the experience of certain other European Union countries (Denmark, the Netherlands and the United Kingdom) (Charpentier, 1996).

5.2　Pension Expenditure Projections

Demographic and economic prospects: a large increase in the dependency ratio

The majority of the difficulties with which the pay-as-you-go pension schemes will be confronted in the medium and long term result from the ageing of the population. The share in the population of elderly people over the age of 60 years will increase rapidly in the years to come. According to demographic projections carried out by INSEE (1992), the ratio of the population aged over 60 years to the population aged 15 to 59 years would increase from 0.31 in 1990 to 0.43 in 2015 and to 0.63 in 2040.[47] This means that, at this time, there would be six potential pensioners for every ten potential contributors, compared with three in 1990. Moreover, the financial situation of the pension system depends on such factors as the activity rate and the situation on the labour market, which determine the growth of the wage bill and, as a result, the resources of the pension schemes. Furthermore, legislation influences the level of pensions disbursements.

On the basis of alternative scenarios involving trends in participation rates and in the rate of unemployment, the Forecasting Department (Direction de la prévision), using the Margaret model, has evaluated developments in the dependency ratio and the rate of social security contributions required in order to balance the social accounts. Whichever scenario is used, the dependency ratio will clearly increase during the period (see Table 8.22). In the best-case scenario, the dependency ratio would increase by 0.3 points between 2000 and 2040, rising from 0.48 to 0.77. In the worst-case scenario, this ratio would reach 0.9 points in 2040. In this year, there would only be 1.1 contributors per pensioner compared with two in 2000 and three in 1990. It is around the years from 2005 to 2010, which correspond to the arrival at retirement age of the baby-boom generation, that the growth of the dependency ratio would begin.

The effects of the July 1993 reform

The projections presented by Briet (1995) show that the 1993 reform of the general scheme allows the financial prospects of the pension system to be improved up to 2005. Under certain macroeconomic hypotheses, the savings resulting from this reform can be estimated at approximately FRF 45 billion (1993 value) between now and 2005, which would allow 70 per cent of the projected net borrowing to be covered. This net borrowing would then be no more than 0.9 points of the social security contributions. However, by 2015, the rise in the demographic ratio will be such that the reform would not be sufficient to check the increase in the deficit, which would amount to 4.3 contribution points (see Tables 8.23 and 8.24).

Table 8.22 Projected development of dependency ratios

| | Birth rate 1.8 | | | | Birth rate 2.1 | | | |
| | Low activity rate | | High activity rate | | Low activity rate | | High activity rate | |
	Stability[1] Alternative 1	Absorption[1] Alternative 2	Stability Alternative 3	Absorption Alternative 4	Stability Alternative 5	Absorption Alternative 6	Stability Alternative 7	Absorption Alternative 8
2000	0.50	0.48	0.49	0.48	0.50	0.48	0.49	0.48
2040	0.91	0.84	0.90	0.82	0.85	0.78	0.83	0.77

Note: [1] 'Stability' and 'Absorption' refer to unemployment.

Source: Briet (1995).

Table 8.23   Principal macroeconomic hypotheses (% change per year, unless otherwise indicated)

	1995–2000	2000–2005	2005–2010	2010–2015
GDP growth	3.5	2.5	2.0	1.75
Labour productivity	2.25	1.25	1.75	2.0
Real wage per capita	1.0	1.5	2.0	2.0
Numbers employed	1.25	1.25	0.25	–0.25
Unemployment rate at end of period (%)	11.0	9.0	8.5	8.5
Compensation of employees	2.25	2.75	2.25	1.75

Source: Briet (1995).

Table 8.24   Net borrowing of the general scheme before and after reform (billion FRF (1993 value))

		1993	1995	2000	2005	2010	2015
Before reform	Net borrowing	25.2	42.0	55.5	62.9	120.0	191.0
	expressed in contribution points	1.7	2.8	3.2	3.1	5.3	7.8
After reform	Net borrowing	25.2	9.5	18.4	17.8	55.4	107.0
	expressed in contribution points	1.7	0.6	1.1	0.9	2.4	4.3

Source: Briet (1995).

Consequences of the ageing of the population

The increase of the dependency ratio will weigh significantly on the financial balance of the pension schemes (see Table 8.25). The consequences of the projected development in the dependency ratio on the equilibrium contribution rate[48] have been simulated for a fictional single scheme, representative of the whole pension system, using the Margaret model. Taking into account the reform of the general scheme, the net borrowing of this fictional single scheme would increase by nearly 22 contribution points between 1990 and 2040. Although the reform has the effect of significantly limiting the pension level of pensioners, their financial situation would improve relative to that of employees during the period; assuming parity of income is achieved in 1990 between pensioners and the working population, the average pensioner pension would be 55 per cent higher in 2040 than the net average earned income. An extension

*Table 8.25   Equilibrium contribution rate and relative income of
pensioners*

	Reform of the general scheme		Extended reform[1]	
	Equilibrium contribution rate[2]	Relative income of pensioners[3]	Equilibrium contribution rate	Relative income of pensioners
1990	18.9	100	18.9	100
2040	40.8	155.5	33.6	114.1

Notes:
[1] Hypothesis of the extension of the reform of the general scheme to all pension schemes.
[2] This concerns an apparent contribution rate. This rate is calculated as the ratio of total benefits to total gross earnings.
[3] Ratio of the average pension to the average earned income net of old age contributions.

Source: Briet (1995).

of the reform of the general scheme to all the pension schemes would limit to approximately 15 points the increase in contributions needed to maintain the balance of this fictional scheme. In this case, in 2040, the relative income of pensioners would be 14 per cent higher than that in the 1990s.

The projections presented by Briet (1995) update the projections in the White Paper (1991). They are based on less favourable demographic and economic hypotheses which lead to less encouraging results in respect of both the expected dependency ratios and the development of the financial accounts of the pension schemes. However, as underlined by Franco and Munzi (1996), such estimates of future pension expenditure must be treated with care as they are dependent on underlying macroeconomic and demographic hypotheses. The demographic prospects are fairly uncertain in the long term. Birth rates may fluctuate significantly and unpredictably even in the short term; death rates and migratory movements are also difficult to predict. Uncertainties also surround macroeconomic developments. The influence of demographic and economic factors on pension expenditure, changes in social behaviour and legislation necessitate periodic reviews of the projections (Franco and Munzi, 1996).

Differing financial prospects depending on the scheme
The long-term financial prospects vary by scheme. They partly relate to specific demographic prospects of the population in each scheme, and partly to the average pensions paid by each scheme, and to the wage bill of the population covered by each scheme.

(i)   The private sector schemes (general scheme, ARRCO and AGIRC supplementary schemes) would experience financial difficulties from 2005. In fact, from this date, the pensioners/contributors dependency ratio would rapidly increase with the arrival at retirement age of large post-war cohorts. The application to the general scheme of the July 1993 reform and the measures adopted for the supplementary schemes would nevertheless tend to halt the development of the costs of these schemes.

(ii)   The situation of the special schemes would deteriorate significantly from 2000. This development would result from the deterioration of the demographic ratio and a relatively higher increase in the average pension than in the private sector.

(iii)   The scheme for farmers and that for the SNCF should see their net borrowing stabilize, due to the stability of the ratio of contributions to disbursements. By contrast, the local authorities' scheme will, under the assumption of unchanged legislation, see its net borrowing increase significantly from 1994.

The private sector schemes which are sensitive to the economic situation could experience contrasting developments depending on economic growth. By contrast, a more favourable macroeconomic environment would not solve the financial problems of the special schemes which face negative demographic prospects.

A similar situation to that in the other European Union countries
The ageing of the population is a phenomenon which is affecting all the European Union countries. The dependency ratio in the European Union is expected to increase from 22.9 per cent in 1995 to 25.8 to 28.7 per cent in 2010 and to 30.8 to 40.6 per cent in 2025 according to the projections of various international organizations. The increase of the dependency ratio is causing concern in the member states in terms of the sustainable nature of the pay-as-you-go pension schemes. The analysis of the pension expenditure projections carried out recently in the member states makes it possible to distinguish three periods. Between now and 2000, the pressures exerted by pension expenditure on public finances should be fairly limited in most member states. During the 2000–2010 period, the prospects of the pension schemes will deteriorate. But it is particularly after 2010, with the arrival at retirement age of the baby-boom generation, that the situation of the European pension systems will probably deteriorate most dramatically. The financial prospects for the French pension system appear to be in line with those of the European schemes. The differences in the forecasting methods, in the reference periods and in the demographic and economic hypotheses make

comparison of the national estimates difficult. Nevertheless, the results of the forecasts lead to the same conclusion: given the anticipated changes in the demographic structure, the sustainability of the current pension levels would require a substantial increase in the national resources allocated to the pension systems (Franco and Munzi, 1996).

6. CONCLUDING REMARKS

The Juppé plan presented by the French government on 15 November 1995 is certainly the most ambitious social security reform plan since the creation of the social security system in 1945. In spite of its complexity and its considerable scope, the plan has been implemented within a very short time and almost in its entirety. The reform of the special pension schemes is the main provision which has been abandoned.

A central objective of this plan is to bring the social security accounts back to balance and to secure a lasting balance within the social security system. This falls within the context of the government's budgetary strategy, defined in 1993 and aimed at reducing the general government deficit to 3 per cent of GDP in 1997 and achieving a sustainable situation in the public finances over the medium term. In the short term, the discretionary measures adopted for the 1996–97 period were designed to restore to balance the social security accounts by 1997. However, although the results of these measures have been very close to initial estimates, the deficit objective was overshot in 1996, due to unfavourable economic developments which caused revenue shortfalls. In the long term, containing social, and specifically health, expenditure growth must ensure the sustainability of equilibrium in the social security accounts.

The reform of the health insurance system constitutes the key element of the Juppé plan. This reform has numerous common features with reforms carried out recently in other industrialized countries. The objectives pursued are the same: to contain the health insurance spending growth in the long term while improving the quality of care and increasing the equity of the health-care system. A salient feature of the 1995 plan in relation to previous reforms in France is the emphasis placed on the microeconomic efficiency objective: this implies providing better-quality health care at a lower cost than is currently the case, through, among other measures, the creation of a system of accreditation of hospitals or the reinforcement of the control of medical practices. Efficiency considerations have led certain countries (the United Kingdom, the Netherlands, and the United States) to introduce more competition between care providers and insurers. The 1995 reform plan remains cautious in this area and seeks more specifically to make the social security funds and the health professionals more responsible through a network of contracts.

The health insurance reform focuses on supply-side measures to control spending growth. It reinforces budget constraints on the two main items of health expenditure – hospital and ambulatory care spending. The 1983 reform of hospital financing in France and, more recently, the reform of the German health-care system have shown that budget ceilings are an effective cost containment mechanism in the short term. The marked slowdown in health expenditure in 1996 is an encouraging result. However, it is too early to evaluate the long-term impact of the reform in terms of cost containment. The structural measures adopted will produce their effects only gradually. Ultimately, the success of the reform from a budgetary perspective will depend on its credible and determined implementation, notably as regards the application of the sanctions specified against physicians as well as the introduction of incentive mechanisms such as the *réseaux de soins coordonnés*.

Until 2005, and conditional on a favourable macroeconomic environment, the social security system should not be subject to significant pressures. Until this time, the social security net borrowing would result mainly from the health insurance system, whereas the pension schemes, due to the effects of the July 1993 reform, would not as a whole experience financing difficulties (Cornilleau et al., 1996). On the other hand, beyond 2005, the social security accounts will again experience severe financial difficulties. The arrival at retirement age of the many post-war cohorts will weigh heavily on the financial position of the pay-as-you-go pension system. The 1995 reform introduced a major change with the adoption of measures favouring the creation of private pension funds. Nevertheless, it is unlikely that such pensions funds will become prominent in France in the near future. Thus, the reform of the pay-as-you-go pension scheme remains to be completed.

NOTES

1. This chapter is a revised translation of a study originally prepared in French under the title 'La réforme du système français de sécurité sociale: enjeux et perspectives'. I am particularly grateful to Tassos Belessiotis who encouraged me and provided many valuable comments and suggestions on a first draft, and to Daniele Franco who read thoroughly a subsequent draft of this chapter; thanks are also due to Antonio Cabral and Mirella Tieleman for helpful comments, and to Donatienne Dernouchamps for assistance with the data. The views expressed in this chapter are exclusively those of the author and do not necessarily correspond to those of the European Commission.
2. See European Commission (1995, 1997).
3. Average for EU 12 (Eurostat, 1995).
4. OECD (1994b). In 1992, Finland together with France had the highest ratio of health spending to GDP in the European Union.
5. This chapter was completed in March 1997 and, consequently, it does not review the developments occurring beyond that date.
6. Protection mechanisms were set up from the end of the nineteenth century, basically for employees (law of 30 April 1930 creating 'social insurance' in France). After World War

II, it was considered necessary to generalize protection against social risks for the whole population.

7. The social security systems play a contra-cyclical role through unemployment benefits. The majority of sickness benefits and pensions contribute to supporting household incomes.

8. The social security system according to current French meaning forms only a part of the social security system according to the definition of national accounts. In French national accounting, the social security authorities encompass, in addition to the compulsory schemes (basic and supplementary pension schemes), the unemployment benefit scheme and the bodies depending on social insurances, that is, the hospitals participating in the public hospital service and the social works integrated within the social security bodies. The social protection system according to the European system of integrated social protection statistics (Esspros), used by Eurostat, also includes, among others, optional supplementary protection.

9. If the expenditure on the invalidity risk is added to these benefits, a different classification is obtained. According to the Esspros data, the share in GDP of expenditure on sickness–industrial accident–invalidity benefits in 1993 amounted on average to 9.2 per cent in the European Union (excluding the new member states). The Netherlands had the highest ratio (14.3 per cent), followed by Germany (11.4 per cent) and France (9.9 per cent).

10. According to OECD data, in 1992 France was in first place, together with Finland, within the European Union for the share of health expenditure in GDP. France and Finland, with a ratio of 9.4 per cent, were followed by Austria (8.8 per cent), Germany (8.7 per cent), the Netherlands (8.6 per cent), Italy (8.5 per cent) and Belgium (8.2 per cent). Within the OECD, France and Finland were in third place, behind the United States (14.0 per cent) and Canada (10.2 per cent).

11. The density of doctors per 100 000 inhabitants was 270 in 1994 and was above the OECD average.

12. For an analysis of the strengths and weaknesses of the French social protection system, see French Government (1995a) and, in particular for the health-care system, Commissariat général du plan (1994).

13. However, if one compares the average level of the pension with that of the final earned income, the loss in remuneration is relatively higher.

14. The United States, which is in first place among the countries of the OECD for the share of health expenditure in GDP, also has a health performance which is little different from the average of the European countries (see Table 8.7).

15. Public spending on health accounted for 74.7 per cent of total health expenditure in 1992, which is close to the European average. Within the European Union, Belgium had the highest ratio (88.9 per cent), followed by Sweden (85.6 per cent) and the United Kingdom (84.4 per cent) (Oxley and MacFarlan, 1994).

16. In France, so-called solidarity expenditure has developed since 1956. After the creation of the old-age minimum (*minimum vieillesse*), allowances were introduced for other categories of the population: allowance for handicapped adults, single parent allowance, specific solidarity allowance, then *revenu minimum d'insertion* for the unemployed.

17. In 1994, the rate of employees' contributions on the gross wage amounted to 20.6 per cent at the level of the social security ceiling, 18.8 per cent for a wage equal to four times the SMIC and 17.7 per cent for a wage equal to eight times the SMIC. The rate of employers' contributions on the gross wage amounted to 39.6 per cent at the ceiling level, 37.6 per cent for the part of the wage between one and four times the ceiling and 31.1 per cent for the part of the wage above four times the ceiling.

18. Until 1979, the setting of a ceiling on social security contributions was the rule, that is, the main part of the contributions affected the part of the wage below the social security ceiling.

19. As noted by Moghadam (1995), empirical analysis suggests that the minimum wage has a negative impact on employment in general and on youth employment in particular. The minimum wage is high in France by international standards. To the extent that the productivity of the less skilled is below that justified by the SMIC, the latter constitutes an

obstacle to the employment of these workers. Moghadam (1995) shows empirically that a reduction in the real minimum wage would help to lower long-term unemployment.

20. CSERC (1996) estimates that, for wages below 1.33 times the SMIC, the elasticity of labour demand with respect to the cost of labour is –0.34 where possibilities of substitution between labour categories are fewer, and –0.72 where the substitution elasticity is unity.

21. For Wilsford (1994), the reform of hospital financing in 1983 has been a success thanks to a combination of favourable circumstances.

22. Part of the expenditure remaining to be paid by the individual after reimbursement by the social security and the voluntary supplementary insurances.

23. Kopits (1997) shows that in several member states the position of social finances may constitute an impediment to meeting the Maastricht Treaty convergence criteria for the general government net borrowing and gross debt. In the short term, deficits in the social security accounts may be accommodated with expenditure cuts and tax increases. However, far-reaching reforms will be necessary in several countries in order to ensure sustainable budgetary consolidation in accordance with the provisions of the Stability and Growth Pact.

24. In June 1995, the government fixed a timetable for reducing public deficits, planning to reduce the government deficit to 5 per cent of GDP in 1995, 4 per cent in 1996 and 3 per cent in 1997. At the time, restoring to balance social security accounts in 1997 was viewed as an essential condition for achieving these objectives.

25. The revenue forecasts were based on the assumption of a wage bill growth of 5.3 per cent in 1996 and of 5 per cent in 1997.

26. The social security debt is composed of the following items: FRF 110 billion of debt taken over by the state at the end of 1993, the cumulated deficits for the 1994 and 1995 financial years (FRF 120 billion), the projected deficit for 1996 (FRF 17 billion) and the deficit of the national health insurance fund, that is, in total, FRF 250 billion.

27. Also exempt from the RDS are industrial accident allowances and military disability pensions.

28. The decree of 24 April 1996, introducing the new mechanisms for the control of ambulatory care spending, was subsequently transcribed and supplemented by the two medical agreements (for general practitioners and specialists) concluded in March 1997 between the health insurance funds and the doctors' unions.

29. Families are taxed more heavily but are also the main beneficiaries of social spending.

30. This reform, intended to re-establish in ten years the financial balance of the unemployment benefit scheme, consisted mainly of the creation of the special regressive allowance.

31. To evaluate more precisely the redistributing effects of the emergency measures, it would be necessary to analyse microeconomic data which were not available at the time this chapter was written.

32. For a presentation of the QUEST model, see European Commission (1987).

33. The government's plan set balance objectives solely for the general scheme. Furthermore, the balance objective is established on a cash accounts basis. The main item of deviation between the cash accounts balance and the net borrowing according to national accounts is constituted by capital operations which are not taken into account in the cash accounts balance.

34. The government's initial forecast was based on a hypothesis of a wage bill growth rate of 5.3 per cent in 1996. In September 1996, the Commission des comptes forecast a growth rate of 2.3 per cent. The slowdown of growth in 1996 occurred quite independently of the restrictive impact of the adjustment measures adopted in the framework of the social security reform.

35. The government has presented, in the annex to the social security financing law of 1997, a forecast for the balance of the general scheme in 1998 and 1999. Under the hypothesis of a wage bill growth of 4.3 per cent, equivalent to nominal GDP growth, and a tight control of social expenditure (+0.7 per cent in volume terms in 1998 and 1999), the general scheme would be slightly in deficit in 1998, by FRF 12.3 billion, and would record an FRF 7.9 billion surplus in 1999.

36. For a description of this reform, see Henke et al. (1994) and for the analysis of the circumstances favouring the adoption of this reform, see Wilsford (1994). The main similarity presented by the Seehofer reform and the Juppé plan concerns the financial control of ambulatory care expenditure. The German reform stipulated that medical expenses should not grow faster than the revenue of the health insurance funds during the 1993–95 period. In the event of the overrun of the expenditure ceilings, a reduction in doctors' fees was specified. A system of control of doctors by the doctors' associations and funds was established. The reform also sought to control the medical demography and to favour family doctors over specialists. The Seehofer reform also introduced cost containment measures for hospitalization, dental care and drug expenses. Cost-sharing by patients was increased.

37. However, it is not proven that the reinforcement of competition between providers and/or insurers leads to greater efficiency in the allocation of resources (Reinhardt, 1989; Jönsson, 1996). In addition, the pursuit of greater efficiency through market mechanisms may compromise the achievement of the equity objective (Jönsson, 1996).

38. In the case of the introduction of care networks, the government has opted for a prudent approach. The coordination of care risks encountering opposition in France as it may jeopardize certain principles of independent medical practice to which patients and physicians are attached: freedom of choice on the part of the patient, confidentiality and fee-for-service payment (Commissariat général du plan, 1994).

39. According to the government, the cost of this reform would not be high for two reasons: first, the number of people not contributing is relatively low, due to the progressive generalization of health insurance since 1974; and, second, the harmonization of benefits should not lead to an improvement in the average health insurance coverage of people already insured.

40. The objectives set by the government for the growth of the global hospital allocations and ambulatory care expenditure were 2.1 per cent for 1996. These objectives were slightly overshot for the general scheme: the ambulatory care expenditure increased by 2.3 per cent; however, payments to hospitals under the *dotations globales hospitalières* increased by 2.7 per cent. For all the schemes, the growth in hospital expenditure was in line with the objective.

41. If the reduction in social security contributions concerns employers, the results of the general equilibrium model used by the IMF are significantly different. In the short term, a reduction of 1 point in employers' contributions, whose effects on the budget would be neutralized in the short term, leads to an increase in employment by 0.4 per cent. The net income of employees falls. In the long term, this reform leads to significant favourable effects on employment. The negative effects of increased taxes on capital income are offset by the positive effects of lower social security contributions. The results of the model depend critically on the hypotheses used, in particular on the elasticity of wages with respect to unemployment.

42. For a description of the French pension system, see the White Paper (1991).

43. For a comparison of the pension systems in the European Union member states, see Thomas (1997).

44. This reform concerns solely the basic scheme and the aligned schemes. The special schemes are outside the scope of this reform. In terms of the supplementary schemes, in 1993–94 and in 1996 the social partners – the managers of these schemes – adopted agreements to redress their financial situation. These agreements provide for staggered reductions in the rate of return of the pension point and a progressive increase in contractual contribution rates.

45. Until the end of 1995, the FSV also had the exceptional task of ensuring the repayment of the capital and the interest for the debt of the basic scheme taken over by the state in 1993. The repayment of the debt was transferred to the *Caisse d'amortissement de la dette sociale*, created by the decree of 24 January 1996 (see Section 3.2.2).

46. The retirement savings plans (*plans d'épargne retraite* – PER), contribution to which is voluntary, will allow employees in the private sector to receive an income on their retirement. They benefit from a favourable tax system. The employer can supplement the

sums paid in by its employees and, in this case, does not pay any social security contributions on its payments up to a sum of 85 per cent of the annual social security ceiling. The employee can deduct from his/her taxable income his/her own payments and those of his/her employer.

47. Results were obtained using the following demographic hypotheses: birth rate of 1.8, extension until 2000 of the increase in life expectancy and positive balance of migration movement of +50 000 people per year.

48. This is the contribution rate required to finance all the old-age benefits. It is defined as the ratio of the total benefits to the gross earned incomes (total remuneration of employees, including employers' contributions and the trading profit of individual enterprises).

REFERENCES

Barr, N. (1992), 'Economic theory and the welfare state: a survey and interpretation', *Journal of Economic Literature*, June.

Briet, R. (1995), *Perspectives à long terme des retraites*, Commissariat général du plan, Paris: La Documentation Française.

Charpentier, F. (1996), *Retraites et fonds de pension: l'état de la question en France et à l'étranger*, Paris: Editions Economica.

Chassin, M. et al. (1987), 'Does inappropriate use explain geographic variations in the use of health-care services?', *Journal of the American Medical Association*, November.

Commissariat général du plan (1993), *Santé 2010*, Paris: La Documentation Française.

Commissariat général du plan (1994), *Livre blanc sur le système de santé et d'assurance-maladie,* Paris: La Documentation Française.

Commission des comptes de la sécurité sociale (1996), *Les comptes de la sécurité sociale – Résultats 1995 et prévisions 1996*, July.

Comptes de la nation (1996), *Rapport sur les comptes de la nation 1995*, Paris: INSEE.

Cornilleau, G. and Sterdyniak, H. (1995), 'Les retraites en France: des débats théoriques aux choix politiques', in Cocheme, B. and Legros, F. (eds), *Les retraites – Genèse, acteurs, enjeux*, Paris: Armand Colin.

Cornilleau, G., Echevin, D. and Timbeau, X. (1996), 'Perspectives à moyen terme des finances sociales', *Revue de l'OFCE*, No. 56, January.

Cotis, J.P. and Loufir, A. (1990), 'Formation des salaires, chômage d'équilibre et incidence des cotisations sociales sur le coût du travail', *Economie et Prévision*, Nos 92–3.

CSERC (Conseil supérieur de l'emploi, des revenus et des coûts) (1996), *L'allègement des charges sociales sur les bas salaires*, Paris: La Documentation Française.

Cutler, D.M. (1994), 'A guide to health-care reform', *Journal of Economic Perspectives*, No. 3, summer.

Documentation Française (1995), *La protection sociale en France*, Paris.

Dormont, B. (1994), 'Quelle est l'influence du coût du travail sur l'emploi?', *Revue Économique*, **45** (3), May.

Enthoven, A.C. (1980), *Consumer Choice Health Plan: The Only Practical Solution to the Soaring Cost of Medical Care*, Reading, MA: Addison-Wesley.

European Commission (1987), 'Estimation and simulation of international trade linkages in the QUEST model', *European Economy*, No. 31.

European Commission (1995), 'The future of social protection: a framework for a European debate', communication from the Commission (COM(95) 466, 31.10.1995).

European Commission (1996), *Social protection in Europe*, Directorate-General for Employment, Industrial Relations and Social Affairs.

European Commission (1997), 'Modernising and improving social protection in Europe', communication from the Commission (COM(97) 102, 28.2.1997).

Eurostat (1992), *Enquête sur les coûts de la main d'œuvre*, Luxembourg.

Eurostat (1995), *Dépenses et recettes de protection sociale 1980–1993*, Luxembourg.

Evans, R.G. (1996), 'Vendre le marché ou réglementer la régulation: Qui y perd? Qui y gagne?', *Études de Politique de Santé*, No. 8, OECD, Paris.

Feldstein, M.S. (1974), 'Social security, induced retirement and aggregate capital accumulation', *Journal of Political Economy*, October.

Foucault, J.B. de (1995), *Le financement de la protection sociale*, Commissariat général du plan, Paris: La Documentation Française.

Franco, D. and Munzi, T. (1996), 'Public pension expenditure prospects in the European Union: a survey of national projections', *European Economy, Reports and Studies*, No. 3.

French Government (1995a), 'Rapport du Gouvernement au Parlement sur la protection sociale', October.

French Government (1995b), 'La réforme de la protection sociale', dossier de presse, November.

Henke, K.D., Murray, M.A. and Ade, C. (1994), 'Global budgeting in Germany: lessons for the United States', *Health Affairs*, autumn.

Henry, J., Leroux, V. and Muet, P.A. (1988), 'Coût relatif capital–travail et substitution: Existe-t-il encore un lien?', *Observations et Diagnostics Économiques, Revue de l'OFCE*, No. 24, July.

INSEE (1992), *Projections de la population totale pour la France métropolitaine*, document de travail, November.

Jönsson, B. (1996), 'Comprendre la réforme des systèmes de santé', *Études de Politique de Santé*, No. 8, OECD, Paris.

Kopits, G. (1997), 'Are Europe's social security finances compatible with EMU?', *IMF Working Paper*, PPAA/97/3, February.

Kotlikoff, L. (1989), 'On the contribution of economics to the evaluation and formation of social insurance policy', *American Economic Review*, No. 2, summer.

Lachaud, C. and Rochaix, L. (1995), 'Équité dans le financement et la prestation de soins de santé en Europe', *Revue d'Économie Financière*, No. 34, autumn.

Levy, J.V. (1995), 'Some considerations relevant to prefunded pensions in France', ch. 6 in Masson (1996).

Masson, P.R. (ed.) (1996), *France: Financial and Real Sector issues*, Washington, DC: IMF.

Moghadam, R. (1995), 'Why is unemployment in France so high?, ch. 1 in Masson (1996).

Newhouse, J.P. (1992), 'Medical care costs: How much welfare loss?', *Journal of Economic Perspectives*, No. 3, summer.

Newhouse, J.P. (1994), 'Symposium on health-care', *Journal of Economic Perspectives*, No. 3, summer.

Nolan, B. (1996), 'Qualité, efficacité et équité des soins médicaux par rapport aux capacités financières: Quels compromis?', *Études de Politique de Santé*, No. 8, OECD.

OECD (1990), 'Employer versus employee taxation: the impact on employment', *Employment Outlook*.

OECD (1992), *Les systèmes de santé des pays de l'OCDE, faits et tendances 1960–91*, Vols I and II, Paris.

OECD (1994a), *Études économiques de l'OCDE, France*, Paris.

OECD (1994b), *La réforme des systèmes de santé – Étude de dix-sept pays de l'OCDE*, Paris.

Pierson, P. (1996), 'The new politics of the welfare state', *World Politics*.

Reinhardt, U. (1989), 'Economists in health-care: saviours or elephants in a porcelain shop?', *American Economic Review, Papers and Proceedings*, May.

SESI (1996), *Comptes nationaux de la santé, 1993–1994–1995*.

Thomas, G. (1997), 'Retirement income financing reform: a general issues paper', this book, ch. 7.

Viossat, L.C. (1995), 'Protection sociale et institutions sociales', in Documentation Française (1995), p. 51.

Weisbrod, B.A. (1991), 'The health-care quadrilemma: an essay on technological change, insurance, quality of care and cost containment', *Journal of Economic Literature*, June.

White Paper (1991), *Livre Blanc sur les retraites*, Paris: La Documentation Française.

Wilsford, D. (1994), 'Path dependency, or why history makes it difficult but not impossible to reform health-care systems in a big way', *Journal of Public Policy*.

PART VI

Demography and the Welfare State

9. Ageing and fiscal policies in the European Union

Daniele Franco and Teresa Munzi

1. INTRODUCTION[1]

Changes in birth rates, life expectancy and migration flows are modifying the level and structure of the population of European Union member states. The increase in the old-age dependency ratio, which is reaching historically unprecedented levels, is one of the most evident and important trends (see European Commission, 1995 and 1996; OECD, 1988a). In the coming decades, demographic changes will produce pervasive effects on labour and capital markets, goods and services markets, macroeconomic aggregates and relative prices (see European Commission, 1994; Börsch-Supan, 1991; Hagemann and Nicoletti, 1989; OECD, 1996). They will also affect public budgets, through their effects on the demand for public services and transfers and, indirectly, through their effects on the above-mentioned economic factors.

Significant pressures towards higher public expenditure are expected in the pension and health sectors. On the other hand, the decline in the share of young people in total population tends to reduce the demand for public services and transfers in other areas, namely education, maternity and child allowances. Overall, there is a widespread consensus that demographic changes tend to increase public expenditure and produce negative effects on public budgets (see Heller et al., 1986; OECD, 1988a; Leibfritz et al., 1995). These pressures, unless offset by policy changes, might endanger the fiscal framework designed in the Maastricht Treaty and the Stability and Growth Pact.

Both at national and EU level, studies are needed to evaluate, well in advance, the budgetary effects of these demographic changes. At national level, such evaluations should guide the adjustment of expenditure programmes to the new demographic conditions. At Union level, systematic evaluations of the medium- and long-term prospects for public budgets would contribute to signal trends which could potentially undermine the rules introduced for deficits and debts. This is particularly relevant since budgetary pressures arising from demographic changes will vary very much across the EU according to different national demographic trends and public expenditure structures. More specifically, indicators of medium- and long-term trends in public budgets could provide a framework for the assessment of the stability and convergence programmes.

Objectives

The study has two objectives:

(a)   to provide some preliminary estimates of the budgetary effects of demographic changes in some EU member states over the coming decades;
(b)   to develop a methodological framework for monitoring budgetary trends in member states over the medium and long term.

More specifically, as to the first objective, the study provides elements to assess the sustainability of current EU member states' fiscal policies, that is, the possibility of maintaining present expenditure and revenue policies without excessive debt accumulation, taking the impact of expected demographic changes into account. It also estimates the adjustments required to ensure the implementation of the 'close-to-balance' rule outlined in the Stability and Growth Pact.

The problem of developing indicators of long-term trends of public budgets should obviously be approached with a great deal of caution. While these trends depend on many factors, their interactions and policy reactions, budgetary policy indicators can only capture the effects of a few relevant factors. They are also extremely sensitive to underlying economic and demographic assumptions and to the specification of the projection model. This study, which follows the approach of work carried out within IMF and OECD, takes the view that 'a good indicator of sustainability is one which sends clear and easily interpretable signals when current policy appears to be leading to a rapidly growing debt to GDP ratio' (Blanchard et al., 1990, p. 8).

It would, however, be extremely useful to complement the indicators developed here with other indicators developed within alternative and more complex approaches, like generational accounting and dynamics general equilibrium models (see Raffelhüschen, 1997). Generational accounting would allow a broader view to be taken of the budgetary situation (including revenue trends and public sector net wealth) and of its intergenerational implications. General equilibrium models would allow the consideration of the implications of demographic and public finance changes for relative prices, factors' income, saving decisions, and so on. It should be pointed out that this study is based on the same building blocks underlying generational accounting studies, that is, age-related public expenditure profiles.

Two additional points should be stressed before outlining the methodology of the work. First, the study focuses on unchanged policy projections. Although these projections cannot be considered as realistic forecasts of future public finance trends, since policies will obviously change to cope with unsustainable trends, they provide a useful benchmark for evaluating the need for reform. Second, in assessing the sustainability of budgetary trends, attention should focus on expenditure trends for a country over time rather than on comparisons of public expenditure levels across countries (see Heller et al., 1986).

Methodology

The first part of the study considers alternative indicators of long-term budgetary trends and examines the characteristics and results of the main international studies which have examined long-term public expenditure prospects in recent years. Some projections carried out by public institutions in EU member states are also taken into consideration.

The study then provides some tentative estimates of the changes in the ratio of public primary expenditure to GDP in some EU member states over the period up to 2030 by integrating:

(i) the results of the most recent pension expenditure projections carried out by national authorities (see the report by Franco and Munzi, 1996) and

(ii) mechanical estimates of the effects of demographic changes on the other main age-related expenditure items (such as health care, education and family allowances). At present, these estimates are provided for only eight member states for which data are available (Belgium, Denmark, Finland, Germany, Italy, the Netherlands, Spain and Sweden). The estimates are produced by combining data on per capita expenditures for different age groups and for different budgetary items, expressed in terms of per capita GDP, with Eurostat's new demographic projections for the period 1995–2050. Age-related profiles of public expenditure have usually been obtained from generational accounting studies. Alternative demographic scenarios are considered, as well as alternative dynamics of age-related per capita expenditure.

An indicative measure of the primary balance trend is then obtained by adding the projected changes of age-related public expenditure to the primary balance level expected for 1997, assuming that revenues and age-unrelated expenditure are constant in GDP terms at their present levels. The estimates for the primary balance are finally used to project the ratio of public debt to

GDP on the basis of assumption on interest rates and productivity growth. For an outline of the projection procedure, see Figure 9.1.

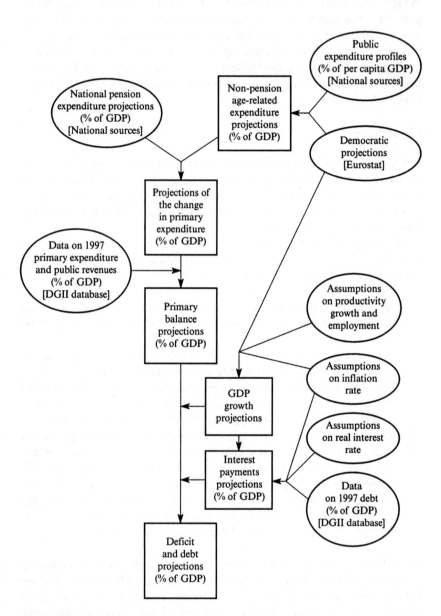

Figure 9.1   Projection procedure

The estimates for the primary balance are also used to evaluate the adjustments required on the primary balance over the period 1997–2030 to achieve the 'close-to-balance' rule indicated in the Stability and Growth Pact.

In order to have a concise and comparable measure of the adjustment required for each country, the study also estimates the 'tax gap' consistent with the implementation of the 'close-to-balance' rule outlined in the Stability and Growth Pact (that is, the change in the tax to GDP ratio immediately required in order to reach, by the end of the projection period, the debt to GDP ratio that would be reached by implementing the 'close-to-balance' rule).[2] The tax gap concept allows a comparison of the adjustments required by the 'close-to-balance' rule with those that would be required to keep the debt to GDP ratio by the end of the projection period at the present level (that is, the 'sustainable tax gap' *à la* Blanchard). It also allows comparisons of alternative macroeconomic scenarios.

Notes of Caution

The limitations of this methodology should be stressed.

(a) National pension projections are taken at face value; no attempt has been made to evaluate the reliability of the projections presented in the preceding sections. An indirect indicator of the reliability of projections is, however, provided by the adjustments implemented in projections over time. The fact that estimates have usually been revised upwards may suggest that there is a tendency to underestimate expenditure trends (Franco and Munzi, 1996). Moreover, the economic and demographic assumptions underlying the national projections are not homogeneous and may also differ from those used for projecting non-pension expenditure items.

(b) The approach used for projecting non-pension expenditure items is purely mechanical and takes only demographic factors into consideration. Demographic factors actually affect public budgets through several more complex channels. Moreover, public expenditure and revenue dynamics largely depend on non-demographic factors. Therefore, the estimates indicate only the broad direction of the impact of demographic change and the broad dimension of required policy adjustment.

(c) Some estimates of per capita expenditure for different age groups and for different budgetary items are still rather unsatisfactory (for instance, the expenditure profiles for Spain consider only three large age groups, those for Belgium refer to 1988 data, education expenditure is not considered for Spain and Sweden).

(d) Some assumptions (for example productivity growth, interest rates) are necessarily arbitrary. Sensitivity analysis is carried out to evaluate the implications of alternative assumptions.

(e) Present ratios of non-age-related expenditure and revenue to GDP are assumed to remain constant over time. Some expenditure and revenue items are actually temporary (for example the expenditure related to German reunification and the one-off tax measures implemented by some governments). In order to evaluate the adjustment required by demographic changes under unchanged policies, expenditure and revenue ratios should be corrected for the most important of these temporary items.

(f) Labour force participation rates and unemployment rates are at present assumed constant over the projection period, as well as age-related per capita expenditure for unemployment benefits. As indicated in some national reports on long-term expenditure trends, unemployment rates and unemployment benefit expenditure are likely to decline.

Structure of the Paper

The paper is structured as follows. Section 2 presents alternative indicators of long-term budgetary trends and examines the characteristics and results of the main international studies which have examined long-term public expenditure prospects in recent years. Some national projections are also taken into consideration. Section 3 presents the methodology for the estimates of age-related public expenditure trends; it also presents some estimates of the burden that these expenditures will represent for the working-age population. Section 4, drawing from a survey of national pension expenditure projections carried out within the European Commission, examines expected pension expenditure trends. Section 5 provides some tentative estimates of the ratio of age-related public expenditure to GDP by integrating national pension projections with the mechanical estimates of the effects of demographic changes on the age-related expenditure items. It also estimates primary balance trends under the assumption that revenues and age-unrelated expenditure remain constant as a share of GDP. Finally, it provides estimates of the adjustments required on the primary balance over the period 1998–2030 to implement the 'close-to-balance' rule indicated in the Stability and Growth Pact. The implications of the exclusion of some expenditure and revenue items of a temporary nature, as well as of different interest rates and productivity growth rates are also considered. Comparisons of different scenarios are presented in terms of tax gaps. Section 6 outlines the main results of the study and points to directions for further work.

2. INDICATORS OF MEDIUM- AND LONG-TERM TRENDS IN PUBLIC BUDGETS

Since the mid-1980s, when it became apparent that western countries were experiencing major changes in their demographic structure, an increasing number of studies have examined the long-term prospects for public budgets. The studies were prompted by the widespread perception that population ageing was going to increase the demand for public expenditure and produce negative effects on public budgets.

Two lines of research have been followed: one group of studies has evaluated the prospects of the main age-related expenditure programmes and has produced projections of the ratio of age-related expenditure to GDP; projections of the primary balances have also been derived assuming age-unrelated expenditures and revenues to remain constant as a percentage of GDP.[3] Another group has taken all budgetary items into account in the generational accounting framework developed by Auerbach and Kotlikoff.[4] These two lines of research are examined in Sections 2.1 and 2.2 respectively.

2.1 Projections of Age-related Public Expenditure

The studies examining the prospects of age-related expenditure programmes focus on those public expenditure items which are particularly dependent on population age structure (such as pension, health, education). They combine data on per capita expenditure for different age groups and for different budgetary items with demographic projections. Some studies consider only the effects of demographic changes, while others also try to capture some non-demographic factors such as pension scheme maturation and long-term trends towards higher health expenditure. Some studies go further and develop projections for the primary balance and estimates of the adjustments required to ensure budgetary sustainability.

2.1.1 Mechanical projections of the effects of demographic changes

The most basic approach provides estimates of the effects of demographic changes on public expenditure under the assumption that age-related per capita expenditure levels remain constant in real terms or in per capita GDP terms on the initial level over the projection period. In other words, it is assumed that present standards of transfers and services are maintained for all population age groups and that there is no behavioural response from governments or households to demographic changes and their budgetary effects.

Some mechanical projections aimed at evaluating the pure impact of demographic changes were carried out by OECD in 1988 for 12 countries (see

OECD, 1988a). The burden for the financing of the main social programmes per working-age citizen was projected up to 2040 (see Box 9.1). Demographic pressure on pension and health expenditure was expected to be very large in all the countries considered. Education and family benefits, which are mostly related to younger age classes, were expected to decrease in all countries, but not enough to offset the increase in pension and health expenditure. Over the period 1980–2040 the burden would grow by 54 per cent in Germany, 39 per cent in Italy and the Netherlands, 32 per cent in France, 20–26 per cent in Belgium, Sweden and Denmark and 11 per cent in the UK (Table 9.1). At the end of the period, the ratio of social expenditure to GDP would be in the 37–49 per cent range in all the above-mentioned countries (Table 9.2), with the only exception of the UK (24 per cent). The pressure of ageing on social expenditure was expected to increase substantially from 2010 onwards, when the baby-boom generation reaches retirement age. A breathing space would therefore be available for taking corrective action.

Box 9.1   Main international projections of age-related public expenditure

At the international level, two major studies were carried out by IMF and OECD in the second half of the 1980s; a third was carried out by OECD in 1995 and updated in 1996. By combining data on per capita expenditure for each age group within the various social programmes with demographic projections, OECD (1988a) evaluated the pure impact of demographic changes while the IMF study (Heller et al., 1986) and the second OECD study (Leibfritz et al., 1995 and Roseveare et al., 1996) also considered some additional factors influencing pension and health expenditure. Both the earlier studies covered the five major social programmes: education, health care, pensions (old-age, survivors' and invalidity), unemployment compensation and family benefits. OECD (1996) also projected total public expenditure, OECD covered 12 countries in the first study and 20 in the second; IMF considered only the seven major western countries.

    OECD (1988a) baseline population projections were based on the assumptions of: (a) gradual convergence of fertility rates to replacement level, (b) an increase in life expectancy of two years for each sex between 1983 and 2030, (c) zero of low levels of net migration. IMF's baseline scenario was somewhat similar: (a) gradual increase in total fertility ratio that by 2010 reaches the replacement level in five out of the seven countries, (b) increase in life expectancy at birth of 3.4 years for males and 2.5 for females between 1980 and 2010, (c) limited net emigration from Germany and immigration to Canada and the United

States. Two more scenarios were considered in the IMF paper. They both envisage a 'greater ageing' situation with fertility broadly constant at 1980 levels and with a life expectancy increase of 6.7 years for males and 4.8 years for females. One scenario shares the baseline economic assumptions, while the other takes a more pessimistic view of growth and employment. In OECD (1988a), the proportion of the elderly (65 and over) in total population for the whole OECD was projected to rise from 12.2 per cent in 1980 to 15.4 per cent in 2010 and 22.1 per cent in 2040. For the seven major countries it was projected to rise from 12.5 per cent in 1980 to 16.4 and 22.8 per cent respectively.

The proportion of the elderly to the working-age population was expected to grow at a faster rate. In the IMF projections the ageing process was slower; in the seven countries the share of population aged 65 and over was projected to rise from 12.5 per cent in 1980 to 15.9 per cent in 2010 and 19.5 per cent in 2025 (respectively 17.3 and 22.3 per cent in the greater ageing scenario).

OECD (1988a) follows a two-step approach: first it estimates the change in expenditure in real terms implied by projected demographic changes (that is, what would be the expenditure level in the base year under different demographic conditions, all other factors being equal); then it takes into consideration the capacity to finance public expenditure by dividing the index of projected expenditure levels by the index of the number of working-age citizens (15–64 age group).

IMF (Heller et al., 1986) projections of pension and health expenditure also considers some non-demographic factors. The growth in the number of pensioners and the dynamics of the average pension are projected taking the maturity of the different systems into consideration. More specifically, the average pension was expected to grow faster than implied by indexation arrangements for Italy, Japan and the United Kingdom. As to health expenditure, the study outlines a baseline scenario in which average medical costs increase in line with productivity and an alternative scenario, more closely corresponding with historical experience, in which they grow by 0.3 to 0.9 percentage points per year faster than productivity.

In the new projections produced within OECD in 1996 (see Roseveare et al., 1996 and OECD, 1996, that extend the results of Leibfritz et al., 1995), the impact of population ageing on public pensions, public health expenditure and the overall budget position were examined under the assumption of constant expenditure and revenue policies. As to pension expenditure, a simulation model was developed for each country taking legislated reforms into account. Despite the efforts to capture the institutional arrangements, simplifying assumptions were necessary. Projections were carried out for a baseline and four alternative scenarios. Two alternative approaches were taken for health expenditure projections. In the first, expenditure trends were estimated by multiplying present per capita public health expenditure levels by the total number of elderly people; in the second, they were estimated by multiplying per capita health expenditure by the number of deaths among the elderly population. The latter approach is based on the consideration that consumption of health care is concentrated in the period preceding death, so that increases in life expectancy determine an increase in the healthy portion of life. Three alternative assumptions on the growth of per capita health expenditure were considered for each approach (with expenditure growing at the same rate of real GDP, 1 per cent slower and 1 per cent faster). In order to estimate the effects of ageing on the overall fiscal position, the other expenditure items and public revenues were assumed to remain constant as a percentage of GDP. In Leibfritz et al. (1995), specific projections were also carried out for education expenditure; spending per pupil was assumed to grow in line with productivity growth.

However, it should be stressed that estimates combining data on per capita expenditures for different age groups and for different budgetary items with demographic projections are only indicative measures of the likely effects of demographic change on public expenditure, since they do not take all relevant effects of demographic changes into account.[5]

(a)   Mechanical estimates are based on the implicit assumption that the marginal cost of providing services to a smaller or a larger number of individuals in each age group in the future will be equal to the present average cost of these services.[6] In other words, it is assumed that there are no economies or diseconomies of scale in the production of public services. This assumption is surely implausible over relatively short periods, because of time-lags in the adjustment of inputs to changes in demand for public services.

(b)   Mechanical estimates implicitly assume that demographic changes do not modify present age-related per capita expenditure levels, while they can actually affect them through many different channels. Demographic changes can influence the cost of inputs used in services (for example, a relative shortage of young workers may increase the cost of public services employing them)[7] and the demand for some services (for example, a reduction in the number of children per household may, in the

Table 9.1   Public expenditure projections: IMF (1986) and OECD (1988)

Country	IMF (1986) Index of the ratio of social expenditure to GDP, 1980–2025[1] (1980 = 100)					OECD (1988) Index of financing burden of social expenditure per head of 15–64 age group, 1980–2040[2] (1980 = 100)				
	Pensions	Health	Education	Family benefits	Total social expenditure	Pensions	Health	Education	Family benefits	Total social expenditure
Belgium						158	116	84	87	120
Denmark						178	136	83	87	126
France	130	140	90	87	113	177	123	82	86	132
Germany[3]	154	159	82	67	125	200	143	84	95	154
Italy	171	130	75	—	138	174	140	81	83	139
Netherlands						184	157	80	79	139
Sweden						138	131	93	94	122
United Kingdom	144	144	80	85	116	131	122	86	87	111
USA	110	172	74	—	110	171	141	81	91	131
Canada	123	152	75	42	102	236	169	80	85	145
Australia						181	151	80	79	130
Japan	319	168	86	—	176	252	161	87	85	154

Notes:
1   Baseline economic and demographic scenario. Calculated from Table 14.
2   Medium fertility variant. Calculated from Tables 19 and 22.
3   West Germany.

Table 9.2   Public expenditure projections: IMF (1986) and OECD (1988)

Country	IMF (1986) Share of total social expenditure to GDP[1] (%)				OECD (1988) Share of total social expenditure to GDP[2] (%)				
	1980	2000	2010	2025	1980	2000	2010	2020	2040
Belgium					38.2	36.3	37.1	39.3	45.8
Denmark					34.9	30.7	33.2	35.9	44.0
France	31.0	32.4	32.6	35.1	28.3	28.3	29.4	32.8	37.4
Germany[3]	31.1	33.2	35.3	38.8	30.8	32.6	34.8	38.2	47.4
Italy	25.1	27.7	30.2	34.7	26.9	26.6	28.5	31.2	37.4
Netherlands					35.5	35.5	36.9	40.5	49.3
Sweden					32.5	30.9	32.5	35.8	39.7
United Kingdom	22.9	22.9	24.0	26.5	22.0	20.5	21.1	22.2	24.4
USA	17.7	16.4	16.6	19.4	20.7	19.9	20.5	24.2	27.1
Canada	20.3	17.4	17.4	20.7	21.0	21.6	22.9	26.3	30.5
Australia					18.6	18.6	19.2	20.8	24.2
Japan	15.4	21.1	25.9	27.2	16.9	19.4	23.2	24.0	26.0

Notes:
[1] Baseline economic and demographic scenario. Calculated from Table 14.
[2] Medium fertility variant. Computed on the basis of the share of social expenditure in GDP in 1980 calculated in Table 21 and the index of the financing burden per head of 15–64 age group as calculated in Table 22.
[3] West Germany.

Sources: Heller et al. (1986) and OECD (1988a).

long run, increase the demand for elderly care).[8] They can also affect productivity trends, wage rates and savings ratios.

Economies/diseconomies of scale and the effects of demographic changes on the level of age-related per capita expenditure are not usually taken into account in expenditure projections. While the failure to consider economies and diseconomies of scale may compromise short period estimates, that concerning system-wide effects may affect long-period estimates.

Moreover, it should be stressed that demographic change is just one of the several factors affecting public expenditure dynamics. The contribution of mechanical estimates of the effects of demographic changes to the assessment of the prospects for public expenditure is therefore necessarily limited.

2.1.2 Projections considering non-demographic factors

In order to take non-demographic factors into consideration, it is necessary to remove the assumption that age-related per capita expenditure levels remain constant in real terms or in per capita GDP terms on the initial level over the projection period. This implies assuming that standards of transfers and services will change over time.

While several economic, political and social factors can obviously affect the dynamics of per capita transfers and services, the studies examining the prospects of age-related expenditure usually focus only on two rather specific factors: the effects of changes introduced in legislation, but not yet embodied in present expenditure profiles, and the continuation of structural expenditure trends. These two factors are considered because they are consistent with a constant policy approach, while there is usually no attempt to predict the effects of changes in behaviours and policies.

The effects of changes introduced in legislation, but not yet embodied in present expenditure profiles, are particularly relevant for pension expenditure projections, since pension eligibility and transfer ratios[9] can change considerably over time due to the maturation of schemes, i.e. the process of adjustment of all pensions to present retirement rules.[10] On the one hand, pension coverage extensions and benefit improvements usually only produce their full effects on the two ratios after many decades. On the other, quite often pension benefit curtailing reforms are implemented gradually and only display their full effects a long time later (OECD, 1988b). Therefore, the assumption that age-related per capita expenditure levels remain constant is not equivalent to a constant policy assumption. It implies that all the effects of changes introduced in legislation are reflected in present age-related per capita expenditure levels.

The continuation of structural expenditure trends (that is, the assumption that some non-demographic factors relevant in the past would continue to affect expenditure dynamics in the future) is especially relevant for health care expenditure projections. In several countries the health sector has for long periods recorded a price deflator substantially higher than the GDP deflator and a tendency towards a continuous increase in per capita consumption.[11]

Projections integrating the mechanical effects of demographic changes with estimates of some additional factors influencing pension and health expenditure were produced by the IMF in 1986 for the seven main western economies (see Box 9.1 and Heller et al., 1986). The growth in the number of pensioners and the dynamics of the average pension were projected taking the maturity of the different systems into consideration. As to health expenditure, the study outlined a scenario in which average medical costs were rising more rapidly than productivity. For France and Germany the IMF's estimates for total social expenditure were similar to those of OECD (1988a). The IMF

Table 9.3   Public expenditure projections: OECD (1996)

County	Expenditure/GDP Change in the period 2000–2030		Effects of the demographic changes on net primary balance				
			Net primary balance/GDP				Change in the period 2000–2030
	Health	Pensions	1995	2000	2015	2030	Total
Austria	2.8	5.8	−2.7	0.9	−2.3	−7.7	−8.6
Belgium	2.2	4.2	4.3	5.9	5.7	−0.5	−6.4
Denmark	1.6	4.5	2	3.8	1	−2.3	−6.1
Finland	2.8	8.3	−4.3	2.3	−2.5	−8.8	−11.1
France	2	3.7	−1.6	1.2	−0.1	−4.5	−5.7
Germany	1.5	5	−0.6	−0.1	−0.2	−6.6	−6.5
Ireland	0.7	−0.1	1.8	0.6	0.6	0.0	−0.6
Italy	2	7.7	3.4	3.8	4.0	−5.9	−9.7
Netherlands	3.3	5.5	1.4	2.8	0.0	−6.0	−8.8
Portugal	1	6.1	0.6	1.5	−0.4	−5.6	−7.1
Spain	1.3	4.6	−1.1	1.5	0.5	−4.4	−5.9
Sweden	1.7	3.9	−5.1	2.9	0.2	−2.7	−5.6
United Kingdom	0.9	1	−2.8	0.5	−0.1	−1.4	−1.9
USA	1.6	2.4	0.4	0.2	−0.6	−3.8	−4
Japan	1.3	5.9	−3.4	−1.5	−6.0	−8.7	−7.2

Source: Roseveare et al. (1996).

projected larger increases than OECD for Italy, Japan and the United Kingdom and more limited increases for the United States (Table 9.2).[12]

New projections were produced by OECD in 1995 for the seven major western economies; they were updated and extended to 20 countries in the following year (see Box 9.1).[13] Pension expenditure was projected up to 2070 taking present expenditure levels and the expected effects of major legislated changes in pension rules into account. Health-care projections were carried out up to 2030 under six alternative scenarios. Contrary to previous projections, the ratio of education expenditure to GDP was assumed to remain constant.

In OECD's recent projections, under the baseline scenario, over the period 2000–2030 in most countries the increase in pension expenditure would range between 4 and 6 percentage points of GDP; the only exceptions would be Ireland, the United Kingdom and the United States with lower increases, and Finland and Italy with an increase of about 8 points of GDP (see Table 9.3). Health expenditure would also increase substantially, with most of the countries in the 1–3 per cent bracket (Ireland and the United Kingdom would record lower increases). The burden for pension and health expenditure would increase mostly in the period 2015–30.

Growing awareness of population ageing has also led to a substantial increase in the resources devoted to national long-term public expenditure projections.[14] Most projections consider only one expenditure sector, with pensions, health and education being the most frequently considered. The projections for pension expenditure are examined more extensively in Section 4. Projections for all the main public expenditure items are available for only some countries. Four studies produced by Belgian, Danish, Finnish and Italian public institutions are examined in Box 9.2.[15] The Belgian and Italian projections appear less pessimistic than those carried out by IMF and OECD.

Box 9.2   National projections of age-related public expenditure

The Belgian Bureau du Plan (Englert et al., 1994) projected total public expenditure up to 2050 with the MALTESE model that allows non-demographic factors to be taken into consideration (that is, the macroeconomic framework, socioeconomic behaviour of agents and social policies). The projection considers the main age-related items (pensions, health care, unemployment benefits, family allowances, other social transfers) as well as the remainder of public expenditure. According to the most favourable scenario considered, the share of total public expenditure to GDP would increase from 41.6 per cent in 1990 to 45.4 per cent in 2030 and then decline to 43.8 per cent by 2050 (see table below). The increase in expenditure ratio would depend on pensions and health care, since expenditure for the other items is expected to decline.

Belgium – Englert et al. (1994)

	Social public expenditure					Other public expenditure			
Year	Pensions	Health	Unemploy-ment	Family allowances	Other social transfers	Public consump-tion	Transfers to firms	Other transfers	Total
1991	10.5	5.2	2.2	1.9	4.1	14.7	2.3	0.7	41.6
2000	11.6	5.7	2.2	1.6	3.9	14.5	2.1	0.9	42.5
2030	15.7	7.4	0.6	1.0	3.3	14.5	2.1	0.9	45.4
2050	14.7	7.6	0.5	0.8	3.0	14.3	2.1	0.9	43.8

Note: Favourable scenario assuming that private employment grows at 0.75 per cent p.a. and GDP at 2.35 per cent p.a.

The Danish Ministry of Finance (1995) projected public expenditure on transfers and services to elderly and young citizens. The share of public expenditure to GDP is expected to rise from 18 per cent in 1995 to about 19.5 per cent in 2005 and to more than 24 per cent in 2030 (see table below). The increase in the expenditure for the elderly would not be compensated by a reduction of the expenditure for young citizens, which would also increase, particularly over the period up to 2010. The assumptions underlying these projections imply that changes in the burden for elderly and young citizens reflect changes in the size of these population groups. Sensitivity analysis was carried out to evaluate the effects of changes in unemployment rates, average retirement age, productivity growth in public services and life expectancy.

Denmark – Ministry of Finance (1995)

Year	Public expenditure for young citizens	Public expenditure for old citizens	Total
1995	4.9	13.1	18
2005	5.8	13.7	19.5
2030	6.2	18.3	24.5

Note: It is assumed that the unemployment level is constant from 1995 onwards, that the ratio of the number of employees in services for the elderly to the number of elderly citizens is constant, and that public wages and transfers are adjusted in line with private sector wage dynamics. The estimates for public expenditure for the elderly have been updated in Ministry of Finance of Denmark (1996). Expenditure is estimated at 13.3 per cent for 1995, 13.6 per cent for 2005 and 18.0 per cent for 2030.

The Finnish Ministry of Social Affairs and Health (1994) carried out social expenditure projection for the period 1990–2030 on the basis of three macroeconomic scenarios. In the baseline scenario, the share of social expenditure to GDP is expected to increase from 27.2 per cent in 1990 to 36.6 per cent by 2030 (see table below). Pension expenditure would increase from 11.1 per cent of GDP in 1990 to 18.8 per cent in 2030. Unemployment benefit expenditure would increase substantially over the first ten years of the projection period (from 1.2 per cent in 1990 to 5.3 per cent in 1995 and 4.4 per cent in 2000), and later decline to a level close to the initial one.

Finland – Ministry of Social Affairs and Health (1994)

		Social expenditure				
Year	Pensions	Sickness insurance	Unemployment benefits	Social and health services	Other	Total
1990	11.1	3.5	1.2	10.2	1.2	27.2
1995	14.9	4.0	5.3	12.6	1.2	38.0
2000	15.0	3.8	4.4	11.8	1.1	36.1
2050	18.8	3.5	1.4	12.1	0.8	36.6

Note: Baseline scenario: GDP growth = 2.7 per cent from 1996 to 2000, 2 per cent from 2000 to 2010, 1.9 per cent from 2010 to 2020 and 1.2 per cent from 2020 to 2030.

Italy – State General Accounting Office (1996a, b, c)

	Social expenditure			
Year	Pensions	Health	Education	Total
1995	13.6	4.4	5.3	23.3
2000	13.6	4.5	4.7	22.8
2030	16.0	5.8	3.9	25.7
2045	14.7	6.6	4.2	25.5

Note: Baseline demographic scenario developed by the General Accounting Office. Pension expenditure estimates refer to the scenario including the effect of the 1995 reform and assuming the indexation of pensions to price dynamics and the adjustment of pension coefficients to changes in life expectancy. Health expenditure projections refer to the scenario assuming that expenditure per member of each age group increases as per worker productivity. Education expenditure estimates assume an increase in school attendance rates, an increase in the students/teachers ratio and wages in the education sector increasing in line with per worker productivity in the economy.

In order to evaluate the dynamics of the three most important age-
related expenditure items (pensions, health and education), the Italian
State General Accounting Office (1996a, 1996b, 1996c) carried out
projections based on different demographic and policy scenarios. In
the baseline scenario, the share of pension and health expenditure to
GDP would increase over the period 1995–2045 respectively from
13.6 to 14.7 per cent and from 4.4 to 6.6 per cent (see table above).
Education expenditure would decline from 5.3 per cent to 4.2 per
cent. Total expenditure for these three items would increase from
23.3 per cent of GDP in 1995 to 25.5 per cent in 2045.

These estimates were updated in 1997 (see State General Accounting Office, 1997) on the basis of the new demographic projections
carried out by the Italian National Statistical Office. The new estimates
point to smaller increases in pension and health expenditure and to a
smaller decline in education expenditure.

2.1.3　Estimates of sustainable primary balances and tax gaps

Projections of age-related public expenditure can be used to produce estimates of the changes to be expected in the primary balance under the
assumption that revenues and age-unrelated expenditures remain constant as
a percentage of GDP. Estimates of primary balances can then be used to
assess the sustainability of current budgetary policies taking expected GDP
growth and the burden for the public debt into consideration. Blanchard
(1990) introduced the concept of tax gap, that is, the gap between the current
tax to GDP level and the sustainable tax to GDP level, the latter being the
level which, if constant, would achieve an unchanged debt to GDP ratio by
the end of the projection period given expected expenditure trends (for a
description of the methodology used to compute the 'tax gap', see Annex A,
which refers to Blanchard, 1990, and Blanchard et al., 1990).[16]

In a study carried out within OECD, Blanchard et al. (1990) estimated the
long-term tax gap for 18 countries over a 40-year horizon taking long-term
projections of pension and health-care expenditure into account. The ratio of
pension expenditure to GDP was assumed to change in line with demographic trends,[17] while medical care expenditure was assumed to be affected
by changes in population structure and increases in the relative price of
medical care.[18] The study also estimated the short- and medium-term tax
gaps which are not affected by demographic changes: the former is computed
on a one-year time horizon and does not require projections; the latter relies
on five-year projections of economic activity and public spending and considers expected cyclical effects.

Assuming that the difference between the interest rate and the growth rate is 2 per cent and relative medical inflation is 1 per cent, the long-term tax gap was positive (that is, an increase in revenues was required) in five out of the eight EU member states for which both pension and health expenditure trends were considered (see Table 9.4). The gap was particularly high for Italy (6 points) and the Netherlands (4 points). For France, Sweden and Germany it was in the 1–2 per cent bracket. Negative gaps were estimated for Belgium, Denmark and the United Kingdom (that is, revenues could have been reduced). For most countries, the medium-term gap was more favourable than either the short- or long-term gap. The worsening between the medium- and long-term gap was usually very large.

Delbecque and Bogaert (1994) carried out a similar analysis for Belgium for the period up to 2050. In a first stage, on the basis of current budgetary

Table 9.4   Indicators of sustainability of fiscal policy: OECD (1990) (percentage of GDP)

		Long-term gap (1989–2029)				
Country	Pensions only	Pensions and health, assuming a medical cost differential of:			Short-term gap (1989)	Medium-term gap (1989–94)
		0%	1%	2%		
Austria	0.3	—	—	—	1.1	−0.7
Belgium	−2.2	−2.2	−1.5	−0.7	0.3	−1.5
Denmark	−3.1	−3.1	−2.4	−1.4	−2.3	−2.7
Finland	1.5	—	—	—	−2.5	−1.5
France	0.6	0.9	1.9	3.1	−0.1	−0.6
Germany	0.1	0.2	1.0	2.0	−2.0	−2.8
Greece	9.4	—	—	—	11.9	11.1
Ireland	−6.2	—	—	—	−0.9	−3.2
Italy	5.4	5.6	6.1	6.7	5.2	4.6
Netherlands	2.5	3.1	4.1	5.4	1.3	0.6
Portugal	—	—	—	—	—	—
Spain	1.4	—	—	—	0.3	0.6
Sweden	−0.4	−0.2	1.0	2.5	−3.4	−2.5
United Kingdom	−3.8	−3.6	−3.0	−2.2	−3.5	−3.7
USA	0.1	0.6	1.4	2.3	−0.3	−0.6
Japan	0.7	1.4	2.2	3.3	−3.0	−3.1

Source: Blanchard et al. (1990).

data from national sources and assuming a nominal GDP growth of 5 per cent, they computed the required minimum primary surplus, that is, the level of the primary surplus that could be maintained forever without giving rise to an explosion of the public debt. As a result, under the assumption of a difference between the interest rate and the GDP growth rate of 2.5 per cent (which was considered the most realistic, given historical trends), the Belgian primary surplus should have been maintained constant from 1994 onwards at a level of 4.2 per cent of GDP (see Table 9.5). This would imply that Belgium, which then had a surplus of 5.2 per cent of GDP, was in a sustainable position.

As a second stage of the analysis, Delbecque and Bogaert calculated the recommended primary surplus, that is, the level of the primary surplus that would guarantee the long-term sustainability of fiscal policy, given the actual pension expenditure projections. This indicator was calculated on the basis of long-term public finance projections carried out within the MALTESE model (see Englert et al., 1994 and Lambrecht et al., 1994). The recommended primary surplus allows pension expenditure increases to be fully offset by a decline in interest payments caused by a fast reduction in the debt to GDP ratio. In this case, under the same economic assumptions, sustainability would be assured only if the level of the primary surplus is increased to 7.6 per cent of GDP by 1997.

Underlying the minimum surplus and the recommended surplus there are different approaches to the expected increases in pension expenditure. The attainment of the minimum surplus would imply a year-by-year compensation of the expenditure growth with tax increases or expenditure cuts; the attainment of the recommended surplus would imply a bigger immediate effort with a view to preserving present pension arrangements. If reforms were introduced to curb pension expenditure growth, the recommended surplus would decline.

The overall impact of ageing populations on government budget positions up to 2030 was examined in the studies carried out by OECD in 1995–96 (see Leibfritz et al., 1995, Roseveare et al., 1996 and OECD, 1996). For the period 1995–2000, the net primary balance was projected on the basis of OECD's medium-term reference scenario. For the period 2000–2030, long-term projections of the primary balance were carried out on the basis of the pension and health care projections examined in Section 2.1.2.[19] Revenues and other expenditure items were assumed constant to GDP. Under these assumptions, in most countries primary balances improve up to 2000 and deteriorate thereafter, particularly after 2015. Over the period 2000–2030, primary balances deteriorate by 11 percentage points of GDP in Finland, 10 points in Italy, 9 points in Austria and the Netherlands, 6 to 7 points in Belgium, Denmark, France, Germany, Japan, Portugal, Spain and Sweden, 4

Table 9.5 Projections of the primary surplus in Belgium

Difference between the interest rate and the GDP growth rate	Required minimum primary surplus		Recommended primary surplus	
	Level of the surplus required in 1994	Gap with respect to the 1994 level (5.2%)	Level of the surplus required in 1997	Gap with respect to the 1996 level (6.5%)
1	2.2	−3	6.6	0.1
1.5	2.9	−2.3	6.9	0.4
2	3.5	−1.7	7.2	0.7
2.5	4.2	−1	7.6	1.1
3	4.9	−0.3	8	1.5
3.5	5.6	0.4	8.4	1.9
4	6.2	1	8.9	2.4

Source: Delbecque and Bogaert (1994).

313

314   *Demography and the welfare state*

points in the United States, 2 in the United Kingdom and less than 1 point in Ireland (see Table 9.3).

On the basis of these projections and different assumptions on interest rates on the public debt, the OECD's studies estimated the increase in tax revenues required to keep the debt to GDP ratio constant from 2000 onwards.[20] In other words, they estimated the increase in tax rates which, in each year, would offset the increase in public expenditure determined by ageing.[21] Assuming constant interest rates, in the period up to 2015, in most countries, the adjustment required was in the 1.5–3 per cent range, the exceptions being Austria and Japan, where larger tax increases would be needed, and Belgium and Italy, where tax revenues could be reduced (see Table 9.6). By 2030 increases in tax revenues of 5 to 10 percentage points of GDP would be required in most countries. Greater increases would be needed in Austria and Italy, while smaller increases would be required in Denmark, Ireland, Sweden and the United Kingdom.

Table 9.6   Public expenditure projections: OECD (1996)

Increase in tax/GDP ratios required to keep debt constant

	Interest rate constant			Interest rate–growth rate differentials constant		
Country	2005	2015	2030	2005	2015	2030
Austria	3.8	7.3	15.4	3.8	7.2	15
Belgium	-2	-0.9	5.9	-2	-1.5	4.7
Denmark	-1.9	0.5	3.8	-1.9	0.4	3.7
Finland	-1.4	2.7	8.8	-1.4	2.7	8.9
France	0.8	2.9	7.1	0.8	2.5	6.6
Germany	2.8	2.6	9.7	2.8	2.5	8.8
Ireland	-0.3	1	1.8	-0.3	0.3	1.1
Italy	1.8	-0.4	11.4	1.8	0.4	10.2
Netherlands	0.8	3.1	9	0.8	2.9	8.5
Portugal	0.5	2.2	8.2	0.5	2	7.4
Spain	0.9	2.3	7.4	0.9	1.9	6.6
Sweden	-0.6	1.4	4	-0.6	1.3	3.9
United Kingdom	1.7	1.8	3.5	1.7	2	3.1
USA	-0.3	1.4	5.3	-0.3	1.1	4.6
Japan	3.5	6.9	9.6	3.5	6.7	9.5

Source: Roseveare et al. (1996).

2.2 Generational Accounting Studies

Generational accounting is a new technique used to study the effects of fiscal policy on different generations.[22] More specifically, it can assess the distributional implications across generations of changes in budgetary policies and highlight the effects of policy changes that do not affect the conventional deficit. Generational accounting also provides estimates of long-term sustainability of budgetary policies on the basis of present expenditure and taxation policies, present net public debt and expected demographic and macroeconomic trends. The methodology of generational accounting is briefly presented in Box 9.3

Box 9.3   The methodology of generational accounting

Generational accounting assess the present value of transfers, services and taxes received and paid for by different generations (annual cohorts of the population) under the intertemporal budget constraint requiring that the present value of future taxes is equal to the present value of future government consumption, less the initial stock of debt. Future taxes are split into the amount to be paid by all existing generations from the base year to the end of their lives and those that are to be paid by all future generations. Cash transfers (for example pensions) are considered as negative taxes and detracted by future taxes.

The budget constraints can be expressed as:

Present value of all future government consumption		Stock of current government net wealth	+	Present value of all future net tax payments of all living generations	+	Present value of all net tax payments of all future generations
	=					

or, in algebraic form:

$$\sum_{s=b}^{\infty} G_s (1+r)^{b-s} = W_b^G + \sum_{s=0}^{D} N_{b,b-s} + \sum_{s=1}^{\infty} N_{b,b+s}$$

where G_s = government consumption in period s;

W_b^G = government net wealth in the base year b (minus in case of net debt);

$N_{b,k}$ = present value in the base year b of all future net tax
      payments of the generation born in the year k;

r = real interest rate;

D = maximum age (constant value).

More specifically, the present value in the base year b of all future net
tax payments of the generation born in the year k, $N_{b,k}$ can be expressed as:

$$N_{b,k} = \sum_{s=\max(b,k)}^{k+D} T_{s,k} P_{s,k} (1+r)^{b-s}$$

where $T_{s,k}$ = average per capita net tax payments in year s of the
          cohort born in year k;

$P_{s,k}$ = number of surviving members in year s of the cohort
          born in year k.

Generational accounts are constructed so that no policy changes are
envisaged for present generations (even if present policies are unbal-
anced), while future generations bear the burden for restoring the
sustainability of public finances. It is also assumed that the adjustment
of budgetary policies take place on the tax side. The difference between present and future generations' net taxes provides a measure of
the imbalance in present fiscal policy.

More specifically, generational accounting compares the net discounted taxes paid by the new-born generation on the basis of present
expenditure and revenue policies, with the net discounted taxes paid by
future generations on the basis of present expenditure policies and the
increase in tax rates required by the intertemporal budget constraint.

The first step in the development of generational accounts for all
living and future cohorts of the population consists in the attribution
of present government revenues and outlays to the different age groups.
On the revenue side, generational accounting studies usually consider
labour and capital income taxes, social security contributions and
indirect taxes; on the expenditure side, they consider the main social
transfers (pensions, family allowances, unemployment benefits) and
age-related public consumption programmes (health, education). For
each item, an age-related profile of the ratio of revenue or expenditure
to per capita GDP is developed. For revenue and expenditure items
that cannot be assigned to specific age groups a uniform distribution
on age groups is assumed.

The generational accounting methodology was first applied in the United States by Auerbach et al. (1991). In the United States (Office of Management and Budget, 1994) and Norway[23] (Ministry of Finance) it has also been introduced in official budget documents. Estimates have since been produced for Denmark (Jensen and Raffelhüschen, 1995 and Raffelhüschen, 1997), Finland (Prime Minister's Office, 1994), Germany (Gokhale et al., 1995 and Raffelhüschen, 1997), Italy (Franco et al., 1994), the Netherlands (Ter Rele, 1997) and Sweden (Hagemann and John, 1995).

In 1995 OECD produced estimates for the United States, Germany, Italy, Norway and Sweden. The main results are reported in Table 9.7. The imbalance in fiscal policy is extremely large for Italy, where future generations would be expected to pay net taxes more than five times higher than those paid by the new-born generation under present policies.[24] In the United States taxes on future generations would be twice as high as those on the new-born generation.[25] In Germany, Norway and Sweden the increase in net taxes would range between 27 and 53 per cent.[26]

Generational accounting, as already pointed out, evaluates the long-term sustainability of budgets taking the interaction of demographic and macro-economic scenarios into account. However, it is liable to the same limitations listed above for public expenditure projections; it does not consider the future effects of past changes in legislation, the changes in economies/diseconomies

Table 9.7   Generational accounting: OECD (1995)

Present values of future net tax payments per capita (males)
(thousands of dollars)[1]

	Generation's age in 1993					Future generations	Percentage difference[2]
Country	0	20	40	60	80		
Germany	197	374	203	−150	−68	250	27%
Italy	65	196	88	−148	−115	354	446%
Sweden	156	259	253	−29	−29	204	31%
Norway	110	177	134	−29	−43	171	53%
USA	121	218	168	−58	−89	243	100%

Notes:
[1] In constant prices, adjusted for income growth. Assuming real income growth of 1.5 per cent and a discount rate of 5 per cent.
[2] Between future generations and the generation born in 1993.

Source: Leibfritz et al. (1995).

of scale, the effects of demographic developments on relative prices and work, consumption and investment decisions.[27]

The usefulness of generational accounting, as against traditional expenditure and deficit projections, in estimating the effects of demographic changes and monitoring budgetary trends in member states is limited by the fact that generational accounting does not provide indications about the timing of the effects of demographic changes, nor does it outline budgetary trends over the short and medium term. Moreover, its results are not intuitive, which may hamper their use for policy objectives, and are very sensitive to assumptions about the determination of private consumption, productivity growth and discount rates.[28]

For these reasons, and in order to provide a framework consistent with the conventional budgetary indicators, and more specifically with the stability and convergence programmes presented by EU governments, this study follows the approach outlined in Section 2.1. However, it makes extensive use of the age-related expenditure profiles developed within generational accounting studies. Generational accounts, which provide considerable insight into the impact of fiscal policy on the lifetime budget constraints of households of different generations, would represent a useful complement to the indicators presented in this study.

3.   MECHANICAL EFFECTS OF DEMOGRAPHIC CHANGES ON PUBLIC EXPENDITURE

This section provides some estimates of the direct effects of demographic changes on public expenditure in eight EU member states for which age-related expenditure profiles are available. As already mentioned, it is a mechanical exercise projecting future expenditure trends on the basis of initial age-related expenditure profiles and changing demographic population structures. These estimates update and improve the results of the studies mentioned in Section 2.1 and are obviously subject to the same limitations.

The methodology of the estimates is presented in Section 3.1. The results of the projections are presented in Section 3.2. More specifically, Section 3.2.1 outlines the baseline estimates for the burden of age-related public expenditure on the working-age population. Sections 3.2.3 and 3.2.4 consider alternative estimates, based respectively on different dynamics of per capita expenditure and demographic scenarios.

3.1   The Methodology

The mechanical effects of demographic changes are assessed, identifying the major items of public expenditure particularly dependent on population age structure. Data on per capita expenditure for different age groups and for different budgetary items are combined with demographic projections. More specifically, the estimates, which cover the period 1995–2050, are based on the following two sets of data:

(a) demographic scenarios developed by Eurostat for the 15 EU member states for the period 1995–2050 (see Annex B). Three scenarios are considered: the baseline and, in order to identify the range of possible effects of demographic changes, two extreme scenarios (the 'youngest population' and the 'most-aged population' scenarios).

(b) national estimates of the per capita amount of public expenditure concerning the citizens of each age group. Eight European countries are taken into consideration: Belgium, Denmark, Finland, Germany, Italy, the Netherlands, Spain and Sweden. Most estimates have been produced in research work on generational accounting. According to the availability of the data, the coverage of the profiles in terms of expenditure items is different between countries.

3.1.1 The expenditure profiles

Citizens of different sex and age groups consume different amounts of public services. They also receive different amounts of public transfers. Expenditure for educational and health services, pension benefits and child allowances are the budget items most dependent on the age structure of the population. This study considers all age-related expenditures as reported in Annex C. The outlays considered differ across countries; therefore, as already indicated, the results are not fully comparable. In order to compare different countries and periods, the amount spend for each age group has been expressed as a percentage of per capita GDP (see Box 9.4).

Box 9.4   Age-related expenditure profiles

In order to evaluate the effects of demographic changes on public expenditure, it is necessary to estimate the average amount spent for the members of each age group and sex within each expenditure programme. Total expenditure in the base year should be allocated among males (*M*) and females (*F*) following the following identity:

$$GG_k^b = \left[\sum_i \left(gg_{ik}^b \times P_i^b \right) \right]^M + \left[\sum_i \left(gg_{ik}^b \times P_i^b \right) \right]^F$$

where GG_k^b = total age-related public expenditure for budgetary item k
in the base year b;

gg_{ik}^b = expenditure for budgetary item k per member of each
age group i in national currency in the base year b;

P_i^b = population in each age group in the base year b;

i = 0, 90;

b = base year;

k = budgetary item (for example, pension expenditure, health
care expenditure).

In recent years age-related public expenditure profiles have been estimated for some countries either within studies projecting the effects
of demographic changes on public budgets (Belgium, Spain) or within
research work on generational accounting (Denmark, Finland, Germany, Italy, the Netherlands and Sweden). The profiles for Finland and
Italy cover all public expenditure; those for the other countries cover
only some important age-related items (Table 8). Different male and
female profiles have been computed for Denmark, Germany, Italy and
Sweden. The profiles for Finland, Denmark, Germany, Italy and the
Netherlands refer to 1-year age groups, those for Belgium and Sweden,
respectively, to 5-year and 10-year age groups. Spanish profiles consider only three large age groups.

For the purpose of this paper, per capita expenditure for each age
group (gg_{ik}^b) has been divided by base-year per capita GDP obtaining
the following identity:

$$G_k^b = \left[\sum_i\left(g_{ik}^b \times P_i^b\right)\right]^M + \left[\sum_i\left(g_{ik}^b \times P_i^b\right)\right]^F$$

where G_k^b = total age-related public expenditure for budgetary item k
in the base year b in terms of the base-year per capita
GDP;

g_{ik}^b = expenditure for budgetary item k per member of each
age group i in national currency in the base year b in
terms of the base-year per capita GDP.

The national profiles for the different age-related expenditure items are
presented in Annex C. Figures 9.2a and 9.2b outline the profiles for male and
female total age-related expenditure. As an example, the estimate for total
age-related expenditure for the 0–4-year age group in Belgium (0.221) means
that in the base year (1988) the public sector spent 22.1 per cent of per capita

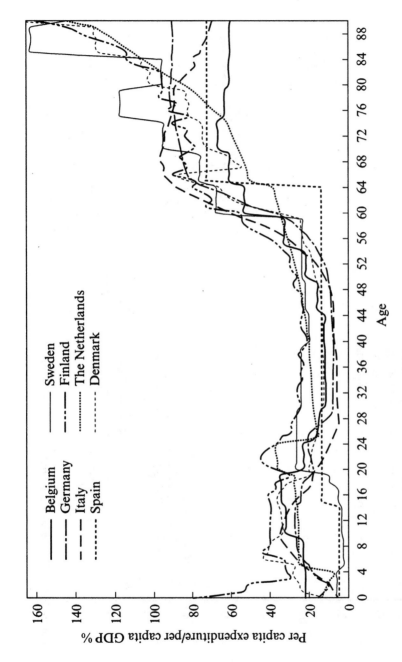

Figure 9.2a Total age-related public expenditure profiles for males (percentage of per capita GDP)

Legend:
Belgium — Sweden
Germany — Finland
Italy — The Netherlands
Spain — Denmark

321

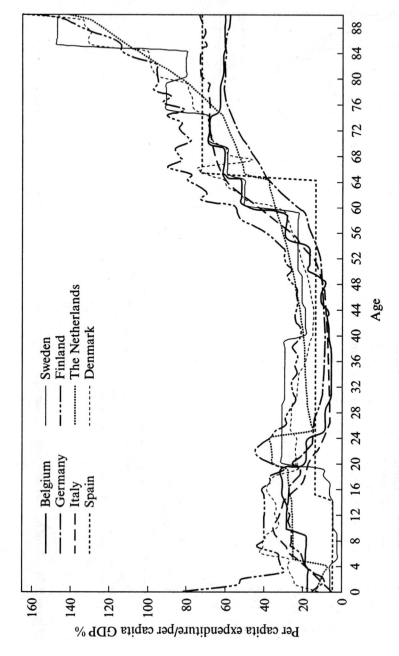

Figure 9.2b   Total age-related public expenditure profiles for females (percentage of capita GDP)

GDP in order to provide services to each 0–4-year-old citizen. The profiles are not fully comparable since national estimates differ in terms of coverage of expenditure items. Education expenditure, for instance, is not covered for Spain and Sweden. The expenditure programmes considered represent about 50 per cent of total public expenditure (net of interest payments) in Spain, 55 per cent in Germany and Sweden, about 65 per cent in Belgium, Denmark, Italy and the Netherlands and nearly 80 per cent in Finland.

Profiles including all main items are typically two-peaked. The first peak occurs in the 10–25-year age group with education expenditure as the most important item.[29] The second peak, reaching higher levels, occurs for the 60–80-year age groups and is largely determined by pension and health expenditure trends. The lowest expenditure levels are usually recorded for the 30–50-year age groups. Female expenditure levels are lower than male levels. The Finnish profile in addition shows very high expenditure in the first year of life and in the over 80-year age group.

Figures 9.3a and 9.3b compare the male and female profiles for pension expenditure in the eight countries considered. Separate male and female profiles are available only for Denmark, Germany, Italy and Sweden. Per capita expenditure increases earlier in Finland, Italy and Sweden, where, on average, 61-year-old male[30] citizens receive pension payments amounting to about 55 per cent of per capita GDP. For most countries expenditure peaks for the 65–80-year age group. The Italian and Swedish male profiles peak at about 80 per cent of per capita GDP, the Finnish and the German profiles at about 70 per cent and the Belgian and Spanish at about 60 per cent. Expenditure is lower in the Netherlands. Female profiles are much lower than for male; they peak at 50 per cent of per capita GDP in Sweden and 40 per cent in Italy and Germany. The Danish profile is rather peculiar, since it includes expenditure for elderly care, which increases substantially with age.[31]

In each country health expenditure increases gradually with age (see Figures 9.4a and 9.4b). Some countries also record a peak for new-born children (about 8–9 per cent of per capita GDP). Expenditure for children in the 5–15-year age group is very limited; in most countries it is in the 2–3 per cent range. Thereafter expenditure grows steadily: in most countries it is in the 4–6 per cent range for people aged 40,[32] in the 6–9 per cent range for people aged 60 and in the 13–19 per cent range for people aged 80. Expenditure for the very elderly is particularly high in Denmark and Finland. The Dutch profile also includes home care and cannot be compared with the other profiles. Males and female profiles are rather similar.

Education expenditure profiles are not available for Spain and Sweden (see Figures 9.5a and 9.5b). Expenditure peaks at about 35 per cent of per capita GDP in Denmark; at 25–30 per cent in Belgium, Finland and Italy and at 18 per cent in Germany and the Netherlands. While for most countries

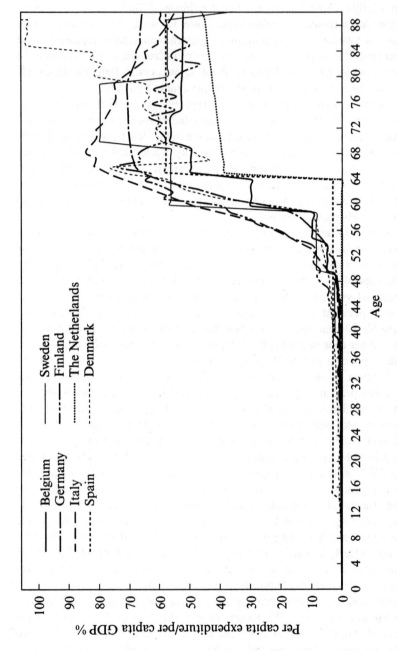

Figure 9.3a A comparison of national pension expenditure profiles for males (percentage of per capita GDP)

The legend contains:
Belgium   Sweden
Germany   Finland
Italy   The Netherlands
Spain   Denmark

Y-axis: Per capita expenditure/per capita GDP %

X-axis: Age

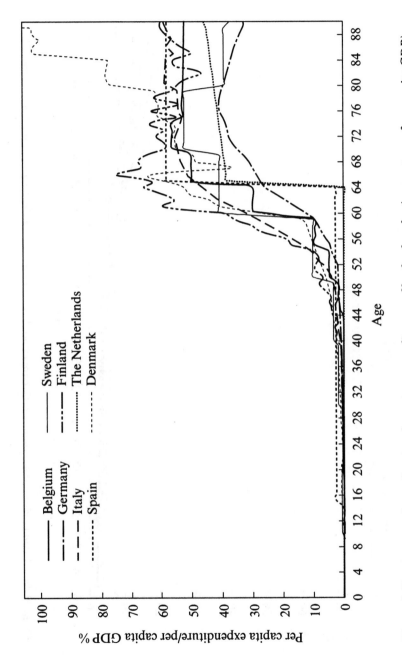

Figure 9.3b   A comparison of national pension expenditure profiles for females (percentage of per capita GDP)

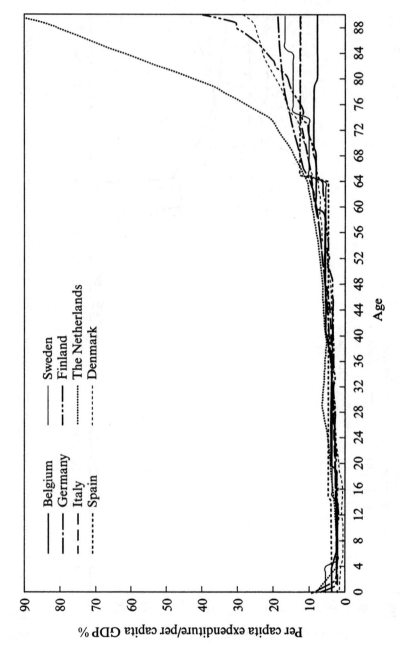

Figure 9.4a A comparison of national health-care expenditure profiles for males (percentage of per capita GDP)

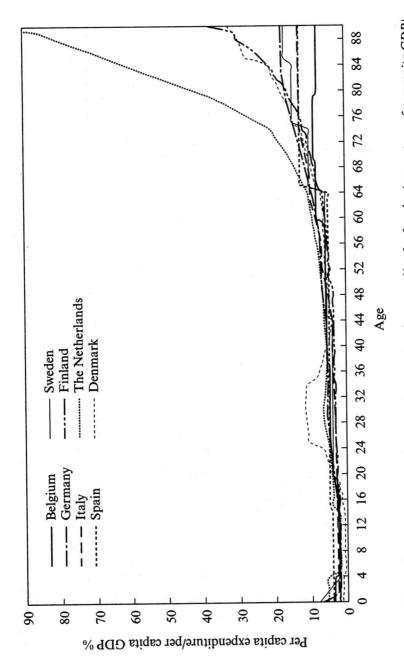

Figure 9.4b A comparison of national health-care expenditure profiles for females (percentage of per capita GDP)

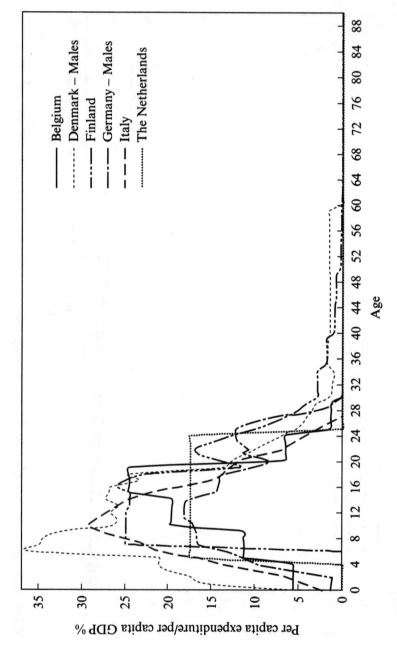

Figure 9.5a *A comparison of national education expenditure profiles for males (percentage of per capita GDP)*

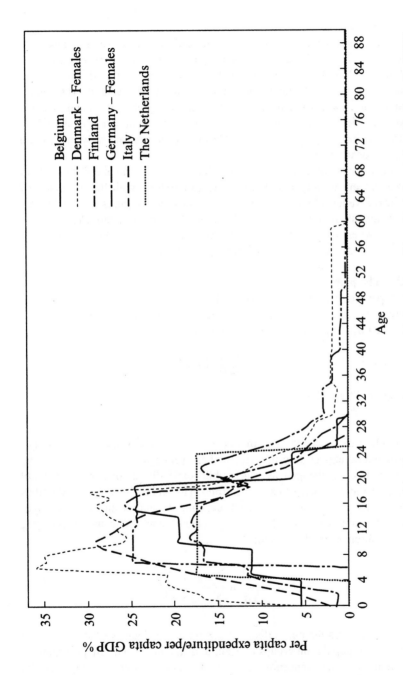

Figure 9.5b   A comparison of national education expenditure profiles for females (percentage of per capita GDP)

Demography and the welfare state

expenditure is higher than the 6–16-year age groups, in Belgium it peaks for the 15–19-year age group.

The profiles for unemployment benefits and labour market assistance are rather different (see Figures 9.6a and 9.6b).[33] In most countries there is a peak for the 20–30-year age group and a second peak for the 55–60-year age group. Where separate male and female profiles are available (Denmark, Germany and Sweden), male profiles are usually higher. Finnish and Swedish expenditure levels are particularly high (over 7 per cent of per capita GDP) for most working-age groups, while German levels are relatively low (in the 1–3.5 per cent range).

Profiles for family and maternity allowances are also rather different. Child allowances are usually imputed directly to children, with the exception of Italy and Sweden where they are imputed to parents (Figures 9.7a and 9.7b). Allowances are relatively high for Belgium, Denmark, Finland, Germany and Sweden, where they are often in the 5–10 per cent range, and modest for Italy and Spain (less than 1 per cent of per capita GDP).

3.1.2 The projections

The expenditure profiles (g_{ik}^b) reported in Figures 9.2–9.7 and in Annex C (expressed in percentage terms of the base-year per capita GDP) have been multiplied by the population in each age group for the years 1995–2050 (P_i^j).

$$G_k^j = \sum_i \left(g_{ik}^b \times P_i^j \right)$$

where j = 1995, 2050
  b = 1995.

By dividing by the 1995 data, this provides an index of the change in age-related public expenditure in terms of base-year per capita GDP under the assumption of unchanged average public expenditure (in per capita GDP terms) for the members of each age group. This index (henceforth defined as index A) can be computed for each expenditure item k and for total age-related expenditure (by calculating the weighted average of the indices referring to the different expenditure items).

$$A_k = \frac{G_k^j}{G_k^b} = \frac{\sum_i \left(g_{ik}^b \times P_i^j \right)}{\sum_i \left(g_{ik}^b \times P_i^b \right)}$$

Index A measures the pure effects of demographic changes (that is, changes in the size of population groups relevant to different expenditure programmes and changes in the proportion of population in the different groups) on the

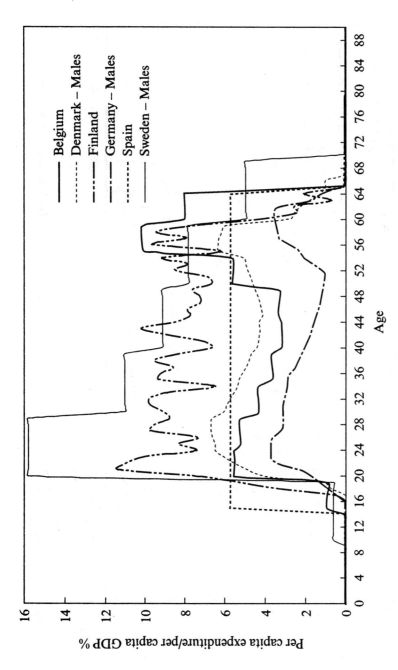

Figure 9.6a A comparison of national unemployment benefits and labour market assistance profiles for males (percentage of per capita GDP)

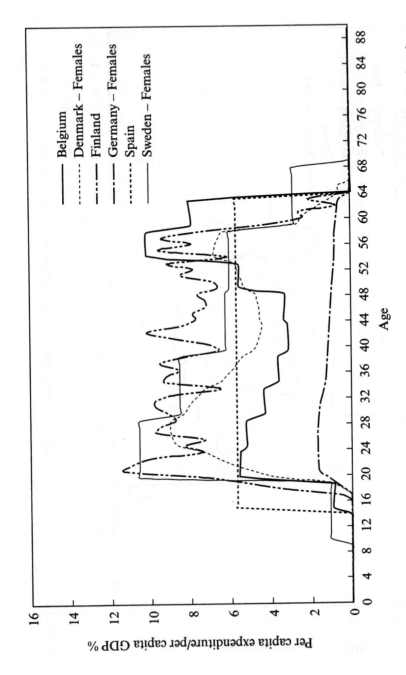

Figure 9.6b   A comparison of national unemployment benefits and labour market assistance profiles for females (percentage of per capita GDP)

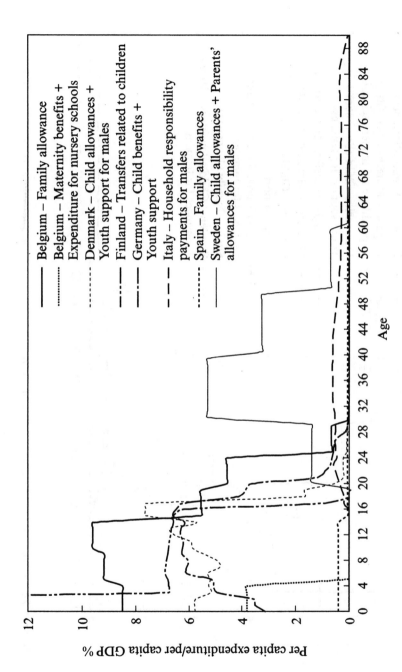

Legend:

— Belgium – Family allowance

⋯⋯ Belgium – Maternity benefits +
Expenditure for nursery schools

⋯⋯ Denmark – Child allowances +
Youth support for males

–·– Finland – Transfers related to children

–··– Germany – Child benefits +
Youth support

– – Italy – Household responsibility
payments for males

⋯⋯ Spain – Family allowances

— Sweden – Child allowances + Parents'
allowances for males

Per capita expenditure/per capita GDP %

Age

Figure 9.7a   A comparison of national family allowances profiles for males (percentage of per capita GDP)

333

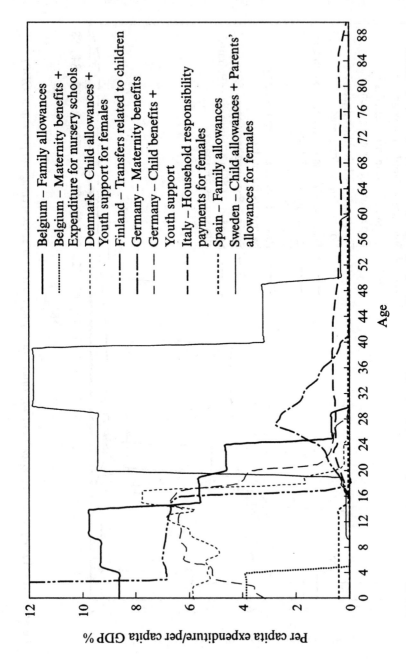

Figure 9.7b A comparison of national family allowances profiles for females (percentage of per capita GDP)

'demand' for public services and transfers, under the above-mentioned assumption.

Index *A* does not measure the burden that will be carried by workers and taxpayers, since the number of workers and taxpayers will also be affected by change in demographic structure. An assessment of this burden requires that trends in the size and productivity of the labour force (that is, trends in GDP) are also taken into account.

Two indices (*B* and *C*) have been developed in order to consider these factors (for a brief overview of the formulae used for the computation of the two indices, see Box 9.5).

Box 9.5   Indices of the burden of age-related expenditure on citizens of working age

The indices of the ratio of age-related public expenditure to GDP have been estimated for each age-related expenditure item considered in Section 3, on the basis of the following assumptions:

(a)   the change in the number of workers and taxpayers has been assumed to be proportional to the change in the number of working-age citizens, which is equivalent to assuming that the aggregate labour force participation rate and unemployment rate remain constant over the projection period.

(b)   The rate of growth of GDP has been determined on the basis of the change in the number of working-age citizens and the rate of increase in their productivity (r_w), which has been assumed constant over time (even though demographic changes are actually likely to have repercussions on productivity growth). Because of the changes in population structure, per capita GDP growth (which depends on the population structure) is different from per worker GDP growth.

(c)   Age-related public expenditure profiles have been projected into the future on the basis of two alternative assumptions:

(i)   public expenditure for the members of each age group increases at a yearly rate equal to the rate of growth of per capita GDP (index *B*);

(ii)   public expenditure for the members of each age group increases at a yearly rate equal to the rate of growth of GDP per worker (index *C*).

The indices can be expressed as:

$$B_k = \frac{\dfrac{\sum\limits_{i=0}^{90}\left(g_{ik}^b \times gdp_C^b(1+r_c)^{j-b} \times P_i^j\right)}{\sum\limits_{i=0}^{90}\left(g_{ik}^b \times gdp_C^b \times P_i^b\right)}}{\dfrac{\sum\limits_{i=0}^{90}P_i^j \times gdp_C^b(1+r_c)^{j-b}}{\sum\limits_{i=0}^{90}P_i^b \times gdp_C^b}} \quad \text{and} \quad C_k = \frac{\dfrac{\sum\limits_{i=0}^{90}\left(g_{ik}^b \times gdp_C^b(1+r_W)^{j-b} \times P_i^j\right)}{\sum\limits_{i=0}^{90}\left(g_{ik}^b \times gdp_C^b \times P_i^b\right)}}{\dfrac{\sum\limits_{i=20}^{64}P_i^j \times gdp_W^b(1+r_W)^{j-b}}{\sum\limits_{i=20}^{64}P_i^b \times gdp_W^b}}$$

where gdp_C^b = per capita GDP in the base year b;
 gdp_W^b = GDP per worker in the base year b;
 P_i^b = population in each age group in the base year b;
 j = 1995, 2050;
 r_W = growth rate of GDP per worker;
 r_c = growth rate of per capita GDP.

The two indices can be expressed as follows:

$$B_k = \frac{\dfrac{\sum\limits_{i=0}^{90}\left(g_{ik}^b \times P_i^j\right)}{\sum\limits_{i=0}^{90}\left(g_{ik}^b \times P_i^b\right)}}{\dfrac{\sum\limits_{i=0}^{90}P_i^j}{\sum\limits_{i=0}^{90}P_i^b}} = \frac{A_k}{\dfrac{\sum\limits_{i=0}^{90}P_i^j}{\sum\limits_{i=0}^{90}P_i^b}} \quad \text{and} \quad C_k = \frac{\dfrac{\sum\limits_{i=0}^{90}\left(g_{ik}^b \times P_i^j\right)}{\sum\limits_{i=0}^{90}\left(g_{ik}^b \times P_i^b\right)}}{\dfrac{\sum\limits_{i=20}^{64}P_i^j}{\sum\limits_{i=20}^{64}P_i^b}} = \frac{A_k}{\dfrac{\sum\limits_{i=20}^{64}P_i^j}{\sum\limits_{i=20}^{64}P_i^b}}$$

The two indices can therefore be calculated as the ratio of index A to the index of the growth of total population (index B) or to the index of the growth of working-age population (index C). This implies that no assumptions are actually required for the level of r_W. The two indices B and C also represent the burden of age-related public expenditure on the working-age population.

Index B measures the trend of the ratio of public expenditure to GDP, based on the assumption that per capita expenditure grows as per capita GDP. This index is suitable for evaluating the burden for transfer expenditure aimed at ensuring that benefit recipients have a living standard comparable to that of other citizens.

Index C measures the trend of the ratio of public expenditure to GDP, based on the assumption that per capita expenditure grows as GDP per worker. This index is suitable for expenditure programmes mostly represented by wages, such as education and health care.

A fourth 'mixed' index (D) has been computed by projecting expenditure profiles for transfers on the basis of per capita GDP growth (that is, of index B) and expenditure profiles for public services on the basis of per worker GDP growth (that is, of index C). While indices A, B and C are computed for each expenditure item as well as for total expenditure, index D is computed only for total expenditure. The baseline projections presented in the following sections refer to this mixed index.

Before analysing the results of the projections, some notes of caution should be addressed.

(a)   The coefficients g_{ik}^{1995} have been estimated on the basis of 1988 data for Belgium, 1991 data for Spain, 1994 data for Italy, 1995 data for Denmark, Germany, the Netherlands and Sweden.

(b)   As already pointed out, the ratios are not directly comparable since not all the same items are taken into account for each country (Table 9.8). For instance, the fact that Spanish and Swedish estimates do not take education expenditure into account tends to overestimate the effects of ageing on public expenditure in these countries.

3.2   The Results: The Burden on Working-age Population

The first part of this section focuses on the results referring to index D in the baseline demographic scenario; the second on indices B and C in the same demographic scenario; the third on index D under alternative demographic scenarios. The results for index A (that is, the change in the 'demand' of public expenditure determined by demographic changes) are presented in Annex D.

3.2.1   Baseline economic and demographic projections
As indicated in Section 3.1, in the baseline economic projection the burden of age-related public expenditure on working-age population is computed assuming that present per capita expenditure for education and health grows in line with GDP per worker, while expenditure for transfers grows in line with per capita GDP (that is, index D).

Index D depends on the effects of demographic changes on the 'demand' for public expenditure (that is, index A) and on the number of working-age

Table 9.8   Main features of national age-related expenditure profiles

Country	Source	Year of reference	Main items included				Child allowances attributed to	Share of age-related expenditure to		
			Pensions	Health	Education			Total public expenditure (net of interest payments)		GDP
Belgium	Lambrecht et al. (1994)	1988	YES	YES	YES		Children	62		28.8
Denmark	Raffelhüschen (1997)	1995	YES	YES	YES		Children	66		35
Finland	Mäki et al. (1996)	1993	YES	YES	YES		Children	78		43
Germany	Raffelhüschen (1997)	1995	YES	YES	NO		Children	54		25
Italy	Franco et al. (1994)	1994	YEs	YES	YES		Parents	65		28.3
Netherlands	Ter Rele (1997)	1995	YES	YES	YES		–	63		30
Spain	Barea and Fernández (1994)	1991	YES	NO	NO		Childten	49		20.3
Sweden	Hagemann and John (1995)	1995	YES	YES	NO		Parents	39 } 16 } 55	23.6 9.4 }	33
	Committee on Health Care (1995)	1994	NO	YES	NO		–			

338

citizens, that is, the number of potential workers. Over the period 1995–2050, in the baseline demographic scenario the number of working-age citizens is expected to decline substantially in Italy (29 per cent), Spain (21 per cent) and Germany (19 per cent). In Finland and Belgium it would decline by about 10 per cent. Limited reductions are expected for Denmark (4 per cent) and the Netherlands (1 per cent). In Sweden it would increase by 8 per cent.

The burden of total age-related expenditure would increase substantially over the next decades in all the eight countries considered (see Figure 9.8). By 2010 the burden would increase by 10 per cent in Germany and Italy, 7 per cent in Finland and the Netherlands, and 4–6 per cent in Belgium, Denmark, Spain and Sweden. The rate of increase would accelerate over the following 15 years. By 2025 the burden would be higher than in 1995, by 25 per cent in Germany and Italy, 18–20 per cent in Finland, the Netherlands and Spain, 13–16 per cent in Belgium, Denmark and Sweden. Over the period 2025–2040 national trends would be rather different; while the burden would increase substantially in Italy, Germany, the Netherlands and Spain, its growth would slow down in the other four countries. By 2040 the burden

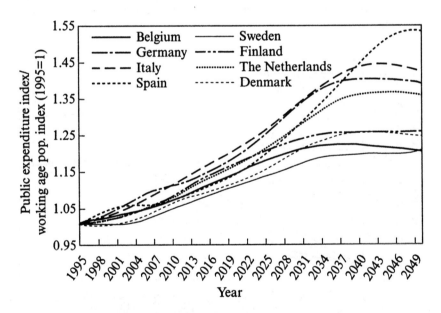

Note: Education and health expenditures grow as GDP per worker, other expenditure items grow as per capita GDP

Figure 9.8   Burden of age-related public expenditure on working-age
population (baseline economic and demographic scenario)

would have peaked in most countries, with the major exception of Spain where it would still be growing fast.[34]

Pension expenditure trends, which contribute substantially to the expected increases in total expenditure, are rather homogeneous (see Figure 9.9a). By 2010 the burden of pension expenditure on working-age population would increase by 10 per cent in Denmark and Sweden, by 13–17 per cent in Belgium, Italy, the Netherlands and Spain, and by 22–24 per cent in Finland and Germany. By 2035 it would increase by 25 per cent in Sweden, 45–50 per cent in Belgium, Denmark and Finland, 60–70 per cent in Germany, Italy and Spain, and 90 per cent in the Netherlands.

In most countries, the burden for health care increases gradually up to the period 2035–40. The increase is particularly high for the Netherlands (75 per cent) and relatively limited for Belgium, Denmark and Sweden (18–32 per cent). In the remaining countries, it is in the 30–50 per cent range (see Figure 9.9b).

Education provides some scope for expenditure cuts. The pattern of the burden for education is similar for Belgium and Finland: declining in the period up to 2010–15, then stable for about a decade, then increasing again up to the period 2035–40, and eventually declining again at the end of the projection period (see Figure 9.9c). The pattern for Denmark, Italy and the

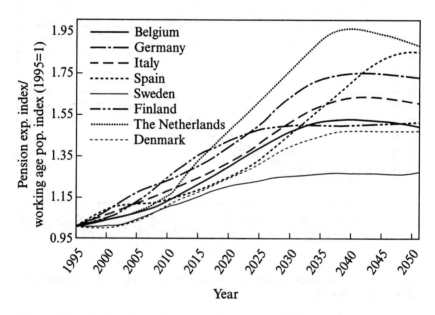

Figure 9.9a Burden of pension expenditure on working-age population (baseline economic and demographic scenario)

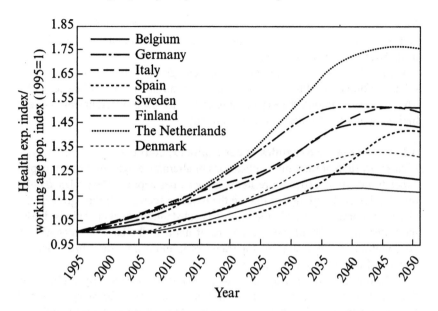

Figure 9.9b Burden of health expenditure on working-age population (baseline economic and demographic scenario)

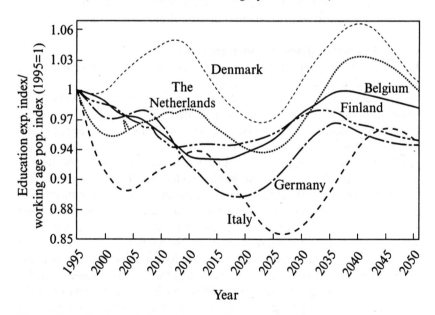

Figure 9.9c Burden of education expenditure on working-age population (baseline economic and demographic scenario)

Netherlands is less smooth, with two troughs, in 2000–2005 and 2025–30, and two peaks, in 2010–15 and 2040–45. The German pattern is similar but troughs and peaks are anticipated.

Figures 9.10a–h report the effects of demographic changes on each age-related public expenditure item for the six countries in the baseline scenario. The dispersion among the expenditure trends for each different item is very high in Spain, the Netherlands and Germany.

3.2.2   Alternative dynamics of per capita expenditure

Figures 9.11a–h present the implications of alternative dynamics of per capita expenditure. If all expenditure items grow as per capita GDP (index *B*), the total burden is slightly lower than in the baseline scenario. If they grow as the GDP per worker (index *C*), the burden is substantially higher. This is due to the different weights of the two groups of items in the baseline scenario: in all countries, the expenditure for transfers is more important than that for services, like health and education.

In the optimistic scenario, the burden is expected to grow only slightly less than in the baseline case. The difference is substantial in Germany, Italy and the Netherlands, while in Sweden there is almost no difference with the burden expected in the baseline scenario. More important divergences from the burden expected in the baseline scenario are to be recorded within the pessimistic scenario, with the highest in Italy, Germany and Spain.

3.2.3   Alternative demographic scenarios

Figures 9.12a–h compare the expenditure trends under the baseline economic scenario and three different demographic scenarios. For all eight countries, the prospects for the burden of total age-related expenditure on working-age population are much more pessimistic under the assumption of an older population ('most-aged population' scenario), while they are more optimistic in the youngest population scenario.

More specifically, in the six countries for which education expenditure is considered, the dynamics of the burden under the different scenarios are rather close up to 2020, since, under the most-aged scenario, the increase in pension expenditure is partly offset by the decrease in education expenditure and, in the same way, under the youngest population scenario the lower increase in pension expenditure is aggravated by a lower decrease (or even an increase) in education expenditure. Over the longer term, the burden is expected to diverge more substantially according to the demographic scenario, due to the fact that after 2040 demographic trends start to converge and the opposite effects of young-related and old-related expenditure are less pronounced.

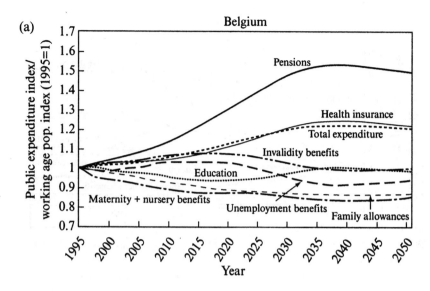

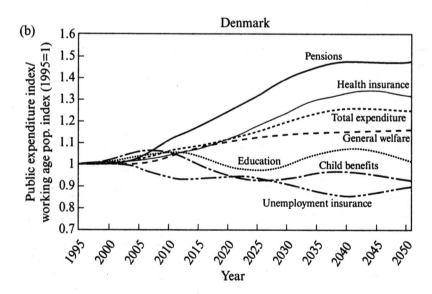

Figure 9.10   Burden of age-related public expenditure on working-age population (baseline economic and demographic scenario)

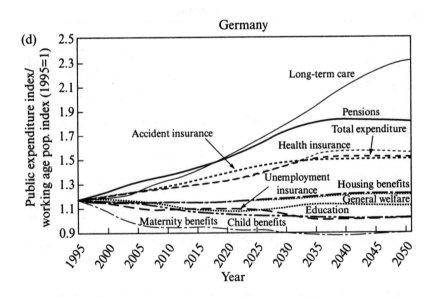

Figure 9.10   continued

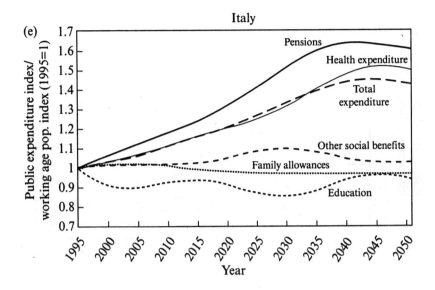

Italy

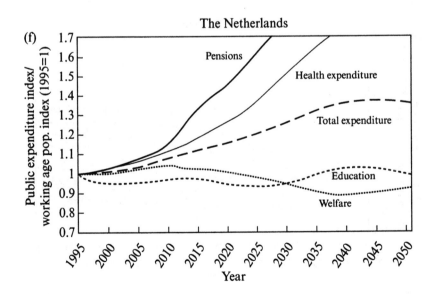

The Netherlands

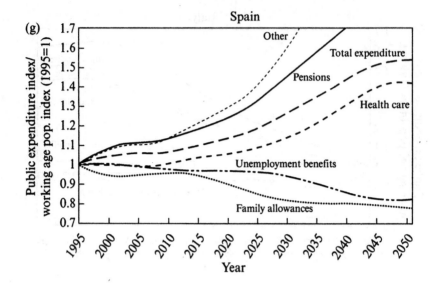

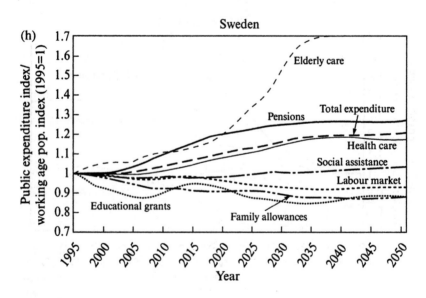

Figure 9.10   continued

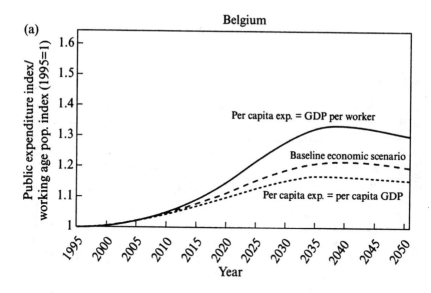

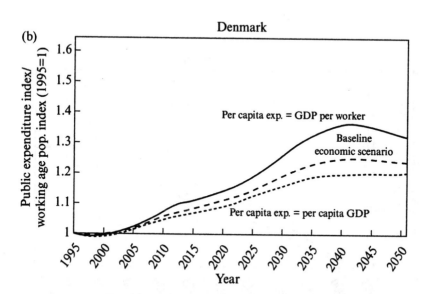

Figure 9.11   Burden of age-related public expenditure on working-age population with different assumptions on per capita expenditure growth rates (baseline demographic scenario)

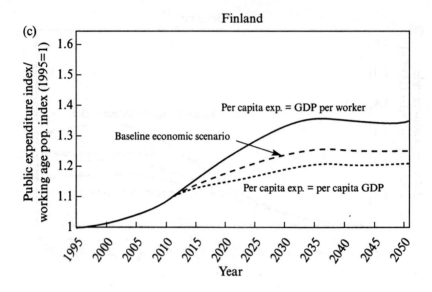

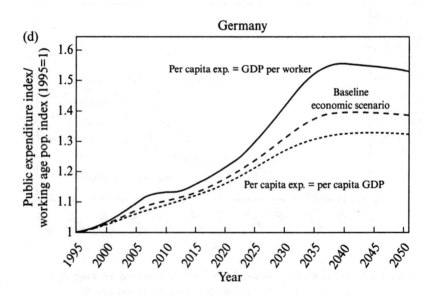

Figure 9.11   continued

(e)

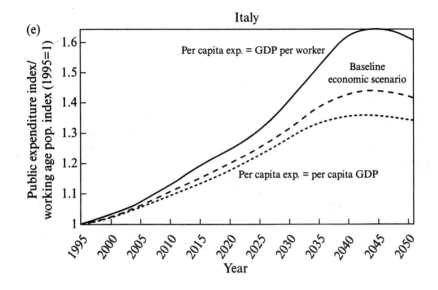

Italy

(f)

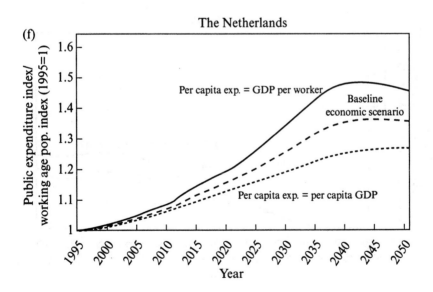

The Netherlands

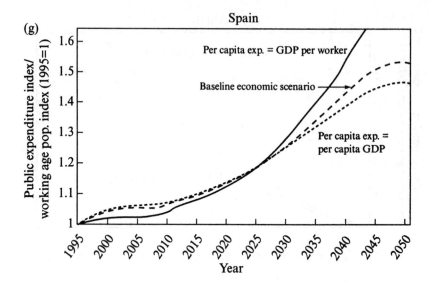

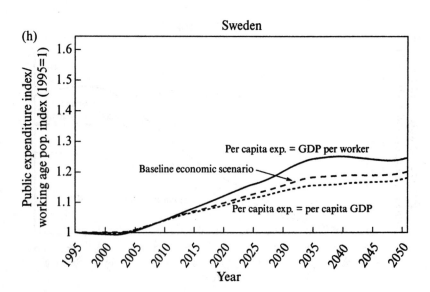

Figure 9.11   continued

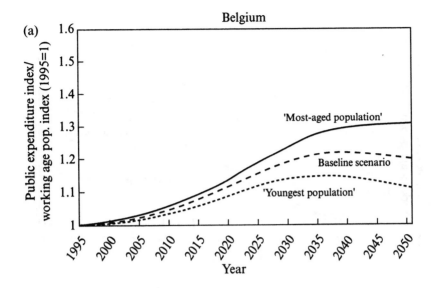

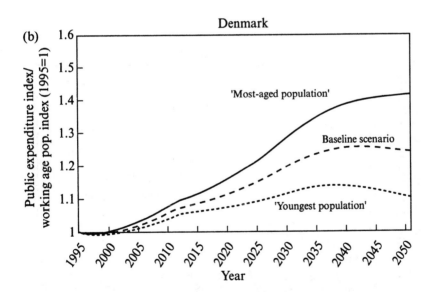

Figure 9.12   Burden of age-related public expenditure on working-age population with different demographic scenarios (baseline economic scenario)

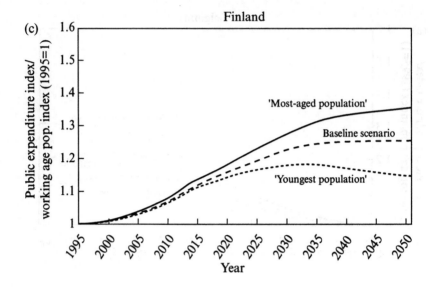

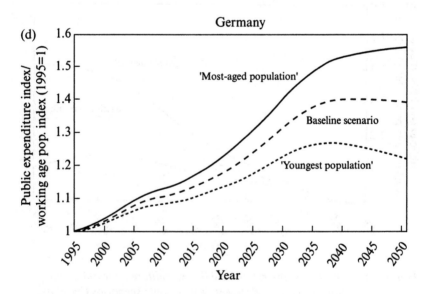

Figure 9.12 continued

(e)

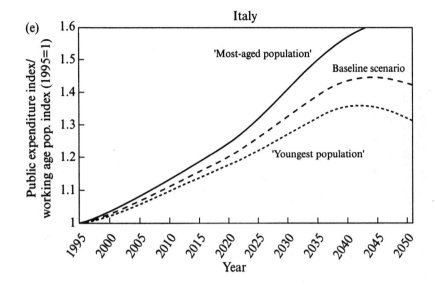

Italy

(f)

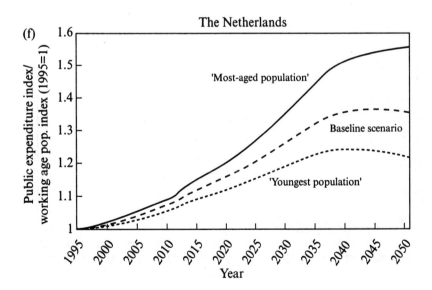

The Netherlands

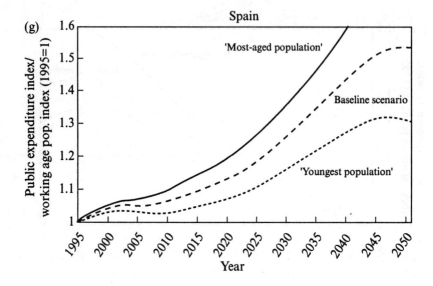

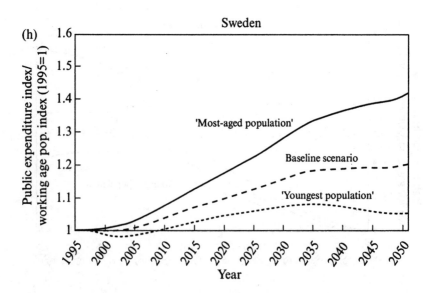

Figure 9.12   continued

4. NATIONAL ESTIMATES OF PENSION EXPENDITURE TRENDS

Pension expenditure growth cannot be accurately forecast on the basis of demographic trends alone. Pension expenditure dynamics are also influenced by changes in legislation (that defines eligibility rules, the amount granted to new pensioners, indexation mechanisms, and so on), past and present employment (that influences the length of workers' membership in pension schemes and the distribution of workers among the different schemes), and social attitudes (such as those towards early retirement and the demand for disability benefits).[35] While legislation basically determines the supply of pensions, the other factors define the demand for them stemming from citizens.

Any assessment of future pension expenditure must therefore consider the likely changes in the eligibility and transfer ratios, respectively the ratio of the number of pensions to the number of elderly citizens and the ratio of the average pension to per capita or per worker GDP (see Box 9.6). While from the 1960s to the mid-1980s these changes increased expenditure in most countries, in the future they are likely to work both ways. In some countries the effects of past extensions and improvements to pension schemes are still expanding expenditure; in others, the recently introduced reforms are reducing eligibility and transfer ratios. The latter might also be negatively influenced by the present widespread unemployment, which limits the contribution record of future pensioners.

Box 9.6 Factors influencing pension expenditure

In order to highlight the problems faced in projecting pension expenditure, one can refer to some simple accounting identities. Following the OECD (1988b) approach, the ratio of pension expenditure (EXP_p) to GDP can be expressed on the basis of the four following ratios:

(a) The old-age dependency ratio = population of pensionable age (POP_p) divided by the population of working age (POP_w).
(b) The eligibility ratio = number of pension beneficiaries (NPEN) divided by the population of pensionable age (POP_p).
(c) The transfer ratio = average pension per beneficiary (p_a) divided by GDP per worker (gdp_w).
(d) The employment ratio = population of working age (POP_w) divided by employment (NWOR).

The ratio of public expenditure on old-age pensions to GDP can therefore be written as:

$$\frac{EXP_p}{GDP} = \left(\frac{POP_p}{POP_w}\right) \times \left(\frac{NPEN}{POP_p}\right) \times \left(\frac{p_a}{gdp_w}\right) \times \left(\frac{POP_w}{NWOR}\right)$$

Ratio (a) represents the pure demographic component of expenditure dynamics. Ratios (b) and (c) depend on legislation and economic factors. Ratio (d) is affected by economic factors. Ratios (b) and (c) can change considerably over time because of the 'maturing' of pension schemes, that is, the process of adjustment of all pensions to present retirement rules. On the one hand, pension coverage extensions and benefit improvements usually produce their full effects on the two ratios after many decades. On the other, quite often pension reforms curtailing benefits are implemented gradually and only display their full effects a long time later.

Changes in the relative number of workers enrolled in the different schemes are also likely to influence ratios (b) and (c). In many countries, for instance, in the last decades public employment has grown faster than total employment and, since public employees frequently have better retirement rules, the shift in employment increases pension expenditure.

According to OECD (1988b), between 1960 and 1985 in the OECD countries the old-age dependency, eligibility, transfer and employment ratios respectively contributed to 25.6, 38.0, 33.2, and 3.2 per cent of the total change in the pension expenditure to GDP ratio. Among the 15 EU countries, only in Denmark and the United Kingdom was the old-age dependency ratio the most relevant factor in contributing to expenditure growth. These data reflect the widespread process of expansion of pension coverage and improvement of benefits that took place in many European countries from the 1950s to the 1970s.

In order to take the non-demographic factors affecting pension expenditure dynamics into consideration, this section draws on the results of the most recent public pension expenditure projections carried out in each country by a public institution.[36] This also allows consideration of the maturation of pension schemes, that is, the fact that pension expenditure dynamics over the next decades will be influenced by changes already introduced in legislation. The projections taken into consideration are based on the assumption of unchanged policies. This approach may lead to some unrealistic outcomes, since policies will obviously adapt over time to new demographic and economic circumstances, but it is helpful in identifying the dimension of required policy adjustment.

National projections are not homogeneous in their coverage of pension expenditure. Therefore, although they provide some useful indications about trends in future pension expenditure in the EU member states, they do not provide an estimate of the impact of the future evolution of public pension schemes on general governments' accounts. Franco and Munzi (1996) tried to fill this gap by applying each country's projected expenditure trend to an estimate of its 1995 ratio of total public pension expenditure to GDP.[37]

The results of these estimates for the eight countries considered in this chapter are presented in Figures 9.13a and 9.13b. Wherever additional scenarios were considered in the national projections, the most favourable and the least favourable are used to provide a range for future pension expenditure growth.

The data can be examined over three periods: the next five years, the period 2000–2010 and the period after 2010. Between 1995 and 2000, the ratio of public pension expenditure to GDP would grow by 0.7 percentage points in Germany and by 0.5 to 0.7 points in Belgium; it would remain almost stable in Denmark and Spain, while in Italy and the Netherlands it would remain stable in the best scenario and increase respectively by 1.4 and 0.6 points in the worst. In Finland and Sweden the best and the worst economic scenarios point to a decline in the expenditure ratio of 0.5 points and to an increase of 0.6 to 0.8 points respectively.

Expenditure growth would accelerate in the period 2000–2010. Over the decade, the expenditure to GDP ratio would grow by 1.7 percentage points in Denmark; 1.2 points in Germany; 1–2.4 points in Finland; 0.7–2.2 points in Italy; 0.6–1.3 points in Belgium; 0.4–1 point in Sweden. In Spain the ratio would be nearly stable in the best scenario and increase by 0.5 point in the worst, while in the Netherlands it would remain stable in both scenarios.

After 2010 expenditure pressure would rise substantially in most countries. The increase expected for the period 2010–30 is 3.5 points for Germany, 3–3.2 points for Belgium, 2.8–3.8 points for the Netherlands, 2.2–4.6 points for Italy, 1.8 points for Denmark, 0.6–2.4 points for Finland. Expenditure pressures would be more moderate in Spain (0.3–1.4 percentage points of GDP) and Sweden (0–0.5 point).

By comparing the expected trend of the old-age dependency ratio with those of the expenditure to GDP ratio, it is possible to evaluate the expected future effects of the non-demographic factors (more specifically the effects of changes in the eligibility and transfer ratios). Figures 9.14a–h plot the two ratios for the eight countries. An old-age dependency ratio line above the expenditure line points to a reduction in the eligibility and transfer ratios. This implies that restrictive reforms, counterbalancing the ageing trend, have already been implemented in the pension system. An old-age dependency

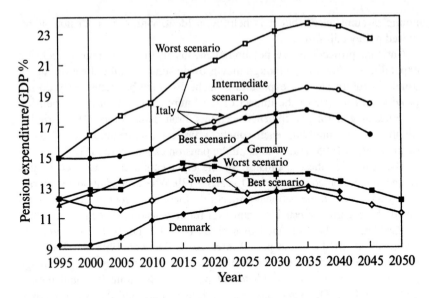

Figure 9.13a   Estimates of total public pension expenditure – part I
(percentage of GDP)

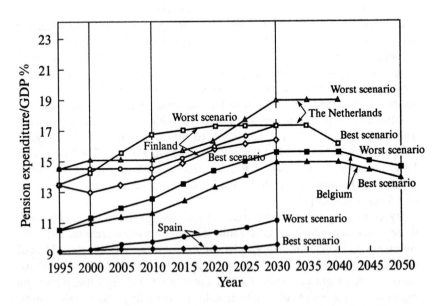

Figure 9.13b   Estimates of total public pension expenditure – part II
(percentage of GDP)

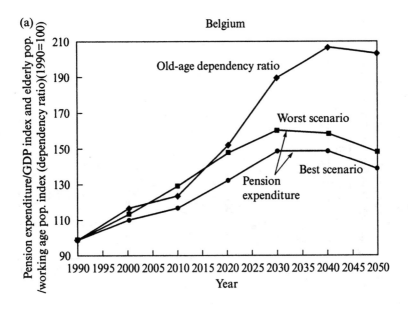

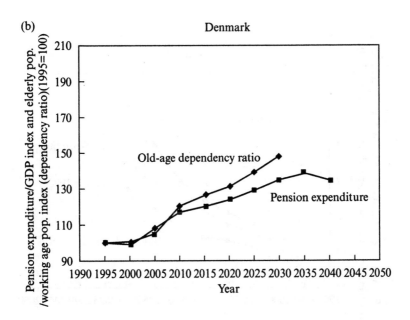

Figure 9.14   Pension expenditure dynamics: demographic and non-demographic factors

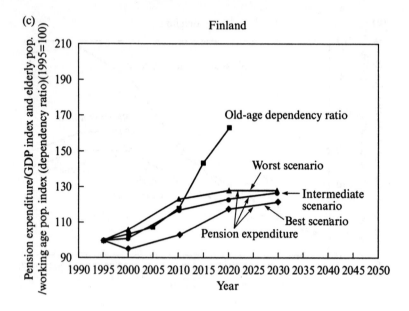

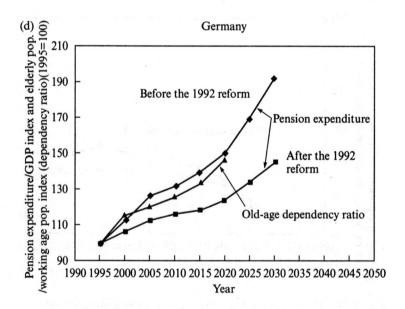

Figure 9.14   continued

(e)

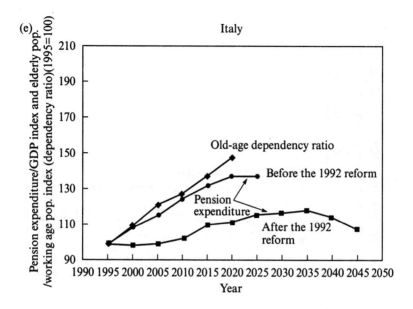

Italy

(f)

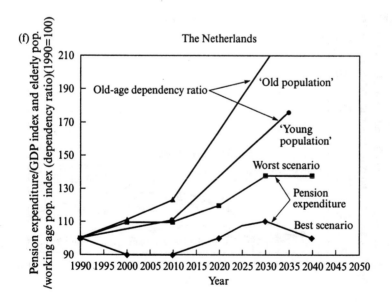

The Netherlands

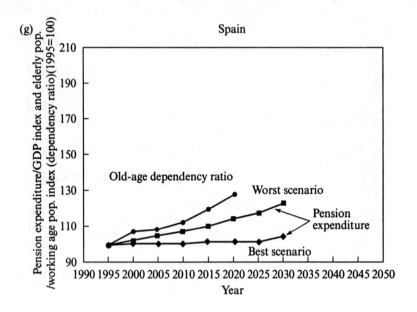

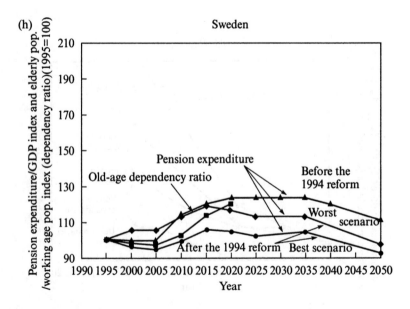

Figure 9.14   continued

(a)

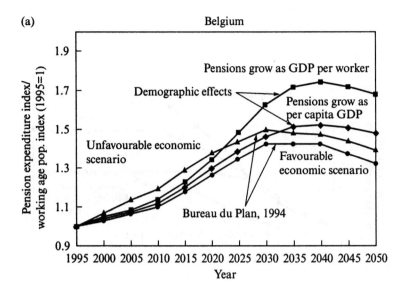

(b)

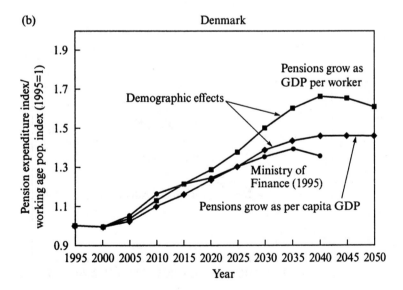

*Figure 9.15 Pension expenditure dynamics: burden on working-age
population compared with national projections*

Demography and the welfare state

(c)

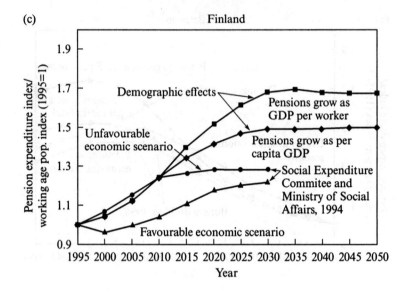

(d)

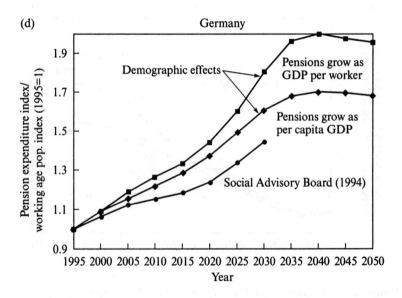

Figure 9.15   continued

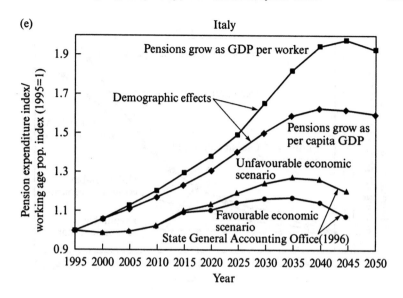

(e)

Italy

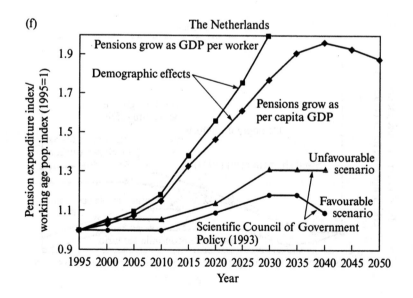

(f)

The Netherlands

Demography and the welfare state

(g)

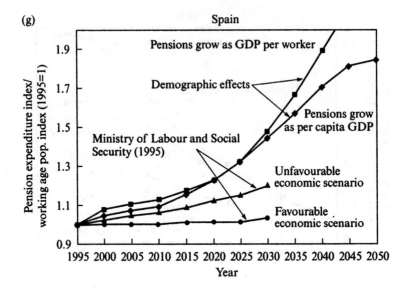

(h)

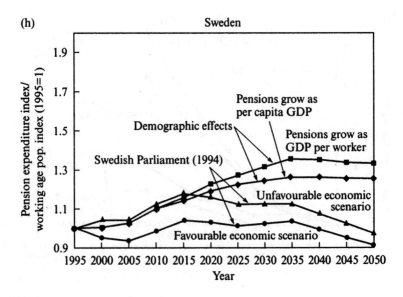

Figure 9.15 continued

ratio line close to the expenditure line points to stable eligibility and transfer ratios, and therefore to a mature pension system in which expenditure growth depends mostly on demographic change. An old-age dependency ratio line under the expenditure line points to an increase in the eligibility and transfer ratios. This implies that the effects of demographic changes will be increased by the improvements introduced in pension rules in the past or by the gradual increase in workers' contributory records.

In the eight countries studied, the old-age dependency line is expected to lie above the expenditure line, particularly in the long term. This is due to a radical change in pension policies with respect to previous decades: the phase of extension of coverage and improvement of benefits is over, while several reforms have been implemented to curb expenditure. According to national projections, only demographic trends are presently exerting an upward pressure on the expenditure to GDP; non-demographic factors are actually going to partly offset the effects of demographic trends.

The effects of non-demographic factors can also be evaluated by comparing the national pension expenditure projections with the mechanical projections estimated in Section 3 (see Figures 9.15a–h). In all the countries considered, the mechanical projections of pension expenditure tend to be substantially higher than the estimates produced by national authorities, which also consider non-demographic factors. The differences are particularly large for Italy, the Netherlands, and Spain.

5. PRIMARY BALANCE TRENDS AND BUDGETARY ADJUSTMENTS: TENTATIVE ESTIMATES

The first part of this section integrates the mechanical estimates of the effects of demographic changes on non-pension items presented in Section 3 with the pension expenditure projections considered in Section 4 in order to provide some tentative estimates of the share of total age-related public expenditure to GDP and to derive primary balance and public debt trends under unchanged policy scenarios. The base year is 1997. The first part also provides estimates of the adjustment required on the primary balance over the period 1998–2030 to implement the 'close-to-balance' rule indicated in the Stability and Growth Pact. The dimension of the adjustment is also assessed on the basis of the tax gap concept, that allows comparisons with alternative fiscal policies, such as keeping the debt to GDP ratio by the end of the projection period at the present level.

The second part of the section examines some alternative scenarios. More specifically it considers the implications of the exclusion from the unchanged policy scenario of some expenditure and revenue items of a temporary nature and the possible failure to implement the pension reform planned in one of the countries considered. It also examines the implications of different interest rates on the public debt and different productivity growth rates. Finally, it evaluates the effects of taking 1996 rather than 1997 as the base year for deficit and debt statistics, and the implications of different ways of implementing the close-to-balance rule.

The third part of the section briefly considers the implications of alternative budgetary strategies for the problems raised by population ageing. It shows how the fast contraction in the debt to GDP ratio determined by the implementation of the close-to-balance rule would allow EU member states to meet the worsening of the demographic situation after 2010 on a sounder fiscal footing.

5.1 Public Expenditure, Primary Balances and Budgetary Adjustments: Baseline Scenario

5.1.1 Age-related public expenditure[38]
In order to project the share of total age-related public expenditure to GDP, the share of pension expenditure to GDP is derived from the national pension expenditure projections, while that of each non-pension item is estimated by multiplying the base-year expenditure to GDP ratio by the baseline index presented in Section 3.2.1.[39] It should be noted that the total age-related expenditure to GDP ratios for the different countries are not comparable in their levels since, as already mentioned, different items were considered for the eight countries.[40]

Under the baseline demographic and economic scenarios defined in Section 3, the share of total age-related expenditure to GDP is expected to grow substantially in all the eight countries taken into consideration.[41] Over the period 1995–2030, it would increase by 4.9–5.6 percentage points in Belgium (respectively according to the most favourable and the most unfavourable pension expenditure scenario defined in Section 4), by 6.5 points in Denmark, 6.1–6.9 in Finland, 6.1 in Germany, 3.8–5.0 in Italy and 4.6–5.3 in the Netherlands (see Table 9.9). Expenditure growth would be more limited in Spain and Sweden, respectively 1.2–2.9 and 2.3–3.7 points. For Sweden, these less pessimistic prospects are related to the demographic trends and to the expected effects of the pension reform outlined in 1994.[42] For Spain, they are related to the limited increases of pension expenditure projected by Ministry of Labour and Social Security (1995).

5.1.2 Primary balances
The projections for age-related expenditure items can be used to estimate the changes to be expected in primary balances, on the assumption that age-unrelated expenditure items and revenues are constant as a share of GDP.

Table 9.9 Age-related public expenditure trends

| | Baseline economic and demographic scenario | | | | | | | | Change over the period | |
| | Share to GDP | | | | | | | | | |
	1995	2000	2010	2020	2025	2030	2040	2050	1995–2030	1995–2050
Belgium										
Health insurance	5.4	5.5	5.6	5.9	6.2	6.5	6.7	6.6	1.1	1.2
Invalidity benefits	2.6	2.6	2.8	2.8	2.7	2.7	2.6	2.6	0.1	0.0
Education	4.5	4.4	4.3	4.2	4.2	4.4	4.5	4.4	-0.1	-0.1
Pensions	*10.3*	*10.8/11.0*	*11.4/12.4*	*13.1/14.2*	*13.9/14.8*	*14.7/15.5*	*14.7/15.2*	*13.7/14.4*	*4.5/5.2*	*3.4/4.1*
Unemployment benefits	3.3	3.3	3.4	3.4	3.3	3.1	3.0	3.1	-0.2	-0.2
Family allowances	2.5	2.4	2.3	2.2	2.2	2.2	2.1	2.2	-0.3	-0.3
Maternity & nursery benefits	0.2	0.2	0.2	0.2	0.2	0.2	0.2	0.0	0.0	0.0
Total expenditure	*28.8*	*29.2/29.4*	*29.3/30.9*	*31.8/32.9*	*32.7/33.7*	*33.7/34.4*	*33.8/34.3*	*32.7/33.4*	*4.9/5.6*	*3.9/4.6*
Denmark										
Pensions	*14.2*	*14.0*	*16.6*	*17.7*	*18.4*	*19.3*	*19.3*		*5.2*	
Health insurance	6.2	6.2	6.4	6.9	7.3	7.7	8.2	8.2	1.4	1.9
Unemployment insurance	3.4	3.4	3.1	3.1	3.1	3.0	2.9	3.0	-0.3	-0.4
General welfare	2.5	2.5	2.6	2.8	2.8	2.8	2.9	2.9	0.3	0.4
Child benefits/Youth support	1.4	1.4	1.4	1.3	1.3	1.3	1.3	1.3	-0.1	-0.1
Education	7.4	7.4	7.8	7.3	7.2	7.4	7.9	7.5	-0.1	0.1
Total expenditure	*35.0*	*34.9*	*37.9*	*39.1*	*40.1*	*41.5*	*42.5*		*6.5*	
Finland										
Education	5.9	5.8	5.6	5.6	5.6	5.7	5.7	5.6	-0.2	-0.3
Health care	5.1	5.2	5.6	6.4	6.9	7.3	7.7	7.7	2.2	2.6
Social services	3.6	3.6	3.8	4.4	4.8	5.2	5.7	5.7	1.6	2.2
Net investments	1.4	1.4	1.4	1.4	1.5	1.5	1.5	1.5	0.1	0.1

Table 9.9   *continued*

<table>
<thead>
<tr><th></th><th colspan="10">Baseline economic and demographic scenario</th></tr>
<tr><th></th><th colspan="8">Share to GDP</th><th colspan="2">Change over the period</th></tr>
<tr><th></th><th>1995</th><th>2000</th><th>2010</th><th>2020</th><th>2025</th><th>2030</th><th>2040</th><th>2050</th><th>1995–2030</th><th>1995–2050</th></tr>
</thead>
<tbody>
<tr><td>*Finland continued*</td><td></td><td></td><td></td><td></td><td></td><td></td><td></td><td></td><td></td><td></td></tr>
<tr><td>Transfers related to children</td><td>2.9</td><td>2.8</td><td>2.5</td><td>2.5</td><td>2.4</td><td>2.4</td><td>2.3</td><td>2.4</td><td>-0.5</td><td>-0.5</td></tr>
<tr><td>*Pensions*</td><td>*14.0*</td><td>*13.4/14.8*</td><td>*14.6/17.4*</td><td>*16.5/17.9*</td><td>*16.8/17.9*</td><td>*17.1/17.9*</td><td></td><td></td><td>*3.1/3.9*</td><td></td></tr>
<tr><td>Unemployment benefits</td><td>4.9</td><td>4.9</td><td>4.7</td><td>4.5</td><td>4.3</td><td>4.2</td><td>4.3</td><td>4.3</td><td>-0.7</td><td>-0.6</td></tr>
<tr><td>Other social transfers</td><td>3.6</td><td>3.6</td><td>3.6</td><td>3.7</td><td>3.7</td><td>3.8</td><td>3.8</td><td>3.8</td><td>0.2</td><td>0.3</td></tr>
<tr><td>Transfers to households</td><td>1.7</td><td>1.7</td><td>1.7</td><td>1.7</td><td>1.8</td><td>1.8</td><td>1.9</td><td>1.9</td><td>0.1</td><td>0.2</td></tr>
<tr><td>*Total expenditure*</td><td>*43.0*</td><td>*42.5/43.9*</td><td>*43.5/46.3*</td><td>*46.7/48.1*</td><td>*47.8/48.9*</td><td>*49.1/49.9*</td><td></td><td></td><td>*6.1/6.9*</td><td></td></tr>
<tr><td>**Germany**</td><td></td><td></td><td></td><td></td><td></td><td></td><td></td><td></td><td></td><td></td></tr>
<tr><td>*Pensions*</td><td>*10.1*</td><td>*10.7*</td><td>*11.7*</td><td>*12.5*</td><td>*13.5*</td><td>*14.6*</td><td></td><td></td><td>*4.5*</td><td>2.8</td></tr>
<tr><td>Health insurance</td><td>6.5</td><td>6.7</td><td>7.3</td><td>7.7</td><td>8.0</td><td>8.6</td><td>9.4</td><td>9.4</td><td>2.1</td><td>0.2</td></tr>
<tr><td>Accident insurance</td><td>0.5</td><td>0.5</td><td>0.5</td><td>0.6</td><td>0.7</td><td>0.7</td><td>0.7</td><td>0.7</td><td>0.2</td><td>-0.3</td></tr>
<tr><td>Unemployment insurance</td><td>1.8</td><td>1.7</td><td>1.6</td><td>1.6</td><td>1.6</td><td>1.5</td><td>1.5</td><td>1.5</td><td>-0.2</td><td>0.0</td></tr>
<tr><td>General welfare</td><td>0.5</td><td>0.5</td><td>0.5</td><td>0.5</td><td>0.5</td><td>0.5</td><td>0.6</td><td>0.6</td><td>0.0</td><td>0.0</td></tr>
<tr><td>Housing benefits</td><td>0.2</td><td>0.2</td><td>0.2</td><td>0.2</td><td>0.2</td><td>0.2</td><td>0.2</td><td>0.2</td><td>0.0</td><td>0.0</td></tr>
<tr><td>Maternity benefits</td><td>0.2</td><td>0.2</td><td>0.2</td><td>0.2</td><td>0.2</td><td>0.1</td><td>0.1</td><td>0.1</td><td>-0.1</td><td>-0.1</td></tr>
<tr><td>Child benefits/Youth support</td><td>1.3</td><td>1.3</td><td>1.2</td><td>1.1</td><td>1.1</td><td>1.1</td><td>1.1</td><td>1.1</td><td>-0.2</td><td>-0.2</td></tr>
<tr><td>Education</td><td>3.7</td><td>3.6</td><td>3.5</td><td>3.3</td><td>3.3</td><td>3.4</td><td>3.5</td><td>3.5</td><td>-0.3</td><td>-0.2</td></tr>
<tr><td>Long-term care</td><td>0.2</td><td>0.2</td><td>0.2</td><td>0.3</td><td>0.3</td><td>0.3</td><td>0.4</td><td>0.4</td><td>0.1</td><td>0.2</td></tr>
<tr><td>*Total expenditure*</td><td>*25.0*</td><td>*25.6*</td><td>*27.0*</td><td>*28.0*</td><td>*29.4*</td><td>*31.2*</td><td></td><td></td><td>*6.1*</td><td></td></tr>
<tr><td>**Italy**</td><td></td><td></td><td></td><td></td><td></td><td></td><td></td><td></td><td></td><td></td></tr>
<tr><td>Education</td><td>5.3</td><td>4.8</td><td>4.9</td><td>4.8</td><td>4.6</td><td>4.5</td><td>4.9</td><td>5.0</td><td>-0.8</td><td>-0.3</td></tr>
<tr><td>Health expenditure</td><td>5.6</td><td>5.8</td><td>6.2</td><td>6.7</td><td>7.0</td><td>7.3</td><td>8.3</td><td>8.4</td><td>1.7</td><td>2.8</td></tr>
</tbody>
</table>

Pensions	15.5	15.3	16.0	*17.2/17.7*	*17.8/18.6*	*18.1/19.4*	*17.8/19.7*		*2.6/3.9*	0.0
Family allowances	0.3	0.3	0.3	0.3	0.3	0.3	0.3		0.0	0.0
Other social benefits	1.6	1.6	1.6	1.7	1.7	1.8	1.7		0.2	
Total expenditure	28.3	27.8	29.1	*30.7/31.2*	*31.4/32.2*	*32.1/33.3*	*33.0/34.9*		*3.8/5.0*	
The Netherlands										
Health	8.9	9.3	9.9	11.2	12.1	13.3	15.4	15.6	4.5	6.8
Welfare	11.1	11.3	11.6	11.2	11.0	10.5	9.9	10.3	-0.6	-0.9
Education	4.5	4.3	4.4	4.3	4.2	4.3	4.6	4.5	-0.2	0.0
Pensions	5.2	*5.2/5.5*	*5.2/5.5*	*5.7/5.9*	*5.9/6.1*	*6.1/6.8*	*5.7/6.8*		*0.9/1.6*	
Total expenditure	29.7	*30.1/30.4*	*31.0/31.3*	*32.3/32.6*	*33.2/33.4*	*34.3/35.0*	*35.6/36.8*		*4.6/5.3*	
Spain										
Health care	6.2	6.2	6.2	6.5	6.7	7.0	8.1	8.8	0.9	2.6
Pensions	9.9	*10.0/10.1*	*10.0/10.6*	*10.1/11.2*	*10.1/11.5*	*10.3/12.0*			*0.4/2.1*	
Unemployment	3.8	3.8	3.8	3.8	3.7	3.6	3.2	2.9	-0.2	-0.9
Family allowances	0.1	0.1	0.1	0.1	0.1	0.1	0.1	0.1	0.0	0.0
Other	0.3	0.3	0.4	0.4	0.4	0.5	0.6	0.6	0.2	0.3
Total expenditure	20.3	*20.4/20.5*	*20.5/21.1*	*20.9/22.0*	*21.1/22.4*	*21.5/23.2*			*1.2/2.9*	
Sweden										
Pensions	13.7	*13.2/14.4*	*13.6/15.5*	*14.3/16.0*	*14.0/15.5*	*14.1/15.5*	*13.7/14.8*	*12.6/13.4*	*0.4/1.8*	*-1.1/-0.3*
Labour market	5.5	5.5	5.4	5.3	5.2	5.1	5.1	5.1	-0.4	-0.4
Family allowances	2.4	2.4	2.2	2.2	2.2	2.2	2.1	2.1	-0.2	-0.3
Educational grants	0.6	0.6	0.5	0.6	0.5	0.5	0.5	0.5	-0.1	-0.1
Social assistance	1.3	1.3	1.3	1.3	1.3	1.3	1.4	1.4	0.0	0.0
Health care	6.0	5.9	6.0	6.4	6.6	6.8	7.0	7.0	0.8	1.0
Elderly care	3.5	3.6	3.8	4.1	4.6	5.2	5.9	6.2	1.7	2.7
Total expenditure	33.0	*32.4/33.6*	*32.9/34.8*	*34.2/36.0*	*34.5/36.0*	*35.3/36.7*	*35.7/36.8*	*34.9/35.7*	*2.3/3.7*	*1.9/2.7*

Note: Data in italics are derived from national pension expenditure projections. Where two sets of data are presented, the left assumes the most favourable pension expenditure scenario and the right the most unfavourable one.

371

This assumption implies that the revenues and expenditures of a temporary nature are substituted with permanent revenues and expenditures (Section 5.2.1 considers the implication of removing this assumption for two countries). More specifically, the share of total primary public expenditure to GDP over the next decades has been estimated by adding to its current share the increase in age-related public expenditure projected above.[43] An indicative measure of the primary balance is obtained by subtracting from the expected share of total primary expenditure to GDP, a constant share of revenues to GDP.[44]

In all the countries considered present primary surpluses would be gradually eroded by expenditure increases (see Figures 9.16a–h). In Finland, Germany and the Netherlands primary balances become substantially negative over the next three to four decades. In Germany, the present surplus (0.7 points of GDP) turns into a deficit at the beginning of the next century; the deficit grows over time, reaching a level of more than 5 percentage points by 2030. In Finland and the Netherlands, primary balances become negative between 2015 and 2030 and continue to worsen thereafter. Over the period 1997–2030, Finland would move from a 3.9 per cent surplus to a 2.3–2.6 per cent deficit; the Netherlands from a 3 points surplus to a 1.6–2.2 per cent deficit.

In Belgium, Italy, and Sweden present primary surpluses would be eroded over the next three to four decades, but worrying deficit levels would not be reached. The three countries would record small deficits only in the worst scenario and for short periods between 2030 and 2040. Thereafter they would again attain surplus positions.

The Danish present surplus (6.1 per cent of GDP) would turn into a deficit by 2030; the deficit would increase up to 1.5 points in 2035 and stabilize thereafter. The Spanish surplus (2.2 per cent) would turn into a small deficit by 2030 only in the worst scenario. Since pension expenditure projections are not available for a longer time span, it is not clear whether in Spain the tendency towards a worsening of the budgetary position would continue or would be reversed after 2030.

5.1.3   Debt to GDP ratio

On the basis of the primary balance trends presented above and some assumptions on real GDP growth, interest rates and inflation, it is possible to estimate the dynamics of the debt to GDP ratio under unchanged policies.

More specifically, it has been assumed that in all countries:

(a)   productivity per worker increases by 1.5 per cent per year (the standard assumption in OECD's recent studies on long-term economic prospects);[45]

(b)   GDP growth depends on productivity growth and the rate of change in the number of working age citizens (that is, aggregate labour force

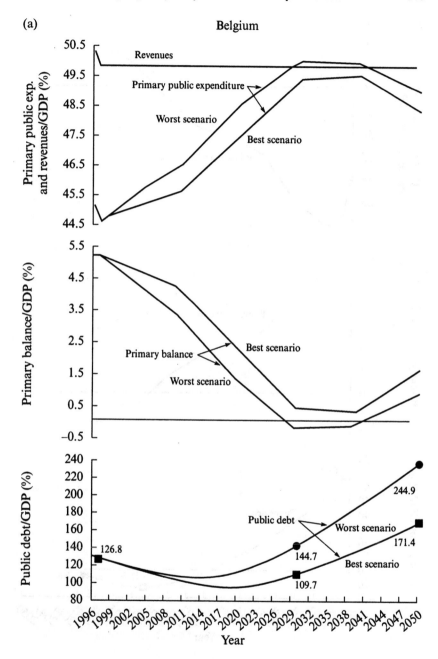

Figure 9.16 Primary balance and public debt trends under constant
policies (percentage of GDP)

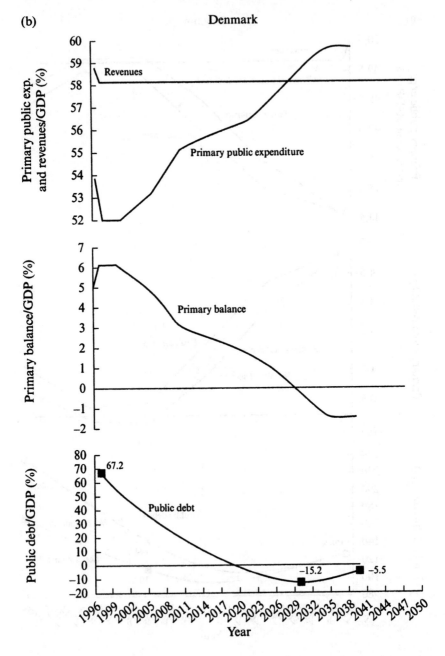

Figure 9.16   continued

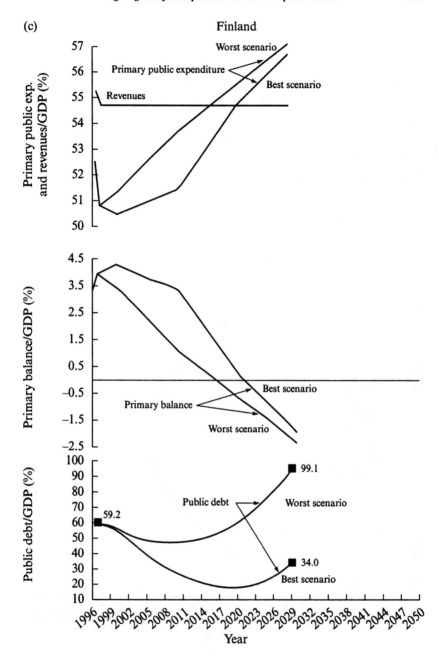

(c)

Finland

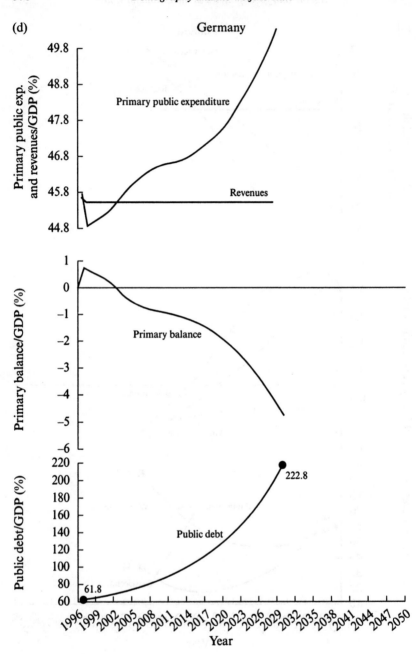

Figure 9.16   continued

(e)

Italy

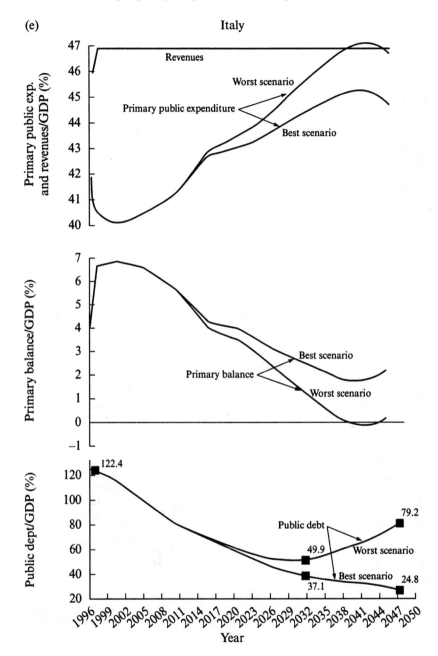

(f)

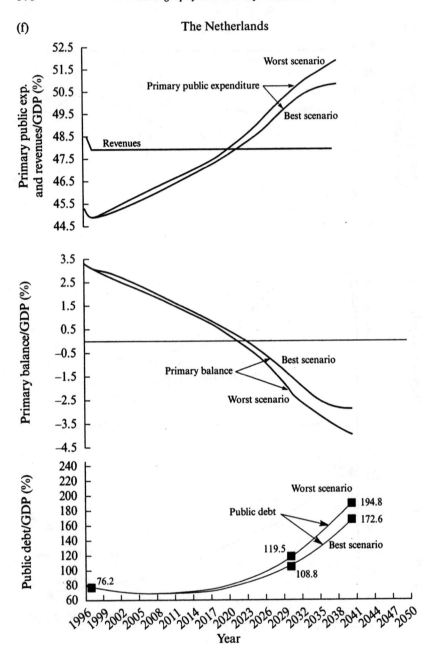

Figure 9.16   continued

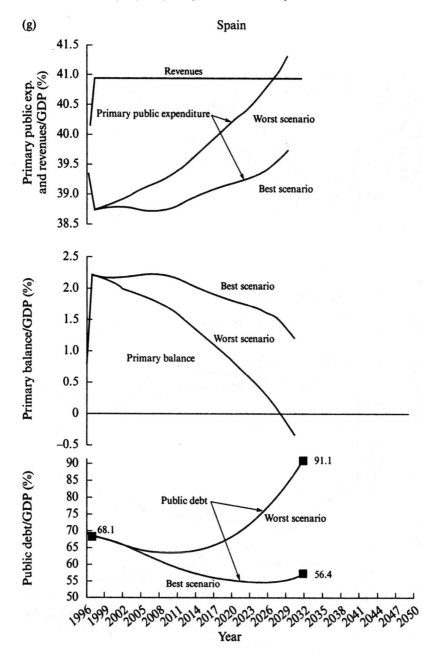

Demography and the welfare state

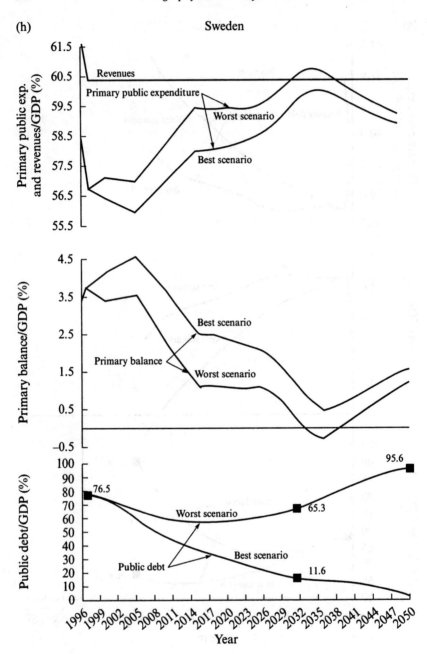

(h)   Sweden

Figure 9.16   continued

participation rates and unemployment rates remain constant over the projection period);

(c) inflation and the real interest rate on public debt are respectively 2 and 4 per cent over the whole projection period;[46]

(d) the stock-flow adjustment is systematically zero (that is, other possible influences on the gross debt ratio, such as privatization receipts or the building-up by general government of stocks of financial assets, are ignored).

In most of the countries considered the debt to GDP ratio (under unchanged policies) would follow a U-shaped curve, with the debt decreasing until the second or third decade of the next century and increasing thereafter (see Figures 9.16a–h). In Belgium, Finland and Spain the ratio projected for 2030 would be higher than the present level in the unfavourable pension expenditure scenario and lower in the favourable scenario. More specifically, over the period 1997–2030, in Belgium the ratio would either decline from 127 to 110 per cent or increase to 145 per cent; in Finland it would decline from 59 to 34 per cent or increase to 99 per cent; in Spain it would decline from 68 to 56 per cent or increase to 91 per cent.

Regardless of the pension scenario considered, the debt to GDP ratio projected for 2030 would be lower than the present level in Denmark, Italy and Sweden and higher in Germany and the Netherlands. More specifically, in Italy, where the primary surplus expected for 1997 is relatively high (6.6 per cent of GDP), the ratio would decline from 122 per cent in 1997 to 37 per cent in 2030 in the best scenario and 50 per cent in the worst scenario. Sweden would have a similar trend, with the debt ratio declining from 76 per cent to 12 and 65 per cent. In Denmark the debt (67 per cent of GDP in 1997) would turn into a net credit position by 2018; the net credit position would improve up to 2030 and then decline. In the Netherlands the ratio would increase in both scenarios (from 76 per cent to 109–120 per cent). In Germany it would increase continuously from 62 per cent in 1997 to about 223 per cent in 2030.

In conclusion, under unchanged policies, in spite of the decline of primary surplus due to the increase in age-related expenditure, the debt to GDP ratio would decline substantially in most countries over the next two or three decades. Thereafter, it would increase in most countries.

In evaluating these results, two points should be considered. First, the projections depend very much on the primary balance level in the base year (that is, on the levels expected for 1997); as will be pointed out in Section 5.2.4, budgetary outlooks for most countries considered would be substantially worse if projections were based on 1996 primary balances. Second, the temporary nature of some expenditure and revenue items is not considered.

The tentative estimates presented in Section 5.2.1 for Germany and Italy highlight the importance of this factor; more specifically, they point to a more favourable scenario for Germany and less positive prospects for Italy.

5.1.4   The adjustment required by 'close-to-balance' policies

According to the Stability and Growth Pact approved at the Dublin summit of December 1996, EMU members should set medium-term budgetary targets of close-to-balance or in surplus (see Buti et al., 1997). These targets would allow them to respect the 3 per cent ceiling even during economic downturns. Taking the close-to-balance indication and the likely effects of downturns into consideration, the average deficit of these countries over the cycle is likely to be in the 0 to 1 per cent of GDP range. It would be close to 0 for countries running surpluses during favourable cyclical phases (which could be the countries with bigger cyclical swings and/or greater automatic stabilisers) and close to 1 for countries aiming at balanced budgets while in favourable cyclical phases (which could be the countries where the impact of economic cycles on government budgets is relatively limited).

Assuming that over each cycle the average deficit is stable at a certain level from 1998 onwards and taking interest payments into account, it is possible to derive the primary balance level required by the close-to-balance rule. In this section the average deficit is assumed to be 1 per cent of GDP. Section 5.2.5 will consider the 0 per cent case.

With a 1 per cent average deficit, in the six non-heavily indebted countries the required primary surplus would decline from an initial value of 2.5–5 points of GDP in 1998 to about 1–2 points by 2030 (see Figures 9.17a–h). In the two heavily indebted countries it would decline from 6.4 per cent of GDP in Belgium and 7.9 per cent in Italy, to about 3 per cent of GDP. In some countries the reduction is particularly fast over the period 1998–2001, due to the assumption that the real interest rate on the public debt converges to 4 per cent. In all countries the primary balance level required by the close-to-balance rule is reduced by the decline in interest payments related to the fast contraction in the level of the debt to GDP ratio.

The difference between this required primary balance and the trend primary deficit provides an indicative measure of the adjustment required by the implementation of the close-to-balance rule. For all the countries considered, the adjustment, which reflects the changes in age-related expenditure and the decrease in interest payments determined by the reduction in the debt to GDP level, is positive over most of the period 1997–2030. In other words, over that period, measures should be taken to improve the primary balance (see Figures 9.17a–h).

In Germany and the Netherlands the adjustment is always positive and increases continuously over most of the period, reaching a peak, respectively,

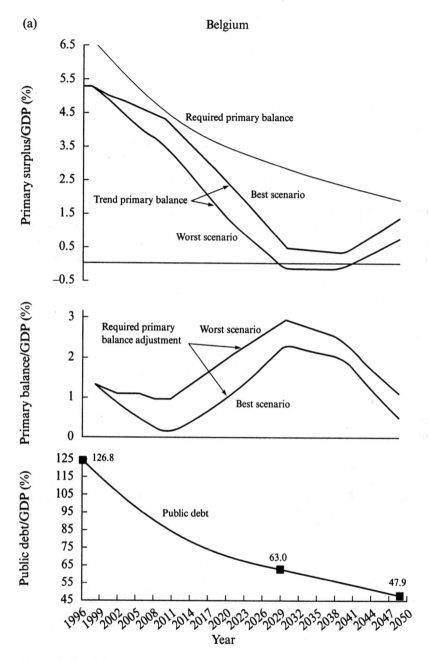

Figure 9.17   Adjustment in primary balances required for the implementation of the close-to-balance rule (percentage of GDP)

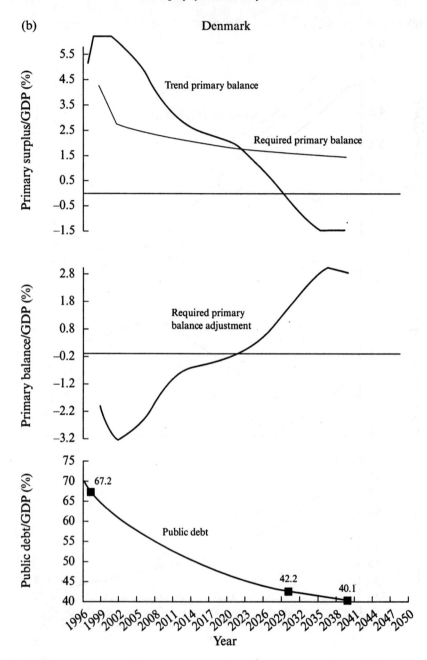

Figure 9.17   continued

(c)

Finland

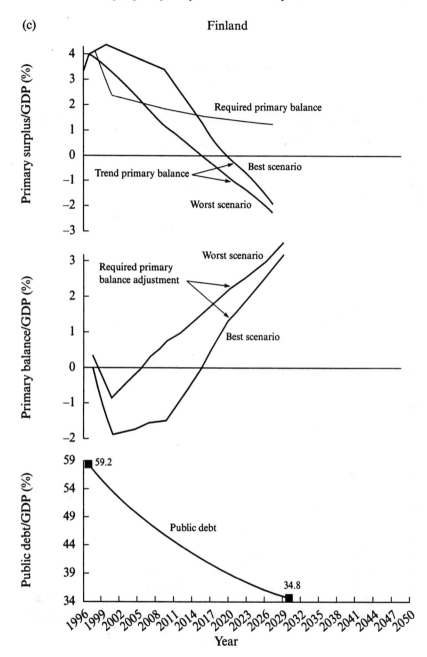

(d)   Germany

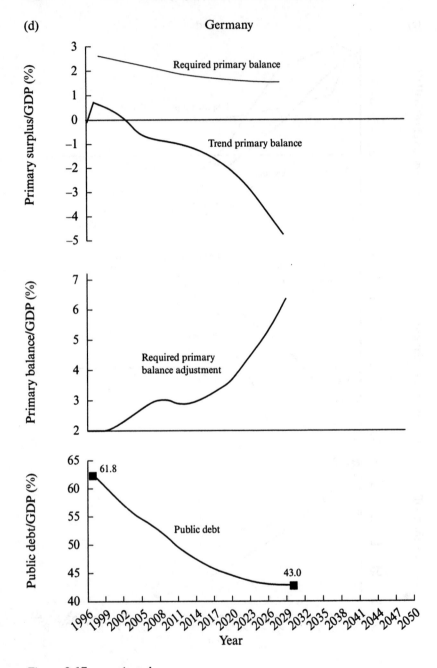

Figure 9.17   continued

(e)

Italy

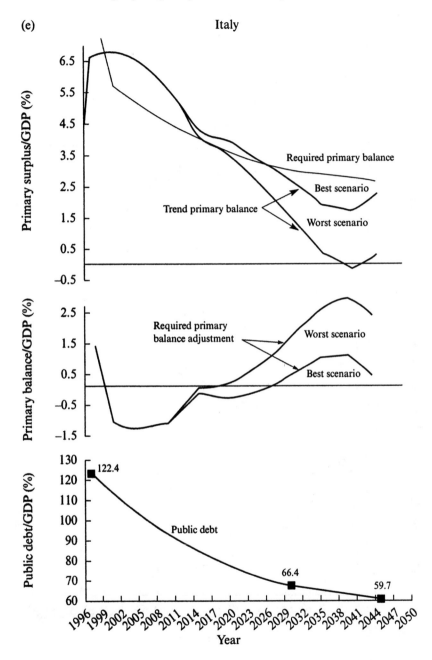

(f)   The Netherlands

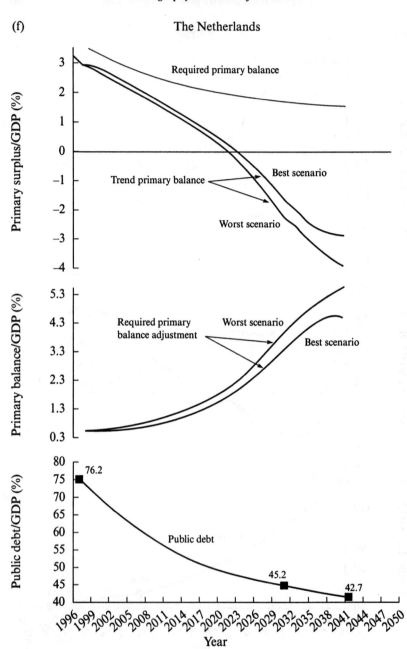

Figure 9.17   continued

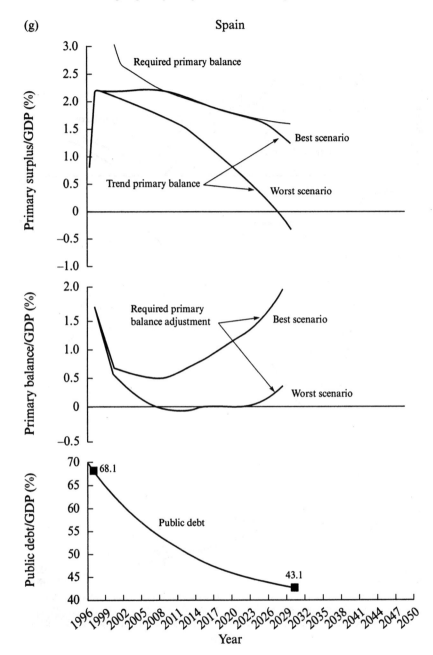

(g) Spain

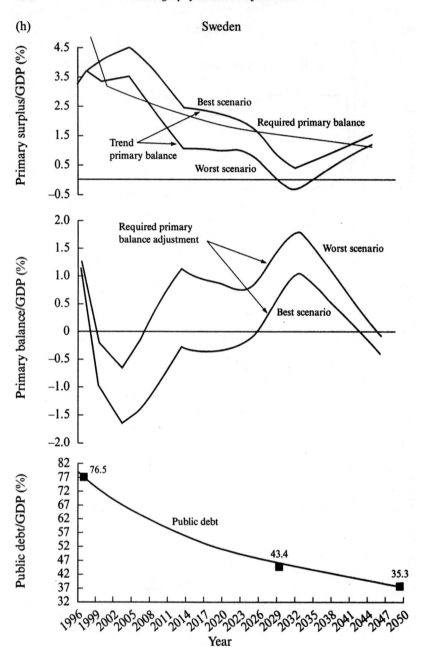

Figure 9.17   *continued*

in 2030 (6.7 per cent of GDP) and in 2040 (4.5–5.5 per cent according to the pension scenario). In Belgium the adjustment is also always positive, but the trend is more complex; the adjustment decreases until 2010, then it increases up to 2030 (with a peak of 2.2–2.9 per cent of GDP), thereafter it decreases again. In Spain the adjustment declines up to 2010; thereafter it increases up to 0.4–2.1 per cent of GDP by 2030.

In Finland, Italy and Sweden the adjustment changes from positive to negative (that is, budgetary policy could be relaxed) over the initial part of the projection period, when real interest rates converge to 4 per cent; thereafter it becomes positive again between 2010 and 2030. Denmark retains a negative adjustment from the beginning of the projection period until 2010; thereafter the adjustment required increases continuously until 2035 when it reaches a peak of almost 3 percentage points.

In conclusion, even assuming that the average deficit over the cycle is 1 per cent of GDP, in several countries the implementation of the close-to-balance rule would require significant adjustments of primary balances over most of the period considered. In all the countries considered substantial adjustments would be required in the period 2020–40. The notes of caution presented at the end of Section 5.1.3 (that is, the reference to 1997 expected primary surpluses and the temporary nature of some budgetary items) should be considered also for the evaluation of these results.

5.1.5 Tax gaps and comparisons of alternative fiscal policies

The adjustments required to implement the close-to-balance rule change over time, according to primary deficit trends and interest expenditure dynamics. A concise measure of the adjustment required for a country over a certain period is provided by the tax gap, that is, the change in the tax to GDP ratio immediately required in order to reach, by the end of the period considered, the debt to GDP ratio that would be reached by implementing the close-to-balance rule outlined in the Stability and Growth Pact.[47] The choice of the period over which tax gaps are computed obviously affects the estimates. In this study, in order to allow cross-country comparisons, tax gaps are computed over the period 1997–2030 for all countries.

The tax gap concept also allows comparison of the adjustment required by the close-to-balance rule with those required by alternative policies, such as keeping the debt to GDP ratio by the end of the projection period at the present level (that is, the 'sustainable tax gap' *à la* Blanchard – see Section 2.1.3) or bringing it to the 60 per cent level indicated in the Maastricht fiscal framework.

Under the above-mentioned assumptions on productivity growth, GDP growth, inflation and interest rates, the tax gap allowing for the respect of the close-to-balance rule (interpreted as requiring an average deficit of 1 per cent

Table 9.10 Tax gap computed over the period 1997–2030[1]

	Close-to-balance rule[2]		60% debt criterion		Stable public debt	
	Favourable pension scenario	Unfavourable pension scenario	Favourable pension scenario	Unfavourable pension scenario	Favourable pension scenario	Unfavourable pension scenario
Belgium	0.9	1.5	0.9	1.6	−0.3	0.3
Denmark	−1.1	—	−1.5	—	−1.6	—
Finland	0.0	1.2	−0.5	0.7	−0.4	0.8
Germany	3.3	—	3.0	—	3.0	—
Italy	−0.5	−0.3	−0.4	−0.2	−1.5	−1.3
Netherlands	1.1	1.3	0.9	1.1	0.6	0.8
Spain	0.3	0.9	−0.1	0.6	−0.2	0.4
Sweden	−0.6	0.4	−1.0	0.1	−1.3	−0.2

Notes:
[1] Baseline macroeconomic scenario: real interest rate = 4 per cent, productivity growth = 1.5 per cent. Base year 1997.
[2] It is assumed that the rule implies an average deficit over the economic cycle of 1 per cent of GDP.

of GDP over economic cycles) over the period 1997–2030 is highest in Germany (3.3 points). According to the different pension scenarios, it is in the 0.9–1.5 range in Belgium, in the 1.1–1.3 range in the Netherlands, in the 0–1.2 range in Finland and in the 0.3–0.9 range in Spain (See Table 9.10). In Denmark, Italy (both pension scenarios) and Sweden (favourable pension scenario) the tax gap is negative, implying that, given spending trends and current revenues, no adjustment is needed over the whole of the period considered for the implementation of the close-to-balance rule.

The reference to a longer time period (for example, 1997–2050) would in most countries imply bigger tax gaps, since primary balances under unchanged policies in the period 2030–50 are on average substantially worse than average primary balances in the period up to 2030. For instance, the tax gaps for Denmark, Italy and Sweden would worsen substantially and in some cases turn from negative to positive. This aspect should be considered in comparing tax-gap levels with the adjustments outlined in Figures 9.17a–h.

For all eight countries, the close-to-balance rule obviously implies bigger adjustments than those required for keeping the debt to GDP ratio at the end of the projection period at the present level. For the less indebted countries it also requires bigger adjustments than those required for maintaining the debt level at 60 per cent. For Belgium and Italy the adjustments required by the implementation of the close-to-balance rule are slightly lower than those required to bring the debt to GDP ratio to the 60 per cent level, implying that, even if the rule is respected, the level of the debt to GDP ratio would still not have declined below 60 per cent by 2030. In Denmark and Italy all tax gaps are negative, implying that current fiscal policies (that is, 1997 primary balances and projected expenditure trends) allows for the fulfilment of the debt-stability condition, the 60 per cent debt criterion and the close-to-balance rule. In Sweden, debt stability is ensured irrespective of pension scenarios, while current fiscal policies allow for the respect of the 60 per cent debt criterion and the close-to-balance rule only in the favourable pension scenario.

5.2 Alternative Scenarios

5.2.1 Temporary expenditure and revenue items

The estimates presented in Section 5.1 are based on the assumption that, under constant policies, revenues and age-unrelated expenditure items are constant as a share of GDP at their 1997 level. Therefore, the temporary nature of some revenue and expenditure items is not taken into consideration. This section provides some tentative estimates of the effects of the removal of this assumption. Two cases are considered: the expenditure related to German reunification and the one-off revenues included in the 1997 Italian budget.

Public expenditure related to German reunification has been estimated by the German Ministry of Finance (1996) as 4 to 5 per cent of West German GDP. If the reduction of the burden for reunification were to allow German public expenditure to decline by, say, 0.2 per cent of GDP per year over a 15-year period, the expected primary balance trend would change radically: rather than worsening continuously, it would improve for 15 years and worsen thereafter (see Figure 9.18). Accordingly, the debt to GDP ratio would increase substantially only after 2020.

The adjustment to be implemented in the primary balance would also be substantially smaller than in the scenario assuming a constant expenditure to GDP ratio. While in the latter scenario the tax gap allowing for the implementation of the close-to-balance rule is 3.3 per cent, in the scenario including reduction of the burden for reunification the tax gap is only 1.2 per cent.

The 1997 Italian budget includes revenues of a temporary nature amounting to about 1.5 per cent of GDP. The exclusion of these revenues from 1998 onwards would reduce the primary surplus and modify the debt dynamics in the unchanged policy scenario. The debt to GDP ratio would decline up to 2010 and then gradually increase; by 2030 it would be in the 120 to 133 range (see Figure 9.19).

The adjustment required by the implementation of the close-to-balance rule would be substantially increased. Over the whole projection period, the unchanged policy primary surplus would be smaller than that required by the rule. The tax gap would be in the 1–1.2 range, as against the negative values indicated in the estimates including temporary tax revenues.

These tentative estimates point to the necessity of considering the temporary nature of some budgetary items while evaluating future budgetary trends.

5.2.2 The Swedish pension reform

In June 1994 the Swedish Parliament endorsed a proposition for a radical reform of the pension system (Ministry of Health and Social Affairs of Sweden, 1994). According to the projections of the Swedish Parliament (1994), the pension benefits measures contained in the reform are expected to reduce the ratio by about 1 point in 2015, by 2.5 per cent in 2025 and by 3 points in 2050. The rather favourable prospects for Swedish public finances projections reported in the previous sections depend to a large extent on this reform.

Nevertheless, the reform has not yet been implemented and still needs some legislative action for approval. The failure to implement it would substantially worsen Swedish budgetary prospects. If national projections of pension expenditure as estimated without accounting for the reform were considered, the debt to GDP ratio would decline only very slightly up to 2010 and then gradually increase. It would reach 86 per cent of GDP by 2030 and 174 per cent of GDP by 2050 (see Figure 9.20).

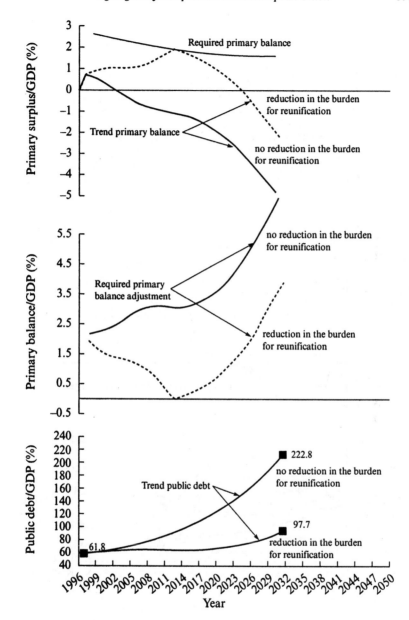

Figure 9.18   *Adjustment in primary balances required for the implementation of the close-to-balance rule in Germany: tentative evaluation of the reduction in the burden for reunification (percentage of GDP)*

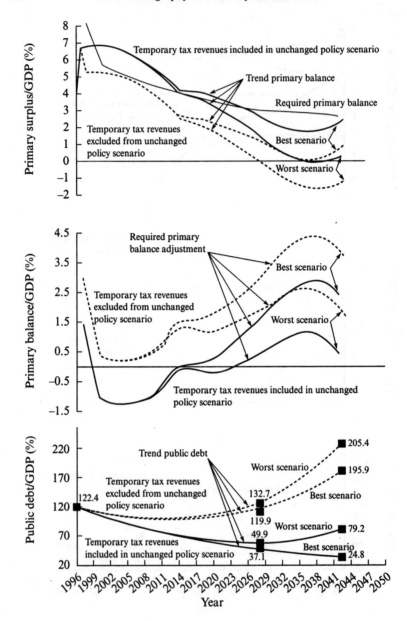

*Figure 9.19   Adjustment in primary balances required for the
implementation of the close-to-balance rule in Italy: exclusion
of 1997 one-off tax revenues from unchanged policy scenario
(percentage of GDP)*

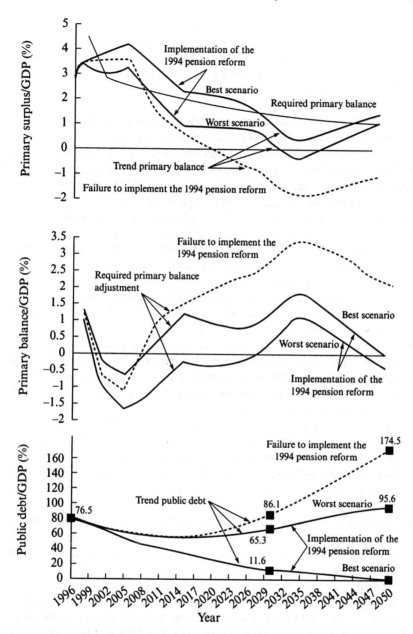

Figure 9.20   *Adjustment in primary balances required for the implementation of the close-to-balance rule in Sweden: failure to implement the 1994 pension reform (percentage of GDP)*

The adjustment required by the implementation of the close-to-balance rule would be substantially increased. Over most of the projection period, the unchanged policy primary balance would be smaller than that required by the rule. The tax gap would be 0.9, as against the −0.6–0.4 range indicated in the estimates including the effects of the reform.

5.2.3   Different macroeconomic scenarios: sensitivity analysis

As already mentioned, the results presented in the previous sections are based on primary expenditure projections and macroeconomic assumptions. As to the latter, it has been assumed that, for all the countries considered, productivity per worker increases by 1.5 per cent per year, GDP growth depends on productivity growth and the rate of change in the number of working age citizens. It is also assumed that inflation and the real interest rate on public debt are respectively 2 and 4 per cent over the whole projection period.

The long-term economic outlook is obviously very uncertain. In order to assess the implications of alternative economic scenarios on the adjustments required by close-to-balance rule, sensitivity analyses have been carried out by taking different values for the interest and productivity growth rates. More specifically, two alternative interest rate scenarios have been considered: a more favourable one where the real interest rate on the public debt would be 0.5 percentage points smaller than in the baseline scenario and a more un-favourable one, where it would be 0.5 percentage points higher. As to the productivity rate, an alternative scenario has been examined assuming a yearly growth rate of 2 per cent, as against the 1.5 per cent yearly growth assumed in the baseline scenario.

The results of both analyses are expressed in terms of tax gaps. As to the analysis of the effect of different interest rates, obviously, for all the countries considered, the lower interest rate would allow smaller tax gaps, while the higher would imply larger ones (see Table 9.11). Belgium and Italy would have the biggest differences, with a tax gap 0.3–0.5 percentage points smaller in the more favourable scenario and 0.4–0.5 points bigger in the more un-favourable one. In the Netherlands, Spain and Sweden, the difference between tax gaps in the baseline scenario and in the alternative scenarios would amount to 0.2–0.3 percentage points for both scenarios, and in Denmark and Germany to exactly 0.2. In Finland the difference would be the smallest, with the tax gaps being 0.1 percentage points smaller or 0.2 points bigger.

The 2 per cent productivity growth rate would allow all countries to have smaller tax gaps. Belgium and Italy would again show the biggest differences (0.3 percentage points). In the other countries, the difference between the tax gaps in the baseline scenario and those in the alternative scenario would amount to 0.1–0.2 percentage points.

Table 9.11 *Sensitivity analysis*

Tax gap computed over the period 1997–2030 allowing for respect of the close-to-balance rule:[1]

| | Baseline scenario | | Alternative macroeconomic scenarios | | | | | |
| | real interest rate = 4% productivity growth = 1.5% | | real interest rate = 3.5% productivity growth = 1.5% | | real interest rate = 4.5% productivity growth = 1.5% | | real interest rate = 4% productivity growth = 2% | |
	Favourable pension scenario	Unfavourable pension scenario	Favourable pension scenario	Unfavourable pension scenario	Favourable pension scenario	Unfavourable pension scenario	Favourable pension scenario	Unfavourable pension scenario
Belgium	0.9	1.5	0.4	1.1	1.3	2.0	0.6	1.2
Denmark	-1.1	—	-1.3	—	-0.9	—	-1.2	—
Finland	0.0	1.2	-0.1	1.1	0.2	1.4	-0.2	1.0
Germany	3.3	—	3.1	—	3.5	—	3.2	—
Italy	-0.5	-0.3	-0.9	-0.6	-0.1	0.1	-0.8	-0.6
Netherlands	1.1	1.3	0.9	1.1	1.4	1.6	1.0	1.2
Spain	0.3	0.9	0.0	0.7	0.5	1.1	0.1	0.8
Sweden	-0.6	0.4	-0.9	0.2	-0.4	0.7	-0.8	0.3

Note: [1] It is assumed that the rule implies an average deficit over the economic cycle of 1 per cent of GDP.

5.2.4 Different initial budgetary conditions: 1996 versus 1997

The results presented in the previous sections refer to the latest European Commission public finance estimates for the year 1997 (see European Commission, 1997). In order to highlight the sensitivity of the results to changes in the base-year primary balance and debt to GDP ratio, the adjustments required to implement the close-to-balance rule have also been estimated on the basis of 1996 primary balances and debts.

On the whole, 1996 deficits and debts are worse than those expected for 1997. The 1996 primary balance is better than that expected for 1997 only for the Netherlands, equal for Belgium and worse for the other countries. The 1996 debt ratio is higher for all countries except Finland and Germany, where it is slightly lower.

As a consequence, for seven of the eight countries considered, the adjustment required by the implementation of the close-to-balance rule on the basis of 1996 data is substantially higher than that required on the basis of 1997 data (see Table 9.12). The change is particularly significant for Italy and Spain (where the tax gaps are respectively 2.5 and 1.5 percentage points

Table 9.12   Different initial budgetary conditions: 1996 versus 1997[1]

| | Tax gap computed over the period up to 2030 allowing for respect of the close-to-balance rule[2] | | | |
| | Base year: 1996 | | Base year: 1997 | |
	Favourable pension scenario	Unfavourable pension scenario	Favourable pension scenario	Unfavourable pension scenario
Belgium	1.0	1.7	0.9	1.5
Denmark	−0.1	—	−1.1	—
Finland	0.4	1.9	0.0	1.2
Germany	4.1	—	3.3	—
Italy	2.0	2.2	−0.5	−0.3
Netherlands	1.0	1.2	1.1	1.3
Spain	1.7	2.4	0.3	0.9
Sweden	−0.3	0.9	−0.6	0.4

Notes:
[1] Baseline macroeconomic scenario: real interest rate = 4 per cent and productivity growth = 1.5 per cent.
[2] It is assumed that the rule implies an average deficit over the economic cycle of 1 per cent of GDP.

greater on the basis of 1996 data). Only for the Netherlands the tax gaps calculated on the basis of the 1996 data are slightly smaller.

These estimates point to the substantial contribution of the efforts undertaken in 1997 to the achievement of sustainable budgetary positions. If the estimates for 1997 are confirmed, then a significant part of the budgetary adjustment required by demographic changes will already have been achieved in 1997.

5.2.5 Different implications of the close-to-balance rule

As pointed out in Section 5.1.4, the implementation of the close-to-balance rule may be consistent with different budgetary policies. Some countries may consider that, in order to respect the 3 per cent deficit ceiling during economic downturns, they need to run a surplus while in favourable economic conditions. Other countries may consider that a balanced budget is sufficient. These different options imply different average deficits over economic cycles. The estimates presented in Sections 5.1.4 and 5.1.5 are based on the assumption that, taking also recessions into account, the average deficit is 1 per cent of GDP. This section evaluates the implications of a 0 per cent average deficit.

The achievement of a 0 per cent deficit would require a primary surplus greater than in the 1 per cent deficit scenario over the initial part of the period considered (see Figures 9.21a–h). The required surplus would, however, decline faster than in the 1 per cent scenario due to the faster decline in the debt to GDP ratio. After 2025, when the reduction in interest payments would exceed 1 per cent of GDP, the 0 per cent scenario would imply a lower surplus.

In the 0 per cent scenario, the changes to be implemented in present budgetary policy would be smoother than in the 1 per cent scenario. Over the next 25 years, some countries would have to tighten their policies even more, while others would have less scope to relax them. In the long run, these efforts would allow them to offset a greater part of the likely increases in pension and health expenditure with reductions in interest payments.

5.3 Debt Reduction and the Ageing Process

A sound budgetary position before joining the single currency and budgetary prudence once in economic and monetary union (EMU) are at the core of the budgetary policy provisions of the Maastricht Treaty. More specifically, once in EMU, governments are required to achieve a balanced budget or a surplus position in order to avoid excessive deficits during recessions.

While this close-to-balance rule has been introduced primarily to avoid budgetary imbalances in monetary union, its implementation will have

(a)

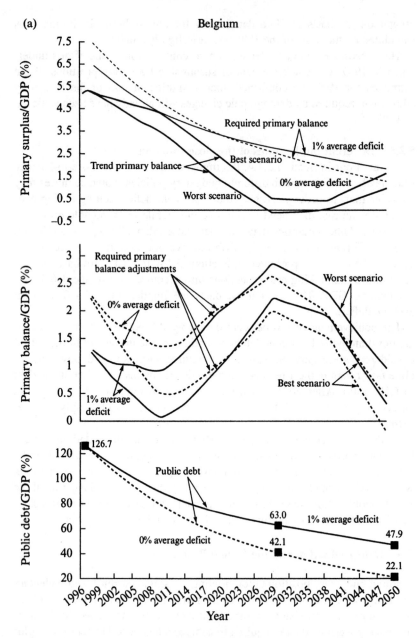

*Figure 9.21   Primary balance adjustments required for the implementation
of the close-to-balance rule: different interpretations of the
rule (percentage of GDP)*

(b)

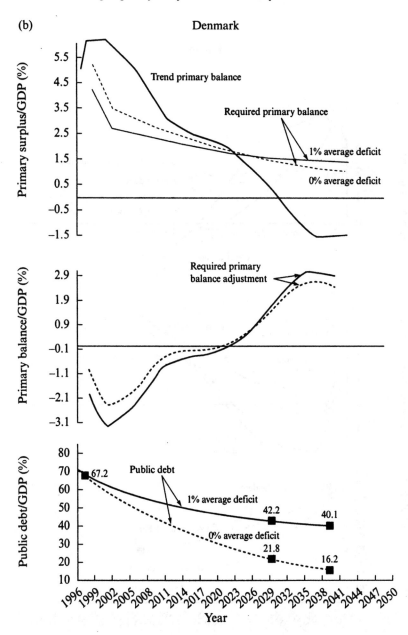

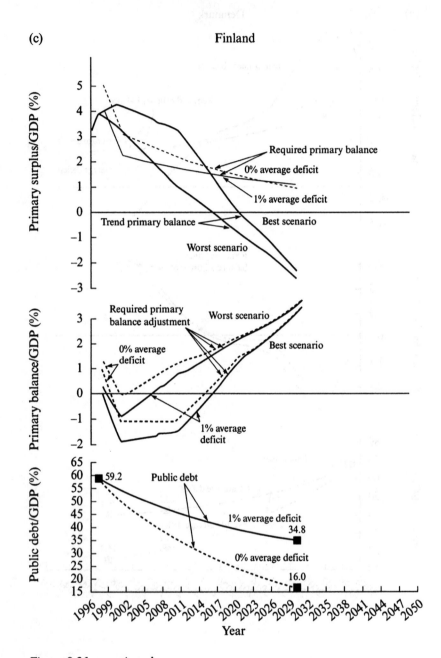

Figure 9.21   continued

(d)

Germany

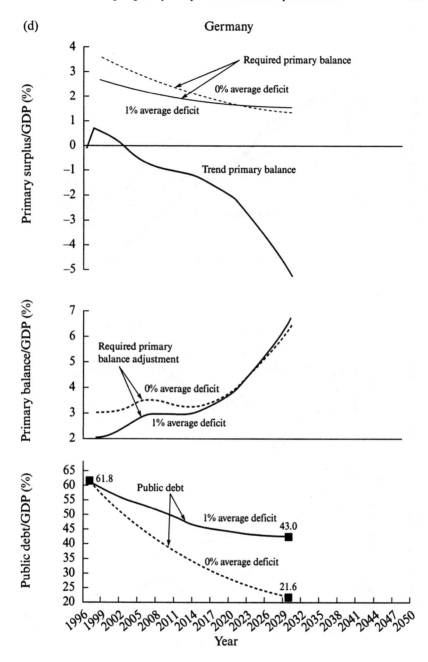

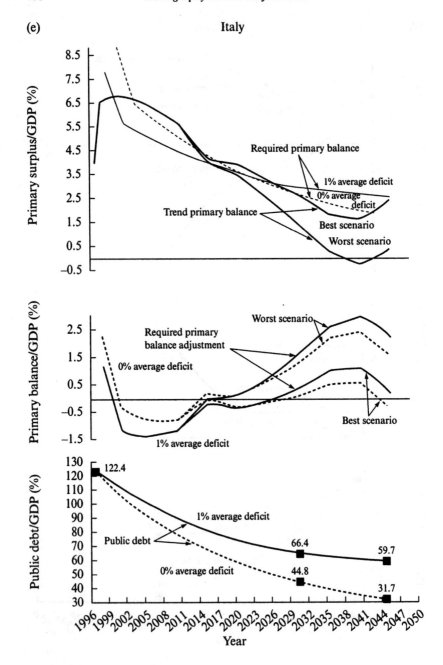

Figure 9.21   continued

(f)   The Netherlands

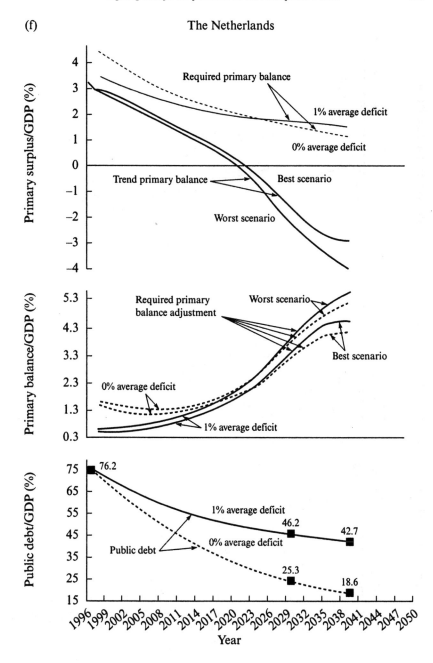

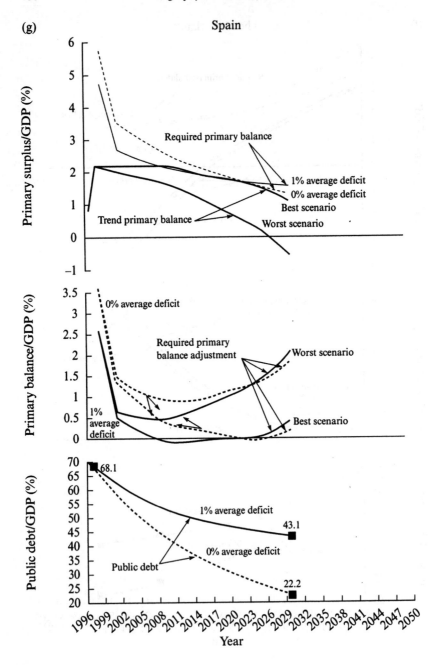

Figure 9.21   continued

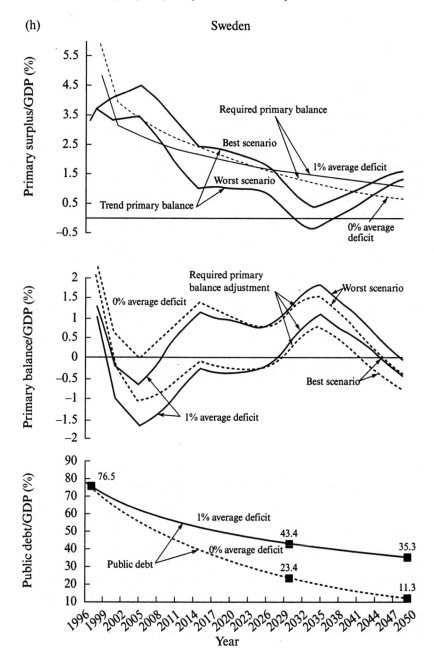

(h)   Sweden

substantial implications for the way in which governments will meet the worsening of the demographic situation after 2010 (when the baby-boom generation will retire). By inducing a fast contraction in the level of the debt to GDP ratio, the ratio, the close-to-balance rule will move budgets to a sounder position.

An indication of this effect is provided by Figures 9.22a–h, that compare the primary balances required for ensuring the stability of the debt to GDP ratio at the present level with those required for the implementation of the close-to-balance rule. For all countries considered, debt stabilization would require lower primary surpluses in the period up to 2010–25 and higher primary surpluses in the following period. The difference between the two scenarios is particularly relevant for the highly indebted countries.

This implies that the close-to-balance rule would smooth the changes to be implemented in present budgetary policy as compared with the scenario in which adjustments are delayed to the period in which ageing will be more accentuated.[48] More specifically, the rule would allow member states to offset part of the likely increases in pension and health expenditure with reductions in interest payments. About half of the increase in public expenditure determined by population ageing in the two most heavily indebted countries considered would be offset by reductions in interest payments.

In conclusion, the implementation of the close-to-balance rule would force governments to make use of the 'breathing-space' available over the next decade to meet the ageing of the baby-boom generation on a sounder fiscal policy footing.

6.   CONCLUSIONS

Before presenting the main results of the study, its major limitations should be enumerated. National pension expenditure projections have been taken at face value and are not homogeneous. The expenditure trends of the other age-related items have been projected mechanically. Some expenditure profiles used for the projections are rather unsatisfactory. It also should be stressed that demographic factors affect public budgets through several complex channels and that public expenditure and revenue dynamics largely depend on non-demographic factors. For these reasons, the estimates presented in this study indicate only the broad direction of the impact of demographic change on public budgets and represent only a starting point for the analysis of the prospects of public finance in the EU member states.

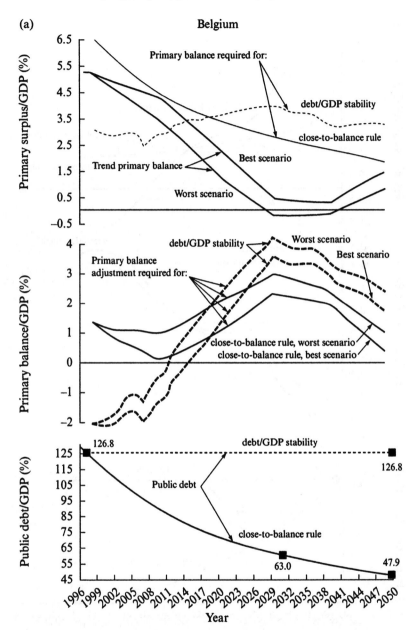

Figure 9.22   Primary balance adjustments required for the debt/GDP stability and the implementation of the close-to-balance rule (percentage of GDP)

Demography and the welfare state

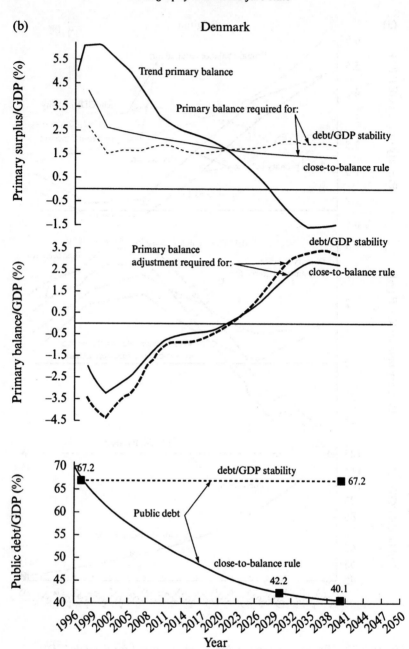

Figure 9.22   continued

(c)   Finland

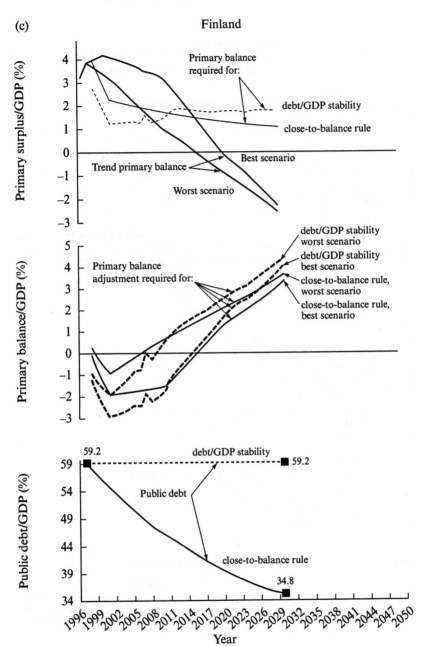

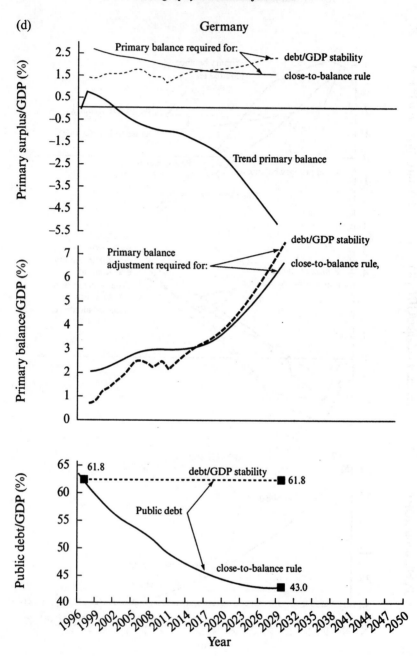

Figure 9.22   continued

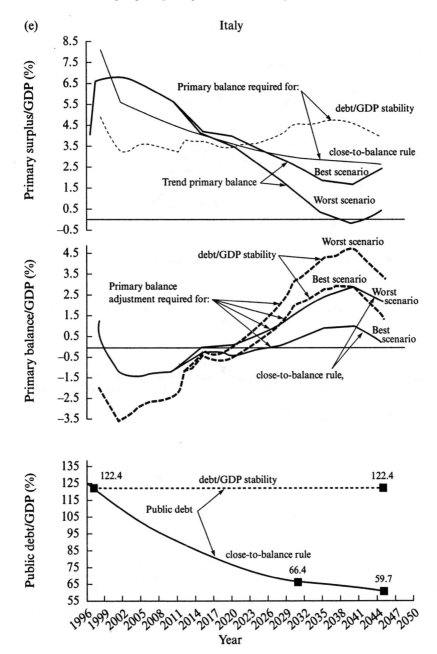

(e)

Italy

(f)   The Netherlands

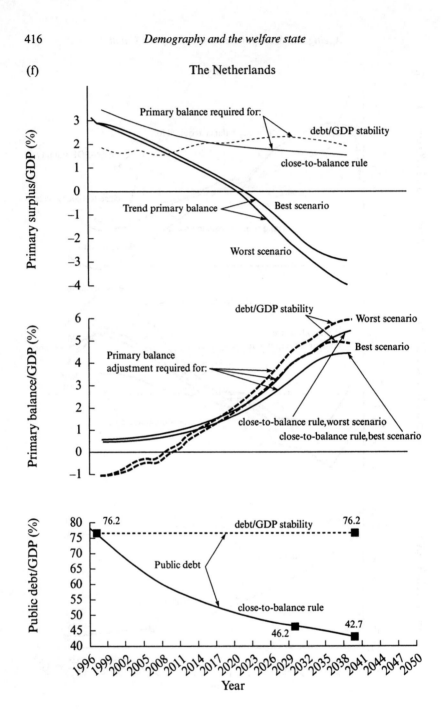

Figure 9.22   continued

(g)

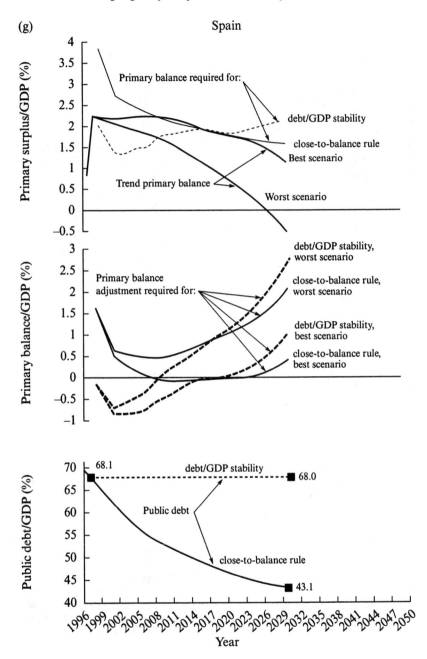

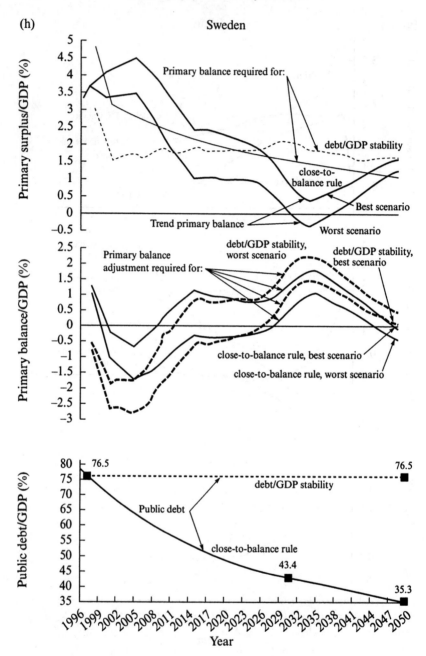

Figure 9.22   continued

6.1 Main Results

The main results are the following.

(a) Citizens of different sex and age groups consume different amounts of public services, and receive different amounts of public transfers. Expenditure for educational and health services, pension benefits and child allowances are the budget items most dependent on population age structure. The profiles of per capita expenditure for different age groups of the eight countries considered are typically two-peaked. The first peak occurs in the 10–20-year age group with education expenditure as the most important item. The second peak, reaching higher levels, occurs for the 60–80-year age group and is largely determined by pension and health expenditure trends. The lowest expenditure levels are usually recorded for the 30–50-age group. Female expenditure levels are usually lower than male levels.

(b) According to studies produced by national institutions, over the period 1995–2030, the ratio of public pension expenditure to GDP would increase by about 5 percentage points of GDP in Belgium and Denmark, 2.5–4 points in Finland, Germany and Italy, 0.5–2 points in the Netherlands, Spain and Sweden. Expenditure pressures are expected to be rather limited up to 2000. The outlook worsens in the first decade of the next century and deteriorates even further after 2010, when the baby-boom generation retires. In several countries the effects of demographic trends will be partly offset by reforms already introduced, aimed at restraining expenditure growth.

(c) The integration of the estimates of pension expenditure trends with mechanical projections of the effects of demographic changes on the other main age-related expenditure items point to the following increases in the share to GDP of total primary expenditure over the period 1997–2020: 6–7 percentage points in Finland and Germany, 5–5.5 points in Belgium, 4–5 points in Italy and the Netherlands, 2–4 points in Sweden and 1–3 in Spain. This implies that in most countries the effects of ageing on pension and health expenditure would not be offset by the reduction in the demand for the public services and transfers directed to young citizens (education, maternity and child allowances).

(d) Under the assumption that age-unrelated expenditure items and revenues are constant as a share to GDP at the levels currently estimated for 1997, in all the countries considered, present primary surpluses would be gradually eroded by expenditure increases. As a result, assuming a real interest rate on public debt of 4 per cent, the debt to GDP ratio (under unchanged policies) would follow a U-shaped curve in most countries.

(e) In order to respect the 3 per cent deficit ceiling even during economic downturns, EMU members should set medium-term budgetary targets of close-to-balance or in surplus. Assuming that the average deficit over the cycle is 1 per cent of GDP from 1998 onwards and taking interest payments into account, it is possible to derive the primary balance level required by the close-to-balance rule. In the non-heavily indebted countries the required primary surplus would decline from an initial value of 2.5–5 per cent of GDP to 1–2 per cent by 2030. In the two heavily indebted countries it would decline from 6.5–8 per cent to about 3 per cent of GDP. The reduction would be determined by the decline in interest payments related to the fast contraction in the level of the debt to GDP ratio.

The difference between the required primary balance and the trend primary balance provides an indicative measure of the changes in current budgetary policies required by the implementation of the close-to-balance rule. In several countries adjustment would be required over most of the period taken into consideration. In all the countries considered measures should be taken to improve the primary balance over most of the period 2020–40.

The achievement of a 0 per cent average deficit over the economic cycle would require primary surpluses greater than in the 1 per cent deficit scenario in the period up to 2025 and smaller in the following years. This would smooth the changes to be implemented in present budgetary policy.

(f) For several countries the outlook would be substantially different taking 1996 budgetary outcomes as a starting point. The improvement of the primary balance expected for 1997, if consolidated in the following years, substantially contributes to the adjustment of budgetary policies to demographic changes and to the implementation of the close-to-balance rule.

(g) Some expenditure and revenue items are of a temporary nature and should not be kept constant over the whole projection period. The public expenditure related to German reunification and the one-off tax measures included in the 1997 Italian budget are two of the most relevant cases. Tentative estimates assuming a gradual reduction of the burden for reunification point to a substantial reduction of the fiscal adjustment required in Germany for the implementation of the close-to-balance rule. Estimates excluding temporary tax revenues from the Italian unchanged policy scenario point to the need of implementing fiscal adjustment over the whole period in question.

(h)   In case of failure to implement the Swedish pension reform (which still needs some legislative action for approval), Swedish budgetary prospects would worsen substantially. If the projections of pension expenditure not accounting for the reform were considered, the adjustment required by the implementation of the close-to-balance rule would be substantially increased. Over almost the whole projection period, the unchanged policy primary balance would be smaller than that required by the rule.

(i)   Lower (higher) interest rates on public debt would obviously reduce (increase) the dimension of the adjustment required for the primary balance. For instance, a reduction of about 0.5 percentage points would reduce the adjustment required for 2030 by 0.3–0.5 percentage points of GDP for the heavily indebted countries and by 0.2–0.3 points for the other countries. Higher productivity growth would also reduce the dimension of the adjustment.

(j)   The achievement of a close-to-balance budget over the next few years would allow member states to meet the worsening of the demographic situation after 2010 (when the baby-boom generation will retire) with smaller public debts. This would allow them to offset part of the likely increases in pension and health expenditure with reductions in interest payments. Assuming that the average deficit over the cycle is 1 per cent of GDP, about half of the increase in public expenditure determined by population ageing in the two heavily indebted countries considered would be offset by reductions in interest payments.

The close-to-balance rule would force governments to make use of the breathing-space available over the next decade to meet the ageing of the baby-boom generation on a sounder fiscal policy footing. This would allow them to smooth the changes to be implemented in present budgetary policy as compared with the scenario in which adjustments are delayed to the period in which ageing will be more accentuated.

6.2   Further Work

As already pointed out, several aspects of the study need substantial refinement and improvement. The following points are among the most relevant.

(a)   Data concerning public expenditure for different age groups should be updated. The same expenditure programmes should be considered for the different member states. If possible, other member states should be included.

(b)   The results of long-term projection for non-pension public expenditure items carried out by national institutions should be compared with the mechanical projections and, if possible, integrated in the projections. This would allow the impact of some relevant non-demographic factors (for example, long-term health expenditure trends) to be considered.

(c)   The baseline scenario should include the likely decline over time of the main expenditure and revenue items of a temporary nature.

(d)   As already mentioned, labour force participation rates and unemployment rates are at present assumed constant over the projection period, as well as age-related per capita expenditure for unemployment benefits. Alternative assumptions envisaging a reduction in unemployment rates and unemployment benefit expenditure should be taken into consideration.

(e)   The assumptions for interest rates and productivity and employment growth in the member states could be differentiated.

(f)   The average deficit over the economic cycle consistent with the close-to-balance rule and assumed as a reference for evaluating the adjustment to be carried out on the primary balance, which at present is fixed at the same level for all countries, could be differentiated according to the dimension of the output swings and that of the automatic stabilizers. These factors would affect the deficit level to be acquired in non-recession years in order to avoid sanctions.

NOTES

1.   The views expressed in this chapter represent exclusively the positions of the authors and do not necessarily correspond to those of the European Commission. The authors would like to thank M. Jones for valuable comments and suggestions. They also thank C. John, B. Raffelhüschen, H. ter Rele, R. Vanne and J. Walliser for having made available unpublished age-related expenditure profiles and for their several useful suggestions. The authors thank S. Ackerby and L.-L. Teilmand for having provided useful data. Finally, they wish to thank C. Mulligan for her valuable editorial support.

2.   In practice, the adjustment would not necessarily be achieved through raising taxes.

3.   Leibfritz et al. (1995); Roseveare et al. (1996) and OECD (1996) are among the most recent studies on the issue.

4.   See Auerbach et al. (1991, 1994) and Kotlikoff (1992).

5.   This point is made in OECD (1988a), pp. 27–8.

6.   See also the several criticisms expressed in Pearson et al. (1989).

7.   This point is stressed in Pearson et al. (1989).

8.   Elderly people without children are more likely to demand public services (Pearson et al., 1989).

9.   For a definition of eligibility and transfer ratios, see Section 4.

10. The maturation of pension schemes is examined in Franco and Munzi (1996).

11. OECD (1993) decomposed nominal health care expenditure growth over the period 1980–90 for the OECD area (11.8 per cent per year) into the effects of general inflation (8 per cent), medical specific inflation (0.7 per cent), the increase in volume of services (2.9 per cent, of which 2.4 per cent was attributed to the increase in per capita services and only 0.3 per cent was due to the ageing process).

12. The difference in the estimates for the United States is due to the fact that, while the IMF considered the effects of the pension reform introduced in the early 1980s, OECD (1988a)

assumed that real per capita social benefits by age within each programme remained fixed at their 1980 levels.

13. See Leibfritz et al. (1995), Roseveare et al. (1996) and OECD (1996).
14. Some long-term projections were also carried out in the past. The Beveridge Report in 1942 included, for instance, a 30-year estimate of social expenditure in the UK.
15. For the United States see Shoven et al. (1991), who consider expenditure programmes representing 40 per cent of public expenditure and carry out projections for the period up to 2040.
16. The tax gap can be split in two components: the short-term primary gap (that is, the adjustment – positive or negative – required to stabilize the debt in the short term) and the effects of the changes in the primary balance (that is, the adjustment required to offset the effects of the changes expected in expenditures and revenues).
17. More specifically, the expenditure to GDP ratio was assumed to change in line with changes in the old-age dependency ratio, which implies that the transfer and the eligibility ratio were assumed as constant.
18. Three assumptions were considered, with relative price inflation of medical care equal to 0.1 and 2 per cent per year. Projections of health care were not produced for six countries.
19. As to pension, the primary balance estimate considers the baseline scenario. As to the health care, it refers to the scenario assuming that the cost of health services grows in line with per capita GDP and that health-care consumption depends on population structure and increases in line with the number of elderly citizens.
20. The debt level projected for 2000 is based on the assumption that fiscal consolidation takes place according to the path indicated by the OECD's medium-term reference scenario.
21. This indicator corresponds to Blanchard's short-term gap.
22. For a general presentation of generational accounting and a survey of the studies carried out in Europe, see Raffelhüschen (1997).
23. For the application of generational accounting to Norway, see also Auerbach et al. (1993) and Steigum and Gjersem (1996).
24. This estimate does not consider all the effects of the fiscal consolidation measures and the structural reforms undertaken by Italian governments over recent years.
25. As already pointed out, this indicator provides a measure of the dimension of the budgetary adjustment to be implemented. In practice the budgetary adjustment could also involve expenditure policies and living generations.
26. Updated estimates for several countries are published in Auerbach et al. (1999). New estimates for Denmark, Germany and Spain are included in Raffelhüschen (1997).
27. For a critical review of generational accounting see Haveman (1994) and Buiter (1995).
28. On this issue see Hagemann and John (1995) and IMF (1996).
29. With the exception of the profiles for Spain and Sweden that do not include education expenditure.
30. Males and females in the case of Finland.
31. It also includes early retirement pensions that peak for the 60–66-year age group.
32. The profile for Danish females include maternity allowances that increase expenditure for the 20–40-year age group.
33. In the case of Italy unemployment benefits are included in the item 'Other social benefits'.
34. In comparing the dynamics of age-related expenditure burden in the eight countries, it should be taken into consideration that education expenditure is not considered for Spain and Sweden. This exclusion may overestimate the impact of demographic changes. This applies particularly to Spain, where the fertility rate is relatively low.
35. See OECD (1988b).
36. These projections have been examined in Franco and Munzi (1996). For Italy the more recent projections reported in State General Accounting Office (1996c) have been taken into consideration.
37. More specifically, the expected values of the ratio of pension expenditure to GDP and of the ECR have been turned into an index based on a 1995 value of 1. Then the index has been multiplied by the ratio of public pension expenditure to GDP estimated for 1995.

424   *Demography and the welfare state*

The latter data have been computed in different ways, according to the data available for each country.

38. Since national pension expenditure projections for Denmark, Finland, Germany, the Netherlands and Italy are not available up to 2050, the estimates presented in this section cover only the period up to 2030 for the former three countries, up to 2040 for Denmark and the Netherlands and up 2045 for Italy.

39. More specifically, the estimates for the expenditure to GDP share of the transfer items (excluding pensions) refer to index *B*, while those for the share of expenditure pro- grammes mostly represented by wages (education and health care) refer to index *C*.

40. The comparisons are more significant for the specific expenditure items (pensions, health, education). Nevertheless, these comparisons should also be carried out with some caution, since the same item can include different programmes in each country. Attention should focus on expenditure trends for a country over time rather than on comparisons of public expenditure levels across countries.

41. It should be stressed that these estimates are based on different base years. See Annex C.

42. As pointed out in Section 3.2.1, Sweden is the only country for which an increase in working-age population is expected over the period 1995–2050. See Annex B. On the fiscal prospects for Sweden, see Hagemann and John (1995).

43. Data on current total public expenditure net of interest payments refer to the latest European Commission estimates for 1997 (European Commission, 1997).

44. The share of revenues to GDP is assumed constant on its 1997 level as in the latest European Commission estimates.

45. See Leibfritz et al. (1995) and Roseveare et al. (1996). A similar assumption is considered in the baseline scenario of Delbeque and Bogaert (1994), who assume a 2.5 per cent difference between the real interest rate and GDP growth.

46. It is assumed that the adjustment of interest rates from the present level to the level assumed in the projections takes place gradually over four years.

47. The calculation of the tax-gap has been carried out on the basis of the discrete formula used by Blanchard (1990) adjusted in order to be used for a different level of required debt to GDP by the end of the projection period. The formula used is (symbols refer to Annex A):

$$\tau^* = \left(\frac{r-\theta}{1+r-\theta}\right)\frac{b_0 - b_n(1+r-\theta)^{-n} + \sum_{s=1}^{n}(g+h)_s(1+r-\theta)^{-(s-1)}}{1-(1+r-\theta)^{-n}}$$

48. This approach has been recently recommended in some policy-oriented studies, such as Delbecque and Bogaert (1994) and Ministry of Finance of Denmark (1995). Delbecque and Bogaert, as already pointed out in Section 2.1.3, estimate the primary surplus (*recom- mended primary surplus*) that would allow pension expenditure increases to be fully offset by the decline in interest payments caused by the reduction in the debt to GDP ratio. The Danish report concludes that the downpayment of public debts, via a current surplus, is one of the major policies to be implemented to tackle the problems raised by the growing elderly burden. The generational impact of policies reducing the public debt is examined in Jensen and Raffelhüschen (1996).

REFERENCES

Auerbach, A.J., Gokhale, J. and Kotlikoff, L.J. (1991), 'Generational accounts – a meaningful alternative to deficit accounting', *NBER Working Paper*, No. 3589.

Auerbach, A.J., Gokhale, J. and Kotlikoff, L.J. (1994), 'Generational accounting: a meaningful way to evaluate fiscal policy', *The Journal of Economic Perspectives*, **8** (1), Winter.

Auerbach, A.J., Gokhale, J., Kotlikoff, L.J. and Steigum, E. (1993), 'Generational accounting in Norway: is Norway overconsuming its petroleum wealth?', mimeo.
Auerbach, A.J., Kotlikoff, L.J. and Leibfritz, W. (1999), *Generational Accounting – Around the World*, Chicago: University of Chicago Press.
Barea Tejero, J. and Fernández Moreno, M. (1994), *Evolución demográfica y gasto en protección social en España*.
Bayoumi, T. (1994), 'Ageing population and Canadian public pension plans', *IMF Working Paper*, No. 94/89.
Blanchard, O. (1990), 'Suggestions for a new set of fiscal indicators', OECD, Department of Economics and Statistics, *Working Papers*, No. 79.
Blanchard, O., Chouraqui, J.-C., Hagemann, R.P. and Sartor, N. (1990), 'The sustainability of fiscal policy: New answers to an old question', OECD, *Economic Studies*, No. 15, Autumn, 7–36.
Börsch-Supan, A. (1991), 'Ageing population', *Economic Policy*, April, 103–39.
Bos, E., Vu, M.T., Massiah, E. and Bulatao, R. (1994), *World Population Projections 1994–95*, Washington, DC: The International Bank for Reconstruction and Development/The World Bank.
Buiter, W.H. (1995), 'What do generational accounts tell us about the effects of the budget on intergenerational distribution and saving behaviour?', *Conference papers*, S. 111, Centre for Economic Performance, Seminar, Cambridge.
Buti, M., Franco, D. and Ongena, H. (1997), 'Budgetary policies during recessions: retrospective application of the "Stability and Growth Pact" to the post-war period', European Commission, *Directorate-General for Economic and Financial Affairs, Economic Papers*, No. 121, May.
Chand, S.K. and Jaeger, A. (1996), 'Ageing populations and public pension schemes', *IMF Occasional Paper*, No. 147.
Cruijsen, H., and Eding, H. (1995), 'The 1990-based long term population scenarios for the European economic area and Switzerland. How good were they in the short run?', paper presented at the international seminar 'New long-term population scenarios for the European Economic Area', Eurostat, Luxembourg, 8–10 November.
De Jong, A. (1995), 'Long-term fertility scenarios for the countries of the European Economic Area', paper presented at the international seminar 'New long-term population scenarios for the European Economic Area', Eurostat, Luxembourg, 8–10 November.
Delbecque, B. and Bogaert, H. (1994), 'L'incidence de la dette publique et du viellissement démographique sur la conduite de la politique budgétaire: une étude théorique appliquée au cas de la Belgique', *Bureau du Plan, Planning Papers*, No. 70, November.
Eding, H.J. (1995), 'Long-term demographic scenarios for the European Union', Groningen and Luxembourg, mimeo.
Englert, M., Fasquelle, N. and Weemaes, S. (1994), 'Les perspectives d'évolution à très long terme de la Sécurité sociale (1991–2050)', *Bureau du Plan, Planning Papers*, No. 66, Brussels.
European Commission (1994), 'Some economic implications of demographic trends up to 2020', *Annual Economic Report for 1994, European Economy*, No. 56, Brussels.
European Commission (1995), *The Demographic Situation of the European Union – 1994 Report*, Brussels.

European Commission (1996), *The Demographic Situation of the European Union – 1995 Report*, Brussels.

European Commission (1997), *Statistical Annex of European Economy*, June, Brussels.

Franco, D., Gokhale, J., Guiso, L., Kotlikoff, L.J. and Sartor, N. (1994), 'Generational accounting. The case of Italy', in Ando, A., Guiso, L. and Visco, I., *Saving and the Accumulation of Wealth*, Cambridge: Cambridge University Press.

Franco, D. and Munzi, T. (1996), 'Public pension expenditure prospects in the European Union: a survey of national projections', *European Economy – Reports and Studies*, No. 3, Brussels.

Gokhale, J., Raffelhüschen, B. and Walliser, J. (1995), 'The burden of German unification: a generational accounting approach', *Finanzarchiv*, **52**.

Hagemann, P. and John, C. (1995), 'The fiscal stance in Sweden: a generational accounting perspective', *IMF Working Paper*, No. 105.

Hagemann, R.P. and Nicoletti, G. (1989), 'Ageing populations: economic effects and implications for public finance', *OECD Department of Economics and Statistics, Working Paper*, No. 61.

Haveman, R. (1994), 'Should generational accounts replace public budgets and deficits?', *The Journal of Economic Perspectives*, **8** (1), Winter.

Heller, P.S., Hemming, R. and Kohnert, P. (1986), 'Ageing and social expenditures in the major industrialized countries, 1980–2025', *IMF Occasional Paper*, No. 47.

Henke, K.-D. and Behrens, C. (1989), *Umverteilungswirkungen der gesetzlichen Krankenversicherung. Eine empirische Analyse der differentiellen Einnahmewirkungen*.

IMF (1996), *World Economic Outlook*, May, Washington.

Jensen Hougaard, S.E. and Raffelhüschen, B. (1995), 'Intertemporal aspects of fiscal policy in Denmark', *Economic Policy Research Unit, Working Paper*, No. 22.

Jensen Hougaard, S.E. and Raffelhüschen, B. (1996), 'Public debt, welfare reforms and intergenerational distribution of tax burdens in Denmark', forthcoming in Auerbach, A., Kotlikoff, L.J. and Leibfritz, W. (eds), *Generational Accounting – Worldwide*, NBER series, Cambridge: Cambridge University Press.

Kotlikoff, L.J. (1992), *Generational Accounting – Knowing Who Pays, and When, for What we Spend*, New York: Free Press.

Lambrecht, M. (1981), 'Structure de la population et dépenses sociales (de 1977 à 2000)', *Bilan et Avenir des politiques sociales*, Bureau du Plan, Vol. 1, pp. 127–63, Brussels.

Lambrecht, M., Fasquelle, N. and Weemaes, S. (1994), 'L'évolution démographique de long-terme et son incidence isolée sur quelques grandeurs socio-économiques (1992–2050)', *Bureau de Plan, Planning Papers*, No. 68.

Leibfritz, W., Roseveare, D., Fore, D. and Wurzel, E. (1995), 'Ageing populations, pension systems and government budgets: how do they affect saving?', *OECD Working Paper*, No. 156, Paris.

Long, J.F. (1995), 'Complexity, accuracy, and utility of official population projections', *Mathematical Population Studies*, **5** (3), 203–16.

Mäki, T., Parkinnen, P. and Vanne, R. (1996), 'Kehdosta hautaan – suomalainen hyvinvointiyhteiskuntansa hoivassa (From cradle to grave – In care of the Finnish welfare society)', *Government Institute for Economic Research, Discussion Paper*, No. 119.

Ministry of Finance of Denmark (Finansministeriet) (1995), 'Policy implications of the ageing population in Denmark', *Working Papers*, No. 4. The Working Paper is a translation of Chapter 1 of the report *Pensionssystemet og fremtidens forsorgerbyrde* written by a working group of experts from several Danish ministries and published in March 1995.

Ministry of Finance of Denmark (Finansministeriet) (1996), *Finanredegørelse 1996*, December.

Ministry of Health and Social Affairs of Sweden (1994), *Pension Reform in Sweden – A Short Summary*, Proposal of The Working Group on Pensions in 1994, Stockholm.

Ministry of Labour and Social Security of Spain (1995), *La Securidad Social en el umbral del siglo XXI*, Madrid.

Ministry of Social Affairs and Health of Finland (1994), 'Sociaalimenotoimikunnan Mietintö' (Social Expenditure Committee), Helsinki.

OECD (1988a), *Ageing Populations – The Social Policy Implications*, Paris.

OECD (1988b), *Reforming Public Pensions*, Paris.

OECD (1993), 'OECD health systems – Facts and trends 1960–1991. Vol. 1', *Health Policy Studies*, No. 3.

OECD (1996), 'Ageing in OECD countries – A critical policy challenge', *Social Policy Studies*, No. 20.

Office of Management and Budget (1994), *Budget of the United States Government – Analytical Perspectives – Fiscal Year 1995*, Washington, DC.

Pearson, M., Smith, S. and White, S. (1989), 'Demographic influences on public spending', *Fiscal Studies*, No. 2.

Prime Minister's Office, Finland (1994), 'Intergenerational income distribution', Report of the Working Group on Intergenerational Income Distribution', *Publication*, No. 4.

Raffelhüschen, B. (1997), 'Generational accounting in Europe', study undertaken for the European Commission, mimeo.

Rogers, A. (1995), 'Population forecasting: do simple models outperform complex models?', *Mathematical Population Studies*, 5 (3), 187–202.

Roseveare, D., Leibfritz, W., Fore, D. and Wurzel, E. (1996), 'Ageing populations, pension systems and government budgets: simulations for 20 OECD countries', *OECD, Economics Department, Working Papers*, No. 168.

Shoven, J.B., Topper, M.D. and Wise, D.A. (1991), 'The impact of the demographic transition on government spending', mimeo.

State General Accounting Office, Ministry of Treasury of Italy (1996a), 'Tendenze demografiche e spesa sanitaria: alcuni possibili scenari', *Quaderno Monografico di Conti Pubblici e Congiuntura Economica*, No. 7, Rome, June.

State General Accounting Office, Ministry of Treasury of Italy (1996b), 'Tendenze demografiche e sistema scolastico: alcuni possibili scenari', *Quaderno Monografico di Conti Pubblici e Congiuntura Economica*, No. 8, Rome, June.

State General Accounting Office, Ministry of Treasury of Italy (1996c), 'Tendenze demografiche e spesa pensionistica: alcuni possibili scenari', *Quaderno Monografico di Conti Pubblici e Congiuntura Economica*, No. 9, Rome, June.

State General Accounting Office, Ministry of Treasury of Italy (1997), 'Sanità, scuola e pensioni – Le nuove previsioni basate sugli scenari demografici ISTAT', *Quaderno Monografico di Conti Pubblici e Congiuntura Economica*, No. 13, Rome, February.

Steigum, E. and Gjersem, C.E. (1996), 'Generational accounting and depletable natural resources: the case of Norway', mimeo.

Swedish Parliamentary Committee on Health Care (1996), 'Behov och resurser i våen analys', *Delbetäkande av HSU2000*, SOU, 163.

Swedish Parliament (1994), *Det reformerade pension-systemet*, Stockholm.

Ter Rele, H. (1997), 'Generational accounts for the Dutch public sector', *CPB Netherlands Bureau for Economic Policy Analysis, Research Memorandum*, No. 135, May.
Van Hoorn, W. and De Beer, J. (1995), 'Long-term mortality scenarios for the countries of the European Economic Area', paper presented at the International seminar 'New long-term population scenarios for the European Economic Area, Eurostat, Luxembourg, 8–10 November.
Visser, H. (1995), 'Long-term international migration scenarios for the countries of the European Economic Area', paper presented at the International seminar 'New long-term population scenarios for the European Economic Area', Eurostat, Luxembourg, 8–10 November.

ANNEX A THE 'TAX GAP'

In order to construct an indicator of budget sustainability, the first step is to define the primary deficit d such that

$$d = g + h - t$$

where g is government spending on goods and services, h government transfers and t taxes, all expressed in terms of ratios to GDP.

The change in the ratio of public debt (b) to GDP is then expressed by

$$\frac{db}{ds} = g + h - t + (r - \theta)b = d(r - \theta)b$$

where r is the real interest rate and θ the real GDP growth rate.

The public debt to GDP ratio in the year n can be expressed as the debt to GDP ratio in the initial year b_0 accumulated at a rate equal to the difference between the interest rate r and the growth rate θ, plus the accumulated value, at the same rate, of the primary deficits along the way:

$$b_n = b_0 e^{(r-\theta)n} + \int_0^n d_s e^{(r-\theta)(n-s)} ds$$

By discounting to time zero, the equation becomes

$$b_n e^{(r-\theta)n} = b_0 + \int_0^n d_s e^{-(r-\theta)s} ds$$

By substitution of d_s with $(g + h - t)_s$, the equation becomes

$$b_n e^{-(r-\theta)n} = b_0 + \int_0^n \left(g + h - t\right)_s e^{-(r-\theta)s} ds$$

which is equivalent to

$$\int_0^n t_s e^{-(r-\theta)s} ds = b_0 - b_n e^{-(r-\theta)n} + \int_0^n \left(g + h\right)_s e^{-(r-\theta)s} ds$$

Assuming that the tax rate $\bar{t} = t_s$ is constant over time, the equation becomes

$$\bar{t} \int_0^n e^{-(r-\theta)s} ds = b_0 - b_n e^{-(r-\theta)n} + \int_0^n \left(g + h\right)_s e^{-(r-\theta)s} ds$$

It is now possible to solve the integral on the left side of the equation:

$$\int_0^n e^{-(r-\theta)s} ds = \left[\frac{1}{-(r-\theta)} e^{-(r-\theta)s} \right]_0^n = -(r-\theta)^{-1}\left(e^{-(r-\theta)n} - 1\right)$$

The equation thus becomes

$$\bar{t}\left[-(r-\theta)^{-1}\left(e^{-(r-\theta)n}-1\right)\right]=b_0-b_ne^{-(r-\theta)n}+\int_0^n(g+h)_s\,e^{-(r-\theta)s}ds$$

By isolating the tax $\bar{t}$, we obtain

$$\bar{t}=\frac{b_0-b_ne^{-(r-\theta)n}+\int_0^n(g+h)_s\,e^{-(r-\theta)s}ds}{-(r-\theta)^{-1}\left(e^{-(r-\theta)n}-1\right)}$$

which is equivalent to

$$\bar{t}=(r-\theta)\frac{b_0-b_ne^{-(r-\theta)n}+\int_0^n(g+h)_s\,e^{-(r-\theta)s}ds}{1-e^{-(r-\theta)n}}$$

Define $\bar{t}$ as the sustainable tax rate t^* that allows for the debt to GDP ratio at the end of the projection period n to be equal at the initial level of the debt ($b_0 = b_n$); then the equation becomes

$$t^*=(r-\theta)\frac{b_0\left(1-e^{-(r-\theta)n}\right)+\int_0^n(g+h)_s\,e^{-(r-\theta)s}ds}{1-e^{-(r-\theta)n}}$$

which is equivalent to

$$t^*=(r-\theta)\left[b_0+\frac{\int_0^n(g+h)_s\,e^{-(r-\theta)s}ds}{1-e^{-(r-\theta)n}}\right]$$

The sustainable tax rate is thus expressed as follows

$$t^*=(r-\theta)\left[b_0+\left(1-e^{-(r-\theta)n}\right)^{-1}\int_0^n(g+h)_s\,e^{-(r-\theta)s}ds\right]$$

The sustainable tax rate t^* is thus equal to the annuity value of future expected spending and transfers, plus the difference between the *ex ante* interest rate and the growth rate times the ratio of debt to GDP. If the sustainable tax rate is greater than the current tax rate, t, then sooner or later taxes will have to be increased, and/or spending decreased. This latter indicator may be defined as the tax gap and it is given by t^*-t.

ANNEX B   DEMOGRAPHIC PROSPECTS IN THE EUROPEAN UNION

Changes in birth rates, life expectancy and migration flows are modifying the level and structure of the population of the European Union. In recent years national and international institutions have carried out several long-term projections of population. Forecasts for all countries were released in 1994 by the World Bank (see Bos et al.). Forecasts for the European Union member states were produced in 1991 and 1996 by Eurostat. This chapter is based on the latter projections.[1]

Long-term demographic projections are quite uncertain.[2] Fertility rates can fluctuate considerably and rather unpredictably even in the short term.[3] Mortality rates, although the margins of error are relatively smaller, are also difficult to predict.[4] Even greater uncertainties stem from the projection of net migration flows, which depend on several economic and social factors, on political decisions and on the enforcement of policies.[5] The uncertainty of long-term projections is stressed by the Danish Ministry of Finance (1995), which provides the following example: by assuming a higher birth rate and higher net immigration, Denmark's Statistical Department, in its 1994 projection, estimated a population of 5 million people for 2025, as against the 4 million estimate projected a decade earlier.

In order to take the uncertainty of the demographic outlook into account, this chapter refers to three of the five different scenarios developed by Eurostat in 1996: the 'baseline' scenario, the 'youngest population' scenario and the 'most-aged population' scenario.

Box 9B.1   Scenarios

Baseline

Fertility rates are assumed to increase in low fertility countries and remain nearly stable in others (in 2035 total fertility rates in the 15 countries are in the 1.5–1.9 range); life expectancy at birth is projected to increase by 5.5–7.7 years for males and 4.3–6.2 years for females in the period up to 2050; an inflow of 600 000 persons per year for the Union is projected up to 2010 (see Table 9.B1).

Youngest population

Fertility rates are assumed to increase in all countries (with total fertility rates in the 1.8–2.1 range in 2035); life expectancy at birth is projected to increase by 2.0–3.2 years for males and 1.6–2.8 years for females in the period up to 2050; net migration is relatively high (an inflow of 800 000 persons per year up to 2010).

Most-aged population

Fertility rates decline in most countries (with total fertility rates in the 1.3–1.6 range in 2035); life expectancy increases by 8.5–11.4 years for males and 6.7–8.2 years for females in the period up to 2050; net migration is relatively low (400 000 persons per year up to 2010).

In the baseline scenario, total EU population increases from 371.6 million in 1995 to 388.0 million in 2025, declining thereafter to 367.0 million in 2050. In the youngest population scenario, total EU population increases up to 2044 (to 414.3 million) and remains nearly constant afterwards (413.6 million in 2050). In the most-aged scenario, total population reaches a peak in 2010 (378.6 million) and thereafter declines to 331.6 million in 2050.

A significant ageing of EU population occurs under all scenarios. The change in the population structure is clearly shown in the population pyramids that refer to the baseline scenario (Figures 9B.1a–c). In this scenario the ratio of the citizens aged 65 and over to total population increases from 15.4 per cent in 1995 to 27.3 per cent in 2040 and remains stable thereafter.

The ratio of the elderly to working-age population, which provides a first measure of the burden represented by the former group, increases even more substantially: in the baseline scenario it rises from 25.3 per cent in 1995 to 38.1 per cent in 2025 and 51.4 per cent in 2040. In the 'youngest population' scenario it reaches a peak at 41.4 per cent in 2040; in the 'most aged population' scenario it grows continuously to 65.1 per cent in 2050 (see Figure 9.B2a). This process affects all countries considered in this study, with Italy and Spain reaching the highest ratios in all scenarios and Sweden recording the lowest ratios (see Figures 9B.3a–h).

The composition of the elderly and working-age population will also change substantially; both groups will gradually age (see Figures 9B.1a–c). In the baseline scenario, in the EU the ratio of people aged 80 and over to people aged 65 and over increases from 25.1 per cent in 1995, to 27.2 per cent in 2025 and 36.3 per cent in 2050. The ratio of people aged 50–64 to people aged 15–64 increases from 27.6 per cent in 1995 to 37.6 in 2025; thereafter it declines to 34.9 in 2040.

In the baseline scenario the ratio of the EU citizens aged 0–19 to working age population declines from 39.4 per cent in 1995 to 34.7 per cent in 2025. Thereafter it rises to 36.6 per cent by 2040. In the youngest population scenario the ratio increases to a 44.0 per cent peak in 2040. In the most-aged population scenario it declines to 30.0 per cent in 2025 and remains stable

Table 9B.1 *Key assumptions on fertility, mortality and migration rates*

	Total fertility rate				Life expectancy at birth								Net migration (× 1000)		
					Males				Females						
	1994	2035			1990–94	2050			1990–94	2050			2010		
		Low	Baseline	High		Low	Baseline	High		Low	Baseline	High	Low	Baseline	High
Austria	1.5	1.4	1.6	1.9	72.7	75.5	80.0	83.0	79.2	81.5	85.0	87.0	15	23	30
Belgium	1.6	1.5	1.8	2.0	73.0	76.0	80.0	83.0	79.7	82.0	85.0	87.0	10	15	20
Denmark	1.8	1.5	1.8	2.0	72.5	75.0	79.0	82.0	77.9	79.5	83.0	85.0	5	10	15
Finland	1.9	1.6	1.8	2.1	71.7	74.5	79.0	82.0	79.5	81.5	85.0	87.0	0	5	10
France	1.7	1.6	1.8	2.1	73.1	76.0	80.0	83.0	81.2	84.0	87.0	88.0	30	50	70
Germany	1.3	1.3	1.5	1.8	72.5	75.0	79.0	82.0	78.9	81.5	84.0	86.0	150	200	250
Greece	1.4	1.4	1.7	1.9	74.8	77.5	81.0	84.0	79.7	82.0	85.0	87.0	20	25	30
Ireland	1.9	1.6	1.8	2.1	72.5	75.0	79.0	82.0	78.0	80.5	84.0	86.0	–5	–3	0
Italy	1.2	1.3	1.5	1.8	73.7	76.0	80.0	83.0	80.3	82.5	85.0	87.0	60	80	100
Luxembourg	1.7	1.5	1.8	2.0	72.3	75.5	80.0	83.0	78.9	81.5	85.0	87.0	1	2	3
Netherlands	1.6	1.5	1.8	2.0	74.1	76.5	80.0	83.0	80.2	82.0	85.0	87.0	20	35	50
Portugal	1.4	1.4	1.7	1.9	70.6	73.0	78.0	82.0	77.8	80.0	84.0	86.0	20	25	30
Spain	1.2	1.3	1.5	1.8	73.5	75.5	79.0	82.0	80.7	82.5	85.0	87.0	40	60	80
Sweden	1.9	1.6	1.9	2.1	75.4	78.0	82.0	85.0	80.7	83.0	86.0	88.0	10	20	30
United Kingdom	1.7	1.6	1.8	2.1	73.4	76.5	80.0	83.0	78.8	81.5	85.0	87.0	20	45	70

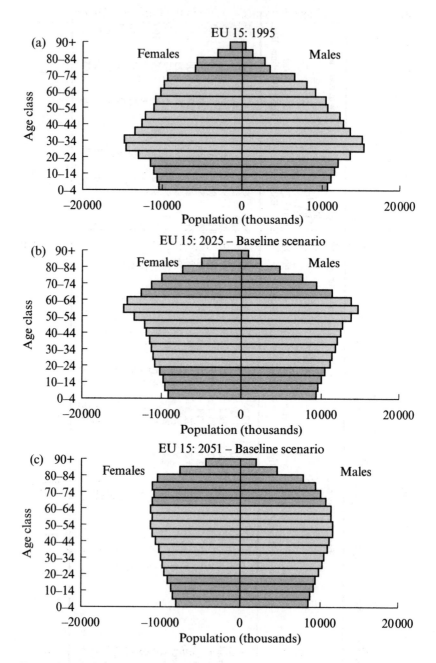

Figure 9B.1 Population pyramid

(a)

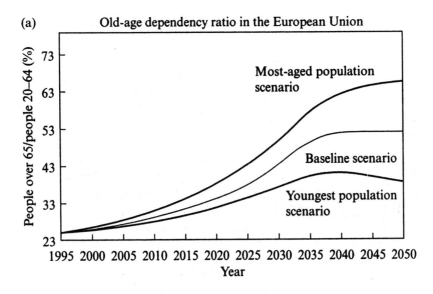

(b)

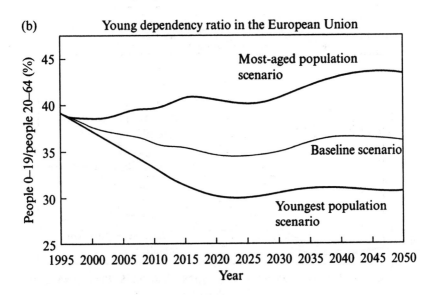

Figure 9B.2 Old-age and young dependency ratios in EU 15: the three Eurostat scenarios

(a)

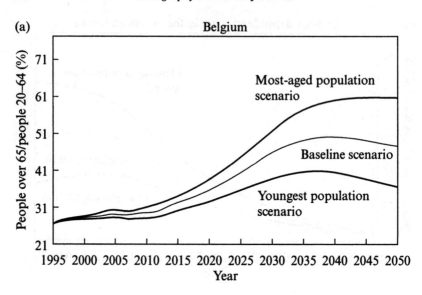

(b)

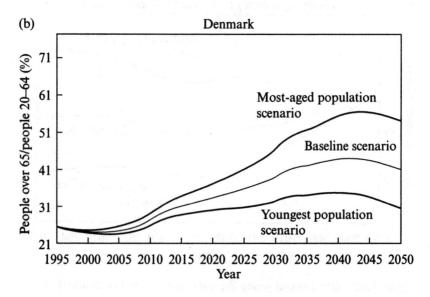

Figure 9B.3   Old-age dependency ratio: the three Eurostat scenarios

(c)

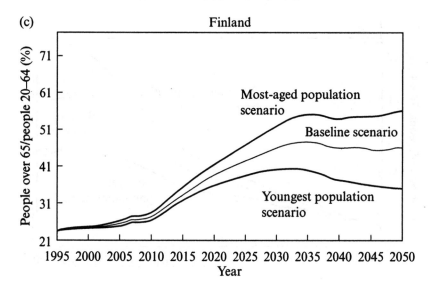

Finland

(d)

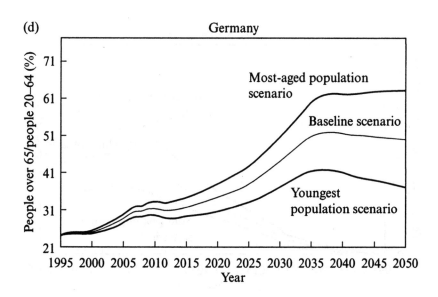

Germany

(e)

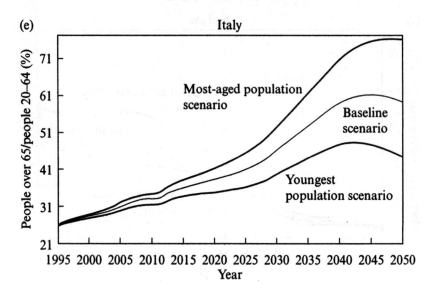

Italy

(f)

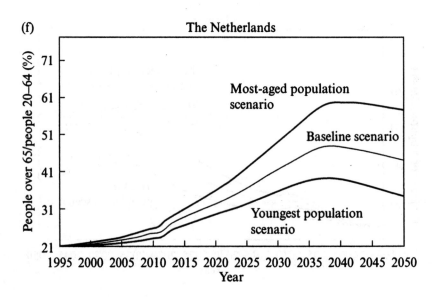

The Netherlands

Figure 9B.3   continued

(g)

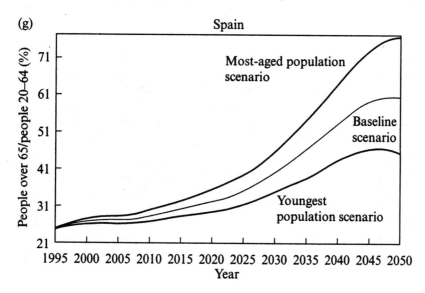

(h)

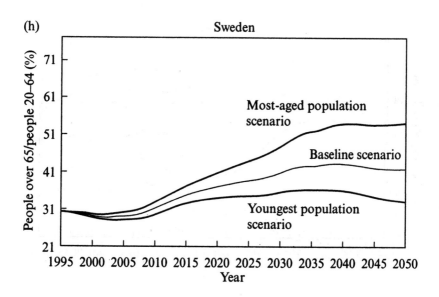

(a)

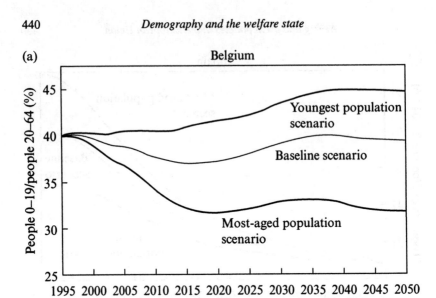

(b)

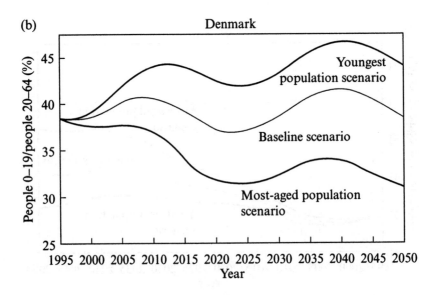

Figure 9B.4   Young dependency ratio: the three Eurostat scenarios

(c)

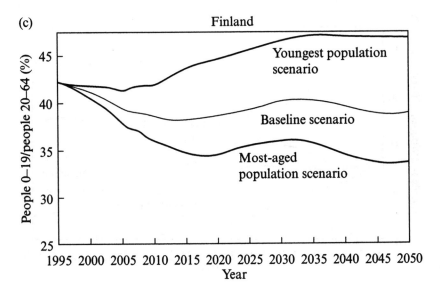

(d)

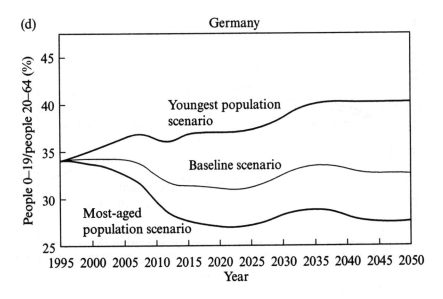

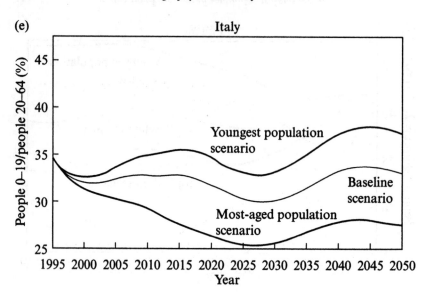

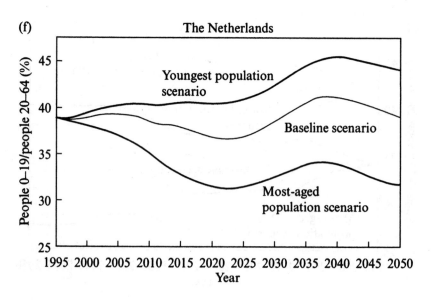

Figure 9B.4   continued

(g)

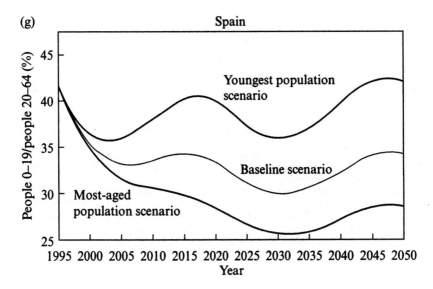

(h)

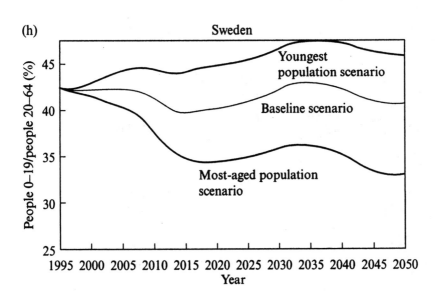

thereafter (see Figure 9B.2b). Similar trends are expected for all the eight countries examined, with Italy and Spain recording the lowest levels and Finland and Sweden recording the highest ones (see Figures 9.B4a–h).

Notes

1. See Eding (1995) and the papers presented at the seminar 'New long-term population scenarios for the European Economic Area', Eurostat, European Commission, Luxembourg, 1995.
2. Long (1995) and Rogers (1995) evaluate the methodological problems underlying long-term population projections. Long also analyses the accuracy of official population projections used for government planning.
3. In the early 1990s, for instance, the number of births in the European Union was lower than that predicted by Eurostat in 1991 in the low-fertility scenario. See De Jong (1995) and Cruijsen and Eding (1995). According to the latter paper (p. 4), 'fertility showed once again its capricious and unpredictable nature'.
4. See Van Hoorn and De Beer (1995) and Cruijsen and Eding (1995).
5. The topic is examined in Visser (1995).

ANNEX C   NATIONAL AGE-RELATED EXPENDITURE PROFILES

Belgium

The expenditure profiles for Belgium are based on the estimates provided by Lambrecht et al. (1994).[1] The aggregate 1988 values for the main social expenditure items have been allocated by 5-year age classes (0–4 to 95–99 years). These data have been used to compute the average per capita expenditure in Belgian francs for each age group in 1988. The following items were considered: health care, invalidity benefits,[2] education, pensions (for public and private sector workers), unemployment benefits,[3] family allowances, maternity benefits and expenditure for nursery schools.

In 1988, the programmes considered by Lambrecht et al. accounted for about 62 per cent of general government expenditure net of interest payments and represented 28.8 per cent of GDP.[4]

The per capita expenditures reported in Lambrecht et al. have been expressed in terms of per capita 1988 GDP. Figure 9C.1 outlines the resulting age-related profiles. The total age-related expenditure profile has two peaks for the 15–19 and the 70–74 age groups. Educational expenditure largely contributes in determining the increase in total expenditure from the 0–4 to the 15–19 age group. Expenditure then gradually declines, reaching a minimum level with the 30–34 age group. It remains relatively low up to the 45–49 age group. Thereafter it increases fast, because of the substantial increase in disability and unemployment benefits (in the 50–64 age range) and in pensions (which become the most relevant expenditure item from the 60–64 age group). Expenditure peaks in the 70–74 group and declines afterwards.

Denmark

The age and sex expenditure profiles for Denmark were estimated by Raffelhüschen (1997) on the basis of 1995 data. Public expenditure profiles have been computed for a number of age-related items, and have then been grouped in six main categories: expenditure for the elderly, social welfare, education, health benefits, housing benefits, child allowances and youth support, and unemployment insurance.[5]

In 1995, the programmes considered by Raffelhüschen accounted for DKK 339 billion, that is, about 66 per cent of general government expenditure net of interest payments, and represented 35 per cent of GDP.

The profiles have been expressed in terms of per capita 1995 GDP. Figures 9C.2a and 9C.2b outline the age-related profiles of the expenditure items

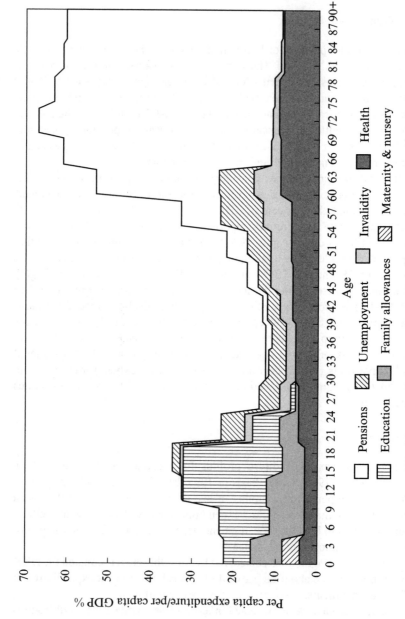

Figure 9C.1   Age-related public expenditure profiles in Belgium (percentage of per capita GDP)

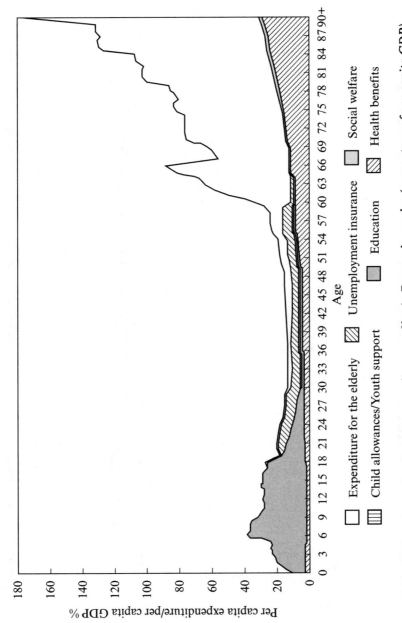

Figure 9C.2a   Age-related public expenditure profiles in Denmark – males (percentage of per capita GDP)

447

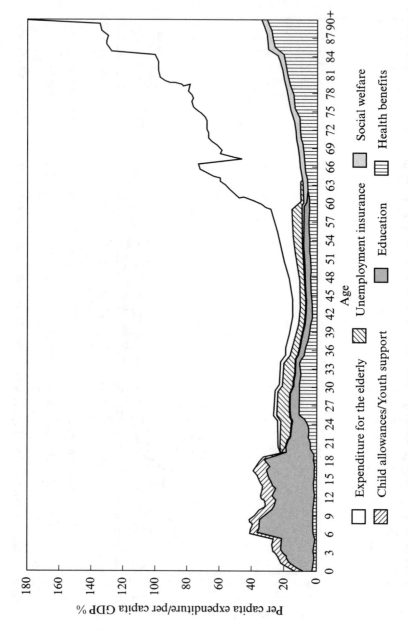

Figure 9C.2b   Age-related public expenditure profiles in Denmark – females (percentage of per capita GDP)

Legend:
- Expenditure for the elderly
- Child allowances/Youth support
- Unemployment insurance
- Education
- Social welfare
- Health benefits

Y-axis: Per capita expenditure/per capita GDP %
X-axis: Age (0 3 6 9 12 15 18 21 24 27 30 33 36 39 42 45 48 51 54 57 60 63 66 69 72 75 78 81 84 87 90+)

taken into consideration. They both present three peaks, one for the 6–20 age group due to education expenditure, one for the 60–66 age group due to early retirement pensions, and a much higher one for the very elderly mainly related to pensions, elderly care and health care. The female profile is very similar to the male one, with the exception of higher expenditure for child allowances and youth support up to the 20 age group, and higher expenditure for health expenditure in the 20–40 age group due to maternity benefits. The large expenditure for the elderly is due to the inclusion, on top of pensions, of other services and benefits, such as home help and residential institutions.

Finland

The age expenditure profiles for Finland have been estimated in Mäki et al. (1996). The aggregate 1993 values for the main social expenditure items have been allocated by age classes (0–108 years). These data have been used to compute the average per capita expenditure in Finnish markka for each age group in the year 1993. General government payments, net of interest payments, have been broken down into spending on 11 age-related items (health, education, pensions, social services, transfers related to children, unemployment benefits, other social transfers, transfers to households, transfers to non-profit organizations, transfers to farmers and firms, net investments) and on the remaining age-unrelated public consumption. The net investment profile is based on the profile for public consumption.

In 1993, the programmes considered by Mäki et al. (1996) accounted for about 78 per cent of general government expenditure net of interest payments and represented 43.0 per cent of GDP.[6]

The per capita expenditures reported in Mäki et al. have been expressed in terms of per capita 1993 GDP. Figure 9C.3 outlines the resulting age-related profiles. The total age-related expenditure profile is U-shaped. Transfers related to children and social services determine a high level of expenditure for the 0–2 age group (over 50 per cent of per capita GDP). For the 7–18 age group education is the main expenditure item, with total expenditure amounting to about 40 per cent of per capita GDP. Total expenditure remains high for the 20–25 age group, for which unemployment benefits and other social transfers add up to the gradually declining education expenditure. The lowest expenditure levels (20–25 per cent of per capita GDP) are recorded for the 30–50 age group. For the following generations expenditure gradually increases, reaching 55 per cent of per capita GDP for 60-year-olds, 78 per cent for 65-year-olds, 95 per cent for 80-year-olds. This profile is determined by the high level of pension benefits (over 50 per cent of per capita GDP for all classes over 60) and by the rising level of health and social services expenditure.

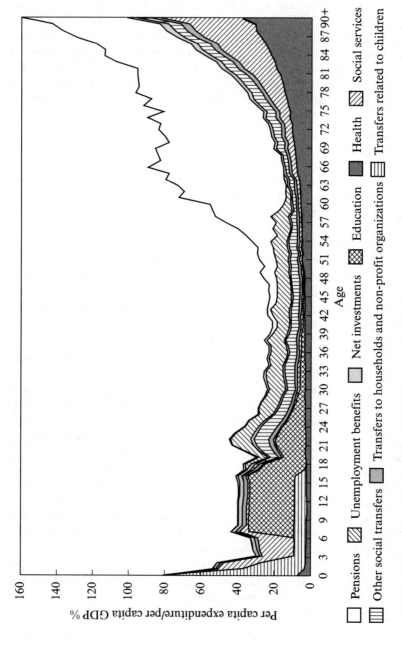

Figure 9C.3   Age-related public expenditure profiles in Finland

Germany

The age and sex expenditure profiles for Germany were first estimated for both western and eastern Germany by Gokhale et al. (1995). Most of the data were obtained from the German Socioeconomic Panel. The health expenditure profile was a smoothed version of data collected by Henke and Behrens (1989).

Public expenditure profiles were computed for the main age-related items: social security, health, accident insurance, unemployment insurance, general welfare, housing benefits, maternity benefits and child benefits. The profiles were presented in terms of indexes (c_{ik}^j) based on the expenditure recorded for a 40-year-old male in the base year 1992.

$$G_k^j = \sum_i \left(c_{ik}^j \times P_i^j \right) \times V_{40}^j$$

with c_{ik}^j = (expenditure for budgetary item k per member of each age group i in the base year j)/(expenditure for budgetary item k per male of the age group 40 in the base year j);

V_{40}^j = expenditure for budgetary item k in national currency per male of the age group 40 in the base year j.

In 1992, the programmes considered by Gokhale et al. (1995) accounted for DEM 725 billion, that is, about 43 per cent of general government expenditure net of interest payments, and represented 19.5 per cent of GDP.

In 1997, these profiles were updated by Raffelhüschen (1997). The new profiles referred to Germany as a whole and considered two extra items (education and long-term care). In 1995, the programmes considered by Raffelhüschen accounted for DEM 865 billion, that is, about 54 per cent of general government expenditure net of interest payments, and represented 25 per cent of GDP. Of the additional 5.5 percentage points of GDP taken into consideration with respect to Gokhale et al. (1995), 4 points are due to the inclusion of education and long term care expenditure, while the other 1.5 points are due to an increase in pension expenditure.

Figures 9C.4a and 9C.4b outline the age-related profiles of the expenditure items taken into consideration. The profiles have been expressed in terms of per capita 1995 GDP. As all other national profiles, they present two peaks, one in the younger age groups due to education expenditure and a higher one for the elderly due to pensions and health care. Expenditure is rather high (between 20 and 30 per cent of per capita GDP) for the 3–30 age groups mainly because of education. Thereafter it is rather limited up to the 50 age group, increasing from 9 to 11 per cent because of a rise in health services, unemployment and welfare benefits. Pension benefits affect male and female

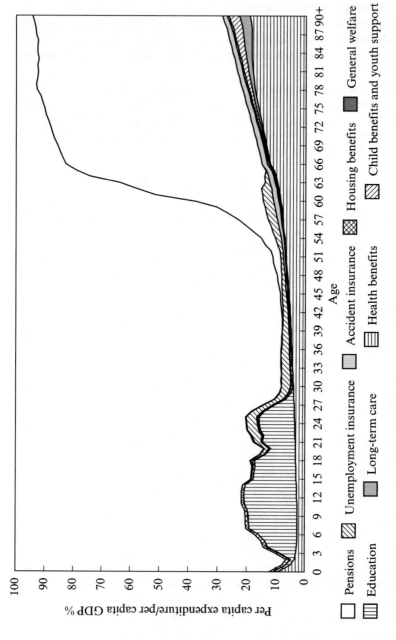

Figure 9C.4a   Age-related public expenditure profiles in Germany – males (percentage of per capita GDP)

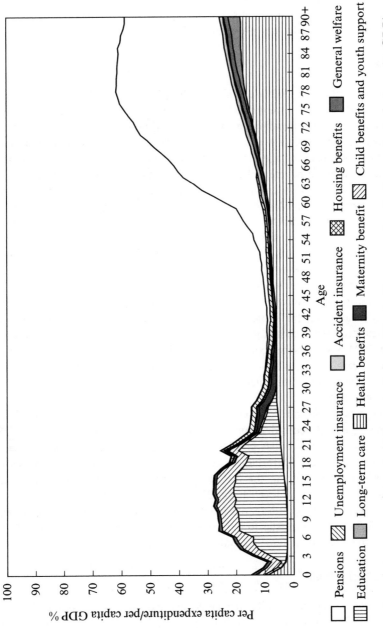

Figure 9C.4b   Age-related public expenditure profiles in Germany – females (percentage of per capita GDP)

453

expenditure profiles from the 50 year group; they peak in the 66–80 group for males and in the 70 and over group for females. Accident insurance benefits substantially affect the male profile in the 65–70 age group. Because of differences in pension benefits, the male profile is substantially higher than the female one for the age group over 55.

Italy

The age and sex expenditure profiles for Italy have been estimated in Franco et al. (1994). General government payments, net of interest payments, have been broken down into spending on five age-related items (health, education, pensions, household responsibility payments and other social security transfers) and on the remaining age-unrelated items. The aggregate 1990 values of each of these different payments have been allocated by age (0–90 years and over) and sex according to cross-section age–sex profiles. As for German public expenditure, the profiles are presented in terms of indexes with the index 1 representing the expenditure for a 40-year-old male in the base year 1990.

In 1990, the age-related programmes considered by Franco et al. accounted for about 66 per cent of general government expenditure net of interest payments and represented 27.4 per cent of GDP.

Within the present study, the data have been updated on the basis of 1994 general government aggregate outlays (G_k^{1994}) and 1994 population (P_i^{1994}). This means that the projection is based on the 1990 indexes of relative expenditure for each age group within each expenditure item (c_{ik}^{1990}), but on the 1994 level of the expenditure.[7] In 1994 the age-related programmes considered by Franco et al. (1994) accounted for about 65 per cent of general government expenditure net of interest payments and represented 28.3 per cent of GDP.

Figures 9C.5a and 9C.5b outline the age-related profile of the expenditure items taken into consideration expressed in terms of per capita 1994 GDP. Both the male and female profiles have a peak for the 10-year-old age class. Educational expenditure largely contributes in determining the changes in total expenditure up to the 20–24 age group. Expenditure then declines, reaching a minimum level in the 27–48 age group. Thereafter it increases fast, because of the substantial increase in pension expenditure. Health expenditure also contributes to this trend. The male profile peaks for the 65–70 age group, while the female profile is nearly flat after the 65 age group.

The Netherlands

The age expenditure profiles for the Netherlands have been estimated by Ter Rele (1997) for the year 1995. Per capita expenditure in Dutch guilders has

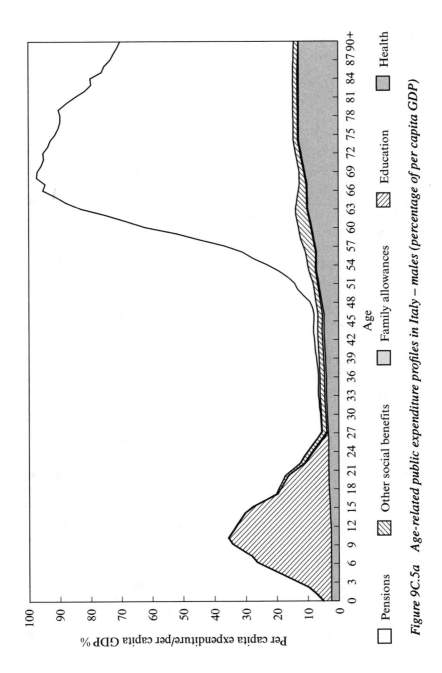

Figure 9C.5a   Age-related public expenditure profiles in Italy – males (percentage of per capita GDP)

Pensions   Other social benefits   Family allowances   Education   Health

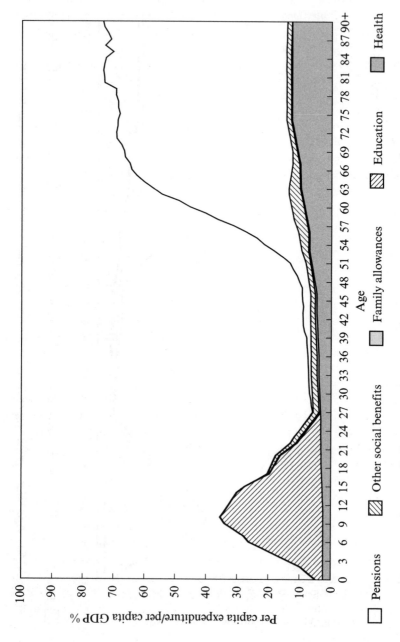

Figure 9C.5b   Age-related public expenditure profiles in Italy – females (percentage of per capita GDP)

been computed for one-year age groups from 0–99 years and over.[8] Profiles have been provided for the following items: pensions, welfare benefits (including expenditure on unemployment, disability and sickness benefits, child allowances and social assistance), health care (including home care and services for the elderly) and education.

In 1995, the age-related programmes considered by ter Rele accounted for about 61.4 per cent of general government expenditure net of interest payments and represented about 29.7 per cent of GDP.

Figure 9C.6 outlines the age-related profile of the expenditure items taken into consideration expressed in terms of 1995 per capita GDP. The profile is characterized by a first peak for the 7–25 age group mainly due to education expenditure, and by a very large increase in the right end of the profile, due to a substantial increase in health and pension expenditure.

Spain

The expenditure profiles for Spain are based on the estimates provided by Barea Tejero and Fernández Moreno (1994). The average per capita expenditure in Spanish pesetas for three age groups (0–14, 15–64 and 65 and over) results from the allocation of the aggregate 1991 values for the main social expenditure items over each age group. The following five items were considered: health care, pensions, unemployment benefits, family allowances, other social benefits. Different profiles were not computed for males and females.

In 1991, the age-related programmes considered by Tejero and Moreno accounted for about 49 per cent of general government expenditure net of interest payments and represented about 20.3 per cent of GDP.

The per capita expenditure reported in Tejero and Moreno have been expressed in terms of 1991 per capita GDP. Figure 9C.7 outlines the resulting age-related profiles. Expenditure increases from 5 per cent of per capita GDP for the 0–14 age group to 14 per cent for the 15–64 group and to 73 per cent for the older age group. Pensions and health care account for most of the changes in expenditure levels.

Sweden

The age and sex expenditure profiles have been estimated by combining profiles from two different sources: (a) Hagemann and John (1995) provided profiles for a number of items excluding services, (b) the profiles for health expenditure were presented in a report by the parliamentary committee on health care.[9] Profiles for education are not available.

As to the first source, the profiles have been produced according to the results of an income and expenditure survey undertaken by the Swedish

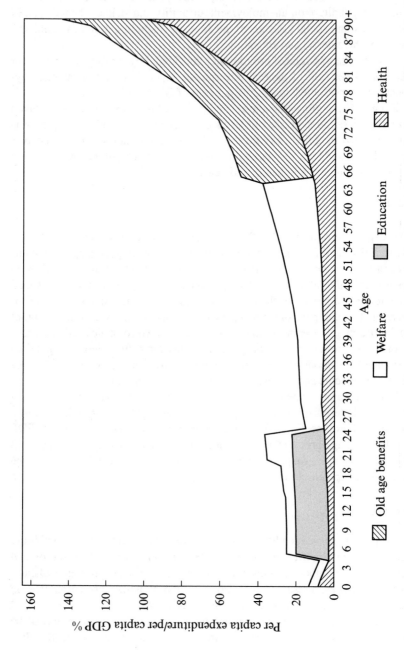

Figure 9C.6   Age-related public expenditure profiles in the Netherlands – males and females (percentage of per capita GDP)

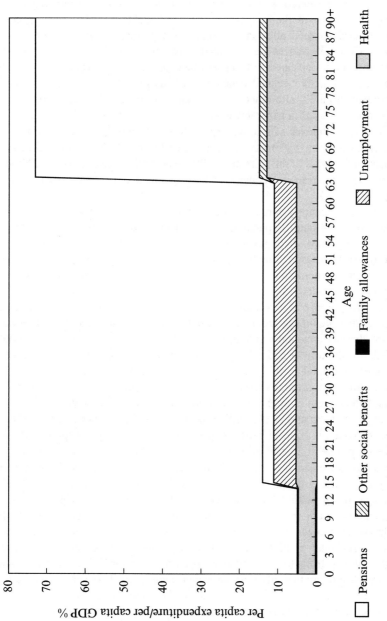

Figure 9C.7   Age-related public expenditure profiles in Spain – males and females (percentage of per capita GDP)

Per capita expenditure/per capita GDP %

Age

☐ Pensions   ▨ Other social benefits   ■ Family allowances   ▨ Unemployment   ▨ Health

459

Statistical Office. The survey refers to 1992. Per capita expenditure in Swedish kronor have been computed for ten age groups for each sex. Only cash transfers have been considered. Profiles have been produced for the following items: pensions, labour market assistance, sickness benefits, social assistance, child allowances, parents' allowances, educational grants, accommodation allowances. Child allowances are attributed to parents. For the scope of this paper, labour market assistance and sickness benefits have been grouped as a single item (labour market-related benefits), such as parents and child allowances (grouped in family allowances) and social assistance and accommodation allowances (grouped in general welfare).

The 1992 indexes of relative expenditure for each age group within each expenditure item (c_{ik}^{1992}) have been updated by the above-mentioned economists on the basis of an estimate of 1995 level of the expenditure. In 1995 the age-related programmes considered by Hagemann and John represented 23.6 per cent of GDP.

The parliamentary committee on health care presented health care profiles based on 1994 data. Expenditure in Swedish kronor has been computed for seven age groups, distinguishing expenditure on health care in county councils (mainly corresponding to hospital expenditure) and expenditure on elderly care in local municipalities (that is, home care).[10] In 1994 the health programmes considered by the report represented 9.4 per cent of GDP.

For the purpose of this chapter, per capita expenditure for each of the seven items (five stemming from the estimates of Hagemann and John and two from the parliamentary committee) has been divided by per capita GDP (1995 for the former and 1994 for the latter), and has been considered as part of the same total profile for Swedish age-related public expenditure. The expenditure programmes considered represent about 33 per cent of GDP and about 55 per cent of total public expenditure net of interest payments in 1995.

Figures 9C.8a and 9C.8b outline the age-related profile of the expenditure items taken into consideration expressed in terms of per capita GDP. As already pointed out, education expenditure is not included and child allowances are attributed to parents. This underestimates public expenditure devoted to younger age-groups. The male and female profiles have a peak for the 20–30 age group, with labour market related benefits representing the major expenditure item for males and labour market related benefits and family allowances representing the major ones for females. Expenditure then declines, reaching a minimum level for the 40–50 age group. It increases substantially from the 60 and over age group onwards with pensions and health care being the only relevant expenditure items: between 60 and 75 the increase is mainly due to pensions, while from the 75 age group also health expenditure increases become consistent; for the over-85 age group, home care becomes the major expenditure item, inducing a peak of almost 150 per

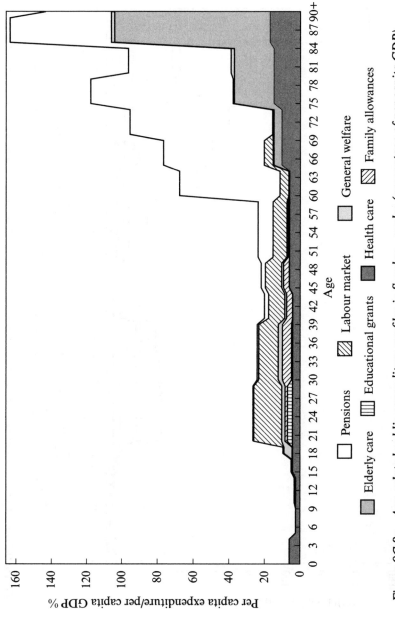

Figure 9C.8a   Age-related public expenditure profiles in Sweden – males (percentage of per capita GDP)

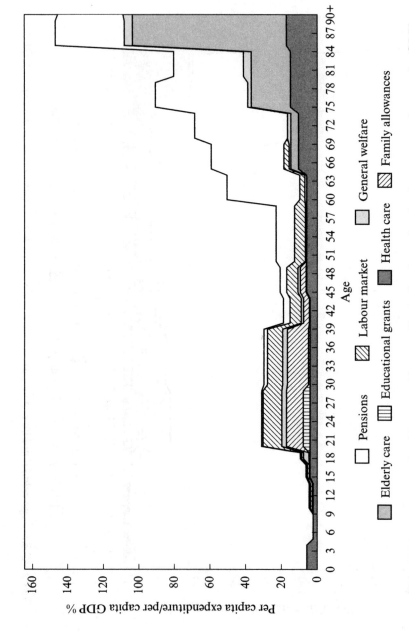

Figure 9C.8b Age-related public expenditure profiles in Sweden – females (percentage of per capita GDP)

cent of per capita GDP for females and 160 per cent for males (the difference being due to different pension levels for males and females, since health profiles are not split according to gender).

Notes

1. The study updated and improved some estimates of the effects of demographic changes on public expenditure carried out in 1981 (see Lambrecht, 1981).
2. These include benefits for temporary work disability, invalidity, work accidents, professional diseases and handicaps.
3. Expenditure for unemployment also includes expenditure for early retirement pensions and active employment policies.
4. The total amount of public expenditure for the items considered in Lambrecht et al. (1995) have been computed multiplying the age-related per capita amounts indicated in the study by the number of people in each age group resulting in Eurostat statistics.
5. Expenditure for the elderly includes old-age pensions, civil servants' pensions, supplementary pensions, early retirement pensions, old people's homes, home helps, expenditure for residential institutions for pensioners. Social welfare includes cash benefits, social assistance act benefits, family allowances, rent subsidies. Education includes primary schools, lower secondary schools, upper secondary schools, third level schools (university and non-university type), vocational schools, folk and juvenile high schools, school-care schemes, adult education, labour market training courses. Health expenditure includes expenditure for general and specialist practitioners, dentists, medicines, sickness and maternity benefits, other sickness protection schemes, hospitals, rehabilitation institutions, rehabilitation benefits, day care. Child allowances and youth support include clubs and play-area expenditure and education grants.
6. The total amount of public expenditure for the items considered by Mäki et al. (1996) have been computed multiplying the age-related per capita amounts indicated in the study by the number of people in each age-group indicated in the same study.
7. The value of V_{40}^{1994} has been computed as $V_{40}^{1994} = \dfrac{G_k^{1994}}{\sum_i \left(c_{ik}^{1990} \times P_i^{1994} \right)}$
8. In order to harmonize the profile to the others considered in this paper, the last ten age groups from 90–99 and over have been substituted with a single group for those aged 90 years and over. It has been assumed that per capita expenditure in that group would equal that of a 92-year-old citizen as estimated by Ter Rele (1997).
9. The parliamentary committee on health care published a report in March 1997 ('Behov och resurser i vå- en analys', *Delbetänkande av HSU2000*, SOU 1996, p. 163).
10. See Tables 5.5 and 5.6 of the above-mentioned report.

ANNEX D   THE 'DEMAND' FOR PUBLIC EXPENDITURE

This annex examines the changes in the 'demand' for public expenditure determined by demographic changes under the assumption of constant expenditure profiles for the members of each age group (that is, index *A*).

In the period 1995–2010 total age-related expenditure would increase by 15 per cent in Denmark, 14 per cent in Germany and 8 to 11 per cent in the other six countries considered. Substantial increments would be recorded over the following 15 years in all the eight countries (see Figure 9D.1). Thereafter it would gradually flatten and decline in most countries after 2035. Projected increases are generally lower for the countries for which education expenditure is taken into consideration: the increase in total age-related expenditure would reach 25 per cent in Belgium, Finland and Italy, 29 per cent in Denmark, 33 in Germany and it would reach 36 to 40 respectively in Sweden and in Spain; the Netherlands is an exception since, in spite of the inclusion of education expenditure, the increase reaches 45 per cent by 2046.[1]

Pension expenditure trends, which contribute substantially to expected increases in total expenditure, are rather homogeneous for seven of the eight countries (see Figure 9D.2a). By 2010 real pension expenditure would increase by 14 to 18 per cent in Belgium, Denmark, Italy, Spain and Sweden, by 24 per cent in the Netherlands and by 28 per cent in Finland and Germany. By 2035 it would increase by 40 to 55 per cent in Denmark, Finland, Italy and Sweden, by 60–73 per cent in Belgium, Germany and Spain, and by 120 per cent in the Netherlands.

Health expenditure trends are rather similar for Belgium, Italy and Spain, with expenditure increasing by about 15 per cent and peaking in the period 2030–35 for the first two countries and ten years later in Spain. Germany records similar trends at slightly higher levels (expenditure increase reaches 22 per cent in 2039 and decreases afterwards). Danish and Swedish expenditure trends are very similar and continously increasing up to 26 per cent by the end of the projection period. Finland and the Netherlands record greater expenditure increases, respectively 38 per cent by 2038 and 74 per cent by 2050 (see Figure 9D.2b).

Over the period 1995–2010 real education expenditure would decline by about 10 per cent in Italy and 2–3 per cent in Belgium and Finland. In Denmark and the Netherlands it would increase by 3 to 7 per cent. By 2035 the reduction would reach 27 per cent in Italy and about 10 per cent in Belgium and Finland (see Figure 9D.2c), while in Denmark and the Netherlands expenditure would be close to the 1995 level. The substantial reduction projected for Germany and Italy is related to their low projected fertility rate (1.5, as against 1.8 for Belgium, Denmark, Finland and the Netherlands).

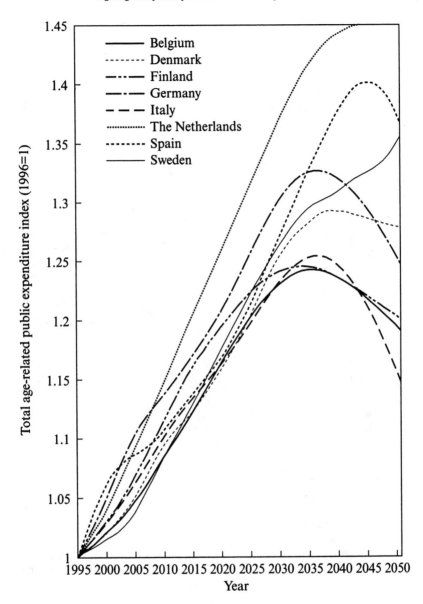

*Figure 9D.1   Effects of demographic changes on real total age-related
public expenditure (baseline demographic scenario)*

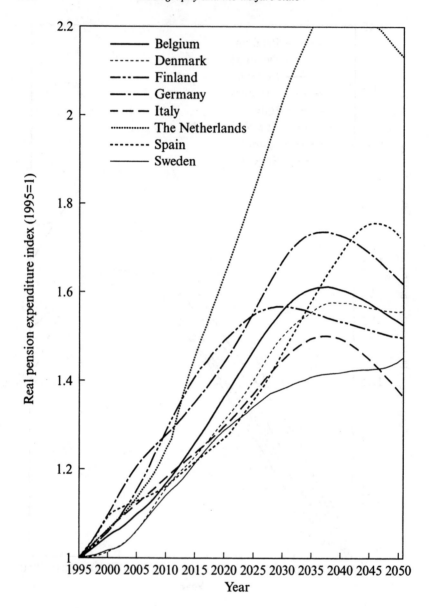

*Figure 9D.2a   Effects of demographic changes on pension expenditure
(baseline demographic scenario)*

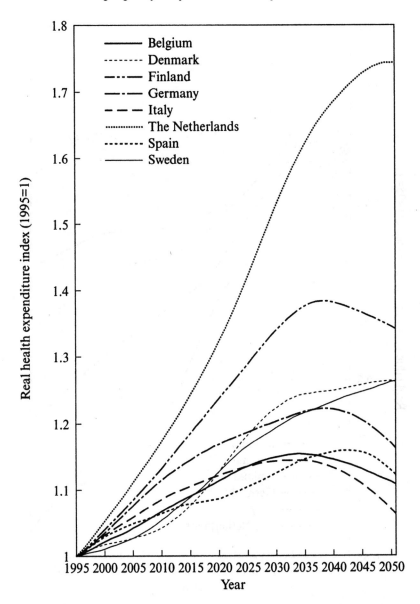

Figure 9D.2b   Effects of demographic changes on health expenditure
(baseline demographic scenario)

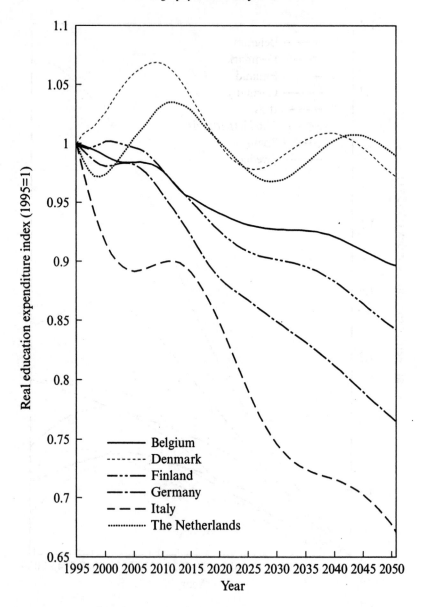

*Figure 9D.2c   Effects of demographic changes on education expenditure
(baseline demographic scenario)*

Note

1. It should be stressed that real expenditure trends also depend on the evolution of total population. The relatively small increases projected for Italy largely depend on the expected decline of Italian population.

Index